Collectible *Silver Jewelry*

Identification and Value Guide

Fred Rezazadeh

COLLECTOR BOOKS
A Division of Schroeder Publishing Co., Inc.

Dedication

To my colleagues, Professors Phillip Dedrick, Dorothy Delman, and Susan Whealler in appreciation for many years of intellectual nourishment and good friendship; and in memory of my mentor, the late distinguished professor and Nobel Prize nominee, Dr. Earl O. Heady.

The current values in this book should be used only as a guide. They are not intended to set prices, which vary from one section of the country to another. Auction prices as well as dealer prices vary greatly and are affected by condition as well as demand. Neither the author nor the publisher assumes responsibility for any losses that might be incurred as a result of consulting this guide.

Cover: top left, Silver necklace by Binder Brothers; top right, Art Nouveau pin; center left, Native American cuff bracelet; center, Silver pin by Viking Craft; center right, Norwegian Sølje brooch by Andersen and Sheinpflug; also center left towards bottom, Japanese 950 silver and porcelain bracelet with matching earrings; bottom left, German marcasite necklace; bottom right, Silver pin by Los Castillo.

Title page: top right, Art Nouveau pin; center, Lapponia necklace (photo courtesy of Lapponia); left, Turkish bracelet; right, Italian cameo necklace; bottom, Mexican cuff bracelet.

Cover design by Beth Summers
Book design by Terri Hunter
Photography by Pitkin Studio

Searching For A Publisher?

We are always looking for knowledgeable people considered to be experts within their fields. If you feel that there is a real need for a book on your collectible subject and have a large comprehensive collection, contact Collector Books.

COLLECTOR BOOKS
P.O. Box 3009
Paducah, Kentucky 42002-3009
www.collectorbooks.com

Copyright © 2001 by Fred Rezazadeh

Contents

Preface

As in my previous book on costume jewelry, my objective for writing this book is to display and price a broad range of silver jewelry, reflecting the breadth of the collectible market and emphasizing the kind of silver jewelry which the average dealer/collector is most likely to encounter in the marketplace. The range covers a broad spectrum, from cheap to expensive, rare to common, U.S. and Continental to Middle Eastern and Oriental, handcrafted to mass produced, urban to tribal, traditional to art moderne, prominent designers to unknown silversmiths. Of course, much of the collectible silver jewelry found in the market was mass produced and mass marketed, and this book aims to be a realistic reflection of this fact.

There are already several excellent books on prominent designers and silversmiths or with a particular focus on Mexican, Native American, and period jewelry such as Art Deco and Art Nouveau jewelry. What is lacking is a book that can serve as a general reference on collectible silver jewelry with a focus on the breadth of the market, covering a wide range of collectible silver jewelry often observed in the market. Much of this type of jewelry was mass manufactured by the major U.S. manufacturers, many of them also involved in the production of costume jewelry; or imported from other countries, sometimes in large quantities and for an extended period, particularly after WWII. Others were imported in limited quantities, sometimes for only a short period, or were brought into the country by immigrants or through the tourist traffic. Over the years, the various ethnic communities of immigrants or specialized ethnic retail or wholesale outlets also served as a source of supply and distribution.

Although some eighteenth and nineteenth century silver jewelry is shown, an overwhelming majority of the jewelry pieces displayed in this book were made in this century, primarily during the 1920s – 1970s period. But a section of the book is devoted to the current designers and silversmiths whose works are already becoming collectible or have a great potential of becoming collectible. Also included are some examples of the recent and/or new mass produced and marketed silver jewelry produced by U.S. and foreign manufacturers in order to provide the readers with an understanding of the current retail market and a glimpse of what may become collectible in the future.

The book is organized according to the geographical areas where the silver jewelry was manufactured with a brief introduction to each chapter which provides basic background information on the history and the type of jewelry manufactured, national silver standards, and hallmarks and manufacturer marks, to facilitate identification and dating. Over all, the book covers the silver jewelry of 30 countries with some countries highlighted because of their special significance and the volume of the jewelry involved. The examples displayed include unmarked silver jewelry as well as those pieces produced by approximately 100 U.S. manufacturers and that of over 150 foreign manufacturers, along with their trademarks and national silver standard marks, and in most cases, supplemented by a brief history and biographies of the major manufacturers and designers. The readers should note that given the nature and broad scope of this work, only a small sampling of the silver jewelry found in the collectible market could be displayed and evaluated. Accordingly, although the breadth of the market is emphasized, it is by no means an exhaustive or fully comprehensive treatment of the collectible silver jewelry market which would have required several volumes.

Since the author's interest in silver jewelry is not merely aesthetic and extends to researching, identifying, and documenting the history, trademarks, and personalities involved in the development of the silver jewelry production and industry in the U.S. and abroad, considerable time and effort were expended to show the trademarks and national silver standards along with the jewelry of the respective companies and countries. This involved intensive research over the course of several years, the survey of much of the relevant literature in several languages, over a thousand correspondences with manufacturers, museums, and knowledgeable sources, without whose help this volume would have not been possible. Given the nature and scope of the task and uncertainties regarding the trademarks and dates, the potential for errors is quite real. But the research continues, and it's the author's hope to correct and improve upon this volume in a future edition provided that this edition is well received by the readers.

Regarding the trademarks in this book, a considerable amount of time was saved in this area because of the kind permission by two publishers to reproduce many of the marks of American manufacturers. In this regard, the author wishes to thank the *Jewelers' Circular Keystone* magazine and the editor, Larry Frederick, for permission to reprint various marks and other material in this book. The

JCK, published by Cahners Business Information, is an indispensable source for serious students and connoisseurs of jewelry and can be contacted at 201 King of Prussia Rd., Radnor, PA 19089. The author also wishes to thank Tran Duy Ly and the Arlington Book Company for permission to reprint various marks from their book, *Trade Marks of the Jewelry and Kindred Trade, 1988*. This book is also an indispensable source for readers who are interested in the trademarks of the early twentieth century jewelry manufacturers and can be directly ordered from the Arlington Book Company at 2706 Elsmore Street, Fairfax, VA. Other marks were acquired from the U.S. Patent and Trademark Office or photographed and drawn directly from the jewelry in the author's collection or that of other collections used to write this book, including all foreign marks with the exception of those provided by the manufacturers and silversmiths, government agencies, and museums.

Special thanks are due to several individuals and museums for their kind assistance in providing invaluable information and/or helping identify foreign marks: Birgitta Martinius, Curator, Nordiska Museet, Stockholm, Sweden; Tone Rasch, Norskfolke Museum, Norway, and Jorunn Fossberg for providing the English synopsis of her book, *Draksølv* and another book, *Arvesølvet*, via Tone Rash and Norkfolke Museum; Jan-Lauritz Opstad, Director, National Museum of Decorative Arts, Trondheim, Norway; Inger Helene N. Stemshaug Kunstindustrimuseet I Oslo, Norway; Poul Dedenroth-Schou, Director, Museet På Koldinghus, Denmark; Ulla Houkjœr, Denmark; Sally Jacobson, Director, The Ephraim Foundation and Anne West for the material provided on Cabin Craft via the Foundation; Eva-Pia Worland, Kalmar, Sweden; Charlotte Modig, Våsterås, Sweden; Margareta Ottosson and Swedac, Sweden; Paula Karvonen, Helsinki, Finland; Silver Forum and its members, particularly Patrick Kapty and Marbeth Schon; author and jewelry expert, Christie Romero; Tim & Vanessa Patterson of Retro Gallery, England; Vladimir Ivanov, Moscow, Russia, for library research and information on Russian and East European jewelry and marks; Phyllis Goddard; Hiro Daiguchi, Japan; Yossef Hakim, Ankara, Turkey; Amir Miryossefi of Hezardastan Gallery, Tehran, Iran; my colleague, Korush Taji, for facilitating correspondence, locating, and interviewing the Persian silversmiths on author's behalf; and my good friend, John Christopher, for his indispensable help in numerous fields.

Many firms and silversmiths provided the author with information and in some cases the images of their jewelry, some were interviewed at length, others were generous with time and knowledge in responding to the author's written inquiries. Their names follow with my sincere gratitude for their assistance: Danecraft Corporation, particularly Victor Primavera III and Victor Primavera, Jr.; James Avery Craftsman Inc., particularly Chris Avery; Leonore Doskow Inc., particularly David Doskow; Hand & Hammer, particularly Chip deMatteo; Stuart Nye Silver Jewelry, particularly Ralph Morris, Jr.; Lapponia, particularly Anne-Maria Simelius; Ola Gorie, particularly Anne Crichton; Zebra Design, particularly, Thomas Auer; Peruzzi Argentieri, Florence, Italy; Sabine Amtsberg; Emanuela Aureli; Laura Evans Bowers; Sandra Buckholz; Kelly Drake; Lee Epperson; J. Erik and Nancy Olson of Silver Artisans; Susan Gifford Knopp; Deb Karash; Marly Malone Company, particularly Frances Malloy; Charlotte Modig; Pat Moses-Caudel; Carrie Nunes; Amy O'Connell; Oliva Rød; Bernard Rosenberg; Dave Stephens; Bryna Tracy; and Randall Wilson.

Much of the jewelry displayed in this book is from the author's collection, but no collection is ever complete and in this case the author's collection was supplemented by the jewelry from other collections for which I am especially thankful to the following individuals: John Christopher; Robin Allison; Joan Welsh; Vicki Fulton; Saman Shams; Shamsi Shamlou; Jim Oneal; Kile Farese; Teina Moran; Kim Cummins; Dale Davis; Christine Kehely; Susan Crosby; and Susan Whealler.

Considerable efforts were expended to develop a more systematic and consistent approach in estimating the prices. The estimated prices are based on asking prices at general and specialized shows, antiques malls and shops, large regional flea markets, on-site and online auctions. Due to the unique nature of the antiques and collectible markets, the actual prices may vary significantly depending on the geographical location, type of market, knowledge and bargaining skills of the parties involved, and should not be construed in the same way as the market prices for other merchandise and commodities which reflect long run average cost in a competitive market. This subject is treated at length in the author's book on costume jewelry by the same publisher and is often misunderstood not only by the novice, but also the experienced dealers and collectors. Accordingly, the values listed should be considered and used as broad price guidelines rather than actual market prices. The author welcomes feedback from the readers, particularly suggestions and corrections, which can be sent via the publisher or directly to Fred Reza@aol.com.

Introduction

The key to the better understanding of our present and future is hidden in our past and understanding and appreciating silver jewelry is no exception. Although the focus of this book is primarily on twentieth century silver jewelry, many of the terms, techniques, and even designs related to silver products and jewelry have their roots in the distant past. It is for this reason that I begin the book with a brief history of the metal, its use in the production of jewelry, and the development and evolution of the craft and its product through the ages. It is written with the hope that it will enrich and enhance the readers' understanding and appreciation of collectible silver jewelry they own, as it has done for the author while researching the subject.

The metal known as silver has been used in the production of precious products, jewelry and ornaments, utilitarian articles, and as money in various forms including coins, since the early times. The chemical symbol that designates silver is Ag, derived from the Latin term *argentum*, though the early Romans actually used the word "luna" for silver and a crescent moon as its symbol, possibly because of the similarity of its color to that of the silvery moon. On modern chemical tables, silver is given the atomic number 47 and the atomic weight of 107.88. In its pure form, it reaches its melting point at 960.5 degrees and boiling point at approximately 2000 degrees Centigrade. After gold, silver is among the most ductile and malleable metals, and it can be made into extremely thin wires or sheets.

In ancient Egypt and Mesopotamia both gold and silver were used as shaving razors by wealthy women, and modern Indian cuisine and delicacies served by a wealthy family are sometimes covered with an exceptionally thin sheet of gold or silver which attests the wealth and generous hospitality of the host rather than enrichment of the taste. There were also many superstitions associated with silver, such as crossing a beggar's or gypsy's hand with a coin for good luck or the bride wearing a piece of silver in her shoe at the time of the wedding.

The first major silver mining technology is attributed to the Chaldeans in Mesopotamia who developed the technology for extracting silver from the lead-silver ore using a method known as the culpellation process. The major sources of silver in ancient times were located in Anatolia (present day Turkey), Armenia, and Elam in southern Iran which supplied silver to the major silver manufacturing centers in Mesopotamia and Asia Minor as well as exports to Egypt and the Greek isles.

We all know about the historic role silver has played until recent times as a form of money, but long before being stamped into coins in Lydia in Asia Minor circa 550 B.C., it was a primary medium of exchange in ancient times. Its first appearance on the market as money can be dated back to the 4th millennium Sumer, the first literate civilization flourishing near the head of the Persian Gulf (present Iraq-Iran border), and southern Iraq, between the rivers Tigris and Euphrates.

The highly developed Sumerian barter economy, relying increasingly on distant trade, required the creation of money by using a universal commodity, easily divisible, to reflect the value of other commodities, and serve as a medium of exchange. Silver and barley were among the first forms of money to facilitate exchange, and the durable nature of silver and gold rendered them as quite suitable forms of money for long distance international trade. Long before silver coins, ingots and rings were used, with the shekel serving as the unit of account, valued at one-eighth of gold in its weight (circa 2600 BC), and measured by the scale. The government even fixed the interest payments on private loans paid in silver at the maximum of 20% per annum and waged war for the control of silver mines of the kingdom of Elam in present day southwestern Iran. Hence, according to Biblical accounts, Abraham received 1,000 pieces of silver from Abimelech for Sara's use (Gen. 20:16), and after her death, paid 400 shekels of silver to Ephron the Hittite buying the cave at Machpelah to bury her (Gen. 23:16).

But the use of silver in making jewelry predates its function as money. Among the earliest silver jewelry and personal ornaments found in ancient times are those excavated at a cemetery in the southern Sumerian city of Ur with graves dating back to at least 3500 BC. In royal graves (dated ca. 2500 B.C.) excavated in late the 1920s by Leonard Wooley, various gold and silver artifacts including jewelry, ornaments, and silver ribbons were found, testifying to a rich society that could support specialized craftsmen. A gold and silver headdress which Wooley attributed to Queen Shub-ad or Puabi so fascinated his wife that she used a female skull to reconstruct in wax and plaster the head and facial features of the ancient queen adorned with the headdress and jewelry found in the grave. These along with other silver and gold artifacts appear to have been made by highly skilled jewelers and artisans exhibiting various techniques, including engraving, relief, and inlay work, decorated with lapis lazuli and carnelian stones. The highly skilled craftsmanship demonstrated by these pieces suggests the development of skills and technology over an extended period perhaps dating back for at least several centuries. Gold and silver jewelry and ornaments found in other tombs in the region, including those at a child's grave in Susa and a silver pin at a Sialak excavation in Iran, dating to even earlier times, all seem to corroborate these postulates and observations. The early Sumerians enjoyed a developed economy relying on distant trade with most of their silver imported from northern Cilicia and Elam, and one can reasonably speculate that silver jewelry, ornaments, vessels, and artifacts were among their varied export products.

Though rich in gold as evidenced by King Tut's treasures (circa 1300s B.C.) discovered in 1922, silver was a scarce metal in ancient Egypt, and the early texts mention silver before gold, implying a higher value and prominence for silver. A decree in the Code of Menes, whose reign is stipulated at circa 3500 B.C., proclaims that "one part of gold is equal to two and one-half parts of silver in value." There were only two silver objects (a vase and a trumpet) among many artifacts found at Tutankhamun's tomb and these as well as a few jewelry pieces were of electrum (natural alloy of gold and silver) quality rather than fine silver. But there is clear evidence of highly revered silver imports from Mesopotamia and Asia Minor. Nevertheless, these and other Egyptian finds reveal the artistic genius and well-developed craftsmanship of the highly skilled Egyptian artisans whose magnificent gold pieces have inspired so many over the centuries.

On the other hand, both Asia Minor and Greece were rich with silver deposits. Some of the gold and silver artifacts, including jewelry, unearthed on mainland Greece, Lemnos, and Cyclades date back before the arrival of the Greek tribes, and the now famed Mycenaean treasures unearthed by Heinrich Schliemann with a gold mask attributed to the Homeric legendary king, Agamemnon, also included silver artifacts, ornaments, and jewelry, many of which are in the collection of the National Museum in Athens. So were silver objects present among the treasures of Knossos in Crete, excavated by Arthur Evans, reflecting the highly developed Minoan civilization. In Asia Minor, during the Bronze Age (ca. 3300 – 1200 B.C.) there developed a group of city-states as evidenced by finds in Lindar, Arsalan Tepe, Kurban, and Troy which were heavily dependent on trade and metalwork. In Troy, also first excavated by Schliemann, there were many gold and silver artifacts among the nearly 9,000 objects unearthed, including exquisitely handcrafted jewelry. Although Schliemann also attributed these to the Homeric Troy of King Priam, they predate the estimated Homeric Troyan era (Troy

IV) by many centuries, dating back to ca. 2500 B.C. (Troy II). In general, these finds in Greece and Asia Minor demonstrate astonishing metallurgical and artistic achievements, utilizing a broad range of techniques, including embossing, repousse, engraving, inlaid, and cloisonne works. They are also among the now increasingly undisputed scientific and archaeological finds that suggest the very early artistic, intellectual, cultural, and commercial interdependence of Eastern Mediterranean's evolving civilizations on the three bordering continents, Mesopotamia, the Indus valley, and central Asia, extending to Britain and China.

Far less speculation is required when we examine the later societies in Western Asia and the Mediterranean Sea coasts, many of which have left behind exquisite works of art and craftsmanship, including jewelry, executed in silver. Among the famous silver mines during the classical period are the Larium silver mines in Greece mentioned by several ancient historians which provided an ample supply of silver, not only for manufacturing silver objects and an abundance of Greek silver coins, but also instrumental in financing the defense of the nation during the Persian Wars; or the Greeks' own foreign military adventures and exploits throughout the Mediterranean Sea. One wonders about the course of history if Themistocles, the leader of one Athenian faction, anticipating the Persian invasion, had not convinced the citizens to spend the revenues from the Larium silver mines on a ship building project instead of distributing it among the freemen at ten drachmas per head, a measure that later proved instrumental in defeating the Persian naval force at Salamis. The extraction at the Larium mines continued until modern times when it was finally closed in the mid nineteenth century. Later the "Hellenistic" era witnessed the development of new styles and production of exquisite gold and silver jewelry which were products of the integration of various techniques, materials, and designs from the vast lands and diverse people conquered by Alexander.

Both the Romans and Byzantines manufactured silver jewelry in a variety of exquisite designs, demonstrating outstanding craftsmanship which has been imitated by or inspired many jewelers and silversmiths throughout the ages. There was already a strong artistic Etruscan tradition, predating the Roman Empire, in jewelry manufacture and designs, itself influenced by the Phoenicians, but with the spoils of the conquest came riches of the east and many cross-cultural influences before the development of distinct Roman artistic expression and domestic jewelry manufacture. The Spanish mines were the main

7

source of silver supply for the Roman Empire, and while initially, Alexandria and Antioch served as the main centers of production for silver products, not long after the age of Caesar and Cleopatra domestic production had taken roots in Rome itself. One can only speculate on Cleopatra's historic and flamboyant visit to Rome and its influence on the Roman taste. During this period, jewelry was increasingly worn by both sexes of the upper class, and the female ornaments included tiaras, rings, bracelets, anklets, necklaces, and earrings employing both silver and gold and a variety of precious stones and material such as ivory. Some of the major improvements in metalwork along with the development of distinct Roman designs occurred during this period, and these exquisite artistic accomplishments in a variety of fields, including jewelry, continued to be discovered and rediscovered, serving as primary sources of inspiration for many centuries to come.

The Eastern Roman Empire, Byzantine, carried on some of these traditions, and with the fusion of Eastern influences, evolved into a highly accomplished society in the field of arts and culture. This was characterized with distinct Byzantine decorative motifs and techniques, particularly in the area of precious metal work and gem jewelry which adorned the churches and satisfied the nobility's demand for luxuries. After the Crusaders sacked Constantinople in 1214, an extraordinary volume of treasures in the form of jewelry and precious objects, looted from the Churches and private homes, were brought back to the West which had a significant impact on the development of the arts in medieval Europe during the next few centuries. The fall of Constantinople to the Turks in 1453 resulted in another flight of treasures as well as intellectuals and artisans to the West, influencing, though to a lesser extent, various fields of arts and crafts in the West. Traces of the Byzantine influence could still be detected in the jewelry of Hungary, Russia, and other East European countries well into the nineteenth century.

Aside from Byzantine and Rome, some of the most beautiful jewelry manufactured in Europe are the products of the Celtic culture, showing traces of influences from a variety of sources, from central Asia, Persia, and Egypt, to Roman, Byzantine, and German. But the Celtic jewelry clearly exhibits exquisite and genuine designs which tell us a thousand tales about an artistically superior and creative people who failed to leave us much of a written record. It should be noted that the Celtic areas in Scotland and Ireland were never subdued by the Romans, and the tradition and motifs found in these areas date back to the very early times. Mention should also be made of the Viking jewelry, primarily executed in gold, with motifs and designs that have inspired many modern Scandinavian silversmiths. Vikings also

were never brought under Roman domination, and their jewelry broadly carried on the early motifs and traditions, which some pundits, lacking taste, classified as mere "barbarian" jewelry. Without the Celts and the Vikings as springs of inspiration for so much of Scottish and Scandinavian jewelry and firms such as Kalevala and Ola Gorie featured in this book, silver manufacturing in these countries would have perhaps taken a different course, denying us the pleasure and leisure of modern renditions and adornments which link mankind to its distant past.

In the Far East, a long tradition in metalwork with superb craftsmanship and use of innovative technologies developed in China and later Japan. As in other fields such as ceramics, the powerful designs and impressive techniques captured the Europeans' imagination and were to influence various schools of arts and crafts, including metalwork, during the last three centuries. So were the arts of civilizations in the "New World," some with a long tradition in gold and silver works, inspiring many modern silversmiths of which the modern Mexican and Peruvian silver jewelry based on pre-Colombian motifs shown in this book are the prime examples.

Renaissance was the age of revival and rediscovery of the lost arts in Europe with its marked influence in every field including metalworks and jewelry, a process which continued its evolutionary transformation and development well into the eighteenth century, spreading in divergent but nevertheless inter-related paths throughout Europe, from Russia to Britain. Some of the most magnificent pieces of jewelry, both in gold and silver, demonstrating astonishing craftsmanship and artistic rendition, were produced during this period, primarily for men, and then increasingly for women. But it should be noted at this juncture that men were the primary consumers of jewelry in the pre-Victorian era and aside from what may be termed as nomadic and peasant jewelry, only the women belonging to the royal and aristocratic class wore jewelry, sparsely, as an ornament. The early sumptuary laws, such as the Code of Justinian in 529, restricted the decorative use of precious metals and stones to the Church and nobility. In order to maintain social hierarchy, sumptuary laws were continually declared or enacted in various parts of Europe.

Actually, the early church fathers frowned at the use of jewelry and luxurious habits and ornaments. According to early church documents, simple habits lacking luxury and ornaments were considered as "womanly gracing" while flamboyant dresses and ornaments were declared as "womanly disgracing" and attire of the prostitutes. But as incomes rose in Europe, more women from the merchant class and the nascent middle class began to wear jewelry and luxurious dresses made of silk and fine fabric. Ironically, as more women began to wear jewelry, laws were instituted to forbid prostitutes to wear silk dresses and ornaments in order to prevent confusion between the chaste wives and the urban harlots. As quoted in Margaret Rosenthal's book, *The Honest Courtesan,* among such early legislation was the Venetian Sumptuary Law of 1562 which forbids the city prostitutes "the use of gold, silver, and silk, as well as that of jewels of any kind, genuine or false, inside and outside of house and even outside this city." Similar sumptuary laws were enacted throughout most of Europe.

With the rise of capitalism and the expanding bourgeoisie, the burgeoning middle class and once taunted merchant class assumed a prominent role in the society and a new degree of respectability. Merchants, entrepreneurs, financiers, and industrialists began to climb the social ladder while the regal aristocratic titles, land-based nobility and past sources of power and wealth, experienced a diminishing role. With this came the "gentlemanly appearance" and attire with some businessmen even trying to capture and emulate the diminishing flamboyance of the nobility, while the "idleness" of women, being denied participation in the political economy and confined to the management of the home and servants, continued to be perceived as a mark of social status and domestic virtue. However, it did not take long before this transformation of the society broadly affected both spheres of production and consumption, including attire and broad use of ornamentation.

The expansion and deepening of industrialization in the nineteenth century led to rising incomes, and mass production and consumption as well as the erosion of artistic individualism and creative freedom, alienating the producer from the product. The century was marked with the dominance of the Victorian taste despite some reactions, but twentieth century was pregnant with many changes, giving birth to, or consolidating, many trends and schools: modern, revivalist, and the synthesis of the modern and traditional.

In the New World, major silver mines of Mexico, Bolivia, and Peru were exploited by the Spaniards and provided a steady source of supply in the form of silver bullions shipped to Europe. Europe was also supplied with large quantities of silver mined in Japan in a trade dominated and controlled by the Portuguese and later the Dutch colonial enterprises. As will be explained in the next chapter, the silver-poor American colonies relied on foreign silver, even in the case of coins, and not until the discovery of the Comstock Lode in Nevada in 1859 did the nation begin to enjoy an ample supply of native silver. As in many fields, it did not take long before America assumed a prominent role in the production of silver products, including jewelry, increasingly employing and applying the most modern methods and tools in the mass production and marketing of silver jewelry.

Although the focus of this book is on twentieth century silver jewelry, in nearly every piece one can see the traces and influences of the distant past, of perfected techniques invented in ancient times, of designs and motifs inspired by the creativity and genius of our ancestors, of the historic and spiritual legacies we so revere, and at the very least, of the rebellion against "all that was" and concrete manifestos on "what ought to be" — all byproducts of creative and imaginative human minds for the purpose of adornment of the human body.

Silver Marks and Identification

Pure silver is too soft for normal use and is consequently mixed with other metals, usually copper, to create a harder alloy. Copper was the choice metal as a hardening agent since it did not affect the color of silver when applied in small quantities, but as such, it also served unscrupulous silversmiths to debase silver without outright detection. This difficulty in assessing the purity of silver has served many unscrupulous silversmiths, even kings and rulers, throughout the ages to deceive the public by debasing silver coins or merchandise. As a consequence, silver standards were gradually developed in Europe to test and assure the purity of silver products.

The process involved weighing a silver sample or scrap before heating it, using bone ash which absorbed the copper. The remaining silver could then be weighed where the pre and post heating weight differential enabled the assayer to measure the silver purity and the degree or percentage of its adulteration. This degree of fineness was then stamped on the metal meeting the minimum standards established in various countries. For example, in England, the term "sterling" was reserved for silver products containing 92.5 percent (925 parts per thousand) silver. Pieces that met this requirement were then stamped with the "King's Mark," a lion or leopard's head, as the official stamp which guaranteed its "sterling" quality. This mark along with other marks, including the silversmith's initials constituted the English hallmark which has evolved over several centuries, enabling us today to identify and date silver objects made in Britain. The term "hallmark" is derived from the fact that the early fourteenth century silver was assayed (tested for quality) in a "hall" serving as the headquarters for the Goldsmiths' Guild and thus the "mark" that guaranteed its "sterling" quality was referred to as the "hallmark." The term "sterling" itself is widely postulated to have been derived from "Easterling," a term then used in reference to German goldsmiths from the East and/or their high quality coins. It should also be noted that no distinction between the goldsmith and silversmith was made until the mid nineteenth century and that the term "goldsmith" referred to a craftsman using both gold and/or silver.

Similar hallmarking traditions evolved in other European countries among which 900, 830, and 800 marks for silver fineness, in addition to other identifying marks, are frequently encountered. Detailed information about these marks is provided in other chapters as they relate to the silver jewelry of a specific country displayed in that chapter.

It should be noted that not all silver jewelry is marked sterling and in the U.S. this practice is primarily a twentieth century practice. Aside from the "sterling" mark, what the collectors should look for are the silver marks, common among which are 925, 900, 830, and 800. Most twentieth century jewelry will have either sterling or one of these conventional identifying silver marks. Exceptions are few and often involve some of the hand-made American Indian or imported jewelry. Turn of the century and nineteenth century U.S. silver jewelry may or may not be marked, and the presence of a particular mark does not necessarily indicate its actual fineness. In such cases the accurate quality and fineness has to be tested. This can be done by employing one of a variety of test kits available in the market today and usually advertised in the collectible journals and supply catalogs. (See appendix.)

Sometimes the jewelry may have no markings other than a number which usually indicates the standard silver fineness, or this number may be incorporated as part of the hallmark. Basic knowledge about these standards in different countries can help to identify the origin of the jewelry, though a number such as 800 is of little use without taking into account other factors such as the designs, production techniques, and the over-all construction of the piece of jewelry being examined. Acknowledging this cautionary note, the table below can be used as the first step in the process of elimination in identifying the jewelry. This is neither an exhaustive nor definitive table but is rather based on the author's many years of research and experience in collecting silver jewelry. The most likely sources are listed first while the remainder are placed in a bracket. The choice is a matter of probabilities based on the volume of imports and the likelihood of encountering such pieces in the U.S. collectible market. For example, a piece of jewelry which is just marked 800 is more likely to be from Italy than from Romania or Belgium. Additional marks, if present, as well as the design and over-all construction, will further help in identifying the jewelry, and these marks and design peculiarities are explained in the relevant chapters which follow.

Table of Standard Silver Fineness

56	Russia	850	Russia, (Bulgaria)
60	Egypt (often in Arabic, see the relevant chapter)	875	Finland, (Poland, Portugal, Romania)
84	Russia, Persia (often in Persian, see the relevant chapter)	900	USA, Germany, Iran/Persia, Turkey
		916	Finland, (Poland, Portugal, Romania)
500	Belgium	925	Many possibilities
583	Russia	935	Germany, Austria/Hungary
750	Czechoslovakia, Poland, (Argentina, Austria/Hungary, Bulgaria, Romania)	950	Mexico, Japan, Germany, Czechoslovakia, (Bulgaria, Italy, Israel)
800	Italy, Germany, (Austria/Hungry, Belgium, Netherlands, Poland, Romania, Czechoslovakia, Switzerland, Egypt, Tunisia, Turkey)	959	Czechoslovakia
		980	Mexico
813	Finland	Silver	China, Japan, Siam pieces from Thailand, (Germany, Middle East), fineness varies
830	Denmark, Norway, Sweden, (Germany, Finland)	Coin silver	USA (implied 900 fineness)
833	Portugal		
835	Germany, Czechoslovakia, (Austria/Hungary, Belgium, Netherlands)		

The readers should also be aware of many other alloys used to imitate silver or misleading marks used to suggest silver or others which are sometimes mistaken for the manufacturer's mark and initials. Among these are:

Alpaco (found on some jewelry, especially Mexican jewelry). This mark is often confused with the maker's trademark. It stands for an alloy similar to German silver which is primarily nickel and not silver. Note that on some pieces, particularly Mexican jewelry such as cuff links, the fastener may be marked Alpaco while the remainder of the piece is made of silver.

B.M. Standing for Britannia Metal and not silver.

EP and **EPNS.** Silver plate. It stands for electroplate on nickel silver.

German Silver (found frequently on mesh and coin purses). Actually an alloy made of nickel, copper, and zinc.

G.S. Standing for German silver.

N.S. Standing for nickel silver.

W.M. Standing for white metal with no silver.

Sterling E.P. (found on rings). Not sterling but actually a silver plated object.

On the other hand, the jewelry may carry a mark in other languages which may indicate silver. Among these, the most common marks are "Argent" and its variants, all of which are derived from the Latin word for silver, argentum; and "Plata" which stands for the same in Spanish. The former is often mistaken for jewelry from Argentina and may be found on both silver and silver plated items while the latter is frequently thought to be the name of a Mexican silver jewelry designer, though there were many silversmiths named Plata, both in Spain and in Mexico.

Production Methods & Decorative Techniques

Many of the decorative techniques used in making silver jewelry were developed in ancient times and perfected over time. Much of modern silver jewelry, particularly in the U.S. and Europe, is mass manufactured by means of advanced and automated machinery, in many cases attempting to replicate the same look and effects as the older handmade silver jewelry.

Some basic knowledge about the decorative techniques and methods used in making silver jewelry may be useful for the readers, not only in enhancing our understanding and appreciation of the jewelry but also in identifying the origin of the jewelry and evaluating the workmanship and quality.

Casting. Whether by machines or by hands, the first step in making most silver jewelry is to create a mold and cast the piece by pouring liquid silver into the mold. Repeat process allows creating multiple pieces which are either used individually to make a ring or pin, or in combination to make a link necklace or bracelet. In manufacturing the modern mass produced silver jewelry, the method used is called centrifugal casting, but the process of casting dates back to the ancient times when both open and hollow casting was invented. Other methods used over time and still practiced by some silversmiths are lost wax, cuttlefish, die, and sand casting. Once the hardened silver piece is removed from the mold, various techniques are employed to enhance, decorate, and develop the design. The surface could be directly decorated by employing various methods or the decorations could be molded separately and applied to the piece. Some of these techniques are briefly described below.

Engraving. This technique, one of the oldest ancient methods, was applied to the surface of the silver piece by using sharp tools to create various designs and motifs.

In modern times, sharp engraving tools referred to as burins or gravers were used by hand while in mass produced jewelry, the same effect or look is accomplished by means of machinery.

Aside from monogrammed pieces, hand engraving can still be seen on some of the Middle Eastern jewelry such as talisman and seal jewelry or contemporary art jewelry.

Chasing. This is a decorating technique using chasing tools to create marks and indentations on the surface, thereby bringing out the details of a motif on flat pieces or to accent and accentuate the design created by other decorating methods. It can be seen on some Middle Eastern and other handmade or semi-handmade jewelry.

Embossing. A decorating technique used to create a design in relief by hammering and punching it on the opposite side, sometimes also referred to as repousse. Specially created metal dies are used which transfer the design to the face of the metal and in case of mass produced silver jewelry, the same effect is accomplished by advanced mechanical means. Embossing can also be used on separate pieces which are then affixed to the surface of the silver piece to create the same effect.

Etching. A decorating technique of creating motifs on the surface by employing chemical processes such as the use of nitric acid. The process is similar to etching in other arts and crafts such as glass and prints and involves covering the surface with an acid resisting substance such as wax and carving the design into it. Once dipped in a pool of nitric acid, the acid will only affect the uncovered (carved) area by corroding it and permanently leaving the impression of the design on the surface while the covered areas will remain unaffected. In modern mass produced silver jewelry, the same process is used en mass to accomplish the effect of chasing and engraving. It can be seen on some of the American and European silver jewelry. When in doubt, in order to distinguish between an engraved and an etched piece, examine it under a magnifying glass. In the former, the lines are cut into the piece and well defined, while in case of etched pieces the lines and curves are not well defined and the surface has a misty or "pitted" look.

Stamping. A decorating technique where a relief design is achieved by means of die stamping or a mechanical stamping machine. In modern production, advanced mechanical press and machinery are used to create the same identical pattern on thousands of mass produced pieces. It can be seen on much American, European, and post WWII Mexican and other silver jewelry.

Filigree. Another ancient decorating and construction technique which involves very fine silver wires that are bent, twisted, coiled, and formed into an openwork design, often floral motifs. The filigree method is also used in conjunction with a solid silver foundation, on the surface, or as a decorative fringe, or complementing other techniques. Such pieces may also include semi-precious stones. This type of construction is more often seen on Italian, Middle Eastern, some German and Mexican jewelry, though its use is not restricted to these areas.

Mesh. A construction method where the piece of jewelry such as a bracelet appears to have been woven of silver thread. The piece may have no other decorations, such as many silver mesh purses, coin purses, and bracelets, and necklaces, or it may serve as the foundation for decorated pieces affixed on the top and sometimes enhanced with semi-precious or simulated stones. Common throughout the world, but seen more frequently among the Italian, German, Turkish, and American silver jewelry.

Granulation. An ancient decorating method first used in Mesopotamia and by the Phoeni-

cians, adopted and perfected by the Etruscans in decorating their famed gold pieces. The process involves decorating the surface with silver grains or beads which could constitute a major or accentuating part of the design.

Niello. Today, the term is broadly applied to a decorating process which consists of emphasizing a design by creating a contrast between black and silver. Originally, the process involved engraving the design on the silver base and filling the indented parts and depression with a metallic sulphide which, after heating, would fuse to the base and when polished, provided a contrast between black and silver, thereby accentuating the design. It was first used by the Egyptians and Romans and continued to be applied in different parts of the world, including Britain, Russia, France, and the Islamic countries. Modern pieces have the surface of the piece covered with a niello compound providing a black background and the design engraved to bring out the silver, hence the contrast between the motif in silver against a black field. Found most frequently on Siamese silver jewelry, and to a lesser extent on Russian and Middle Eastern jewelry such as Persian jewelry.

Enameling. A decorating technique of using colored pigments to fill a part or all of a design on a piece of jewelry, or to completely cover the surface. The process not only provides a great contrast, sometimes of various colors, but also a shiny and glazed surface. There are various categories such as cloisonne, champleve, basse taille, and plique-à-jour. Found most frequently on the jewelry from Norway and Denmark, but also the jewelry from other countries such as France, Germany, and China.

Channel Work. A decorating technique of covering a part or the entire surface of a silver piece with a matrix which outlines the design and filling each compartment with semi-precious stones of contrasting colors to complete the design. The sum of the pieces held in the cells creates the over-all design like a mosaic panel. Found most frequently on Native American jewelry, particularly post WWII Zuni jewelry.

Carving. A decorating technique similar to wood and stone carvings whereby a motif is carved on silver vessels and jewelry. Seen on some Middle Eastern and Oriental jewelry pieces.

Cleaning and Care

Silver can tarnish rapidly. The main reason for the tarnish is the copper which is used in the alloy reacts with air, heat, and other elements, causing tarnish and fire scale. But the presence of copper alone is not the only cause of the tarnish; the reaction

of the two metals when combined is also a contributing factor. For example, gold is also combined with copper but the gold alloy, even though it contains much more copper than sterling silver, does not tarnish. For many years, no other metal was as qualified as copper to create a silver alloy which had superior qualities of being quite malleable but at the same time hard enough to withstand different methods of construction and versatile jewelry applications. New technologies have led to the development of copper free and/or tarnish-free alloys, but these are more expensive, not as versatile or as hard, and require more specialized care in construction, and because of these factors, are not yet well received by the industry.

Concerning the tarnish, two external substances, sulphur and chlorine, are the main culprits. The sulphur that silver is exposed to exists in the air, a problem intensified by modern industrial pollution and smokestacks. Accordingly, when worn and exposed, silver jewelry will eventually tarnish. Interestingly, another source of sulfur emission is wool clothing which is sometimes worn with the jewelry.

Chlorine is another source of tarnish. It is a major component of sodium chloride commonly known as salt. But, unlike silver utensils and tableware, the salt that tarnishes silver jewelry comes from body sweat when the piece is worn. Chemical ingredients of perfumes and cosmetics may also cause tarnish as well as damage to natural material such as pearls and ivory or discolor some porous stones such as turquoise. Other culprits are tap water which is enriched with chlorine, citric liquids, and rubber products. Hence care should be taken to avoid these sources as much as possible, or as an alternative periodically wash and clean the jewelry using unadulterated water and very mild dishwashing soap.

The best method of cleaning silver jewelry which is not badly tarnished is to periodically polish it with a very soft clean cloth or with a damp cloth or a very soft brush using a mix of lukewarm water and a mild detergent and wipe completely dry. Cleaning tarnished antique silver objects and jewelry has always been controversial. Some collectors prefer the uncleaned and tarnished silver and pay lower prices for cleaned pieces. As in the case of other metal objects such as copper and bronze, the preference for uncleaned pieces is because of the value the collectors place on the patina that comes with age and the fact that some of the tarnish and oxidization may have been originally intended by the silversmith and manufacturer to accentuate the contrast of colors and enhance the design. However, those who regularly wear their silver jewelry may find it necessary to clean some of the badly tarnished pieces. For this task, both dipping and rubbing or polishing agents are available in the market. The dipping of silver jewelry must always be approached with care following the instructions that come with the product and certainly avoiding it around certain stones and material such as pearls. It should be used in case of severely tarnished solid silver pieces without gilding or darker shades in crevasses which were originally intended by the designer and silversmith. The piece then should be washed using light soap and water and dried completely. It is always better to hand polish jewelry lightly and selectively, especially when they contain other materials, whether natural or artificial, particularly when ivory, bone, amber, pearls and rhinestones are involved. In case of rhinestones, care should also be taken when the piece is washed, avoiding submerging or dipping the piece in water.

Inventory and Insurance

Unfortunately, jewelry is among the first items that burglars search for, and to avoid a major loss it must be insured. Most home insurance policies have limited coverage for jewelry, often not exceeding $1,000 to $2,000. With the rise in the prices of collectible silver, many surpassing several hundred dollars per piece, even a small collection would exceed these limits. These and certainly larger collections consisting of many pieces should be insured separately. For this purpose, consulting a professional appraiser is strongly advised and this appraisal can then be used by your insurance company to recommend the best coverage . An alternative method, sometimes preferred by collectors/dealers is to purchase a lump sum amount of coverage for the jewelry. In either case, it is advisable to create an inventory of the jewelry. This can be done by taking photographs of the jewelry, individually or in groups when a large volume is involved, and writing a brief, but as specific as possible, description with prices paid, including receipts when available, for each item. The new technology with digital cameras makes this task quite easy and a low cost project. There are also image inventory and organization software that enable you to organize your images in different files and folders, or create an album with easy and accessible thumbnail viewing and cataloging. Like all other important personal and financial documents, a hard or disk copy of this material should be stored in a fireproof safe or somewhere outside of the house.

The storing of the jewelry is also important. Although some people keep their most expensive jewelry in a safety deposit box, many women actually hide them in what they perceive as an inconspicuous place in the house. In case you have the habit of hiding your jewelry, it is advisable to follow several guiding principles that may help in safeguarding it:

1. Make certain that a trustworthy friend or relative knows where the jewelry is hidden and can be recovered in case of unexpected death. An alternative is to write down this information and leave it with the important household documents.

2. Make certain that the jewelry is hidden in a place readily accessible to you but difficult to detect by burglars. Sophisticated burglars use metal detectors and can easily detect a jewelry box hidden under the blankets in the closet. Hence, the pre-

ferred hiding places should be near ordinary and inconspicuous metal objects in the house.

3. Make certain that some inexpensive jewelry is always kept in your jewelry or dresser box.

Although stolen jewelry is seldom recovered and much of the recovered stolen property is auctioned by the police departments without ever being able to notify the actual owners, the chances of recovery are slightly improved by more specific descriptions, noting special features and unique marks and characteristics, which can be used along with the image of the jewelry to identify and reclaim it. You may also wish to visit local pawn shops, flea markets, and auctions where stolen items are sometimes offered for sale immediately after a burglary.

Silver and Jewelry Industry

As pointed out in the introduction, not until the nineteenth century did the wearing of jewelry become popular and widespread among the common people in Western Europe, and silver jewelry found an expanding market only towards the end of the century. This was particularly evident in the U.S. where the supply of silver did not become readily available until after the Civil War. During the Civil War, the shortages of metals and coins had actually forced the government to issue fractional paper currency to supplement the supply of coins.

By the late nineteenth century, the rising demand for practical and affordable jewelry and an increasing supply of silver had led to the establishment of a growing industry and appearance of some of the prominent silver manufacturing firms such

as Tiffany, Unger, Gorham, Kirk, Shiebler, Whiting, Reed & Barton, and International Silver Co. This trend was accelerated with the technological changes which facilitated mass manufacturing and lower cost of production. Over the next century, the industry witnessed many fluctuations, partly related to the fluctuations in the silver market where the metal is traded as a precious commodity and subject to speculative forces, financial panics, and business cycles, and periodic fluctuations in pervading fashion, consumer taste, and demands.

Today, the silver jewelry industry is much less sensitive to the market fluctuation in silver prices, and the cost of the metal actually accounts for less than 20% of the cost of production. Even the efforts of the Hunt brothers to corner the silver mar-

Silver Metal Supply and Demand

| Year | Total Supply | Total Demand | Shortage | Jewelry & Silver Mfg. Demand | | | Market Price $/oz. | | |
				Total	%	US %	High	Low	Avg.
1990	649	717	68	184	26	10	5.39	3.93	4.82
1991	643	715	72	190	27	10	4.53	3.85	4.05
1992	624	730	106	210	29	11	4.31	3.63	3.94
1993	603	781	178	257	33	11	5.37	3.54	4.30
1994	595	773	178	223	29	12	5.75	4.62	5.27
1995	633	774	141	230	30	13	6.01	4.35	5.19
1996	640	826	186	266	32	13	5.79	4.67	5.19
1997	665	863	198	280	32	13	6.21	5.47	4.88
1998(4)							7.31	5.47	6.25

Source: Extrapolated from Shuster, William George. The Silver Boom: While Jewelers Benefit, Suppliers Worry, JCK, July, 1998. Silver figures are expressed in million ounces. All figures except prices are rounded.

ket in 1980, driving prices to as high as $48 per ounce, had a short-lived disruptive effect on the industry, and the recent purchase of 130 million ounces by major investor Warren Buffet, which led to slight increases in the price of silver, was noted in passing in the industry. In fact, during the past few decades the demand for silver jewelry has been on the rise with consumer taste changing in favor of silver.

Mexico, Peru, USA, Russia, Canada, China, Australia, Chile, and Poland account for a sizable portion of the supply of silver metal while much of the silver jewelry supply originates in Mexico, Thailand, Italy, the Scandinavian countries, United States, China, and India.

As the table on page 14 indicates, the production of silver has lagged behind the demand throughout this decade, resulting in an increasing shortage which has been met through disinvestment by investors and others holding silver without a significant impact on the market prices. This secondary source of supply accounted for 149 million ounces in 1996. But theoretically, if this trend continues, other things constant, the depletion of sil-

ver stock held by private investors will eventually exert an upward pressure on the market prices, and this may be the long-term view that prompted a major purchase by Buffet.

As it can also be noted, the demand by the silver jewelry industry is responsible for a significant portion of the increase in demand for silver. This rise in the world wide demand for silver is largely due to the rising popularity of silver jewelry, changes in consumer tastes, and preferences at all age levels, but particularly in the younger population. In the U.S., the retailers have been reporting double digit increases in annual sales causing increased domestic production and imports. The competition among the exporting countries has also intensified with silver jewelry from Italy, Thailand, and Mexico accounting for over 70% of domestic U.S. retail sales, each attempting to capture a larger share of this expanding market.

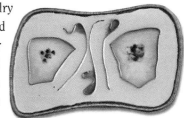

Buying Collectible Silver Jewelry

As in the case of all other antiques and collectibles, there is a hierarchy of markets and sources where collectible silver jewelry can be purchased. These range from garage sales and local flea markets, to classified ads and private individuals, estate sales and auctions, regional flea markets, antiques and jewelry shows, antique malls and shops, and a multitude of online sites and auctions. Prices of silver jewelry vary drastically, depending not only on the geographical area, but more so on the type of the market within the same geographical location. Normally, some of the merchandise found at the lower markets such as garage sales and local auctions turn over many times before reaching the high end of the market and selling at a major show in a large city or in a specialized gallery. Some of it may be bought by dealers from abroad where the price differentials between the U.S. and a particular foreign market allow a reasonable profit margin.

A knowledgeable collector can always find what may be considered a bargain at the best of shows or a well-attended auction, and a significant portion of the silver jewelry at such shows and markets is actually sold to other dealers, many of whom are simultaneously selling at the same market.

If you intend to sell the jewelry you own, there are many alternative outlets some of which are explained briefly here.

1. To antiques and vintage jewelry dealers. There is no transaction cost, but expect offers which are generally 20 to 50% of retail prices considering the fact that the dealers must account for their own cost and allow for a reasonable profit margin.

2. Through consignment to a dealer who provides this type of service and will sell your items in his/her shop or on the Internet. The transaction cost varies, but it usually ranges between 10 to 20% of the sale price. Note that if the items are sold at an auction on the Internet, you may also be charged the auction cost, and in an antiques mall, there may be an additional charge, sometimes a percentage of the sale price charged against the dealer by the mall. Make certain that all these expenses, if any, are accounted for when making the arrangement, and always get a written statement with an itemized list of the merchandise and the relevant fees and charges.

3. Through the classified ads in the local newspapers, specialized national trade papers, or classified sections on the net. The transaction cost varies depending on the location and medium. By the time these lines are printed, there will be major sites on the Internet serving as umbrella sites for classified ads in newspapers throughout the nation, bringing your ad in your local newspaper to the attention of national readership.

4. Through consignment to estate sales and auctions. The transaction cost varies depending on the location and type of auction, and the type of advertisement and promotion of the auction and the merchandise, but on average would range

between 15 to 25% of the final value. Note that unless there is a reserve to protect the items, the auction prices may surpass or fall far below the market prices and in case of certain types of auctions are totally unpredictable.

5. Auctioning the silver jewelry on the Internet yourself. This generally requires a computer, a digital camera or scanner, and a server to connect to the Internet. There are many auction sites and the rules vary somewhat, but nearly all require you to become a registered member in order to participate and agree to the rules outlined in an information statement. Some of the major auction sites are listed in the appendix. The auction cost varies depending on the type of the auction, but for an ordinary auction, the cost ranges from zero at some sites, such as Yahoo or newer sites which are attempting to generate traffic, to an average of 3 to 5% at other sites, such as eBay. You should read the terms of the agreement and a list of different charges for different types of auctions before selecting the one that best suits your needs. Note that even free auctions are not cost free. Holding an auction on the Internet requires creating the images of the jewelry with your camera, uploading them onto a site, and writing a description of the item which along with additional information are entered at the auction site. Once the auction ends, there will be correspondence with the highest bidder, and packing and shipping of the product. All of this takes time and time has value, usually referred to by economists as the "opportunity cost," which is the value of the best alternative such as earnings or leisure time lost as a result of engaging in an activity.

Most of the above channels in addition to flea markets and shows are also utilized by the collectors/dealers to buy and sell collectible silver jewelry. However, the traditional markets are now undergoing a serious change. We are currently experiencing major technological and socio-economic transformation of the world with radical changes which are rapidly uprooting the previous market structures. One dimension of this is the major technological changes in the field of communication along with the integration of the world economy. In the field of antiques and collectibles, some of these changes are already apparent and have affected the buying and selling of collectibles, changing the market structure as well as prices. A collector now has immediate access to thousands of outlets with the opportunity of purchasing some of the rarest pieces of silver jewelry which seldom would have been encountered in local or even regional markets. The seller, at the same time, has the opportunity to reach thousands of potential buyers simultaneously. What are the economic and business implications of these undergoing changes for the antiques and collectible silver jewelry market? Below are some of this author's reflections and observations.

•The traditional markets will not disappear but will account for an increasingly lower share of total activity as online sites and auctions multiply manifold. This will be more so for small items such as jewelry compared to large and heavy items such as furniture.

•The rise in the number of sellers and buyers with direct access to the same online markets will intensify competition and derive market prices toward a more uniform and general price levels. According to some dealers, this increased competition has already placed a downward pressure on prices in the mid to upper layers of the market hierarchy.

•The operation cost of selling will be significantly reduced since some, if not all, of this activity can be undertaken at home using computers. This means savings in both labor time and rental cost, and this reduction in cost will be eventually reflected in the general market prices as well as forcing competitive prices in the stationary outlets such as antique malls, shops, and galleries. This may be another reason for the reported downward pressure on the general market prices.

•Gradually, both dealers and collectors will find it more difficult to buy antiques and collectibles at old bargain prices in the traditional markets since some of this supply will be shifted to and sold on the Internet. As a result, the supply prices will increase, and the cost of replenishing the supply will increase for the dealers. In the short run this increase in cost cannot be passed on to the buyers because the market prices will be subject to the forces of competition and "mark-up" pricing practiced by many dealers in the past will become much more difficult. In the long run, the market prices will eventually reflect this rise in the cost.

•Generally, many sellers in lower markets as well as those in rural and less populated markets will be able to receive much better prices for their collectibles, such as silver jewelry, when selling on the Internet. However, for buyers, the probability of bargain prices on the Internet is far less than buying in these traditional markets.

•The internationalization of the markets will enable both dealers and collectors to buy and sell products which until very recently were not readily available in an average market or even at internationally attended markets. For example, the collectors of Finnish silver jewelry by a particular designer will find it much easier to purchase the type of jewelry they collect and so will international sellers of the same jewelry. Gradually, this will reduce the international price differentials which now induce purchasing in one country and selling in another.

•Commerce on the Internet will increase the risks for buyers and collectors, particularly in the case of auctions and especially for the novice and inexperienced. More on this topic follows.

Cautionary Remarks about Auctions

In the field of antiques and collectibles, the cardinal rule and the primary advice to collectors has always been to "buy from a reputable and established antique dealer," a motto which should apply to all purchases by the beginner and the novice. Auctions were always a risky venture for the inexperienced, and less knowledgeable collectors and auctions on the Internet have multiplied this risk. Auctions with staged bids and/or unscrupulous local and transitory auctioneers selling new merchandise and reproductions can be avoided by reputation or after a few bad experiences, but this would be practically impossible on the Internet and only an experienced and knowledgeable buyer will be able to minimize this risk by deciphering the carefully written descriptions and asking the right questions or noting the possibility of a staged bid. Most items purchased at auctions cannot be returned for a refund, but despite this, even the dishonest seller will refund you if you object strongly, just to keep you quiet. The profits are derived from hundreds of unsuspecting buyers who believe that they have bought an old and antique piece, perhaps never discovering the truth until the item is offered for sale years later. A semi-scientific random survey of several auction sites by the author revealed a serious problem in this area where about half of the silver jewelry auctioned is actually new or recent merchandise, even when, in the author's opinion, a somewhat liberal definition rather than strict dictionary or conventional definitions is used for terms such as antique and vintage. The site with the best result was eBay and as a way of cautioning the readers, the results are summarized below.

Sampling of Antique and Vintage Silver Jewelry Auctioned on eBay

Date	Total # Entries	# New or Recent	Percent
6/14/99	399	78	19.6
7/10/99	197	66	33.5
11/20/99	388	89	22.9
01/14/00	265	49	18.5

The proportion of new and recent silver jewelry classified as antique and vintage on certain sites, especially free auction sites, is as high as 60%. These include mass produced jewelry made in Italy, Mexico, Thailand, Eastern Europe, and other parts of the world which usually wholesale at 50¢ to $1.20 per gram. Some of this new silver jewelry is collectible, depending on the collector's taste and preferences, but it certainly is neither antique nor vintage, though it is auctioned as such, and sold frequently at or even above retail prices.

U.S. Silver Jewelry

By the third quarter of the nineteenth century, the U.S. became a major market for silver products both in terms of supply as well as demand. An 1842 tariff levied against foreign imports and the discovery of Comstock silver in Nevada in 1859 followed by many others in western United States ensured a steady development of the industry. The nation also received a much overdue welcome and recognition in Europe beginning with the 1878 Paris World's Fair where a broad range of U.S. products, both in terms of quality and artistic rendition, matched or surpassed the products of other nations, crowned by the occasion of Tiffany & Co. winning the "grand prix."

Indeed, late nineteenth and early twentieth century was a period of American splendor and grandeur toward which the manifest destiny, expansion, and integration of markets, rising per capita income, and conspicuous consumption were contributing factors — all to be temporarily frustrated by the Great Depression and, so far as silver was concerned, coming to a near halt by WWII because of government restrictions on metal consumption in order to meet the war requirements. Moreover, the Industrial Age provided new technologies and innovative methods to mass produce silver products, hence reducing cost and placing silver within the reach of nearly all but the poorest Americans. Although many jewelry and silverware manufacturers converted their plants to production of war-related products, the production of silver jewelry continued on a much lower scale during the WWII years. In fact, due to heavier war restrictions on other metals, some costume jewelry manufacturers resorted to using silver as a substitute for other base metals.

The post WWII era witnessed a partial recovery in the production of silver jewelry, but the industry also faced heavy competition from imported jewelry, among which Mexico, Thailand (Siam), Middle Eastern and the Far Eastern countries were the major low-cost sources of supply in addition to continued imports from Europe, especially Italy and the Scandinavian countries. Today much of the imported silver jewelry found in the market is manufactured in Italy, Mexico, and Thailand with a trickle from other European countries, Middle East, Far East, and India. The interest in collecting ethnic jewelry, particularly beaded jewelry, is also leading to a larger market for imports

from Africa, central Asia, and the Tibetan highlands as well as other parts of the world. Domestic production is still strong, including Native American and Southwestern silver jewelry which have become increasingly popular during the past few decades though much of what is peddled as Native American is nowadays made outside of the U.S.

As pointed out elsewhere, the product reliability and silver content were implied by the use of hallmarks in various parts of the world though these standards were not always adhered to. The tradition in the U.S., however, was somewhat different. Much of nineteenth century American silver jewelry is not marked, and pieces that were marked for silver content were subject to no laws that guaranteed the validity of the mark. The silver products that were marked often carried the "coin" or later the "sterling" mark sometimes along with pseudo-hallmarks emulating the British system.

The first law regulating the stamping of silver products was enacted by the Massachusetts legislature in 1894 followed by several other states before the National Stamping Act was passed by Congress in 1906 and put into effect in June 13, 1907. This law, enhanced and amended several times over the years, provides the basis for regulating the marking and stamping of silver products. The 1906 act required that any product marked "sterling" or "coin" must contain 925 per 1000 parts pure silver for "sterling" and 900 per 1000 parts pure silver for "coin" silver, permitting a divergence of only 4 parts per 1000 from this standard. An amendment in 1961 required also the maker's trademark to be stamped next to the silver standard mark.

The National Stamping Act, as amended, not only required the use of trademarks, but also specifically requires the registration of such a trademark with the U.S. Patent and Trademark Office (PTO). Despite the law, many regularly used marks on American jewelry are not yet registered trademarks though this situation is gradually improving as a result of the pressures and industry-wide vigilance. For example, many sponsors of major jewelry shows and expos require or strongly encourage their participants' full compliance. Nevertheless, the fact remains that a large volume of U.S. manufactured silver jewelry does not carry the maker's mark, and in many cases, identifying and dating even pieces that are marked is a formidable challenge.

The silver jewelry of approximately 150 U.S. manufacturers and silversmiths is displayed in this section along with a brief history or biography and the images of their trademarks. Aside from the jewelry itself, three sources were indispensable while researching the trademarks, and the kind permission of two publishers, Larry Frederick of JCK and Cahners Business Information and Tran Duy Ly of Arlington Book Company, to reproduce some of the trademarks has saved the author many hours of photographing and drawing these marks or searching the documents filed with the U.S. PTO. The author is especially grateful to all these sources for their kind assistance:

1. Jewelers' Circular Keystone, *Brand Name Trademark Guide,* and various issues of JCK.

2. Jewelers' Circular, *Trade Marks of the Jewelry and Kindred Trade,* reprinted by Arlington Book Company, 1988.

3. U.S. Patent and Trademark Office.

The biographies are drawn from a variety of sources, including author's interviews and communications with many of the extant manufacturers and knowledgeable people who once worked in the industry. For readers who are interested in more detailed biographies, Dorothy T. Rainwater's two excellent books, *American Jewelry Manufacturers* and *Encyclopedia of American Silver Manufacturers,* both published by Schiffer, are still the most comprehensive works in this field and were also relied upon for background information on some of the manufacturers.

American Silversmiths and Manufacturers

A & Z Chain Co.

The firm was founded circa 1905 in Providence, Rhode Island, by Carl Anshen and Saul Zeitlin as a chain manufacturing concern, gradually becoming involved also in the production of jewelry. The ownership changed hands several times before being acquired by Amtel Corporation and reorganized as its Hayward division in Providence. Currently the firm is named A & Z Hayward Company located in East Providence. A & Z sterling silver and vermeil jewelry are usually refined and delicate pieces with stylized floral forms. Various trademarks were used, but they all incorporate the "A & Z" name of the company.

Am Lee

Am Lee Jewelry Company was founded in the mid 1940s in Providence, Rhode Island. Based on the vintage jewelry available on the market, it appears that the firm was a manufacturer of primarily costume jewelry during the mid 1940s to the 1960s. The trademark "Am Lee" was registered with the U.S. PTO claiming first use in January, 1946.

Anson Inc.

Established originally in Providence, Rhode Island, as Anderson Tool & Die Company by Olof Anderson, an emigrant from Tansdorp, Sweden. The firm provided tools and dies for the jewelry industry and after WWII ventured into jewelry business and manufacturing. The current name, Anson Incorporated, was adopted in 1948, and the company was still in business as of the late 1990s. Anson specialized in the production of men's jewelry and accessories such as collar holders, cuff links, tie clips and chains. Women's jewelry was introduced in 1967, but this accounted for an insignificant portion of the firm's aggregate production. A very limited amount of Anson's output was made in sterling silver, and these pieces are occasionally encountered in the market place.

Art Metal Studios

Originally founded as the Chicago Art Silver Shop in Chicago by Edmund Boker (b. 1890) and Ernest Gould (1884 – 1954). Both Boker and Gould were born in Hungary and trained as silversmiths before emigrating to the U.S. and establishing the workshop in 1912. The firm manufactured copper, bronze, and silver products, including silver jewelry. During the 1920s – 1930s it expanded rapidly from a small shop to a wholesaler of silver jewelry which was sold by some of the major department stores such as Marshall Field in Chicago. The firm is still in business.

Atlas Manufacturing Company

Listed in *Jewelers' Circular* as a firm located in New York City, the Atlas appears to have been founded sometime in the 1940s. All of the jewelry marked "Atlas" and seen by the author is either gold-filled, made in sterling silver, or vermeil and appears to have been made during the 1940s to the early 1950s.

The examples shown here are very typical of the type of jewelry manufactured by the firm. The jewelry is always marked on an appliqué.

Avery, James

An art and design teacher at several universities for nearly a decade, James Avery (b. 1921) established his first workshop in 1954 in Texas. The business was launched with a capital investment of $250 in Avery's garage involving a workbench and simple tools, where he worked alone for the next three years making jewelry and building up a long list of clients.

The business expanded rapidly, and by 1968 the firm employed over 25 people and moved to its present location in Kerrville, Texas. By the late 1970s, James Avery Craftsman Inc. had become a major manufacturer of gold and silver jewelry with over 100 employees. Avery is known for its silver charms and religious jewelry made in simple designs "coupled with the integrity of structure and workmanship." The jewelry is usually in solid silver, though some is also set with semi-precious stones. It is marketed throughout the U.S. and in some foreign countries and sold directly through 29 James Avery retail outlets located in Texas, Oklahoma, and Georgia. Chris Avery serves as the current president and CEO of the firm.

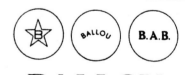

Baldwin & Miller Company

The Baldwin & Miller Company was founded in Indianapolis, Indiana, in the early 1880s.

The firm was a manufacturer of silver products, including jewelry and novelties. The firm was still in business in the 1980s as a division of the Marquis Equestrian with a listed address in Indianapolis, but the 1994 issue of *JCK* had the firm listed with no address, suggesting that it may be out of business.

Ballou & Company

Barton Ballou founded the company in 1876, manufacturing primarily gold, gold filled and plated findings, and jewelry. The firm is also known for its specialty medals and lapel pins. Comparatively, very little silver jewelry was produced. As of 1999, the firm was still in business in Providence, Rhode Island.

N. Barstow & Co. and Barstow & Williams

The firm's history dates back to at least 1880 with Nathaniel Barstow's venture into manufacturing jewelry by founding the Barstow & Luther Company, later joined by a new partner, Walter Williams, and forming the Barstow & Williams Company. The name was changed again circa 1904 to N. Barstow and the firm was in business until the early 1920s. Apparently the firm increasingly specialized in the production of silver jewelry, novelties, and accessories. Several trademarks were used, but the superimposed "BW" is the most common mark found on the silver pieces.

Basset Jewelry Company

Basset was founded in Newark, New Jersey, in the mid 1890s, manufacturing both gold and silver jewelry. The firm was in business until the early 1930s. All Basset jewelry seen by the author is well designed and of high quality. The gold jewelry is found more frequently than their silver pieces.

Beaucraft, Inc.

One of the major U.S. manufacturers of silver jewelry and novelties, the firm was founded after WWII circa 1946 in Providence, Rhode Island, and has been in business continually since that time. There is an abundance of Beaucraft silver jewelry in the collectible market, much of it dating to the 1950s and 1960s, suggesting successful marketing and sales by the company. Several registered trademarks are used by the firm which include the letter "B," "Beau," and "Beaucraft." As of 1999, the firm was still in business in Providence.

Bell Trading Post

The firm was founded circa early 1930s, operating as a branch of the Sunbell Corporation located in Albuquerque, New Mexico. The firm specializes in the production of copper, mixed metal, and silver jewelry, some set with turquoise with Southwestern influence. At least three types of trademarks can be found on the jewelry: "BELL," the image of a bell, and a bell hanging from a post. Based on the author's experience, the non-silver jewelry is more common. The firm was out of business circa late 1980s.

Binder Brothers, Inc.

The Binder brothers were involved in the jewelry wholesale and retail business as far back as 1912 and served as the exclusive U.S. distributors for the German jewelry manufacturer, Ernest Gideon Bek. After WWI, they purchased Gideon Bek and began manufacturing jewelry under the Binder Brothers trademark. This trademark was first used in May 1920. The firm has been continually listed with a New York address in various issues of the *JCK*. It was also listed in the New York City Yellow Pages as late as 1999, but the author's postal inquiries were returned, suggesting that the firm is no longer at that address. The firm's output consisted of primarily silver jewelry and novelties. The quality varies, but the firm made some high quality silver jewelry in stylized floral designs that is relatively scarce.

(B)(B)

Black Hills

The jewelry distinctly recognizable and known as Black Hills jewelry is manufactured by the Black Hills Jewelry Manufacturing Company located in Rapid City, South Dakota. The firm is well known for its gold jewelry with multi-tone leaf motifs, but it also manufactured sterling silver jewelry with applied gold leaf overlay similar to its gold jewelry. The firm is still in business with a market that has been expanding over the past several decades. The black hill trademark, Black Hills Gold J Co., first used in 1962, and several other trademarks registered with the U.S. PTO do not appear on the silver jewelry, but the boxes and tags are marked with the company logo.   L . . .

James E. Blake Company

James E. Blake was the co-founder of the Blake & Calflin Company, in partnership with Edward Calflin and Albert Sturdy, located in Attleboro, Massachusetts. The firm operated under this name from the time of its establishment in 1881 until 1898, increasingly specializing in the production of silver novelties and accessories. The name of the firm was changed to James E. Blake in 1898, and it continued operation until the late 1930s.

Bond Boyd

Manufacturer of primarily costume jewelry which appears to have been made in the 1940s through the 1950s. All the pieces seen by the author are in vermeil similar to the popular floral silver jewelry made during this period. The jewelry is marked on an applied appliqué.

BOND BOYD

Boucher, Marcel

Major designer of primarily costume jewelry avidly sought by collectors, Marcel Boucher was born in France and trained as an apprentice to Cartier before emigrating to the U.S. in the early 1920s. In 1937 he established the Marcel Boucher Company in New York after several years of designing for the Mazer Brothers. Boucher died in 1965, and the company continued for some time under his wife's leadership, Sandra Boucher, also an able and talented designer. As of the late 1990s, the firm was still listed with an active registered trademark of Marcel Boucher. A very limited volume of Boucher jewelry was made in sterling silver, but despite the scarcity,

the pieces are not necessarily of higher value than the costume jewelry. The prices for Boucher jewelry have been rising over the past decade, and this trend is expected to continue.

Bugbee & Niles Company

Bugbee & Niles was founded in 1896 in Providence, Rhode Island. The firm was the manufacturer of gold and silver jewelry, accessories, and watch bands of high quality and durability. The firm's silver jewelry was primarily in traditional designs enhanced with semi-precious stones. Out of business by 1943. The jewelry is marked.

B. & N.

Burch, Laurel

Laurel Burch began her venture in the streets of San Francisco, selling her handmade jewelry in the 1960s, and she rose to create beautiful decorative arts with her distinct designs which received national attention. Most of the jewelry designed by Burch was not in sterling silver although those pieces are also being collected today. Laurel Burch sold her business in San Francisco a few years ago and is reputed to still be doing some designing in Carmel, California. Although the firm was listed in the San Francisco Yellow Pages, the author's postal inquiries in 1999 were returned, indicating that the firm is no longer at that address. Burch's silver jewelry can now be purchased at affordable prices, but the prices are expected to continue to rise in the future. The jewelry is marked with her name in script.

Laurel Burch

Cabin Craft (1933 – 1972)

Cabin Craft Shop was founded in 1933 by Doris Heise (later Miller) in Ephraim, Wisconsin. Originally from Madison, Doris Heise attended the University of Wisconsin, studying art and design and upon graduation, unable to find employment during the Great Depression, decided to open her own shop in the resort town of Ephraim situated in Door County by Lake Michigan, not far from Green Bay, Wisconsin. The cabin she first rented for $85 a season, with no running water and electricity, served both as her home and workshop. The first piece of jewelry she sold was a ring commissioned by a fellow Moravian, Henry Anderson, in exchange for three weeks of free use of his canoe. Doris never used the canoe, but the real compensation came many years later when in a Moravian church service, Anderson showed his hand and declared that he was still wearing the ring. From this meager beginning in 1933, the Cabin Craft Shop grew to include several buildings and became a popular tourist attraction.

Doris met Harvey Miller in Ephraim who was then working for Western Union but the couple did not marry until 1945 after

Harvey had spent two years in Iran working as a telegrapher during WWII. Soon Harvey began managing the business, and since the couple spent their winters in California, many imported gift items, some from Mexico, were added to the merchandise sold by the shop which had by now expanded into several buildings.

Doris made the jewelry herself, frequently commissioned by costumers, initially in an outdoor porch, and later at a specially made workbench under a newly added high tech light fixture. Some of the commissioned jewelry was made in Southern California where the couple spent the winters and bought stock for the shop. Doris Heise Miller's silver jewelry is of the highest quality, all handcrafted, demonstrating exceptional skills in producing the varied pieces and designs commissioned by her clients. It is scarce and usually found in the Midwest and Southern California collectible markets. The Cabin Craft Shop was sold in 1972. Harvey died in 1983, and Doris in 1997.

Carl-Art, Inc.

The firm was founded in Providence, Rhode Island, circa 1938, specializing in the production of gold, gold filled, and silver jewelry, ornaments, and accessories. Much of the jewelry found in the collectible market is gold filled or vermeil sterling silver with delicate traditional floral designs. The firm appears to have gone out of business or reorganized sometime in the mid to late 1980s and was listed without a known address in the 1994 *Jewelers' Circular*.

Carnegie

Founded by Hattie Carnegie (1886 – 1956) in 1918 in New York City, selling apparel and later jewelry designed by her. A very small portion of the jewelry was made in silver and can be occasionally found in the collectible market. Hattie Carnegie was acquired by Chromolloy American Corporation in 1976. The jewelry is usually marked Hattie Carnegie, Carnegie, or with her HC initials within a diamond framed by a semi-oval.

Caron Bros.

A Canadian firm dating back to the 1870s, involved in both importing and manufacturing jewelry. The jewelry is rare in the U.S. market and those seen by the author exhibit either enamel work or gilded sterling silver dating to the turn of the century. Caron appears to have gone out of business sometime in the early 1920s.

Castlecliff, Inc.

Founded by Clifford Furst in New York City sometime in the mid 1940s. Castlecliff was a manufacturer of primarily costume jewelry, including some sterling silver jewelry. These exhibit interesting and refined designs and are usually of good quality. Although not much silver jewelry was manufactured, it is occasionally encountered in the market place.

Caviness, Alice

Alice Caviness began manufacturing costume jewelry after WWII when she was already an established business woman in the garment industry. Only a small portion of Caviness jewelry was made in sterling silver. Although Caviness died in 1983, production of the jewelry continued under the leadership of her partner, Lois Stevens. The firm was still in business as of the late 1990s, located in Malverne, Long Island, New York.

Cellini

Several firms used this trademark, but the manufacturer of the jewelry displayed here was probably the Automatic Gold Chain Company, a producer of jewelry located in Providence, Rhode Island. The registration papers filed with the U.S. patent office claimed first use in 1930.

Ciner

Ciner Manufacturing Company was originally established as a producer of fine jewelry by Emanuel Ciner in 1892. The firm began to manufacture costume jewelry in 1931, and this is the most common Ciner jewelry found in the collectible market. To a much lesser extent, sterling silver jewelry was also manufactured by the firm.

Cini, Gugliemo

Cini was founded in Boston, Massachusetts, by Gugliemo Cini in 1922. Gugliemo was born in Italy and arrived in the U.S. when only 17 years old. Cini jewelry were primarily in sterling silver, reflecting classical and renaissance influences. Some of the jewelry were actually the reproduction of antique jewelry, but many other pieces with the antique look are actually original Cini designs. Different techniques, repousse, filigree, and solid three-dimensional designs, were employed and the jewelry is considered among the best manufactured silver jewelry in America. The company ceased production in 1970, but intermittent production occurred in the 1990s and the trademark and company are listed in *Jewelers' Circular*. The most common marks are **CINI** and **G.CINI**.

Clark & Coombs

The history of this firm dates back to 1872 when it was founded in North Attleboro, Massachusetts. The firm relocated to Providence, Rhode Island, in 1890, and was incorporated in 1903. Coombs died in 1889 while William Clark led the firm until his death in 1918. The firm was still in business as of the late 1990s. Clark & Coombs specialized in the production of gold filled and sterling silver rings set with semi-precious stones, very similar to Scottish jewelry. The double "C" mark found on the sterling silver jewelry has been used since the early years.

Concra

As of this writing, no information on this firm could be obtained. Most of the jewelry seen by the author consists of sterling silver charms and novelties and appears to have been made in the 1960s and 1970s. The jewelry is marked:

CONCRA
STERLING

Cone, Eva Mariam

Born circa 1892, Eva Cone studied art and received her training in metalwork from George Hunt. She subsequently produced silver jewelry for over the next five decades and spent near four of it teaching metalsmithing at Moore College of Art. Given a long period of active silversmithing, Cone's jewelry is extremely rare, suggesting that perhaps much of her jewelry was not marked. The few marked pieces seen by the author are of high quality and show a variety of influences. Her jewelry is usually found in the Philadelphia and New England areas where Cone worked and showed her jewelry. It is usually marked:

CONE
STERLING

Coro (Cohn & Rosenberger)

The history of this company dates back to 1901 when Emanuel Cohn and Gerald Rosenberg began selling jewelry and accessories in a small New York shop. The name "Coro" consists of the first two letters of each partner's name. Over the years Coro rose to become the largest costume jewelry manufacturer in the U.S. with a workforce of over 2,000. A broad range of costume jewelry with variety of designs and different price levels was produced and marketed by Coro over a period of six decades. The firm ceased production in 1979 after the retirement of Rosenberg though the business and trademark abroad were retained by foreign concerns. Only an insignificant portion of the Coro jewelry production was in sterling silver, but the sheer volume of output by Coro has left behind many examples of silver jewelry available in the collectible market. Over 80 trademarks were used by the company, but the most common marks found on the sterling silver jewelry carry the Coro name and can easily be identified. The most common marks are "Coro" and "Corocraft."

Courtly

No definite information could be gathered on the trademark "Courtly." "Courtly Jewels" was the registered trademark used by the Leo Glass & Company, and it is possible that this mark was also used by that company, although this could not be verified. The firm was founded in New York City by Leo Glass sometime in early 1940s, and its "Courtly Jewels" trademark was used beginning in 1946. Leo Glass & Company was primarily the manufacturer of better quality costume jewelry.

COURTLY

cRco

As of this writing no information could be gathered on the company which used the trademark cRco. The jewelry marked as such and seen by the author is better than average costume jewelry set with rhinestones and appears to have been made sometime during the late 1930s to 1950s period.

Curtis Jewelry Mfg. Co.

The Curtis Jewelry Manufacturing Company was founded in Providence, Rhode Island, around 1950.

The firm was a manufacturer of gold plated and sterling silver jewelry. The firm was still in business as of the late 1990s, located in Johnston, Rhode Island. Much of the Curtis jewelry seen on the market dates back to the 1950s or perhaps early 1960s. The pieces are both in sterling silver and vermeil, usually of small and delicate size, with traditional designs.

Curtman Company

The Curtman Company was founded in Providence, Rhode Island, circa 1936. The firm was the manufacturer of primarily gold filled, sterling silver, and vermeil jewelry. Curtman became a division of the Uncas Corporation and its trademark was still active as of the late 1990s.

Danecraft, Inc.

The turn of the twentieth century in America attracted many highly skilled and talented artisans and jewelers from Italy who were instrumental in the development of the American fine and costume jewelry industry, a subject which from the historical perspective deserves independent attention and in-depth research. The history of the founders of Danecraft can be traced back to seventeenth century Italy and the area of Pescara by the Adriatic Sea where the Primavera family of successive jewelers became a well recognized name and supplier of fine jewelry to the Italian wealthy, royalty, and aristocratic families.

As in other crafts in Europe, a common practice was for the artisan to visit the patrons' homes to repair or produce jewelry commissioned by the customers. Another common practice was the learning of the trade and continuation of the business by the sons. Hence, in the late nineteenth century, Thomas Primavera, Sr. was usually accompanied by one of his two sons, Thomas and Victor, who learned the art of design and jewel making trade from their father under the candlelight.

The elder Primavera never saw America, but his son Victor Primavera, Sr. (1896 – 1977) emigrated to the U.S. in 1910 and later with his brother, Thomas, founded the Primavera Brothers Jewelry Company in the 1920s. The firm was one of the early manufacturers of costume jewelry in America and a pioneer in introducing the quality designs used previously in fine jewelry manufacturing in the industry. This point cannot be overemphasized, for one of the primary factors responsible for the acceptance and rapid expansion of the costume jewelry industry in America was the quality of designs and craftsmanship creating jewelry with striking resemblance to fine jewelry. In this respect, Primavera's contributions toward the development of the industry are an integral part of the history of the costume jewelry industry in America, a history that only in recent years has come to be understood and appreciated.

After the death of Thomas Primavera, Jr., Victor Primavera, Sr., founded the Danecraft Corporation in 1934 under a parent company, Felch & Company, in Providence, Rhode Island. The firm manufactured sterling silver jewelry designed by Victor Primavera, Sr., and marketed the jewelry under the Danecraft name. According to the Primavera family, the name Danecraft was adopted because of Victor's preference for, and influences by, the Danish silversmithing tradition and designs.

During WWII, Danecraft separated from Felch & Company and began operating as an independent company with Victor as its president and his son, Victor Jr. (b. 1927), as vice-president. The firm continued to expand in the next few decades, manufacturing a large volume of silver jewelry with varied exquisite designs often inspired by nature. The jewelry was regularly advertised in major national journals and magazines and sold through fine department stores. Both in terms of quality of designs and craftsmanship, Danecraft produced some of the best silver jewelry the industry had to offer during post-war decades.

During the 1970s Danecraft entered the fine jewelry field by introducing its vermeil lines with 24k gold over sterling and expanded its distribution network. It also marketed a collection of 14k jewelry under the name, "Primavera Jewelry," launched in New York. These new vermeil sterling lines were largely smaller pieces with delicate and intricate designs popular during that period and marketed in competition with fine gold jewelry. During the 1980s, the firm continued to expand and acquired Alan Jewelry Company, notable makers of cast fashion jewelry, in Providence, Rhode Island. It also began to diversify by creating jewelry in various classifications, from upscale "Vittorio" line with unique and elegant styling to the "Whimsical & Novelty Pins."

Two senior designers are currently creating most of the new lines for Danecraft. Leslie Block Prip is the main designer of the sterling silver line while Lounne DiBella designs the "Vittorio by Danecraft" line. Danecraft is still privately owned and operated by the Primavera family. Currently, Victor Primavera, Jr. serves as the chairman of the board while his son, Victor III (b.

Danecraft, Inc. (cont.)

1958), is the chief executive officer and his daughter, Gail, the vice-president of the firm. According to Victor III, the firm currently has 425 employees, and 1999 was the most successful year in the history of the company.

To the author's best knowledge, all Danecraft jewelry was marked with the name of the company. The Felch & Co. mark was only used during the early period and never after the separation of Danecraft from the parent company. The fate of Felch & Co. itself after the separation is not very clear. It is assumed that it may have changed its name to Felch & Wehr Co., a manufacturer of shoe and belt buckles.

Because of the large volume of silver jewelry manufactured by the firm, vintage pieces still can be found in the collectible market at bargain prices. These prices are expected to rise, especially for the more elaborate and higher quality pieces, but most vintage Danecraft jewelry would make great additions to any collection of American silver jewelry.

DeRosa

One of the American manufacturers of costume jewelry of highest quality and designs. The firm was founded by Ralph DeRosa in New York City, about 1935. The major period of production was between 1935 through the 1950s though the firm lingered until the late 1960s. Much of the jewelry was not marked and the early marked sterling and vermeil pieces are prized finds. Several marks were used, all of which include the name of the company in block or fancy script letters.

Dieges & Clust

Founded in Providence, Rhode Island, circa 1915, the firm was a prolific manufacturer of pins, badges, and novelties. The firm became a part of the Herff Jones Division of the Carnation Company and was still in business as of the late 1980s, but the 1994 *JCK* issue lists the firm without a known address, suggesting relocation or out-of-business status.

D&C

Doskow, Leonore, Inc.

Founded by Leonore and David Doskow in New York City in the mid 1930s. Leonore was born in Philadelphia in 1910, and her interest in jewelry began at a young age when she was given a jewelry tool set as a gift. After graduating from Bryn Mawr College studying art and archaeology, she returned to Philadelphia and opened a small studio, making jewelry. Among the couple's early customers was the famed Philadelphia Orchestra leader Leopold Stokowski who bought a $40 gold bracelet for his date Greta Garbo. The Doskows moved to New York in 1936, operating the business from a small apartment and then to Greenwich Village in 1937. Around 1960 the firm relocated to Montrose, New York, and by the early 1970s was employing about 50 people.

Leonore and David retired from active participation in the company in 1985, and the management was passed on to the second generation Doskows, David and his wife Lynn Doskow. David Doskow, Sr. died in 1993. Leonore, according to her son David, still comes to the plant a few times a week at age 89.

Doskow manufactured primarily sterling silver jewelry, novelties, and accessories which were personally designed by Leonore Doskow. Initials and gift items constituted a significant portion of the merchandise, but the firm has been gradually moving toward a greater emphasis on jewelry in recent years. Doskow jewelry is of high quality, made of solid silver with interesting and innovative designs. According to David Doskow, the current chairman, "hand craftsmanship is still the basic model of manufacturing with an emphasis on fine polishing and skilled benchwork."

Eisenberg

The best known American manufacturer of rhinestone jewelry and accessories, Eisenberg was founded in Chicago by Jonas Eisenberg in 1914, originally as a manufacturer of ready-to-wear clothing accented and complemented by glittering rhinestone buttons and accessories which were manufactured by other Chicago firms, such as Agnini and Singer. Eisenberg's direct involvement in jewelry production did not begin until around 1930, and the firm rose to manufacture some of the most beautiful and now avidly sought after rhinestone jewelry. Comparatively, a limited amount of jewelry was manufactured in sterling silver and some of these pieces are of WWII vintage due to government restrictions on metal supplies during the war. In 1977, Eisenberg became a division of Berns-Riedmand. Eisenberg International and Eisenberg Jewelry are listed in the Yellow Pages with the same Chicago address.

Ekelund Bros.

Ekelund Bros, Inc. was founded circa 1910 in Providence, Rhode Island, and is still in business. Ekelund's jewelry is primarily in gold though the firm also manufactured sterling silver jewelry. Much of the silver jewelry found in the collectible market consists of rings and to a much lesser degree, pins and pendants.

EKELUND STERLING

Felch & Company (See Danecraft)

Forstner

Originally founded as Forstner Chain Corporation in around 1920 in Irvington, New Jersey.

The firm later changed its name to Forstner Jewelry Manufacturing Corporation. The company was no longer in business by the early 1980s and is not listed in the 1984 *JCK*. A variety of trademarks were used, but most of the silver jewelry is marked with the company name in block letters. This mark was first filed with the U.S. Patent & Trademark Office in 1949 and renewed in 1972.

Forstner

Foster & Baily

Originally founded as White and Foster by Walter White and Theodore Foster in Providence, Rhode Island, in 1873, the company changed names several times before becoming Foster & Baily (1878 – 1898) and finally Foster & Bro. Co. By the turn of the century the firm had grown into a major manufacturer of jewelry in the U.S. and supplier of a wide variety of gold filled and sterling silver jewelry and accessories. The firm's jewelry is of varied quality and reflects the trends over many decades. The Victorian pieces set with precious and semi-precious stones and material as well as the enamel jewelry are most favored by the collectors. The company went out of business sometime around 1950. The most common marks used are the "F &B" inside a flag or separately.

Gorham Corporation

A major American manufacturer of silver products, including jewelry, with a history dating back to the early decades of 1800s. The founder, Jabez Gorham (b. 1792), established his first workshop circa 1820 after a decade of training and experience in the growing silver industry in Providence, Rhode Island. The business expanded after forming a partnership with Henry Webster, manufacturing primarily silver spoons. From this infant beginning, the firm grew to become one of the major and certainly among the most renowned silver manufacturers in the U.S. The firm expanded rapidly under the leadership of Jabez's son John (b. 1820) who introduced the use of machinery, sterling standards, many innovative designs, and an increasing variety of silver products. The late nineteenth century and early twentieth century were an era of mergers and consolidation in the U.S., and this trend seriously affected the silver industry. Like International Silver Company, Gorham expanded as a result of several mergers and acquisitions during this period which included several other well-known American silver manufacturers such as Kerr, Whiting, Alvin, and a retail merger with Black, Starr and Frost in 1929 which lasted for several decades. Gorham itself was acquired by the Textron corporation in 1967.

Much of Gorham's silver production was in the area of cutlery and hollowware, toiletry, novelties, and silver gift products. Generally, jewelry accounted for a very insignificant amount of the firm's production.

Some of the jewelry manufactured at the turn of the century is marked Martele, exhibiting fine craftsmanship and highly creative designs. Others, of more recent vintage, include Christmas pendants and ornaments, and other silver jewelry, including a line known as Gorham Ice which is a combination of silver and crystal glass.

Hamlin-Rice Company

Hamlin-Rice Company was founded in Providence, Rhode Island, sometime during the first decade of the twentieth century. The firm was a manufacturer of jewelry and accessories. The last listing in the *JCK* appears in 1931, and the firm must have gone out of business or reorganized under a different name around this time. The firm's trademark, "H-R. CO" or "H. R. CO," was an early mark used since circa 1910.

Hand & Hammer

The Hand and Hammer Silversmiths was founded in 1979 by Bill and Chip deMatteo and a small group of other craftsmen, including Philip Thorp in Williamsburg, Virginia. But the founding of the company rests on a long history and tradition of fine craftsmanship spanning many decades. William G. deMatteo Sr. (1895 – 1980) was born in Italy and emigrated with his family to the U.S. when he was a young boy. After an apprenticeship at Reed & Barton in New York, he opened his own small workshop in 1919 and subsequently moved to Bergenfield, New Jersey, in 1921 where he continued to manufacture exquisite hand wrought silver and gold products for the next five decades. William deMatteo is considered one of the top American master smiths of this century.

William's son, Bill L. deMatteo (1923 – 1980), learned the craft in his father's studio in New Jersey before becoming a master silversmith at Colonial Williamsburg. During the next few decades, Bill deMatteo created many masterpieces, some as special gifts for royalty, Queen Elizabeth and Princess Anne of England, King Baudoin of Belgium, and King Hussain of Jordan, and also Winston Churchill, President Nixon, and several other heads of state and presidents. For his magnificent craftsmanship and accomplishments, Bill deMatteo was recognized by the American Institute of Architects with a gold medal and became the first American silversmith inducted into the Goldsmiths' Company in London.

Chip deMatteo is the third generation of silversmiths carrying on this long tradition of fine craftsmanship. He began working with silver when he was 10 years old, learning the craft from his father in Williamsburg. The company he and his father founded in 1979 has rapidly evolved into one of the best known names in the silver industry. In recognition of its quality craftsmanship and products, the firm has received many commissioned works. These include designing and making presentation silver for every U.S. President since Kennedy and for many other heads of state. The firm's long list of clients also includes many prominent museums, corporations, and institutions. Among these are gift items and jewelry produced for nearly all major U.S. museums; for institutions and associations such as Harvard and Princeton universities, Phi Beta Kappa, U.S. Marine Corps, and the National Zoo; and for major corporations, such as AT&T, Pepsi, Mass Mutual, Cartier, and Tiffany.

Aside from specialty items and presentation pieces, the main output of Hand & Hammer consists of silver jewelry. These pieces include a broad range of jewelry and charms reflecting a large variety of themes and subjects, including Ann deMatteo's favorite equestrian line. The designs begin with sketches which, according to Chip deMatteo, now involve an increasing use of computers. The designs are then interpreted and rendered in three-dimensional wax sculpture by the firm's current model maker, P.D. Crowe, and a plaster mold and lost wax method is then used by the caster, Mark Moretti, to reproduce the original in silver. Each piece then goes through the final stages of being completed which involve a great deal of handwork.

Hand & Hammer silver jewelry is of high quality and in the author's view, many of the currently produced pieces will soon become the collectibles of tomorrow.

Hayward, Walter E.

The history of Hayward dates back to the mid nineteenth century when several successive partnerships were established in the New England area to manufacture jewelry and accessories. The prominent figures in the company history were Charles E. Hayward, a highly trained silversmith, and his son, Walter E. Hayward. The name Walter E. Hayward was adopted sometime around 1900, but the company was sold several years later to Frank Ryder, an employee of the firm. Frank Ryder and later his son, also named Frank, maintained control until the firm was sold to Amtel Corporation. Amtel, which had also acquired the A&Z Chain Company, reorganized the firms in the early 1970s and Hayward was relocated to East Providence, Rhode Island. The firm is still in business.

Hickok Manufacturing Company

The Hickok Manufacturing Company in Rochester, New York, has been in operation since the early 1900s. The firm specialized in men's jewelry and accessories, including collar buttons, cuff links, cravat ornaments, and tie tacks, of which a very limited volume was manufactured in sterling silver.

The most common trademarks include the company name, Hickok, and to a much lesser extent, the company initials, HMCO.

Hobe

A major American manufacturer of costume jewelry with a history dating back several generations to mid nineteenth century France. The U.S. firm was founded by William Hobe and rose to become a major manufacturer of quality costume jewel-ry in America. Hobe also manufactured some fine jewelry, and others in sterling silver which are primarily of 1930s – 1950s vintage and highly collectible. The firm is still in business with an online catalog at its website.

H.W.K Company

Located in Providence, Rhode Island, and active during the first two decades of 1900s. Manufacturer of primarily sterling and gold filled men's cuffs, clips, and belt buckles. These are rare but not necessarily expensive.

International Silver Company

During the era of mergers and acquisitions which prompted anti-trust laws such as the Sherman Act of 1890, a group of smaller New England firms merged in 1898 to create the International Silver Company. The silver conglomerate included some of the best known nineteenth century silver shops and concerns, such as Meriden Britannia, Holms & Edwards, Rogers & Bros., Webster, and Wilcox. The firm became a major and prolific manufacturer of cutlery, hollowware, and silver products, much of which is silver plated. Limited silver jewelry and nov-elties were manufactured; of particular interest is the post-WWII jewelry designed by La Paglia whose workshop was purchased by International Silver after his death; silver jewelry designed by the Danish silversmith, Kurt Eric Christoffersen, during his short association with the International Silver Company in 1950s; and semi-handcrafted jewelry by Southwestern silversmiths contracted by the company and bearing its trademark.

(W STERLING   *Sterling*

Iskin Manufacturing Company

The firm was founded by Harry Iskin in Philadelphia sometime in late 1920s, originally operating under the name of Harry Iskin Company before assuming the name of Iskin Manufacturing Company sometime in the 1930s. Iskin gradually focused on the production of specialty jewelry, medals, and emblems. The jewelry found on the market dates to the 1930s to 1940s.

Jay Kel

Founded in New York City in the late 1930s to 1940, the firm was active during the decade of 1940s, selling high priced costume jewelry which it regularly advertised in major magazines such as *Vogue*, using a 5th Avenue, New York City address. Sterling silver pieces are rare but not necessarily expensive. The jewelry is marked JAY KEL.

J.H.K Co.

As of this writing, no information has been gathered on the J.H.K Company which appears to have been a manufacturer of primarily sterling silver initials, monograms, and floral type jewelry made sometime during the 1960s to perhaps 1970s.

Jewelart

As of this writing, no detailed information on the manufacturer of the jewelry marked "JEWELART" and no registration records were found with the U.S. Patent and Trademark Office. The jewelry with this mark is primarily silver of average to better than average quality. The examples shown in the following pages are typical Jewelart silver jewelry.

Kabana

Kabana is the registered trademark of Kabana, Inc. founded in Albuquerque, New Mexico, circa early 1970s. The trademark was registered with the U.S. Patent and Trademark Office claiming first use in 1975 for "goods and services jewelry" including catalog order services. Apparently, some of the jewelry is designed by the Greek-born owner and founder, Stavors Eleftheriou, while others are the products of designers who design exclusively for the company. The jewelry marked "Kabana" varies drastically in quality, and it is not clear whether all of these pieces are manufactured at the same plant. Rings abound among the older jewelry, but some of the more recent pieces are outstanding three-dimensional sculptured jewelry in sterling silver that will certainly become prized collectibles in the future. Unfortunately, the author's several inquiries to gather more information on the firm and its jewelry received no response.

Kalo (1900 – 1970)

Kalo was founded by Clara P. Barck (1868 – 1965, Clara Wells after her marriage to another silversmith, George S. Wells) in Park Ridge, Illinois, in 1900. Kalo Shop rapidly grew to become Chicago's most prolific producer of handwrought silver products, including silver jewelry.

The "Kalo girls" operated in a communal setting, true to the arts and crafts movement, highlighting the importance of craftsmanship and training other silversmiths in the arts and crafts tradition. In 1914, Clara Wells moved to Chicago and a salesroom was also opened in New York. With the changing times, Clara refused to adopt new mass production technologies and despite its higher prices, Kalo had a large group of loyal

customers which enabled the firm to continue operations with considerable success. Clara retired in 1940 and in 1959 gave the shop to four of her loyal employees who had been involved with Kalo since its early years at Park Ridge. Kalo continued operations under the new co-owners with Yngve Olsson as the principal designer and finally closed in 1970, refusing to succumb to competitive pressures by lowering its quality standards. Kalo jewelry was made in simple modern designs, sometimes enhanced with semi-precious stones, emphasizing the beauty of the material and fine craftsmanship revealed in artistic forms with soft curves and satin finish.

Keller & Company

The mark of "K" in a lozenge was used by several companies among which King, Raichle & King, and Keller & Company were the best known nineteenth and early twentieth century concerns. The Keller family was involved in the wholesaling and importing of diamonds, watches, and fine jewelry since the Civil War, and one member of the family, Alexander Keller (d. 1873), was the founder of Keller & Untermeyer in 1870 in New York City. The firm entered direct jewelry production around 1885 as Charles Keller & Company located in Newark, New Jersey, producing primarily gold jewelry and discarding the old trademark sometime in early twentieth century. The King, Raichle & King Company was a manufacturer of primarily gold, gold filled and silver jewelry and products. It also used a similar trademark, minutely different from that of the Keller & Company. The firm may have been the manufacturer of silver and enamel jewelry similar to what was popular in Europe, but Keller's involvement in imports would also make it a likely candidate. In either case, the use of the trademark was discontinued by the early twentieth century.

Karen Linne

No information was available on the Karen Linne mark found on vintage jewelry available in the collectible market. All of the jewelry seen by the author appears to have been made in the 1950s to perhaps the 1960s.

Wm. B. Kerr & Company

First founded as Kerr & Thiery in the mid nineteenth century manufacturing a broad range of contemporary silver products, including jewelry. The Kerr jewelry found in the collectible market primarily consists of floral repousse, Art Nouveau, and enamel pieces. This was one of the early American firms which introduced new technology and machinery leading to mass production of jewelry. Kerr was acquired by Gorham in 1906 at which time it was moved from Newark, New Jersey, to Providence, Rhode Island.

Kirk & Son

The oldest American manufacturer of silver products and jewelry with a continuing business, the company was originally founded in Baltimore, Maryland, as Kirk & Smith almost 200 years ago. It subsequently changed its name to Samuel Kirk, Samuel Kirk & Son, before finally being incorporated as Kirk Stieff Corporation in 1979. Samuel Kirk was among the leading American silversmiths and was joined by his son, Henry Child Kirk, who continued the business after his father's death in 1872. Samuel had two other sons who were also associated with the firm for about a decade when the name Samuel Kirk & Son was briefly changed to Samuel Kirk & Sons. Henry Child Kirk incorporated the company in 1896, and his son, Henry Child Kirk, Jr., continued the business after his father's death in 1914.

The Samuel Kirk & Son manufactured a variety of silver products, adjusting to the changing trends and popular fashion during its many decades of operation. Silver jewelry accounted for an insignificant portion of the output. The company was acquired by the Stieff Company in 1972 changing its name to Kirk Stieff which was itself subsequently acquired by the Brown Forman Company in 1990. Many trademarks were used, and the mark shown is one of the more common ones.

Lang Jewelry Company

Lang Jewelry Company, established in Providence, Rhode Island, around 1946, became one of the major, prolific manufacturers of silver jewelry for the next few decades. Lang jewelry is of good quality with floral and figural motifs. The firm was still in business as of the late 1990s.

Two common marks are "LANG" and Lang with a swan (shown), the latter claimed to have been used since 1946.

La Paglia, Alphonse (see Denmark, Georg Jensen)

Born in Italy, La Paglia emigrated to the U.S. in the early twentieth century and during WWII designed jewelry for George Jensen Inc. These pieces are marked with his initials, LP or A.L.P., along with the Georg Jensen USA mark. After the dispute over the Georg Jensen USA operation and its closing in 1950, La Paglia established a workshop in Meriden, Connecticut, circa 1952 and worked briefly in collaboration with the International Silver Company and for the following year produced silver jewelry using some of his designs created for Georg Jensen. La Paglia died in 1953 and his business was purchased by International Silver. Alphonse La Paglia was an exceptionally talented designer, and his silver designs showing Continental and Scandinavian influences are among the best modern jewelry produced in America.

Leach & Miller Company

The Leach and Miller Company was established about the turn of the twentieth century in Attleboro, Massachusetts. The firm was a manufacturer of jewelry and accessories made in gold filled and sterling silver. Leach & Miller jewelry was of high quality, imitating fine jewelry and the styles popular at the time. The sterling silver jewelry made in the 1920s shows strong Art Deco influence. The firm was out of business by the early 1930s.

Several trademarks were used but the two marks shown at right below are the common marks found on the jewelry. The first mark is found only on their earliest jewelry.

L. M. & CO.

Lebolt & Company

Established by brothers John, Joseph, and Nathan Lebolt in Chicago circa 1899, manufacturers of silver products, novelties, and jewelry. John Meyer Lebolt's son assumed leadership in the early 1940s. The firm was among a dozen Chicago firms known for their work in the arts and crafts tradition making handmade silver products and jewelry.

Lewis Bros.

Founded by S.M. Lewis in the mid nineteenth century in Providence, Rhode Island, manufacturer of silver jewelry, accessories, and novelties. The firm was reorganized several times, assuming the Lewis Bros. name sometime in the late nineteenth century. It was out of business around 1913.

Lewis & Paige

Founded by Lewis and Paige circa 1910 – 1914 in Providence, Rhode Island. Manufacturer of sterling silver ornaments, buckles, and buttons and other dress accessories. They were out of business by the mid 1920s.

Lunt Silversmiths (see Rogers, Lunt & Bowlen)

The jewelry shown in this section is marked Lunt, which is the trademark used by the Rogers, Lunt & Bowlen Company since 1936, though the name of the company was not changed to Lunt. The older pieces carried the Rogers, Lunt & Bowlen trademark which is still a registered trademark.

This mark and the company history are covered in following pages under "Rogers." The jewelry produced by Lunt primarily consists of buckles, brooches, and Christmas and Mother's Day jewelry and novelties.

LUNT STERLING

Maisel's Indian Trading Post

Established circa 1930 in Albuquerque, New Mexico, under the ownership of the Maisel family, and manufacturer of Southwestern style Indian jewelry. The jewelry is of fine quality, made in solid silver or in combination with semi-precious stones and is rarely encountered on the market. According to the documents filed with the patent office, the original owners were Edith, Maurice, Cyma, Seymour, and Albert Maisel. The firm was acquired by G.L. Miller in the early 1960s with a new graphic trademark registered in 1966 and renewed in 1986.

Marshall Field

A major department store founded in the second half of the nineteenth century in Chicago and still in business. The company used its trademarks on manufactured products contracted and commissioned by the firm which were marketed through its stores. It also established its own Craft Shop in the early 1900s where the products were marked with the Marshall Field Logo found on handcrafted metalwear. The shop was closed in the late 1940s. Several marks with the company name were used, but the common mark found on small pieces of jewelry was **MF&CO.**

Mary Kay

Some jewelry and silver products found in the collectible market are marked "Mary Kay," the name of the well-known cosmetic corporation which sold its products through thousands of Mary Kay representatives. Those seen by the author are presentation and award pieces given to the representatives for years of service and sales. Given the number of representatives, a large number must have been awarded over the years, and these are collectible both as award pieces as well as silver jewelry. The jewelry is usually marked "Mary Kay" and was probably manufactured for the firm under a special contract.

Joseph Mayer & Bros.

Originally operating under the name of Empire Jewelry Company in Attleboro, the three brothers Joseph, Albert, and Markus Mayer were attracted by the gold and silver strikes in the Northwest and the manufacturing prospects near the supply source and established the Joseph Mayer & Bros. in Seattle, Washington, at the end of the nineteenth century. Manufacturer and wholesalers of gold nugget jewelry discovered in Alaska, fine gold jewelry, silver products, including silverware, souvenir and novelties, specialty jewelry such as medals and emblems executed primarily in gold filled and sterling silver. The firm was acquired by E.J. Towle in 1938.

Mazer Brothers

Two brothers, Joseph and Lincoln Mazer, established the Mazer Brothers Company in New York circa 1927. The name was later changed to Joseph J. Mazer and Company as listed in the 1950 *Jewelers' Circular*. The firm was an important manufacturer of costume jewelry and one of the early employers of Marcel Boucher when he first arrived in the U.S. Andre Fleuridas and Adolfo designed some of the jewelry in the early 1950s.

The firm went out of business in the late 1970s. Unlike some of the other major names in the costume jewelry industry, Mazer was not a prolific manufacturer of jewelry, and vintage pieces, particularly sterling silver pieces, are not as readily available in the collectible market. The earliest pieces are marked Mazer Bros., while the later pieces may be marked Mazer or Jomaz.

McClelland Barclay

McClelland Barclay was born in St. Louis, Missouri, on May 9, 1891 and studied art with H.C. Ives, George Bridgman, and Thomas Fogary before working as an illustrator, sculptor, and painter. A winner of several national prizes for his posters and an illustrator for popular magazines such as *Good Housekeeping* and *Cosmopolitan*, Barclay also ventured into the field of jewelry design and manufacturing. Primarily two types of jewelry were manufactured: Art Deco jewelry in gold plated metals set with rhinestones; and to a lesser extent, sterling silver jewelry with a sculptured three-dimensional look. Both types of jewelry are avidly sought by collectors and command relatively high market prices. McClelland Barclay's life came to an abrupt end during WWII, when a landing ship on which he was a passenger was destroyed by an enemy torpedo on July 18, 1943. His body was never found, and he was reported as missing in action. His jewelry is usually marked "McClelland Barclay" though the mark may show only partially or in abbreviated form. It should not be confused with the trademark of another jewelry manufacturer, Barclay. Based on the author's experience, all McClelland Barclay jewelry carries the mark which contains all or part of his first name. *Jewelers' Circular* listed this name belonging to Rice-Weiner & Co., which may have been the producer of the jewelry or have acquired the trademark after Barclay's death.

Ming

A retail jewelry store first established in Honolulu in the 1940s with over a dozen additional stores opening later in Hawaii and other major American cities such as New York and San Francisco.

Apparently the silver jewelry sold by the stores and marked "MING" was produced for the company, possibly through more than one manufacturer. A significant portion of the silver jewelry was in either solid silver, combined silver with carved natural material such as ivory and coral, or was decorated with pearls and semi-precious stones such as jade. The emphasis is naturalistic with floral and fauna themes showing a strong Oriental influence. The stores owned by the Moon family were gradually closed, and it is the author's understanding that there is no remaining open shop.

There is a small circle of devout Ming jewelry collectors and both auction and asking market prices have risen rapidly during the past decade. The prices for average earrings usually range from $50 to $150 while the unusual pieces are in the several hundred dollar price range. Ming pins are usually in the $150 – $500 price range. The marked jewelry may be stamped or engraved "Ming's."

Mizpah

There is a variety of fine and costume jewelry, both of U.S. and continental origin, marked Mizpah. A jewelry firm owned by Laurie Cybul of New York City is the only company with a current registered trademark of Mizpah at the U.S. Patent Office, claiming commercial use since 1990. But most of the jewelry marked Mizpah is much older, some dating back to the turn of the century if not earlier. Moreover, the variation in the type of the jewelry and the material used suggests that it was not all made by the same manufacturer. As of this date, the author has not been able to locate a single firm which may have been responsible for a significant portion of the jewelry marked Mizpah.

But the mystery of Mizpah may at least be partially resolved by considering the historical and religious significance of the term itself. Mizpah was the name of several ancient cities in Palestine and is mentioned numerous times in the Bible. In ancient times, the word Mizpah basically meant "border" or "watchtower," but over time the term evolved to assume the modern meaning of "farewell" or "God watch over you." There are turn of the century references to Mizpah pins being given to loved ones at the times of separation and departure. Hence, one can speculate that such pieces were marked not by the name of the manufacturer or its trademark, but with a message of love and faith.

Monet

Monet's history dates back to the founding of Monocraft by brothers Michael and Jay Chernow in Providence, Rhode Island, in 1929. Initially the firm manufactured gold plated monograms expanding to production of jewelry and changing its name to Monet in 1937. Monet was among the early American manufacturers of costume jewelry to introduce modern designs, some in sterling silver. The company was acquired by General Mills in 1967 and subsequently by Crystal Brands Jewelry in 1989. The jewelry is marked MONET.

S.F. Myers & Company

A major and prolific manufacturer of jewelry in the latter part of the nineteenth century. Founded by Samuel F. Myers at the outset of the Civil War in New York City. The firm manufactured a broad variety of gold, gold-filled and silver jewelry and accessories. It operated its own wholesale department and was a major East Coast supplier of jewelry by the end of the century. It was out of business circa 1912 – 1913. Many marks were used, most of which include the company name or initials: S.F.M.Co. or S.F.M. & Co.

Napier

The history of this enterprise dates back to the nineteenth century when it was founded as Whitney and Rice in Attleboro, Massachusetts, in 1875. After several changes in ownership and name, including a move to Meriden, Connecticut, in 1890, the leadership of the firm was assumed by James Napier in 1920, and the name of the firm was finally changed to Napier Company in 1922. James Napier led the company for 40 years, during which time the firm became a major manufacturer of costume jewelry, and to a much lesser extent, sterling silver jewelry. Many different trademarks were used, but the most common marks contain the Napier name.

Norseland (see also Coro)

The manufacturers of Coro had many different lines of jewelry and used over 80 trademarks. Norseland was the trademark used on sterling silver jewelry with designs inspired by Scandinavian motifs and frequently imitated Danish sterling silver jewelry. The quality of this jewelry is above most other sterling silver Coro jewelry.

N.S. Company

N.S. Company was founded in Tucker, Georgia, circa 1960. The firm was the manufacturer of jewelry and accessories and was still in business as of the late 1990s. The N.S. trademark has been used since 1962, renewed with the U.S. Patent Office in 1997.

NSco   N. S. C.

Stuart Nye Silver Shop

Stuart Nye (1884 – 1962) founded the company in 1933 in Asheville, North Carolina. Apparently he had no formal training in metal work and had come to North Carolina from New York for treatment of lung disease, possibly tuberculosis, at the Veteran's Hospital. After his release, he began experimenting with metalwork using simple tools and his early hand hammered silver jewelry found buyers, prompting him to open his workshop. Nye's jewelry was simple and inspired by the multitudes of blooming wild flowers and plants in the mountains of western North Carolina. His first handmade piece was a silver pin with a dogwood blossom design, also the state's flower, which has become an easily identifiable Nye symbol and is still being made. Many other lines of silver jewelry depicting flowers and plants were subsequently manufactured and the firm expanded significantly in the 1940s. In addition to the dogwood design, some of the major floral designs introduced were the pansy and lily, poinsettia, trillium, beech, willow, maple, violet, Cherokee rose, ivy, oak, thistle, and pine cone. Copper and bronze pieces were also introduced and are still being manufactured by the company. It is reputed that Nye also briefly made some gold pieces, but the author has never seen an example.

Nye retired in 1948, a year after forming a partnership with Ralph and Annie Morris, who carried on the Nye tradition which survives to this day. This tradition had two important features that characterize Nye silver jewelry: totally handcrafted jewelry reflecting nature. Silver jewelry hand-

Stuart Nye Silver Shop (cont.)

crafted in the old fashioned way was Nye's hallmark, and his designs are as unique and distinct as his craftsmanship. He was so particular about these aspects of his jewelry that it is said he only hired untrained workers so he could train them himself to produce the jewelry using the methods and techniques he had developed.

That same tradition is followed at Nye today where a variety of old Nye designs are still being made, employing the same old tools and techniques. Chisels made of old files, punches made of nail sets, metal shears and hammers, cast iron skillets and anvils, some dating back to the early period, are still the primary tools used to fabricate the Nye silver jewelry. All work is hand

done and hand finished. According to the Nye catalog: "The beauty of our jewelry does not come from the tools. It comes from the inspiration that nature can give to a man who will take the time to look and from the skill and dedication of our craftsmen. We are mountain people with a heritage of craftsmanship. We take pride in our work and in our good reputation." Indeed, nothing better sums up the beauty of Nye jewelry. The jewelry is distinctively American, reminding one of the other American arts and crafts, such as the twentieth century American art pottery, with many similar themes and motifs, celebrating nature, the native plants and fowl, and being blessed with a bounty.

Orb

Orb Silversmiths was founded by Otto R. Bade in New Hope, Pennsylvania, in the late 1950s. Otto Bade was closely associated with Rebajes and served as his foreman in the 1940s and 1950s. Rebajes left the U.S. and relocated in Spain; and a few years prior, he had sold his designs and machinery to Otto Bade. Bade manufactured copper jewelry in the same tradition under

the name of Orbcraft and later relocated to Pennsylvania. Vintage Orb jewelry exhibits very simple modern designs made in silver, usually without stones or ornamentation. Orb is still in business in New Hope, Pennsylvania, specializing in the manufacturing of rings which are executed in both gold and silver.

Pacific Jewelry Manufacturing Co.

Pacific Jewelry Manufacturing Company was a contemporary manufacturer of jewelry, originally located in Culver City, California. The company used a conjoined "JP" trademark which is nearly similar to that used by at least two other companies: the Originals by Pierce & Company; and Phillips Jewelers Inc. The same Pacific trademark shown in 1994 _JCK_ is listed under Pacific Gold Design, a division of American Gold & Diamond Company, located in Los Angeles, California. Most of the silver jewelry examples seen by the author approximately date

to the late 1960s through the 1970s and consist of rings. The marks for all three companies are shown below for comparison.

Pacific Gold Design
Dv American
Gold & Diamond Co

Originals by Pierce & Co

Phillips Jewelers Inc

Panetta

Founded by Benedetto Panetta who began his career as a goldsmith and a jeweler in Naples, Italy, before emigrating to the U.S. in 1908. Panetta worked as a goldsmith for many years as well as for Trifari and Pennino before establishing his own business in New York City in 1945.

The Panetta jewelry exhibits an elegant and refined classical look made usually in sterling silver.

Benedetto died in the 1960s, but his two sons, Amadeo and Armand, both trained by their father, continue the Panetta tradition. The jewelry is marked PANETTA.

Parks Bros. & Rogers

Founded by three partners, George Parks, William Parks, and Everett Rogers in Providence, Rhode Island, around 1892. The company manufactured gold and silver accessories and jewelry with silver jewelry and products becoming its main focus at the turn of the century. Parks Bros. & Rogers used primarily a clover as its trademark on the silver jewelry, sometimes

enclosed in a horseshoe. The extant punch marks on the silver jewelry vary with different types of clover, some without any detail or stem, while others may be enclosed in horseshoes of varying sizes.

Pryor Manufacturing Company

Established perhaps as early as the late nineteenth century, the Pryor Manufacturing Company was a producer of primarily silver and gold-filled accessories and merged with the B.M. Shanley Company sometime in the late 1910s. The latter company was involved in the manufacturing of silver and gold accessories and products similar to that of Pryor and was out of business in the early 1930s.

Reed & Barton

The origin of this firm dates back to the founding of Babbitt & Crossman in Taunton, Massachusetts, in 1824. Though both were in the jewelry business, Isaac Babbit and William Crossman formed the first major U.S. firm manufacturing domestic pewter and Britannia later. After various changes, the firm later named itself Reed & Barton and became a major manufacturer of silverware, maintaining a significant market share in the industry. Post WWII era was marked with the addition of many collectible silver plates, novelties, and giftware. Silver jewelry was also manufactured and marketed on a larger scale including mixed metal and patented Reed & Barton "Damascene" jewelry. All of the firm's products have always been of high quality and craftsmanship.

Reja

Reja Inc. was founded in New York City in the late 1930s. The firm was manufacturer of costume jewelry with a large volume made in sterling silver set with multicolor rhinestones. The jewelry is of relatively high quality with wonderful whimsical designs, many of which are figural depicting insects, birds and animals, usually set with a large central stone. The firm used two registered trademarks, "Reja" in script and in block letters, claiming first use in May, 1940.

Renoir

Renoir of California, Inc., was founded in Los Angeles in 1946 by Jerry Fels. The jewelry designs were inspired by the contemporary abstract and modern art trends and were made primarily in copper. The sterling silver pieces are far more scarce than other Renoir jewelry and command higher prices. The firm was out of business by 1964.

Richards Jewelry Company

H.M. Richards was founded at the turn of the twentieth century in North Attleboro, Massachusetts. The firm was a major manufacturer of jewelry, including gold and silver. Several trademarks were used by the firm, but the two common marks are "WRE" and "Symmetalic." The Symmetalic mark (see page 38) is found on higher quality silver pieces, often with a gold wash or plating. This type of jewelry is more scarce and commands higher prices.

wRE

Richton Jewelry Company (see Coro)

Rogers & Lunt & Bowlen (see also Lunt)

George C. Lunt was an employee of Towle & Son Manufacturing Company where he also apprenticed. After the failure of the company, it was acquired and reorganized by George Rogers, George Lunt, and William Bowlen in 1901. Located in Greenfield, Massachusetts, the firm was the manufacturer of primarily flatware and silver products, and its advertisements appear in the early issues of the *Jewelers' Circular* indicating representation also in New York, Chicago, and San Francisco, and promoting its tableware as "the silver that sells." Over the years the firm acquired several other silver manufacturing companies, and since 1935 has primarily used the Lunt trademark, although its old trademark shown at right and found on its older pieces is still registered.

Rolyn

Rolyn Inc. was founded by Michael A. Ricci in 1963 in Providence, Rhode Island, later relocating to Cranston, Rhode Island. The firm was still in business as of the late 1990s. Rolyn manufactured a broad range of jewelry in 14 kt gold, gold filled, and sterling silver. The firm's major jewelry lines introduced over the years were Radiant and Opalite in both gold and sterling silver using precious and semi-precious stones. A line of men's accessories, Ricci, was primarily in gold while another line, Chante, was gold filled. The firm's common mark on the sterling silver jewelry is the letter "R" enclosing "INC."

S & F

As of this writing, no information on the manufacturer that used the S & F trademark in plain block letters could be gathered. The firm appears to have been the manufacturer of silver products, novelties, and jewelry.

Sarah Coventry, Inc.

Founded by Charles H. Stuart in Newark in 1949, shortly after the establishment of a sister company, Emmons Jewelers, Inc., Sarah Coventry rapidly became a major firm in the costume jewelry industry by successfully marketing its jewelry over the years through home parties attended by millions of American women. Comparatively, a limited amount of silver jewelry was manufactured and marketed under Coventry and Emmons' trademark. The firm ceased operation in 1984, but the rights to the name were purchased by a Canadian manufacturer. All of the sterling silver pieces seen by the author contain all or part of the Sarah Coventry name and can be easily identified. The first trademark was registered with the U.S. Patent Office in February 1, 1956, claiming commercial use since 1949, and renewed under the new ownership of Lifestyle Brands, Ltd., with a Chicago address in 1976. Their second trademark was first registered with the U.S. Patent Office in 1962, claiming commercial use since 1960, and last renewed in 1982. Some of the jewelry was marked with the company "SC" trademark, but the author has never seen this mark on the sterling silver pieces.

SARAH COVENTRY   **SARAH COV**

Schlang, J.D. Co., Inc.

J.D. Schlang Company was established in New York City sometime in the late 1940s. The firm specialized in the production of rings and appears to have gone out of business by the 1970s. The firm's common mark is the stamped or engraved "S" superimposed on "W."

Shiebler & Company

The firm's history dates back to the acquisition of Jahne, Smith & Company in which George Shiebler was a salesman and formed the partnership, Hodenpyl, Tunison & Shiebler circa 1874. In 1876, Shiebler established his own firm and expanded through the acquisition of several other firms. The firm was a manufacturer of flatware, later introducing other silver lines. Jewelry and accessories were introduced in the late nineteenth century which display classical figures and profiles initially used on other silverware. The firm is considered as the first American silver jewelry manufacturer, introducing Renaissance revival motifs adopted in the Victorian era. Silver jewelry accounted for an insignificant portion of the total silver production and is quite scarce, usually with high price tags. The most common mark found on Shiebler silver jewelry is the letter "S" with wings.

Silver Brothers

The firm was founded by the Silver Brothers in the late 1940s and is recognized by its "Silbro" mark on sterling and silver plated silverware. The firm apparently also manufactured some sterling silver jewelry and over the years, and the author has seen a few pieces with this mark.

Silver Cloud, Inc.

The Silver Cloud was founded sometime in the 1970s in Albuquerque, New Mexico. The firm is still in business and manufactures jewelry in the Southwestern style. According to the registration documents filed with the U.S. Patent Office in 1994, the SC mark in a stylized cloud reproduced here was first used in 1979.

Silverman Corporation

The firm was first established in Providence, Rhode Island, by two Russian emigre brothers, Charles (b. 1877) and Archibald (1880 – 1965) Silverman, at the end of the nineteenth century under the name of Silverman Bros. The company apparently ceased operation under this name in 1966 after the death of Archibald Silverman. Several marks were used on silver products, but the most common mark on silver jewelry is the "SB" mark in a circle or oval frame. The jewelry is of average quality with an abundance of figural pins.

Sorrento (see also Uncas)

The trademark Sorrento was registered by the Uncas Manufacturing Company, founded by Vincent Sorrentino in 1911 in Providence, Rhode Island. Nearly all of the jewelry with this mark is either gold plated or sterling and vermeil jewelry, set with semi-precious stones and material. The jewelry is of good quality and normally in traditional and classic designs.

SP Company

The trademark SP Co. was used by the Samuel Platzer Company, Inc., founded in New York City. The firm was still in business as of the late 1990s. The firm's silver jewelry is usually set with semi-precious stones.

Star-Art

Star-Art is the mark found on sterling silver, circa the 1950s through perhaps the 1960s. The jewelry usually has floral designs set with rhinestones and the example shown on the following pages is very typical of the jewelry found under this mark. The Dansal Corporation located in Providence has a "Star Art Jewelry" registered trademark which was still active in the late 1990s, but the author believes this mark belonged to a different company which was in operation during the earlier decades.

Swank

For many years Swank has been the world's largest manufacturer of men's jewelry. The firm was founded in 1897 by Samuel M. Stone and Maurice J. Baer in Attleboro, Massachusetts, and was originally a manufacturer of women's jewelry. By the late 1920s, Swank had abandoned producing women's jewelry and was a major producer of men's jewelry. Since that time, the company has introduced numerous lines made primarily in base metal but also some in sterling silver. In the 1970s, Swank experimented with women's jewelry, but its major market continued to be in the area of men's accessories, including jewelry.

SWANK

Symmetalic (see also W.E. Richards)

Symmetalic was the registered trademark of W.E. Richards Company first used in 1936 and found on the company's high quality sterling silver pieces. The firm also manufactured gold and sterling silver jewelry marked with its WRE trademark. The Symmetalic pieces are usually in vermeil and show Edwardian and Art Deco influences. The jewelry is of high quality and superior to the firm's silver jewelry with the WRE trademark.

Charles Thomae & Son

Charles Thomae (d. 1958) was an employee of the Watson Company, developing several lines which were eventually organized as a separate division of the Watson Company under the name of Thomae Company. Several years later Charles left Watson Company and with his son, Herbert, and established the Charles Thomae & Son, Inc. in Attleboro, Massachusetts, in 1920. The firm was the manufacturer of silver products, including novelties and giftware, medals and medallions, and specialty jewelry. The most common mark found on the Thomae pieces is the crown and lion mark. A crossed "T" superimposed over "C" is Charles Thomae's personal mark and is encountered much less frequently and commands a higher price. Herbert and his younger brother, Charles G. Thomae, assumed the leadership of the company after their father's death in 1958.

Tiffany & Company

Founded by Charles Louis Tiffany in partnership with John Young under the name of Tiffany & Young in 1837. The firm moved on to receive world-wide recognition and prominence for its exquisite designs and quality work in the area of fine jewelry and decorative arts. A limited amount of silver jewelry was manufactured, and pieces seen by the author are primarily of post-WWII vintage and appear as mere tokens when compared to the firm's outstanding fine jewelry. The company was acquired by the Avon Corporation in 1980 and sold to a group of investors in 1984. The more recent mass produced and mass marketed silver jewelry made in Italy, bearing the renowned mark of Tiffany & Company and offered as "designer silver jewelry" is also of lesser quality, failing to exhibit the same imagination and creativity for which Tiffany was world famous. Disregarding the mark, there is little difference between this type of jewelry and the bulk of higher quality mass produced silver jewelry imported from Italy. "Tiffany & Co." is the most common mark found on the silver jewelry.

T & CO . . .   **TIFFANY & CO.**

Towle Silversmiths

The history of this company dates back to the seventeenth century with William Moulton as the first recorded American silversmith. Anthony Towle apprenticed with the descendants of William and in 1857 established a partnership with William Jones, founding the Towle and Jones Company. He and his son Edward later founded the A. F. Towle & Son in 1873 which was subsequently renamed the Towle Manufacturing Company and finally the Towle Silversmiths. The company literature dates its founding to 1690. The firm was a major American manufacturer of silver flatware and products with novelties and jewelry accounting for a very insignificant portion of their output. It was acquired by Syratech Corporation in 1990 and continues operation as one of its subsidiaries.

Trifari-Krussman & Fishel

The history of Trifari can be traced back to the mid 1800s in Naples, Italy, where Luigi Trifari established a workshop manufacturing fine jewelry. His grandson, Gustavo Trifari (b. 1883) learned the trade from his grandfather and in 1910 established Trifari & Trifari with his uncle, Ludovico Trifari, several years after emigrating to America. Several years later, Gustavo established his own company, Trifari, and was eventually joined by Leo Krussman and Carl Fishel, changing the name to Trifari, Krussman & Fishel in 1920. Trifari became a major manufacturer of costume jewelry in America which is avidly collected today. Only a small portion of the firm's output was in sterling silver, mostly designed by a series of talented designers the firm employed throughout the decades. The company was acquired by Hallmark Cards, Inc. in 1964, which was subsequently sold to the Crystal Brands, Inc. in 1988.

Several of its trademarks are still active and registered marks used by the company.

JEWELRY BY TRIFARI

Trueart

Trueart was the registered trademark of the Hingeco Vanities, Inc. founded sometime in the 1940s in Providence, Rhode Island. The jewelry marked as such is primarily in floral designs made of sterling and vermeil. Most of the pieces found in the collectible market date no later than the 1950s, suggesting that the firm may have gone out of business by then.

Uncas Manufacturing Company (see also Sorrento)

The Uncas Manufacturing Company was founded by Vincent Sorrentino in Providence, Rhode Island, in 1911. According to internal company newsletters and current chairman of the board Stanley Sorrentino, Vincent Sorrentino, and John E. Lanigan formed a partnership and established the Sorrentino & Lanigan Company which later was acquired by Vincent and named Sorrento Ring Company, and finally became Uncas Manufacturing Company in 1915. The firm is best known for its finger rings, though it manufactured a wide variety of jewelry using many different trademarks. Vincent Sorrentino retired in 1960 at which time his son, Stanley Sorrentino, assumed the leadership of the company. The firm was still in business as of the late 1990s, owned and operated by John Corsini, an Uncas veteran, who became the firm's president in 1991 when Stanley became the chairman of the board. The common mark found on Uncas silver rings is an arrow through the letter "U."

Unger Brothers

The firm was originally established in Newark, New Jersey, by five Unger brothers, William, George, Frederick, Herman, and Eugene, in 1872 to manufacture pocket knives. By 1878, the two surviving brothers, Herman and Eugene, shifted their focus to manufacturing silver jewelry. However, the famous Art Nouveau silver products, jewelry, and accessories for which Unger is famous were not produced until much later and after Eugene married the highly talented Emma Dickinson who is responsible for many of the sought after designs. By 1910, with the decline of Art Nouveau popularity and the death of the last Unger brothers, the firm ceased production of this type of jewelry and silver products and, not long after, silver production altogether. The enterprise continued as a manufacturer of airplane parts until 1919 when the business was sold.

Unger Brothers are the epitome of Art Nouveau jewelry in the U.S. The silver products and jewelry of no other firm capture the essence of the Art Nouveau movement as those of the Unger Brothers. The jewelry is beautiful, but the accessories and giftwares, including toiletry and brushes, perfumers, cigar and cigarette cases, show outstanding design and craftsmanship. Not all the jewelry was in this style; some of the earlier jewelry had Victorian motifs and was of lower quality. Much of the Unger jewelry was also not marked. Fortunately, recovered old Unger catalogs reprinted in recent years enable collectors to identify many of the unmarked pieces. The common mark is the interwoven "UB" logo. The better Art Nouveau pieces are expected to continue rising in prices.

Van Dell

Van Dell Corporation was founded in Providence, Rhode Island, circa 1938. The firm specialized in the production of delicate silver, vermeil, and gold filled jewelry with floral and retro designs popular at the time. Two somewhat similar script "Van Dell" marks are listed by the *JCK* as belonging to the Van Dell Corporation and Park Lane Associates, but both of these entities have a similar Providence address and apparently are related enterprises. According to documents filed with the U.S. Patent and Trademark Office, the Van Dell trademark was registered by the Park Lane Associates, claiming first commercial use in 1939, renewed in 1993. To the best of the author's knowledge, all pieces were marked with the company trademark.

Vargas Manufacturing Company

Founded in Providence, Rhode Island, sometime in the 1940s, the firm specialized in the production of gold plated jewelry, particularly rings. Other metal jewelry and, to a lesser extent, sterling silver jewelry were also manufactured and are usually found in the collectible market. So are the firm's small children's jewelry, much of which dates back to the 1950s. In 1980, Vargas expanded by acquiring the McGarth-Hamin Corporation which specialized in ring production. The common mark is the letter "V" superimposed on a horizontal diamond.

Vargas

Viking Craft (Albert Horwig Co.)

Albert Horwig Company using the trademark Viking Craft was founded circa 1940 in New York City. The silver jewelry exhibits Scandinavian themes and reflects high quality craftsmanship.

Because of the name and the perception of emulating Scandinavian designs, the firm has not received the proper attention it deserves. In the author's opinion, this company is a real sleeper in the market. Actually, Viking Craft silver jewelry is equal to or better than the average mass produced Scandinavian jewelry.

Warwick Sterling Company

Founded in the first decade of this century in Providence, Rhode Island, Warwick specialized in the production of sterling silverware, toiletry, jewelry, and accessories. The volume of jewelry manufactured is insignificant relative to other silver products, but the accessories are found with a greater frequency. The firm ceased operation sometime in the early 1920s.

Watson Company

The origin of the company dates back to the 1870s and Cobb, Gould & Co. in Attleboro, Massachusetts, but Clarence Watson did not become a principal until the reorganization of the firm under the name of Watson & Newell in 1880. The firm operated as Watson Company from 1920 to 1955. Watson specialized in the production of silver plated and later sterling silver products which included a limited amount of toiletry, novelties, giftware, jewelry, and accessories. Common marks found on jewelry and accessories are reproduced here.

Webster

The Webster Company was first established in 1879 by George K. Webster (1850 – 1894) in North Attleboro, Massachusetts, as G. K. Webster which was changed to Webster Company after his death. The firm was a major manufacturer of silver products, novelties, and accessories. It was acquired by Reed & Barton in 1950 and continued operation as a subsidiary of that company. Its early and most common trademark found on all the pieces shown here is the "WCo" with an arrow.

Wells

"Wells" is the mark found on silver jewelry and novelties made sometime during the late 1950s to 1970s. There were several companies with this name, including Wells, Inc. which was a major manufacturer of charms. The "Wells" and "Wells Sterling" may be the marks used by Wells-Jewelart which was out of business by the late 1970s.

Whiting & Davis

The Whiting and Davis Company was originally founded as a chain manufacturing company in 1876 by William Wade and Edward P. Davis where C.W. Whiting worked as a young boy. Whiting eventually became the owner in 1907, and the firm became one of the major manufacturers of mesh products, handbags, and accessories, and later jewelry. Much of the company's jewelry and accessories were made of silver or were silver plated, though later the company also produced non-silver costume jewelry. The most common pieces found in silver are the firm's mesh purses and accessories. These are usually marked with the firm's trademark W. & D., an early trademark, or its more common mark of "Whiting & Davis" in a cartouche.

41

White Company

The White Manufacturing Company, Inc., was established in North Attleboro, Massachusetts, in the late 1920s, specializing in dress ornaments and accessories with a limited amount of jewelry executed in rolled plated gold and sterling silver. The common trademark found on the jewelry and accessories is the White Co. mark.

Wightman & Hough Company

Founded in the mid nineteenth century by partners Wightman and Hough in Providence, Rhode Island. The firm specialized in the production of gold, gold filled, and sterling silver jewelry and novelties. The firm ceased production sometime in the early 1920s. Several trademarks were used but all incorporate W & H Co. in some form. Several common marks found on silver jewelry are reproduced here.

Wiley-Crawford Company

Established by partners Wiley and Crawford in Providence, Rhode Island, in 1909. The firm specialized in the production of gold and sterling silver giftware, novelties, and to a lesser extent, jewelry and accessories, and was out of business by the early 1920s. The common trademark was the letter W superimposed on the letter C.

Leaf shaped pin and a round monogram pin, both marked A & Z. $20.00 – 30.00 and $8.00 – 12.00.

Pendant and earrings with possibly a matching pin, all marked Am Lee. $60.00 – 75.00 set.

Pair of sterling Anson cuff links. $20.00 – 25.00.

Arts and Crafts period, hand-crafted brooch with a large lapis stone, with Art Metal Studio's mark. $200.00 – 250.00.

Matching set of Anson pin and earrings, usually costume engraved with initials and monograms. $20.00 – 25.00. Two Anson pins, one in vermeil. $10.00 – 12.00 each.

Two 1940s vermeil floral pins made by Atlas. $30.00 – 35.00 each.

Pendant and matching earrings marked with Avery trademark and sterling. $25.00 – 30.00.

Avery mother's pin. These were usually marked with children's names and birthdates. $25.00 – 35.00.

A bracelet, three pins, and two pairs of earrings all marked with Beaucraft trademarks. Bracelet, $30.00 – 40.00; pins $20.00 – 35.00 each; and earrings $12.00 – 20.00 pair.

Beau sterling silver charm bracelet. $50.00 – 70.00.

Large enamel pin with Baldwin trademark. $30.00 – 40.00.

Matching Beau pin and earrings with square dancing couple. $40.00 – 65.00 set.

Beau textured vermeil necklace, bracelet, and earrings set. $65.00 – 90.00.

Three Beaucraft brooches. $30.00 – 40.00 each.

Cuff bracelet and a donkey pin, both marked with Bell trademark and sterling. Pin, $25.00 – 35.00; cuff bracelet, $35.00 – 45.00.

43

Black Hills sterling silver ring with applied two-tone 10k gold leaves, a distinguishing feature of the Black Hills jewelry. $50.00 – 70.00.

Vermeil pin with rhinestones marked BOND BOYD. $25.00 – 30.00.

Marcel Boucher sterling vermeil fur clip, MB mark. $95.00 – 150.00.

Two sterling silver pins, marked with Binder Brothers trademark. $15.00 – 25.00 each.

Pin and earrings set, marked with Bugbee logo. $75.00 – 100.00.

Burch sterling silver pin, marked Laurel Burch. $50.00 – 80.00.

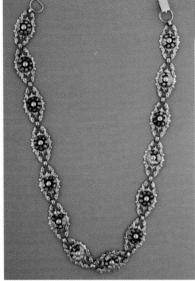

Large floral brooch made by Carl-Art. $40.00 – 50.00.

High quality Binder Brothers necklace, marked with company trademark and sterling. $65.00 – 95.00.

High quality handcrafted necklace with Scandinavian influence marked with Cabincraft logo. $250.00 – 300.00 Inset: Cabincraft logo.
John Christopher collection.

Sterling silver earrings with typical Burch motifs. $50.00 – 80.00 a pair.
Photo courtesy of Pop Beads to Platinum.

Necklace, bracelet and earrings all marked with Cabincraft logo. Necklace: $125.00 – 150.00; bracelet: $75.00 – 100.00; and earrings $40.00 – 60.00.
Courtesy of John Christopher.

Carl-Art pin and pair of earrings set with hematite stones. Pin: $20.00 – 25.00; earrings $25.00 – 30.00.

Turn of century enamel pin, "C3" for Caron Brothers of Canada. $75.00 – 100.00.

Carnegie silver necklace inspired by Asian nomadic silver jewelry. Hattie Carnegie "HC" mark within a diamond framed in a semi-oval, a mark used rarely on her jewelry. $150.00 – 250.00.

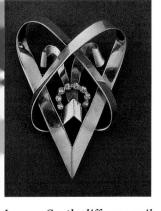

Large Castlecliff vermeil brooch with rhinestone accent. $35.00 – 45.00.

Alice Caviness enamel and marcasite owls pin. $35.00 – 50.00.

Large silver ring set with green crystal stone, marked "CINER." $45.00 – 65.00.

Alice Caviness wheel brooch with large central genuine pearl. $40.00 – 50.00.

Modern enamel cuff links, marked CELLINI. $35.00 – 50.00.

High quality early Cini bracelet, $250.00 – 300.00; and a Cini floral pin with a large central pearl, $125.00 – 165.00.

Two sterling silver pins, marked CINI. $45.00 – 60.00 each.

Cini bracelet with stylized floral design. $150.00 – 200.00.

Cini Crown pin with matching earrings. $125.00 – 175.00.

Exceptionally well made Cini poison ring with classical motif, $250.00 – 300.00; and Cini turtle ring, $50.00 – 75.00.

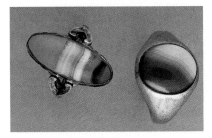

Two early 1900 agate rings in Scottish style with Clark & Coombs trademark. $45.00 – 65.00.

Finely crafted brooch, marked CONE STERLING. $250.00 – 350.00 Photo courtesy of Pop Beads to Platinum.

Three sterling silver Coro pins. $35.00 – 50.00 each.

Two late 1960s charms pin and key chain marked Concra. $18.00 – 25.00 each.

Two identical sterling silver Coro pins, one in vermeil, with singing birds. $40.00 – 60.00 each.

Coro copy of a Georg Jensen pin, $35.00 – 50.00; and two Coro insects with color rhinestones, $35.00 – 50.00 each.

Corocraft sterling silver brooch of salamander in enamel and paste rhinestones with a pearl. $250.00 – 300.00.

Large 1940s vermeil brooch, marked Courtly. $30.00 – 45.00.

Large, well made rhinestone spray floral brooch marked cRco. $40.00 – 60.00.

Matching pin and earrings marked with Curtis trademark. $40.00 – 50.00.

Bracelet, pin, and two pairs of earrings, all marked Danecraft. Bracelet; $40.00 – 60.00; pin, $30.00 – 45.00; and earrings, $25.00 – 30.00 each.

Two pairs of sterling silver and rhinestone earrings, one set with genuine pearls. Curtman trademark. $20.00 – 35.00 a pair.

Sterling Curtis brooch with multicolor rhinestones. $30.00 – 45.00.

Danecraft bracelet with textured surface, $50.00 – 65.00; and two Danecraft brooches, $40.00 – 50.00 each.

Three Danecraft sterling silver bracelets. $35.00 – 50.00 each.

Danecraft bracelet with modern design, $40.00 – 60.00; floral pin, $30.00 – 40.00; and earrings, $25.00 – 30.00.

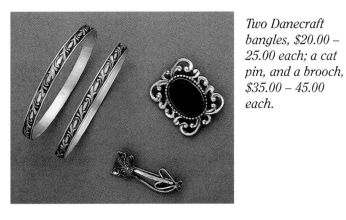

Two Danecraft bangles, $20.00 – 25.00 each; a cat pin, and a brooch, $35.00 – 45.00 each.

Three floral Danecraft pins. $35.00 – 45.00 each.

47

*Variety of vintage Danecraft brooches.
$40.00 – 70.00 each. Photo courtesy of
Danecraft.*

*Danecraft sterling silver set cur-
rently manufactured by the firm.
Retail price. Photo courtesy of Danecraft.*

*Vintage Danecraft bracelets. Lower piece
$50.00 – 65.00; others $80.00 – 120.00 each.
Photo courtesy of Danecraft.*

*1940s and 1950s Danecraft floral pins.
$35.00 – 50.00 each. Photo courtesy of
Danecraft.*

*Vintage Danecraft brooch/pendant,
bracelet, and brooch. Bracelet, $75.00 –
100.00; necklace, $60.00 – 85.00; brooch,
$45.00 – 65.00. Photo courtesy of Danecraft.*

*Danecraft sterling silver set currently
manufactured by the firm. Retail price.
Photo courtesy of Danecraft.*

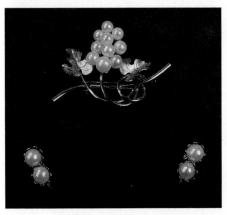

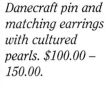

*Danecraft pin and
matching earrings
with cultured
pearls. $100.00 –
150.00.*

*Danecraft pendant
with matching ear-
rings set with car-
nelian stones.
$80.00 – 100.00.*

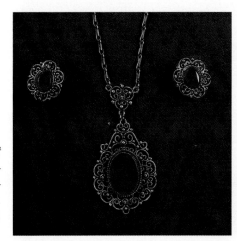

Danecraft sterling silver set currently manufactured by the firm. Retail price. *Photo courtesy of Danecraft.*

DeRosa vermeil and pearl earrings. $120.00 – 160.00.

Doskow monograms which were the specialty of the company. Bracelet, $35.00 – 50.00; pin and pendant, $30.00 – 40.00 each.

Athletic and service award pins, both marked with the Dieges & Clust trademark. Large pin, $35.00 – 45.00; enamel pin, $20.00 – 25.00.

DeRosa trembler brooch with faux pearls. $250.00 – 300.00.

Early Doskow brooch. $45.00 – 65.00.

Doskow sweater guard. $45.00 – 65.00.

Eisenberg sterling clip earrings. Marked sterling and inscribed Eisenberg Original. $40.00 – 60.00.

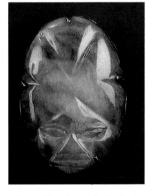

Eisenberg Mexican jade Aztec face and silver brooch. Marked sterling and with early script Eisenberg Original mark. $150.00 – 200.00. Not typical Eisenberg jewelry.

Wonderful Foster and Baily compact. Marked F & B. $350.00 – 450.00.

Sterling silver sweater guard. Felch and Co. mark. $40.00 – 55.00.

49

Foster & Baily handcrafted necklace. F&B mark. $250.00 – 350.00.

Forstner naturalistic brooch. $35.00 – 55.00.

Turn of century Gorham cut glass and sterling perfumer. $100.00 – 125.00. Joan Welsh collection.

Hand & Hammer saddle and sleeping fox pins. These are a few examples of hundreds of figural jewelry pieces made by the company. $30.00 – 35.00 each. Photo courtesy of Hand & Hammer.

Hand & Hammer brooch and matching earrings. $70.00 – 75.00. Photo courtesy of Hand & Hammer.

Gorham unicorn pin. $25.00 – 35.00.

Gorham sterling perfumer marked with the company trademark. $250.00 – 350.00 Robin Allison collection.

Variety of Hand & Hammer silver jewelry in vermeil, but also made in 14K gold. $18.00 – 50.00 Photo courtesy of Hand & Hammer.

Large early Hickok belt buckle with Chinese motif. $30.00 – 45.00.

Hickok sterling belt buckle. $25.00 – 35.00.

Hickok tie tack and pair of earrings. $15.00 – 18.00 each.

Butterfly pin, marked Hobe. $50.00 – 75.00.

Early marked Hobe brooch. $150.00 – 250.00.

Stylized ribbon and flower pin, marked Hobe. $100.00 – 150.00.

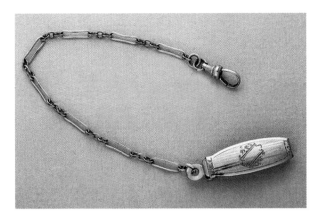

Narrow belt fob, marked H-R.CO. $35.00 – 50.00.

Oval pendant, marked International Silver. $45.00 – 65.00.

Oval International silver pendant. $45.00 – 65.00.

A leaf and two initial pins made by J.H.K. Leaf pin, $10.00 – 15.00; initial pins, $5.00 each.

Pocket liquor casket with International Silver Company logo. $150.00 – 200.00.

Pair of vermeil and rhinestone earrings, marked Jay Kel. $30.00 – 40.00.

Two early 1940s Harry Iskin brooches. $35.00 – 45.00 each.

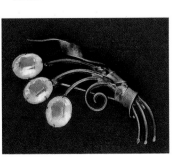

Jay Kel sterling silver brooch with citrine color stones. $40.00 – 50.00.

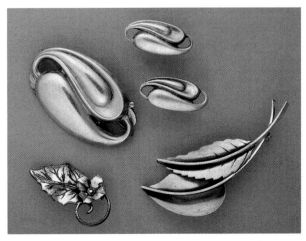

Matching sterling Jewelart pin and earrings, $45.00 – 65.00; marked JEWELART, sterling double leaf pin, $25.00 – 30.00; and small Jewelart pin, $15.00 – 20.00.

Slender Art Deco pin set with cabochon amethyst stone, marked Kalo. $200.00 – 250.00.

Dolphin and inlaid mother-of-pearl rings, marked Kabana. $20.00 – 30.00 each.

Two marked JORDAN pins, one with amethysts. $25.00 – 35.00 and $35.00 – 45.00.

Cuff bracelet with stamped floral motif, marked with Kerr trademark. $45.00 – 65.00.

Marked Karen Linne necklace in traditional classic form. $50.00 – 75.00.

Turn of century enamel brooch, marked with the Kerr trademark. $65.00 – 95.00.

Oriental style dragon silver belt. Marked with "K" in a diamond, possibly the trademark for Charles Keller & Co., but similar mark also used by King, Raichle & King Co. $600.00 – 750.00. Robin Allison collection.

Kerr silver belt depicting demon and swimming lady, marked with the Kerr logo. $600.00 – 850.00. Robin Allison collection.

Kerr demon/lion locket, marked with the Kerr logo. $350.00 – 500.00. Robin Allison collection.

Kerr sterling silver chatelaine, marked with the Kerr logo. $800.00 – 1,200.00. Robin Allison collection.

Kerr Medusa sterling perfumer. $400.00 – 500.00. Robin Allison collection.

Outstanding Kerr vermeil chatelaine with a spider, accented by a cabochon garnet stone and marked with the Kerr logo. $800.00 – 1,200.00. Robin Allison collection.

Marked Lang sterling: necklace, $50.00 – 75.00; sweater guard, $35.00 – 45.00; ballerina pin, $35.00 – 45.00; and bowling pins with a genuine cultured pearl pin accent, $30.00 – 40.00.

Art Nouveau repousse bookmark, stamped with Kirk trademark. $35.00 – 50.00.

Presentation pin depicting a flying bird, marked Mary Kay 1963. Similar pins of various sizes found in the market are often marked Mexico, but much of the sterling silver Mary Kay presentation and award items seen by the author appear to have been made in the U.S. $20.00 – 30.00.

Large Christmas pendant, marked Lunt Sterling Christmas 1972. $30.00 – 45.00.

Floral link necklace and matching bracelet, marked with Lang swan trademark. $70.00 – 95.00.

Small sterling silver perfume bottle with Marshall Field trademark. $75.00 – 100.00.

Leach & Miller Art Deco sterling silver bracelet, marked with the company trademark and patented July 7, 1925. $95.00 – 135.00.

Handcrafted cuff bracelet featuring the 1933 Chicago World's Fair symbol, marked Lebolt. $75.00 – 95.00.

High quality naturalistic pin made by McClelland Barclay. $100.00 – 150.00.

Mazer pin set with faux pearl and rhinestones. $65.00 – 95.00.

Ming Bird of Paradise pin and matching earrings made of silver and carved ivory. $600.00 – 700.00.
Photo courtesy of Jim Oneal.

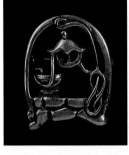

Outstanding sculptured three-dimensional brooch made by McClelland Barclay. This piece is among the earliest sterling silver jewelry designed by this talented artist. $250.00 – 350.00.

Pin and matching earrings, marked MIZPAH. $45.00 – 60.00.

Flying goose brooch of approximately 3" with the Norseland logo. $50.00 – 75.00.

Textured vermeil leaf pin and earrings, marked Monet. $45.00 – 60.00 Monet stylized floral brooch in gold plated sterling silver. $35.00 – 45.00.

Pair of two-tone gold plated sterling silver clip earrings, marked Monet. $25.00 – 35.00. Vermeil floral brooch, marked only sterling but may also have been by Monet. $35.00 – 40.00.

Marked Norseland brooch with lapis stones. $45.00 – 65.00.

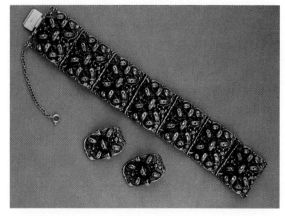

High quality heavy bracelet and matching clip earrings made by Napier. $95.00 – 125.00.

Handcrafted cuff bracelet, stamped with Nye logo. $45.00 – 65.00.

Large handcrafted belt buckle with the N.S. Company trademark. $30.00 – 50.00.

Napier bracelet with simulated shark skin backing that folds up over the sides, $95.00 – 145.00; and pair of marked Napier screw back earrings, $25.00 – 30.00.

Orb brooch. $35.00 – 45.00.

Large handcrafted Nye leaf brooch, $35.00 – 45.00; and leaf screwback earrings, $25.00 – 30.00.

Large Nye naturalistic brooch, $35.00 – 45.00; and two Nye earrings, $25.00 – 35.00 each.

Sterling silver and hematite rings, marked with the conjoined "JP." $25.00 – 35.00.

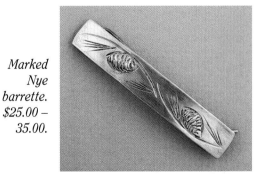

Marked Nye barrette. $25.00 – 35.00.

Pin and matching screwback earrings made by Orb. $45.00 – 70.00 This set is among the most common Orb jewelry seen in the market, and both the auction and asking prices vary widely as in the case of all Orb jewelry.

Panetta heart pendant. $25.00 – 35.00.

Art Nouveau necklace and brooch, marked Pryor Company Sterling. $300.00 – 400.00 each.

Early 1900s Roger & Lunt clip, marked with the company's trademark. $30.00 – 45.00.

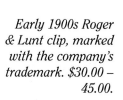

Chatelaine box, pair of cuff buttons, and chatelaine top with three drops, marked with Park's clover trademark, or clover within a horseshoe. Box, $200.00 – 300.00; cuff buttons, $100.00 – 150.00; chatelaine, $700.00 – 1,000.00. Robin Allison collection.

Limited Edition 1973 Reed & Barton Christmas Cross brooch. $35.00 – 50.00.

Sterling silver and multicolor rhinestone, a typical example of Reja jewelry. $75.00 – 100.00.

Large musical note brooch, marked Renoir. $60.00 – 85.00.

Floral pin, marked S & F. $25.00 – 30.00.

W.E. Richards bracelet, $35.00 – 50.00; and Richards screwback earrings. $20.00 – 25.00.

1960s pin with the Rolyn trademark. $20.00 – 25.00.

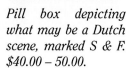

Pill box depicting what may be a Dutch scene, marked S & F. $40.00 – 50.00.

Bracelet set with multicolor stones, marked SARAH COV. $45.00 – 60.00.

Sarah Coventry floral pin. $20.00 – 35.00.

Atypical Shiebler pin, marked with the company logo. $250.00 – 300.00. Photo courtesy of Pop Beads to Platinum.

Three sterling silver rings with channel set square emerald stones, Schlang trademark. $35.00 – 50.00 each.

Two band rings marked with Schlang's "WS" trademark, $20.00 – 25.00 each; and a similar ring with illegible mark, $20.00 – 25.00.

Typical sterling silver Shiebler bracelets and brooch with classic figures. Bracelets, $400.00 – 500.00 each; brooch, $300.00 – 400.00. Robin Allison collection.

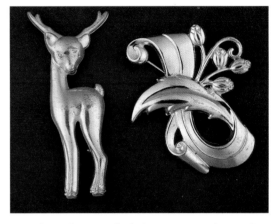

Two brooches, marked "SB" in an oval, standing for Silver Bros. $30.00 – 40.00 each.

Sterling silver ring with a large simulated turquoise stone, Silver Cloud trademark. $25.00 – 35.00.

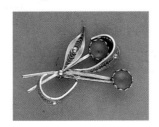

Sterling silver lacy floral pin with genuine jade stones, marked Sorrento. $40.00 – 60.00.

Matching or near matching necklace, bracelet, and earrings set with lacy metalwork and rhinestones marked Sorrento, $95.00 – 120.00; and a Sorrento bracelet, $30.00 – 40.00.

Sterling silver jewelry, marked Sorrento: necklace and earrings set, $40.00 – 50.00; jade earrings, $30.00 – 35.00; and vermeil pin with genuine jade stones, $45.00 – 65.00.

Sterling silver and moss agate pendant marked with SP Co trademark, $30.00 – 40.00; and somewhat similar pin with the same mark. $20.00 – 25.00.

Matching necklace and earrings, marked STAR-ART. $40.00 – 45.00.

Sterling silver tank tie clip, marked SWANK, and a lapel pin. $20.00 – 30.00.

Vermeil necklace, marked Symmetalic, $150.00 – 225.00; and Symmetalic brooch with a central cultured pearl. $200.00 – 260.00.

Wonderful vermeil necklace, marked Symmetalic. $300.00 – 350.00.

Symmetalic silver jewelry; bracelet, $60.00 – 85.00; brooch with aquamarine faceted stones and cultured pearl, $150.00 – 200.00; floral enamel brooch, $70.00 – 90.00; and pin with modern design, $70.00 – 100.00.

"Faith" lapel pin, marked Tiffany & Co. $20.00 – 30.00.

Tiffany textured and creased modern pendant. $90.00 – 135.00.

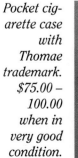

Pocket cigarette case with Thomae trademark. $75.00 – 100.00 when in very good condition.

Tiffany money clip. $65.00 – 95.00.

Early 1970s Tiffany whistle pendant. $50.00 – 75.00.

Tiffany heart necklace with "Gabriel, 77" monogram. $45.00 – 65.00.

Tiffany Ankh pin. $80.00 – 100.00.

Tiffany men's tie pin with words "TRY GOD." $20.00 – 30.00.

Tiffany necklace. $150.00 – 225.00.

Two large Christmas pendants with a different design on each convex side. Right: marked Towle Sterling 1973, $40.00 – 60.00; Left: for 1971 and of lower quality and construction, $25.00 – 35.00.

Trifari floral brooch. $60.00 – 85.00.

Vermeil Trifari pin with red, white, and blue rhinestones. $175.00 – 225.00.

Uncas ring, U and arrow company trademark. $25.00 – 35.00.

Large brooch marked TRUEART. $35.00 – 45.00.

Exceptionally large (about 5") Trueart brooch. $30.00 – 40.00.

Trueart floral brooch. $30.00 – 40.00.

Exquisite late Victorian Unger fob piece, marked with the company logo. $350.00 – 500.00. Photo courtesy of Pop Beads to Platinum.

Marked Unger pocket seal. $75.00 – 100.00.

Art Nouveau Unger mirror. $125.00 – 165.00. These are usually found with some dents and marks which should be discounted. John Christopher collection.

"Love's Dream," Unger jewelry all marked with the Unger logo except the center piece. Large brooch, $450.00 – 550.00; small heart photo locket, $275.00 – 350.00; unmarked round locket, $250.00 – 350.00; lorgnette, $125.00 – 150.00; small round brooch, $175.00 – 225.00. Robin Allison collection.

Large Unger Art Nouveau brooch, marked with the Unger trademark and sterling. $400.00 – 550.00 Robin Allison collection.

Unger sterling silver octopus brooch marked with the Unger logo. $300.00 – 400.00. Robin Allison collection.

Unger possum cuff links and matching tie clip. $300.00 – 450.00. Robin Allison collection.

Unger bracelet with lion head terminals, marked with the Unger trademark and sterling. $400.00 – 500.00. Robin Allison collection.

Unger sterling silver owl pin, marked with the Unger logo. Variety of figural head pins such as this piece were made by Unger. $200.00 – 250.00 Robin Allison collection.

Very large Van Dell brooch. $45.00 – 65.00.

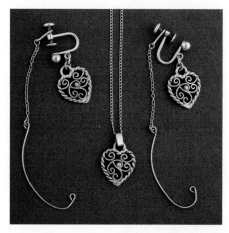

Van Dell pendant with matching earrings. $35.00 – 50.00.

Van Dell necklace. $35.00 – 45.00.

Van Dell pin. $35.00 – 45.00.

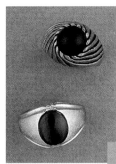

Vargas ring with a blue stone and a Sarah Coventry ring with a hematite stone. $25.00 – 35.00 each.

Webster coin carrier. $50.00 – 75.00.

Two large Viking craft floral brooches in sterling and vermeil. $50.00 – 75.00 each.

Marked Viking craft flying geese brooch. $45.00 – 70.00.

Two match holders with the Watson and Norell Company mark, $12.00 – 18.00 each; and a large repousse pocket cigarette case. $125.00 – 175.00.

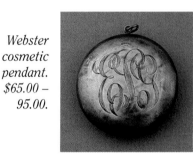

Webster cosmetic pendant. $65.00 – 95.00.

Sterling clip, marked with Webster Company logo. $35.00 – 45.00.

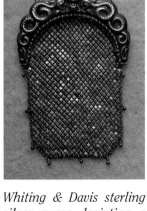

Whiting & Davis sterling silver purse depicting a demon/lion head flanked by serpents. Early W. & D. company trademark. $200.00 – 300.00. Robin Allison collection.

Coin box made by White Co. $50.00 – 65.00.

Webster pocket folding picture album. $50.00 – 75.00 when in very good condition.

American Studio Jewelry

A new form of art expressed through handcrafted jewelry and linked to the modern art movement and known as art or studio jewelry evolved within several artistically rebellious and Bohemian-like post-WWII communities in America. The jewelry has come to be known as "Studio Jewelry," and the inspirational source for the modern American art jewelry. The main centers for this movement were New York's Greenwich Village, Massachusetts's Provincetown, Chicago, Illinois, and the San Francisco Bay area in California. Among the important general characteristics of the movement were lack of formal training or apprenticeship in the jewelry industry; rejection of traditional designs and conventional forms; a search for new ideas and techniques; emphasis on craftsmanship versus the use of machinery; and perceptions concerning jewelry as artistic and expressive objects rather than symbols of status. The movement is directly linked to laying the foundation for art jewelry taught at the American educational institutions and the development of modern jewelry designs and techniques which followed a somewhat distinct and independent path from their counterparts in Europe.

The studio jewelry is finding a much wider circle of attention and appreciation among collectors, and the prices have been rising significantly during the past two decades and are expected to rise drastically in the future. Although some examples are covered in this section, the subject will be covered in detail in the author's planned book on modern studio and art jewelry.

Betty Cooke (b. 1924)

Betty Cooke received her education in fine arts from the Maryland Institute while simultaneously apprenticing with a local jeweler. Subsequently, she taught jewelry making at the same institution for the next 20 years. Parallel to her teaching career, Cooke also began her first business venture by opening a store in Baltimore which sold her own silver jewelry and metalware as well as other arts and crafts merchandise made by her colleagues. She also marketed her jewelry through major shops such as Tiffany and Jensen. The business is still in operation, and Cooke continues to make jewelry.

Cooke's jewelry is skillfully handcrafted in simple, free, and geometric shapes, sometimes superimposed over one another. She is the recipient of many awards including the 1981 De Beers Diamonds Today award.

Hilda Krauss

Hilda Krauss was among the early participants and proponents of the modern studio jewelry movement. She first worked in New York, and later in Westport, Connecticut, and was among a small group of studio jewelers whose work was first exhibited in 1946 at the First National Exhibition of Contemporary Jewelry organized by New York's Museum of Modern Art.

Her jewelry was also displayed in Milan as she is listed in Aloi's 1954 "Esempi di Decorazione Moderna di Tutto il Mondo" (World's Examples of Modern Decoration) in Hoepli, Milan, Italy. Hilda Krauss's jewelry is rare, and the author has only seen a few examples of it. These masterfully display the interplay among form, texture, and color, accomplishing a soft balance and equilibrium which highlight her impressive sense of design and craftsmanship.

Sam Kramer (1913 – 1964)

Educated as a journalist, Sam Kramer worked for a while as a newspaper reporter before returning to his hometown of Pittsburgh and working in a small jewelry factory. This experience and the jewelry making courses he had taken as a college student must have motivated Kramer to move to New York and study gemology; shortly thereafter he opened his first workshop in Greenwich Village. From this beginning, Kramer rose to become a popular and major influence in the American studio jewelry movement and committed the rest of his life to making highly personalized and expressionistic jewelry.

Influenced by surrealism as well as other contemporary movements in art, Kramer's jewelry breaks through the traditional concepts of jewelry, its formality and conventional forms, and treats it, first and foremost, as a means of artistic expression. His jewelry is often in large scale and in mixed metals, displaying simple, modernistic designs, sometimes decorated with irregularly arranged large and exotic stones or with simple non-precious material in a crude assemblage which skillfully and deliberately exhibit rudimentary craftsmanship.

Esther Lewittes

One of the West Coast studio jewelry artists operating in Los Angeles. A prolific and versatile designer and silversmith, Lewittes's jewelry was frequently a uniquely cut and formed silver base with concave surface and smooth flowing corners decorated with asymmetrical linear and curvilinear overlays or applied wire rendered in modern designs; or a silver base in semi-geometric forms inlaid with wood or combined with glass, pearls, and semi-precious stones.

The jewelry is usually marked with her last name in a block and script letters along with "sterling" and sometimes the word "Handmade."

Paul Lobel (1899 – 1983)

Paul Lobel was among the leading studio art jewelers with a versatile background in design and decorative arts. He studied commercial art at the Pratt Institute and initially pursued a career in advertising, but a year of travel in Europe (1925 – 1926) had a major influence on the future course of his career, finalizing a definite shift to design and the field of decorative arts. Lobel used a variety of media in decorative arts, from glass to wooden furniture, and much of his metal work was in steel and bronze. Although Lobel worked with silver before WWII, a definite shift to silver jewelry occurred during the war years and as a result of government restrictions on metals which forced a more frequent use of silver by many U.S. manufacturers. His silver jewelry and small sculptures were well received by the public and displayed at several exhibitions including New York City's Museum of Modern Art.

Lobel also opened a studio and shop in Greenwich Village in 1944 and was one of the early pioneers in the studio art movement centered in Greenwich Village. Lobel's silver jewelry is exceptionally simple in design, frequently reflecting an abstract representation of common objects or animal and plant life. The silver jewelry is of high quality both in design and fabrication which are the two featured elements and the focus of his work, not requiring other materials or stones. Much of the jewelry dates to the 1930s through the 1950s. After a relocation, the New York shop was closed in 1965, and Lobel spent most of the 1960s and 1970s working in other media, such as designing objects in plastic or paper. He died in February 1983. The silver jewelry is usually marked "Lobel" as shown here.

Macchiarini (b. 1909)

Peter Macchiarini is among the notable West Coast studio jewelry artists influencing the post-war modernist movement in the field of jewelry. Born to Italian parents near Santa Rosa, California, Macchiarini received his education and training in marble and stone cutting while residing in Italy with his parents. Returning to the U.S. just before the onset of the Great Depression, in the 1930s he worked and trained under the Works Progress Administration program specifically designed to employ and engage artists and artisans. By the late 1930s Macchiarini was making jewelry which was sold at a shop he opened on Grant Avenue in San Francisco. Macchiarini's jewelry is distinct, frequently displaying his interest and experimentation with form and structure, resulting in pierced or punctured, layered or parallel linear configurations. The silver was frequently used in combination with semi-precious stones or materials, and sometimes a portion was painted to create the illusion of depth. He is still active in San Francisco and collaborates with his son who first learned the trade from him. The jewelry is marked "MACCHIARINI" or with a portion of the name, "MACCH." The jewelry is rare and commands high prices.

Frank Miraglia

One of the East Coast studio silversmiths operating in New York City. Miraglia's work involved subjects rooted in nature including biomorphic shapes with applied metal overlays or stylized fish and plants of similar construction. The jewelry is usually marked "Miraglia" in script, or "F. Miraglia."

Franciso Rebajes (1907 – 1990)

Rebajes was among the most commercially successful modernist jewelry manufacturers. Much of his work was executed in copper which is also avidly collected. But Rebajes also produced silver jewelry with Art Moderne designs which is far more scarce than his copper products. Born in the Dominican Republic, Rebajes moved to New York in 1923 and while seeking employment, began making jewelry using borrowed tools and aluminum cans in a basement apartment. From this meager beginning, Rebajes was able to establish his own company in 1932 and soon became a well recognized name with a store on New York City's fashionable Fifth Avenue which he opened in 1942. By 1953, the firm was employing over 60 workers and its jewelry retailed throughout the country. Rebajes jewelry shows similar influences that inspired the contemporary arts in general, and studio jewelry in particular. The company ceased production in 1960. Frank and his wife, Paula, relocated to Spain where he opened a studio and continued to produce jewelry until his death in 1990. The jewelry is marked REBAJES sometimes with the letters "E" looking like the mathematical identity symbol and a slanted "s" which looks like the numeral 8.

Henry Steig (1906 – 1973)

Educated and trained as a painter and sculptor, Steig explored many fields and careers, including commercial art, music, writing, photography, and business, before experimenting with making and selling jewelry around 1948 – 1949. In 1950 he opened his first shop in Manhattan and a second in Provincetown, Massachusetts, where he took permanent residence during the last decade of his life. Steig's jewelry is small and delicate with curvilinear geometric forms frequently decorated with gemstones. The silver jewelry generally dates to the 1950s and 1960s and is relatively rare.

Pin, marked COOK STERLING. $175.00 – 200.00. John Christopher collection.

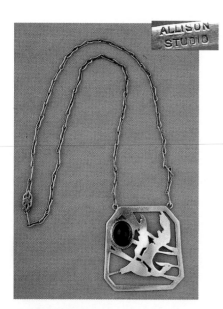

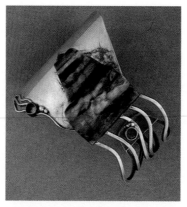

Cuff bracelet in mixed metals, copper and silver, marked D BARNES. $225.00 – 250.00.

Pendant with overlapping geometric forms, marked COOK STERLING. $250.00 – 325.00. John Christopher collection.

Pendant depicting a stylized bird, marked ALLISON STUDIO. $175.00 – $225.00. John Christopher collection.

Two pairs of earrings, one with tension fastener, marked STERLING LEWITTES HAND MADE. $175.00 – 225.00 each. John Christopher collection.

Sam Kramer pin marked with the maker's mushroom mark. $700.00 – 900.00. Photo courtesy of Pop Beads to Platinum.

Marked brooch by Hilda Krauss. $300.00 – 450.00. Photo courtesy of Pop Beads to Platinum.

Pair of wood and silver cuff links, marked in script: Lewittes Sterling. $150.00 – 175.00. John Christopher collection.

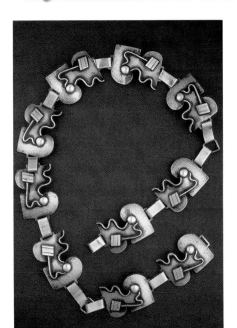

Handcrafted tulip pin, marked LOBEL STER-LING. $300.00 – 400.00 John Christopher collection.

Pendulum shaped pendant with center punched inward and emphasized by oxidization. Marked MACCHIARINI. $650.00 – 850.00. John Christopher collection.

Belt decorated with applied wire and geometric beads, marked STERLING LEWITTES HAND MADE. $500.00 – 650.00. John Christopher collection.

Necklace in free swirl form with three hanging dangles, marked LOBEL STERLING. $650.00 – 750.00. John Christopher collection.

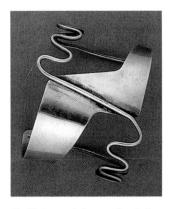

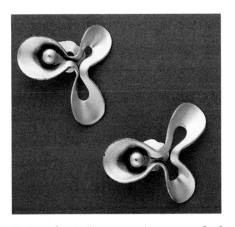

Pair of cuff links with Hebrew motif, marked MARTIN. $85.00 – 125.00. John Christopher collection.

Cuff bracelet emphasizing smooth surface, decorated with applied silver wire, marked in script Miraglia and STERLING. $300.00 – 400.00. John Christopher collection.

Pair of sterling earrings, marked REBAJES STERLING ©. $150.00 – 175.00. John Christopher collection.

Abstract sterling brooch marked "R" for Resnikoff. $350.00 – 450.00 John Christopher collection.

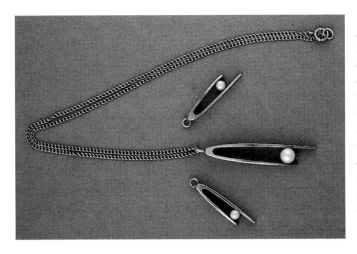

Pendant and matching pair of earrings (fasteners removed) made of forged and bent silver holding a genuine pearl. Marked STEIG STERLING. $250.00 – 350.00 John Christopher collection.

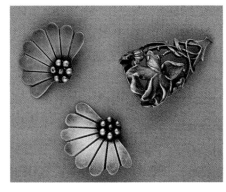

Handcrafted ring with floral motif, marked sterling. $50.00 – 75.00. Pair of clip earrings. $40.00 – 50.00.

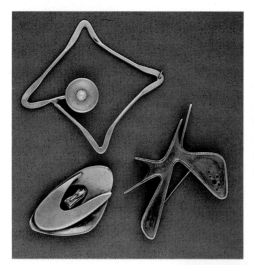

Three hand-crafted pins in biomorphic and abstract shapes, all marked sterling. $100.00 – 150.00 each.

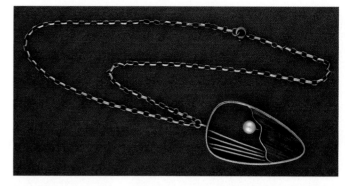

Pendant in a naturalistic design made of silver and wood with a floating pearl. Marked sterling. $125.00 – 175.00.

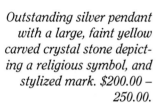

Outstanding silver pendant with a large, faint yellow carved crystal stone depicting a religious symbol, and stylized mark. $200.00 – 250.00.

Unmarked handcrafted abstract tack set with semi-precious stones. $275.00 – 375.00. Photo courtesy of Pop Beads to Platinum.

Large handcrafted ring with modern naturalistic design displaying a central genuine pearl. Marked sterling. $100.00 – 150.00.

Native American Silver Jewelry

Jewelry and ornamentation always had a special place and meaning in the Native American cultures, reflecting a natural bond and special relationship between people and nature. Modern Native American arts and crafts, including silver jewelry, reflect these cultural and religious influences. Although many tribes produced jewelry, including the Sioux, Choctaw, Seneca, and Iroquois, it is the silver jewelry of the Southwest tribes, primarily the Navajo, Zuni, and Hopi, made in the twentieth century which is popular among the collectors and general public.

The Native Americans of the Southwest learned silversmithing from the Mexicans during the second half of the nineteenth century. Atsidi Sani is reputed to be the first Navajo silversmith, having learned the craft from a Mexican metalsmith, Njakai Tsosi. Others, including his son, Red Smith, learned the craft from Atsidi Sani, and making silver jewelry spread by the late nineteenth century.

The early pieces were large and heavy, made of melted down coin silver and completely handcrafted using primitive tools; the crude look is part of the attraction and beauty of the Native

American jewelry. The silver jewelry is characterized by large, often asymmetrical, turquoise stones combined with engraved and stamped motifs drawn from nature or Indian folklore.

The Zuni silver jewelry, first being made circa 1870, is of lighter and finer construction with inlaid turquoise and shells, and in channel work after 1940s. Although employing similar motifs relating the Native American culture, Zuni jewelry designs emphasize the stones and their arrangement rather than the silver.

The Hopi began making silver jewelry around the turn of the twentieth century, and their jewelry had a great resemblance to Navajo and Zuni jewelry though since around 1940, the overlay and sand casting methods have been employed.

Many modern Native American silversmiths are highly trained artisans producing handwrought silver jewelry of the finest quality, some with contemporary designs, executed in both gold and silver. There are also non-Native silversmiths, trained and/or working in the same tradition, whose jewelry is similar to that of the Native Americans or

American firms which specialize in the production of this type of jewelry with some Native Americans and artisans on their staff.

The market for Native American jewelry reached its zenith in the 1960s and 1970s. The high demand generated production by some American firms using modern technologies as well as imports from Mexico and the Far East which were frequently sold as Native American jewelry throughout the nation. The infusion of reproductions became so prevalent that even the galleries and trading posts in the Southwest, as revealed in several surveys and a subject of a report by television's "60 Minutes," were selling imported jewelry as Native American. In 1999, one of the hottest designs offered by the Taxco and other wholesalers was the Hopi designs, and the reproductions from the Far East imitating traditional Native American designs are offered by the importers in the U.S. or can be purchased directly from abroad. These are also sold by major department stores and other distributors under the broad category of Southwestern or Southwestern style silver jewelry. Fortunately, changing technology and Internet access have enabled many Native American pueblos and cooperatives to directly market their arts and crafts on the Internet.

These changes in the past few decades have transformed the collectible market for Native American silver jewelry where, for some, the word Southwestern has now become a substitute for Native American while the purists confine themselves primarily to older and preferably marked pieces.

Nevertheless, the jewelry made by post-WWII and that of many currently living Native American silversmiths is highly collectible and sought throughout the country. Some of the important artists are Preston Monongye, Charles Loloma, Kenneth Begay, Lee Epperson (see Current Silver Jewelry), Allen Kee, George Kee, Roger Skeet, Lambert Homer, Manuel Hayuagawa, Effie Calavaza, Leekya Deyuse, Virgil Dishta, Ralph Quam, Annie Quam Gasper, Edith Tsabetsaye, Calvin Eustace, Tom and Sharon Hannaweeka, Rosita Wallace, Janet and Dewey Gjahate, Josie and Garnet Owaleon, Linda Eustace, Delfina Cachini, Agnes and Hugh Bowekaty, and Anita and Buddy Hattie. Of course, there are hundreds of other skilled and talented Native American silversmiths whose names are not mentioned, and numerous others whose identity is not yet known.

Navajo cuff bracelet with turquoise. $350.00 – 450.00.

Wide handcrafted repousse silver cuff bracelet. Unmarked but tests as silver. $350.00 – 450.00.

Three silver cuff bracelets. $25.00 – 35.00 each.

Zuni silver inlay rings with mother-of-pearl, jet, turquoise, coral, and malachite, some unmarked but test as silver. $40.00 – 90.00 each.

Silver and turquoise watch tips, marked Kakiki. $50.00 – 75.00.

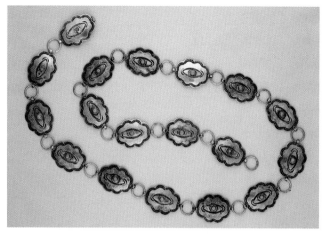

Silver and turquoise concha belt. $300.00 – 375.00.

A group of rings made on both sides of the border. $25.00 – 35.00 each.

A variety of silver and turquoise rings. $20.00 – 50.00 each, depending on age and quality.

Silver concha belt. Unmarked but tests as silver. $275.00 – 350.00.

Marked sterling, bolo set with a large turquoise. $60.00 – 90.00.

Large silver inlay belt buckle, marked "SD" and sterling. $75.00 – 125.00.

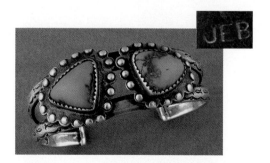

Silver and turquoise cuff bracelet, marked "JEB." $350.00 – 425.00.

Group of rings. $30.00 – 50.00 each.

Large finely handcrafted silver belt buckle set with turquoise. $350.00 – 450.00.

Cuff bracelet with White-Hogan and George Kee logo. Alan and George Kee are among the best known modern Native American silversmiths and their works are avidly sought by collectors. $185.00 – 275.00. John Christopher collection.

Silver necklace set with large irregular cut turquoise. $175.00 – 225.00.

Well crafted silver ring set with turquoise by Bullach. $100.00 – 135.00.

Large finely crafted silver ring with a large polished turquoise. $175.00 – 225.00.

Large silver ring set with turquoise. $75.00 – 100.00.

Top: Silver cuff bracelet with a large smooth bezel set turquoise, $175.00 – 235.00. Bottom: Silver cuff bracelet with thunderbird motif and small central turquoise, $150.00 – 200.00.

Group of scarf pins. $20.00 – 25.00.

Very large and wide silver cuff bracelet set with turquoise. Marked with two back to back "C" letters, and tests as silver. $400.00 – 500.00.

Unmarked silver cuff bracelet with simple motif on top and sides, $40.00 – 60.00; silver cuff bracelet set with turquoise, $45.00 – 65.00; and a silver cuff bracelet with thunderbird motif, $90.00 – 135.00.

Silver shield pin, $25.00 – 35.00; silver and coral earrings, $18.00 – 22.00; silver pendant set with artificial stones and marked with a conjoined double "A," $35.00 – 50.00; lady's silver watch band set with coral and turquoise, $45.00 – 65.00; thunderbird silver pin, $30.00 – 50.00.

Silver cuff bracelet with a central inlay motif. $45.00 – 70.00.

Silver and turquoise ring. $50.00 – 75.00.

Pendant with so called "Sleeping Beauty" turquoise and a silver serpent marked "EFFIE C. ZUNI" standing for Effie Calavaza. Effie has been making jewelry for around five decades, occasionally helped by her daughters in recent years. The usual serpent on the face of her jewelry identifies her work. Pieces marked Juan C. are pre-1970 when Effie and her husband Juan shared the same mark. $45.00 – 65.00.

Ring set with "Sleeping Beauty" turquoise and the usual Effie Calavaza serpent. Marked EFFIE C. ZUNI. $40.00 – 55.00.

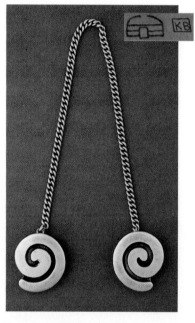

Navajo silver sweater guard marked with White-Hogan and initials "KB" logo standing for Kenneth Begay. Kenneth Begay, now deceased, was among the major post-WWII Native American silversmiths. His jewelry was made in both silver and German silver. $125.00 – 185.00. *John Christopher collection.*

Zuni turquoise needlepoint necklace. $170.00 – 225.00.

Wide cuff bracelet with large bezel set central stone. $400.00 – 500.00.

Silver brooch with textured surface and applied motifs, marked "900" and with the illegible maker's mark, claimed to have been custom made in New Mexico. $60.00 – 95.00.

Silver cuff bracelet featuring inlay heart. $35.00 – 50.00.

Large belt buckle, marked sterling and "AB." $40.00 – 60.00.

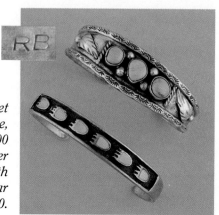

Top: Cuff bracelet set with turquoise, marked "RB," $100.00 – 150.00; and silver cuff bracelet with turquoise set bear claws, $50.00 – 75.00.

Silver cuff bracelet set with turquoise. $100.00 – 150.00.

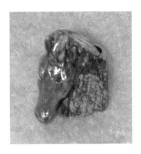

Outstanding sculptured silver and turquoise ring. Marked with a possible road-runner type of symbol. $450.00 – 600.00. *Robin Allison collection.*

Finely handcrafted silver necklace set with mother-of-pearl and matching earrings, marked Don Chee. The Chee family has been making jewelry for decades, and their work is of the highest quality. $125.00 – 175.00.

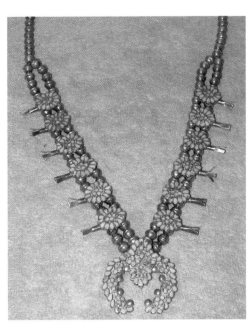

Wonderful Zuni squash blossom made in the 1940s and marked VDISHTA SR. Virgil Dishta was active during the late 1930s to 1950s period. $750.00 – 1,000.00. *Robin Allison collection.*

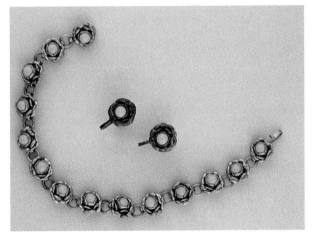

Necklace and matching screwback earrings set with turquoise. $45.00 – 65.00.

Small unmarked handcrafted silver pin. $25.00 – 35.00.

Mexico

Mexican Silver Jewelry

Historically, Mexico has been a major source of the silver supply in the "new world." In fact, until the mid nineteenth century due to a shortage of silver in the U.S., Spanish coins mined in Mexico had wide circulation in the U.S. and the term "dollar" as well as perhaps the symbol "$" are both derived from Spanish, the former itself a corruption of Thaler, a once popular German silver coin first minted in the Tyrolean Jochiem valley and with world-wide circulation, and the latter possibly derived from the abbreviation for Peso, Ps, written vertically for convenience in U.S. documents and transformed into the symbol "$" over time. Mexico has also been known for its fine silver products as attested by many quality pieces preserved in various U.S. and European museums. For example, a silver tureen in the Campbell Museum Collection, dated circa 1750 and executed in a refined simple design with minor ornamentation, reflects the independent Mexican artistic expression and the new world's interpretation of the popular and fashionable "old world" designs and forms.

Mexican silver combined with leather work accounted for the best of saddles, riding gear, belts, buckles, and other ornamentations in the Southwest, often executed by highly skilled Mexican craftsmen. The craft of making silver jewelry and religious relics also dates back to the early colonial years and has been the mainstay of many small village and large urban Mexican silversmiths. Much of this jewelry reflected national and native themes, drawing on the rich Mexican native heritage as well as the Spanish and European, and the urban production was primarily by several major firms in Mexico City. There were also other types of silver jewelry, filigree, engraved, inlaid, and with floral designs and motifs inspired by nature, that were popular throughout the Southwest and northern Mexico, but had not yet attracted the curiosity and attention of the American connoisseurs and pundits. The traditional silversmiths of Iguala, known for their filigree silver jewelry, were among the main workforce for the growing modern silver industry in Taxco.

Modern Mexican silver jewelry to some extent, owes its revival and popularity to the work of two Americans, Frederick Davis and William Spratling, who began living and working in Mexico in the early 1900s. In the English literature, this role is often highly exaggerated, and successful business ventures facilitated by business connections on both sides of the border are credited above artistic leitmotiv and skillful renditions, the main forces responsible for a successful and highly creative Mexican silver jewelry industry. Somehow external marketing and business aspects are treated as the genesis for this revival, superceding the artistic genius and creative expressions of the Mexican silversmiths, while in reality, it was the latter which captured public attention, leaving its indelible impression and motivating enterprising men to successfully market a quality product with extremely low production cost. The recent popularity of Mexican silver jewelry worldwide, the recent recognition of highly talented known Mexican silversmiths, and the long overdue appreciation of many yet unknown artisans are testimonial to this fountain of creativity and superb craftsmanship that captured the imagination of the early American visitors to Mexico.

Davis moved to Mexico in 1910 as an employee of Sonora News Company. He became fascinated by Mexican folk art and began to study and collect it while also selling the objects to American clients as a dealer in arts and antiques. Not long after, with the aid of a Mexican master silversmith, Davis began to design and make silver jewelry inspired by pre-Colombian art utilizing native material such as volcanic glass, obsidian, and amethyst. Spratling, an American architect, arrived in Mexico in 1929 and in 1931 set up a silver smithing workshop, Las Delicias, in Taxco, Mexico (pronounced Tasco which sometimes is the spelling used on some of the marked jewelry). From the outset, Spratling employed several Mexican silversmiths who executed his and their own designs, creating wonderful pieces of silver jewelry exhibiting highly creative designs and superb craftsmanship. Spratling's Las Delicias is usually considered the catalyst of an explosive expansion of silver jewelry production in the Taxco area. Many silver workshops with notable Mexican master silversmiths who are now well known abroad were established in the Taxco area, and a variety of silver jewelry was manufactured for both domestic and expanding export markets. Among these were Los Castillo, Hector Aguilar, Valentin Vidaurreta, Antonio and Sigi Pineda, Rafael Dominguez, Maricela, Margot, Ledesma, Salvador Teran, and Matilde Poulat (MATL), Miguel Melendez, and many other silversmiths, some located in Mexico City.

At the early stages, jewelry made by these silversmiths, particularly pieces made by Davis and Spratling which are prized finds today, were brought back to the U.S. by the tourists visiting Mexico. But during WWII, with the rising popularity of Mexican silver jewelry and the reduction of U.S. import duties, massive quantities were exported. In 1944, Spratling was incorporated with most of the shares held by a group of American investors, and Coro contracted Hector Aguilar to make silver jewelry for the American market. Mexican jewelry remained relatively popular in the U.S. and was imported in large quantities. The recent high recognition of major Mexican silversmiths has multiplied the public demand as well as the supply of the Mexican jewelry and the U.S. imports. Taxco is still thriving with perhaps over a thousand silversmiths working in several hundred workshops, but silver jewelry production was never limited to Taxco. There were major manufacturers in Mexico City with many silversmiths operating small workshops in the northern towns near the U.S. border, and some Native Americans producing handmade jewelry in the U.S. similar to that made across the border by their distant kinsmen.

Most Mexican silver jewelry is marked "Hecho en Mexico" (Made in Mexico) along with either sterling or a silver fineness mark (925 to 980). The word "Taxco" and the workshop or silversmith's name or initials may also appear as part of the mark. These are usually arranged in a circular form framing the name or initials. Some of the old pieces, the majority of which are possibly from Mexico City, are marked only "Silver" and "Mexico" or "Made in Mexico." Some of these unmarked pieces are of the highest quality.

There is a serious problem of attribution since many initials are not yet identified, and many beautiful pieces may not even carry the maker's mark. Many of these marks are reproduced in this book in order to introduce the works of unidentified or unknown Mexican silversmiths and to generate further research leading to eventual identification.

From 1947 to 1979, the Mexican government required an eagle stamp to be used as assay mark on all sterling or higher grade silver jewelry. The eagle stamp, which is seldom clearly visible, carried a number in the center which was supposed to identify the silversmith, but apparently the same numbers were used by other silversmiths, and using these numbers as a method of attribution is highly unreliable. Although these numbers are given below as a reference, they should be interpreted with extreme caution and only as corroborative evidence when all other factors and marks are carefully considered and accounted for.

In 1979, a new registry system which uses two letters and a number, similar to the Italian system, was adopted by the Mexican government. The letters are supposed to represent the initials of the silversmith and the number to reflect the order in which the name was entered on a list of registered silversmiths. For example, TS-24 stands as the mark for the successors to Spratling and TA-01 for Antonio Castillo de Teran. A list of names and addresses of many current Mexican silversmiths and silver shops in Taxco is provided in the appendix.

Classification of the Eagle Marks

Eagle marks with the following numbers are found on the silver products of identified and unidentified Mexican silversmiths:

#1: Generic Mexico City mark, William Spratling, Los Castillo, Hector Gomez (Anita), Santos, AR, ARI, CLS, FCM or ECM, GM (Gustavo Martinez?), GRB, HCV, JSE, and MSR.

#2: Bernice Goodspeed, Ledesma, CF, and ECP.

#3: Generic Guadalajara and Taxco mark, Abriaca, Hector Aguilar, Antonio, Bernice Goodspeed, Chavarrieta, Delfino, Emma (GAR), Jacobo (JNJ), Victor Jaimez (VJC), Ledesma, Maricela, Miguel Garcia (Rancho Alegre), Miguel Melendez,, Nestor, Orvelo, Piedra y Plata, Sigi, BR, JLF, JMT, JS, MR, MRV, RHG, and SC.

#4: FCHH and JGN
#5: Chato Castillo
#7: Possibly Tane
#9: Hector Aguilar

#11: Gonzalo Morenom, Mexico DF
#12: Victoria
#13: William Spratling, Conquistador (Mexico City)
#15: Los Castillo
#16: Margot
#17: Antonio
#22: Bernice Goodspeed
#23: ATE
#26: Lopez
#30: William Spratling
#34: Parra (Conquistador)
#35: Sigi
#36: Sigi and Salvador Teran
#38: Found on high quality silver jewelry without the maker's name or initials.

#40: Reveri Castillo
#47: Los Ballesteros
#56: Possibly Salvador
#58: Combined Antonio and Los Castillo
#60: Ledesma
#63: William Spratling

#82: JGG
#84: Miguel Garcia
#113: E.V.B.
#123: MATL
#124: MATL

Mexican Silversmiths, Designers, and Manufacturers

Aguilar, Hector (active 1937 – 1965)

Hector Aguilar worked as the manager of the Spratling shop, Las Delicias, for two years before leaving with a group of other silversmiths to establish his own workshop, the Taller Borda, in 1939. This move coincided with the war years in 1940s, and the increase in U.S. demand for Mexican silver led to the rapid expansion of the firm. War restrictions on silver and cheap skilled labor brought many American jewelry firms and investors to Mexico, acquiring part ownership or contracting with the Mexican firms to produce silver jewelry for the U.S. market. Coro contracted Aguilar to make silver jewelry and military insignia which are marked "Coro Mexico." The Taller Borda work force increased from 125 to over 300. Exports con-

tinued during the post war years with Aguilar lines of silver jewelry marketed through major U.S. department stores such as Saks Fifth Avenue and Neiman Marcus; the U.S. government also placed large orders for silver insignia for the military.

Superior craftsmanship, outstanding creative stylized designs inspired by nature and Mexican culture characterize Hector Aguilar's silver jewelry. As in the case of Los Castillo, the Taller Borda was responsible for training the next generation of Mexican silversmiths that carried on the tradition of fine silversmithing in Taxco and elsewhere in Mexico. Hector Aguilar retired in 1966 after closing shop and died in the early 1970s.

Antonio (Pineda)

The jewelry commonly marked and referred to as "Antonio" was produced by Antonio Pineda. Antonio had some training as a painter before finding employment as a designer with Spratling. For a few years he also worked for Valentin Vidaurreta in Mexico City, acquiring experience in metalwork before opening his own workshop in 1941. Antonio had several highly skilled master silversmiths with many years of experience at Spratling's Las Delicias and Los Castillo join his workshop which ensured the highest quality of craftsmanship. Most of

Antonio's jewelry has designs that are stylized modern interpretations of pre-Hispanic motifs, executed in pure silver or in combination with native stones. The firm reached its zenith during the 1960s and is still in business. Several marks were used over the years: "AP," 1941 – 1949; "Jewels by Toño," 1949 – 1953; and the most common mark, the crown "ANTONIO."

Ballesteros (1937 – present)

The origin of Talleres de Los Ballesteros and the involvement of the Ballesteros family in the jewelry business can be traced back to several generations of silversmiths with part of the family producing silver jewelry in Iguala using traditional designs. Jalil Majul Ballesteros had learned silversmithing from his grandfather and moved to Taxco to establish a workshop in 1937 and manufacture silver jewelry in the traditional filigree style for which the Iguala silversmiths were famous. The firm later began manufacturing the Taxco type of silver jewelry and expanded during WWII with the rising demand for Mexican silver. After the war, instead of depending on the tourist traffic in Taxco, the Ballesteros family established direct outlets in vari-

ous cities, such as Mexico City and Acapulco, a move which proved instrumental in the survival of the business. There is a broad range of jewelry manufactured by the Ballesteros, many pieces

inspired by the pre-Hispanic motifs and others by the traditional post-conquest themes and designs. In addition to its workshop production, the Ballesteros also used the "put-out" system of contracting many independent silversmiths to produce jewelry for the firm by providing them with materials and designs. The firm is still in business at its workshop on Los Plateros Avenue in Taxco.

Beckman, Carmen

The jewelry marked "Beckman" was designed by Carmen Beckman, circa late 1950s through 1971, and sold in her shop in San Miguel. The jewelry is of average quality with typical designs inspired by the pre-Hispanic motifs.

Castillo, Pedro (b. 1927)

Pedro Castillo began his long career as a young boy at Spratling's Las Delicias and joined Hector Aguilar when he opened Taller Borda in 1939. Pedro Castillo and his brother Carlos opened their own workshop sometime around 1950. Production was concentrated primarily on flatware, some of which was sold through Rancho Alegre and carried the shop's stamp. But silver jewelry was also manufactured and it is marked with the partially superimposed letters, PC, surrounded by Hecho en Mexico. The pieces made by Carlos Castillo were also marked with his initials: CC. Pedro Castillo's jewelry is high quality solid pieces with stylized pre-Colombian motifs or a combination of old motifs rendered in modern forms.

Davis, Frederick (1880 – 1961)

Fred Davis arrived in Mexico in 1910 and found employment with the Sonora News Company. The nature of his job required extensive travel which brought Davis in contact with the Mexican population and instilled in him a growing appreciation for the Mexican popular arts and crafts. Subsequently, he began collecting Mexican arts and artifacts and established a close relationship with a circle of Mexican artisans. But it was the folk silver jewelry worn by the peasantry which most fascinated Davis. Soon Davis began collaborating with Mexican silversmiths in Mexico City to manufacture silver jewelry inspired by the traditional folk and pre-Colombian motifs. This and other silver jewelry along with Mexican folk arts and crafts were sold in his store in Mexico City which also served as a gathering place for a circle of Mexican artists and artisans. Davis purchased and exported antiques and collectibles, Mexican folk arts and artifacts, and contracted Mexican workers to manufacture handcrafted products which he exported to the U.S. with major department stores among his market.

In 1933, Davis formed a partnership with Frank Sanborn in Mexico City which for the next two decades managed the Sanborn department store, offering antiques, collectibles, and Mexican handcrafted products to the growing tourist traffic. Davis also collaborated with the Mexican government which was interested in preserving the Mexican folk art through fostering the development of the crafts as viable business enterprises. In 1951, after retiring from Sanborn, Davis became the first director of the newly established Museum of Popular Arts and Industries; several years later a significant part of his own collection was given to the museum.

Davis's silver jewelry is of superior quality and the designs are directly inspired by the Mexican culture and history. To the end, his business interests never overwhelmed his passion for Mexico and the sources of his inspiration. Much of the silver jewelry and boxes are set with native stones, particularly the popular amethyst. Not all the pieces were marked, and the marked jewelry is extremely rare, commanding high prices.

Delfino

This mark is found on the jewelry made of sterling silver and sometimes set with pearls made by the Mexican designer and silversmith Delfino whose jewelry is finding greater interest among the collectors and is experiencing a rise in prices. Most of the pieces seen by the author are delicate, small pieces with the examples shown on the following pages constituting typical Delfino jewelry found on the market.

Emma (1953 – 1971)

"Emma" is the mark used by Emma Melendez on the jewelry manufactured and sold at her shop. She opened her workshop and store in 1953 and employed at least half a dozen designers. Her first and major designer was Miguel Garcia, and some other talented designers were Victor Jaimez (mark: VJC) and Francisco Rivera (mark: FR). The initials of several yet unidentified designers and/or silversmiths also appear on Emma jewelry. Among these, the mark "MR" belongs to a silversmith who must have also worked independently during the 1940s – 1960s period since several pieces of the period in the author's collection have an identical stamp without the Emma mark. The quality of the MR silver jewelry, both in design and fabrication, is comparable to other major silver-

Emma (Cont.)

smiths of the period. (See MR on page 78.) Other initials are "PCC" or "RCC", "JLF," and "JM."

Emma closed her workshop in 1971. She opened a retail shop in 1977 which sold only the jewelry designed and manufactured by other silversmiths. The vintage jewelry is marked "Emma" and may also be stamped with the initials of the designer.

Garcia, Miguel (active 1950s –)

Like Spratling, Miguel Garcia Martinez became a designer of jewelry with no background in silversmithing. Related to Pedro Perez who was the owner of the most popular silver retail shop in Taxco, Miguel designed jewelry which was manufactured at the retail shop. He apparently also designed jewelry for Emma. Miguel Garcia's jewelry are highly stylized interpretations of the pre-Hispanic motifs and cultural themes with a fashionable modern look.

Goodspeed, Bernice

Bernice Goodspeed's main interest was in pre-Colombian arts and cultural anthropology which initially brought her to Mexico in 1930 to study at the University of Mexico. Her marriage to painter Carl Pappe in 1935 led to relocation in Taxco and her eventual transition to designing and making jewelry. The venture began with opening a studio in the late 1930s where pre-Colombian arts and artifacts were displayed and sold. Of course, in a town like Taxco the natural next step was making silver jewelry. The small workshop manufactured silver jewelry designed primarily by Bernice, and the rising demand during the WWII years led to a prosperous business for the couple.

As an intellectual, writer, and artist, Bernice Goodspeed was quite familiar with and loyal to the pre-Colombian motifs which she had studied and the fusion of the two cultures during the post-conquest era. Her jewelry displays strong pre-Hispanic as well as religious/cultural influences. It is of fine quality with well defined designs and is relatively rare in the market. The jewelry is marked with "B" in a circle.

Ledesma

Originally from Mexico City, Enrique Ledesma was educated and trained as an artist while also learning silversmithing at his father's workshop. He moved to Taxco around 1940 and found employment at Spratling's Las Delicias and later at Los Castillo. Ledesma opened his own workshop around 1950 and proceeded to manufacture some of the most unique and highly technical silver jewelry in Taxco. The jewelry, which often exhibits modern designs inspired by nature, skillfully employs swirls, curls, and curves in a soft harmony with carefully selected and shaped stones. Even the simple pieces demonstrate fine craftsmanship and aptly declare that they are the creations of a master. The jewelry is marked Ledesma with the extended L.

Los Castillo (1939 – 2000)

Antonio Castillo de Teran (b. 1916) and his brothers were among the first handful of young men trained at Spratling's workshop. The four brothers learned every aspect of the business, from management to design and the technical aspects of making and marketing silver jewelry. In 1939, the Castillo brothers set up their own workshop, producing jewelry primarily designed by Margot van Voorhies Carr, an American visitor to Mexico whom Antonio had married. The firm expanded rapidly and is responsible for many technical and artistic innovations among which are stone inlay and fused (married) metal, metal painting, and enameling. These techniques came from the genius and technical expertise of Jorge (Chato) Castillo, one of the best silversmiths Taxco ever produced. Chato's skills in working with the material, Margot's designs, and Antonio's versatility, particularly in management, combined to make Castillo a successful venture.

Many competent silversmiths were trained at Los Castillo who later ventured out to establish their own workshops, including Sigi Pineda, Miguel Melendez, and Salvador Teran. Margot also departed and established her own workshop after her divorce from Antonio around 1948.

Los Castillo's silver jewelry exhibits the finest craftsmanship, beautiful and varied designs resulting from continuous experimentation, and a highly versatile and creative approach to making jewelry. The firm is still in business, and Don Antonio's daughter, Emilia (Mimi) is the major designer for the company with many other silversmiths, including a host of relatives and in-laws who make up the large Castillo family. (Don Antonio passed away as this book was going to press after a long and difficult illness, but his name, contributions, and masterpieces shall live forever, bringing joy and appreciation to collectors around the world. The author expects sharp increases in the prices of his jewelry.)

Margot (d. 1985)

With the changing times, many women entered the field of jewelry design and manufacturing in Europe and America, particularly after WWII. As in many other industries which were closed to women, this process is only at its infant stages even in the more progressive and least chauvinistic cultures. In Mexico, several women paved the way, and Margot van Voohries Carr is among the leading pioneers. Of Dutch and French extraction and born and raised in the U.S., Margot met and married Antonio Castillo after moving to Mexico in 1937. While still working for Spratling, Antonio began moonlighting by making and marketing the jewelry designed by Margot. The jewelry was so well received that Antonio and his brothers left Spratling in 1939 and established their own workshop.

As were many other European designers, Margot was influenced by the Japanese arts and a long tradition in superb metalwork, an influence which affected her early work fabricated by Los Castillo and traces of which are observed in all of her later creations. The marriage with Antonio lasted 10 years and upon her divorce, Margot established her own silver jewelry business.

The business continued to expand and Margot introduced many new lines among which were her now famed silver and enamel jewelry. With a strong demand for her jewelry, her workforce also expanded including several able and experienced silversmiths such as Miguel Melendez and Juan Gonzalez and newcomer Sigi Pineda.

Margot's silver jewelry is solid three-dimensional pieces unique in design and craftsmanship, and her multi-layered enamel pieces, exhibiting depth, not only in execution but also in her spring of creativity. Margot relocated her shop several times, facing declining demand after the fall in tourism aggravated by labor problems; the business was forced into bankruptcy and liquidation in the 1970s. She spent the last years of her life in poverty, frequently depending on the charity of her friends, and died in 1985. The ending is tragic and poignant, but she left behind a rich legacy and beautiful precious objects which shall continue to feed our imagination and aesthetic cravings for many years. Her jewelry is marked "Margot de Taxco" and commands high market prices.

Maricela (Isidro Garcia)

The Mexican silver jewelry marked "Maricela" was manufactured by Isidro Garcia Piña and named after his daughter, Maricela. Isidro Garcia was trained as a silversmith and worked on contract before opening his own workshop in Taxco in 1943. The business flourished for the next three decades before the fall in tourism in Mexico which had a significant impact on all the Tallers and silver production in Taxco. The Taller continued operations, experiencing another setback with the rise of silver prices in 1981 and was finally closed in 1986. Maricela jewelry consists primarily of pins, link and cuff bracelets, and earrings with stylized circular floral motives and others with modern designs reflecting pre-Colombian influence where curves and curvilinear forms dominate. The earliest jewelry was marked "Maricela" in fancy script as shown here. These date back to the 1940s. The last mark used was the name printed in a circle.

Matl (d. 1960)

Matl is the mark used by Matilde Eugenia Poulat on her jewelry, but the name is also used to refer to her jewelry in the collectible market. Matilde was educated and trained as an artist and taught drawing and painting before turning to designing and manufacturing jewelry. She began making jewelry in the mid 1930s and the business grew, helped by the increase in demand for Mexican silver during WWII. In 1950, she opened a retail shop in Mexico City which was kept open by her nephew, Salas Poulat, after her death in 1960.

Matilde's jewelry is characterized by stylized floral and free figural motifs such as birds inspired by Mexico's pre-Hispanic culture and religious themes where large, ornamented crosses dominate. Although the shop in Mexico City was closed, Salas and his family continue to make Matl jewelry in similar styles and fashion.

Melendez, Miguel (active c. 1935 – 1990s)

Miguel Melendez was trained by Antonio Castillo at Spratling's Las Delicias and was among a small group of silversmiths who left Spratling for Los Castillo. Miguel was an exceptionally talented and highly skilled silversmith and was responsible for the development of enamelwork introduced by Los Castillo which later became the hallmark of Margot's jewelry. Melendez was also a master metalworker both in fabrication and techniques and is considered among the best Mexican silversmiths, particularly in the field of repousse. Melendez never established his own workshop but apparently independently designed and manufactured jewelry which is stamped with his

own mark. He spent over a decade at Los Castillo and after Margot established her own workshop, he joined her and helped to produce and launch the now famed Margot enamel jewelry. Melendez's mark is a large script "m," the end of which encircles the letter itself. This mark is seldom seen in its complete form. The jewelry clearly marked with the separate letters "CM" is also attributed to Melendez. These pieces appear to have been made at a later date.

MR (active 1940s – 1960s)

The initials "MR" are found on the jewelry dating to approximately the 1940s through the 1960s. A similar mark is also found on the jewelry marked Emma. It is the author's guess that MR worked as an independent silversmith, sometimes

being contracted by other workshops such as Emma's. Both the designs and fabrication are of high quality, reflecting the work of a highly talented and skilled silversmith.

Rancho Alegre (1956 – 1985)

The Rancho Alegre was perhaps the largest and most popular retail shop in the Taxco area. It was owned by Pedro Perez who had many years of experience in sales and management, including nearly two decades at Spratling's Las Delicias. Rancho Alegre sold both silver jewelry designed and made at its own workshop and marked with the store name as well as pieces made by other silversmiths. Many silversmiths worked at the workshop and their jewelry was then purchased by Perez and

marked Rancho Alegre. Many of the silversmiths made their own designs and the only in-house designer was Miguel Garcia who had his designs executed in silver by several silversmiths such as Melecio Rodriguiz. Perez also sold the silver jewelry and cutlery and hollowware manufactured by independent silversmiths for Rancho Alegre. Perez sold the store in 1985. The jewelry may only be marked Rancho Alegre or also stamped with the name or initials of the maker.

Salvador Teran (active 1934 – present)

Salvador Vaca Teran was among the early group of silversmiths trained at Spratling's Las Delicias. He left Las Delicias in 1939 along with his four cousins, the Castillo brothers, and designed jewelry at Los Castillos before opening his own workshop in Mexico City in 1952. Salvador's jewelry manifests unmistakable pre-Colombian influence and is of very high qual-

ity. Much of the jewelry depicting pre-Hispanic motifs looks like deeply carved pieces of silver, an effect which is highly enhanced with intentional oxidization and emphasis on contrast of colors. The jewelry is marked Salvador in script and is still being made.

Sigi Pineda (b. 1929)

Sigfrido Pineda was trained as a silversmith in Iguala and like many other Mexican silversmiths from this area found employment in Taxco in the late 1940s, acquiring more experience while working for Los Castillo and Margot. He opened his own workshop in Taxco in 1952 which was his first undertaking in a series of shifting artistic and business ventures that involved the production of silver jewelry and products as well as other artistic endeavors including pottery and glass making. Although he has left and returned many times and owned various shops, Sigi still works in Taxco designing jewelry.

Sigfrido Pineda is among a few modern Mexican silversmiths whose work goes beyond the distinct Mexican designs which frequently reflect the pre-Colombian and Mexican cultural influences. His designs are modern and international, finding closer affinity with the modern silver jewelry in other parts of the world such as the Scandinavian jewelry. His vintage jewelry is usually marked "Sigi" along with the inventory number and the eagle mark.

Spratling, William (? – 1967)

While teaching architecture at Tulane University, Spratling spent several summers in Mexico beginning in 1926 and established contacts with many leading Mexican political figures and befriended a circle of progressive Mexican artists such as Diego Rivera, Rufino Tamayo, and Siqueiros who apparently influenced and complemented his world view regarding social responsibility and the place of art in the society. The post Mexican Revolution decades were turbulent years in Mexico with the nation struggling to assume an independent and modern identity, and the pressures for change and transformation of the society gave rise to flourishing artistic and intellectual activities, including the distinct Mexican School in arts, identifying with the peasantry and the Mexican folk traditions rather than the post-colonial aristocracy. Deciding to write a book on Mexico, Spratling moved to Mexico in 1929 and purchased a house in Calle de Las Delicias in Taxco. Impressed by the Mexican arts and crafts tradition and pre-Colombian motifs and as a business venture, Spratling opened a shop in 1931 (La Aduana) which sold handcrafted Mexican products, including silver jewelry. The store also served as a silver workshop manufacturing silver jewelry produced under the guidance of a master goldsmith, Artemio Navarrete, whom Spratling had enticed to leave his own small workshop in Iguala and move to Taxco. Hired with him was also another master smith, Alfunso Ruiz Mondragon, working in Iguala. The workshop produced silver jewelry which according to Spratling was "literal copies of Aztec and colonial motifs," or Aztec seals transformed into silver pins. Throughout his early years, Spratling heavily employed the pre-Colombian and traditional folk motifs as well as domestic stones and materials such as Mexican amethyst and rosewood, later supplemented by lapis, malachite, Mexican "jade," ebony, and tortoise shell. Over the years, this influence gradually declined and became less apparent as Spratling developed his own style and simpler, more stylized designs. The initial workforce included many who later opened their own workshops and became prominent silversmiths in Mexico.

By 1935, the expanding business necessitated the relocation to a larger shop which became known as Taller de las Delicias and within several years a significant portion of the jewelry and silver products were manufactured for the export market,

retailed in the U.S. by upper-end stores such as Neiman-Marcus and Saks Fifth Avenue. By 1941, the firm was employing approximately 120 people. Spratling's success was due to a combination of factors: 1) low labor cost for unskilled as well as relatively skilled labor; 2) proximity to an ample supply of silver; 3) popularity of ancient motifs in jewelry and decorative arts ranging from Egyptian to pre-Colombian; 4) the quality of the products which reflected Spratling's ingenuity, masterful designs, and the skilled craftsmanship of the Mexican silversmiths. For several years in the early 1940s, Spratling also designed products manufactured by the Sislon Company which carry the mark and his name as well as "Sislon Company," but these were not executed in sterling silver.

During the war restrictions on silver in the U.S. and the disruption of the European trade routes, the demand for Mexican silver rose drastically in the U.S. Many major U.S firms and investors turned to Mexico for their silver supply and contracted with or directly acquired part-ownership of some of the Mexican workshops. A group of American investors purchased part of the Spratling company which soon led to frictions and his eventual resignation in 1945. The firm itself did not last very long and it was subsequently dissolved. In 1947, Spratling opened a new workshop at his new ranch in Taxco-el-Viejo, manufacturing silver jewelry with much more stylized and simpler designs. He also designed jewelry which were manufactured by the Conquistador Company in Mexico City in the 1949 – 1951 period. These are marked "Spratling de Mexico." William Spratling died as a result of an automobile accident on August 7, 1967. Ulberto Ulrich purchased his ranch and designs and continued to produce silver jewelry under the company name, "Sucesores de William Spratling," using the last Spratling benchmark and later TS-24. Apparently Spratling designs were also manufactured by others, including some rumored to have been made in the Far East in the 1990s, and reproductions with forged marks are seen increasingly in the market. Spratling jewelry is among the best and highly prized silver jewelry produced in Mexico; Spratling set the direction and tone for the rejuvenated industry in which he played an important pioneering role.

Victoria

Ana Maria Nuñez de Brilianti marked her silver jewelry "VICTORIA" which also served as the name for her silver shop in Taxco. Ana was trained as a painter and taught art in Mexico City before relocating to Taxco with her husband and their five children. Living in a town preoccupied with silver and with the

booming tourist trade, Ana Brilianti began using her talent and artistic background by designing jewelry and having pieces produced in silver. In 1940 she opened her shop, Victoria. Her designs primarily consist of stylized pre-Hispanic and geometric motifs executed in well-defined sculptured structure some-

Victoria (cont.)

times enhanced with fused silver balls or decorative dangles.

In 1953, Ana helped her daughter, Cony, open a shop which sold silver jewelry made at the Plateria Victoria and was stamped with the typical Victoria mark as well as "Cony." As with other Taxco silver enterprises, Brilianti's business was adversely affected by the decline in tourism, and Victoria was closed in 1975 fol-lowed by the liquidation of the workshop in 1978. Later Ana opened a smaller shop which sold jewelry produced by others, some in her own designs. She is still living and working in Taxco, and Cony's shop was in business as of this writing under the name Plateria Cony, Plata Victoria. The vintage jewelry is marked "Victoria" in semi-circular form.

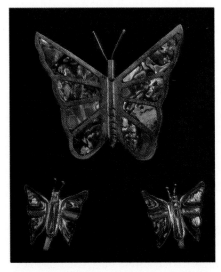

Silver butterfly brooch and near matching screwback earrings, set with abalone shell and marked Hecho En Mexico 925 and the maker's mark, "AFC." Brooch, $30.00 – 40.00; earrings, $20.00 – 25.00.

Pair of .970 silver, pearl, and enamel tie bars, marked with the Antonio crown mark and with original price tags of $75.00. $150.00 – 200.00 each. John Christopher collection.

Floral brooch, marked Hector Aguilar. with Aguilar's conjoined "HA" stamp. $400.00 – 550.00. John Christopher collection.

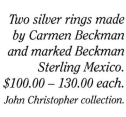

Two silver rings made by Carmen Beckman and marked Beckman Sterling Mexico. $100.00 – 130.00 each. John Christopher collection.

Marked Antonio sterling silver and tortoise bracelet. $750.00 – 1,000.00. Robin Allison collection.

An outstanding bracelet by Hector Aguilar, typical of the master's silver jewelry. Marked with Aguilar's conjoined "HA." $800.00 – 1,100.00. John Christopher collection.

Silver and abalone shell Mexican jewelry, all marked "AP." Bracelet, $30.00 – 45.00; brooch and matching earrings, $35.00 – 50.00.

Solid silver bracelet, marked with Ballesteros's "B" stamp. $130.00 – 165.00.

Silver bracelet made by Pedro Castillo. $275.00 – 350.00.

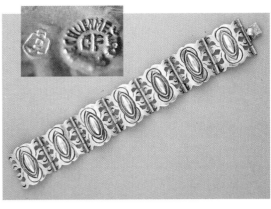

High quality and well executed silver bracelet, marked "CF" and with eagle #2. $90.00 – 125.00.

Silver pill box, marked with Frederick Davis's logo. $250.00 – 350.00. *Photo courtesy of Teina Moran.*

Silver choker, marked with Ballesteros's stamp. $85.00 – 135.00.

Matching bracelet, ring, and screwback earrings, marked Hecho Mexico DAF 900. $60.00 – 95.00.

Silver brooch with applied flying fish and waves on round oxidized concave base. Marked Emma and "CAR" surrounded by Mexico Taxco 925 and eagle #3. In original pouch marked Emma. $100.00 – 130.00.

Three pieces of jewelry decorated with pearl over oxidized base and all marked Delfino. Pendant, $45.00 – 65.00; pin, $60.00 – 85.00; ring, $40.00 – 60.00.

Wide bracelet set with simulated jade stones and marked Iguala Mexico 925 V with the maker's mark, "DR." This is typical Iguala silver jewelry which was also famous for its filigree work. The jewelry is as good as any average Taxco piece. Spratling relied on the talent and skills of the Iguala silversmiths to launch his business. $50.00 – 75.00.

Silver and abalone shell jewelry. All marked with the maker's initials "EAB" and Taxco Mexico 925 and eagle #3. Matching necklace and bracelet, $60.00 – 95.00; brooch, $30.00 – 40.00.

Well-made bracelets, marked Hecho en Mexico 925 and with the maker's initials, "GM" which may be that of Gustavo Martinez. $50.00 – 80.00 each. Sterling earrings, marked "ARA" $18.00 – 22.00.

Left, Mexican silver mask pin, $18.00 – 25.00; round swirl pin, marked A. Garcia, $30.00 – 40.00; round engraved brooch combined with shell inlay, marked "CF" $35.00 – 45.00; unmarked silver and simulated jade bracelet, $35.00 – 45.00; and a large inlay turquoise brooch, marked "JPM," $40.00 – 50.00.

Two marked silver bracelets with simulated jade. Top: marked "JPR" $35.00 – 45.00; bottom: marked "N.S." $35.00 – 50.00.

Silver jewelry marked with the maker's initials "IMP." Brooch, $20.00 – 25.00; earrings, $20.00 – 25.00.

High quality handcrafted matching set marked Hecho en Mexico, Taxco 925, and the maker's initials, "J.S.E" with eagle #1 on applied circle plaque. $250.00 – 350.00.

Two Mexican sterling silver earrings and a tie bar, marked "JFG," with the center earrings also marked F. Caciones. $25.00 – 35.00 each.

Sterling silver brooch with a large agate stone, marked Ledesma. $250.00 – 300.00. *John Christopher collection.*

Pair of sterling silver cuf flinks made by Enrique Ledesma and marked Ledesma. $90.00 – 125.00.

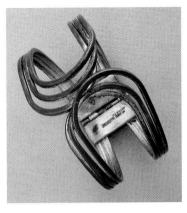

Sterling silver bracelet with modern abstract design, marked Ledesma. $150.00 – 250.00.

Los Castillo mark.

Two round silver pins marked with the maker's initials, "JGN." $30.00 – 45.00 each.

Pair of marked Los Castillo cuff links. $125.00 – 150.00.

Outstanding brooch by Don Castillo and marked Los Castillo. $1,200.00 – 1,800.00. Asking price may be as high as $3,000.00. Photo courtesy of Pop Beads to Platinum.

An exceptional silver and abalone shell set, marked Sterling Taxco Mexico encircling the maker's initials, "LS." $225.00 – 300.00.

An exceptional Los Castillo matching necklace and earrings which can also serve as separate pieces of jewelry once disengaged (shown at left). $800.00 – 1,200.00. John Christopher collection.

Marked Los Castillo brooch. $300.00 – 400.00. John Christopher collection.

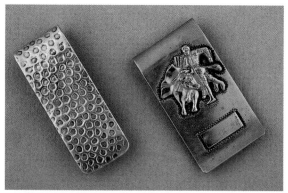

Two Mexican sterling silver money clips, marked "MAP." $25.00 – 40.00.

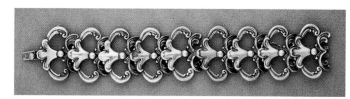

Sterling silver bracelet, marked Margot de Taxco. $350.00 – 450.00. *John Christopher collection.*

Sterling silver earrings, marked MARICELA. $70.00 – 100.00.

Margot de Taxco sterling silver and green enamel set. $1,200.00 – 1,600.00. *Robin Allison collection.*

Wonderful 1950s silver cross typical of Matl's work. Marked Matl Patente 10463 Mexico 925. $650.00 – 800.00. *John Christopher collection.*

Sterling silver brooch, marked Matl. $250.00 – 350.00. *John Christopher collection.*

Sterling silver brooch with amethyst and stamped with Melendez "m" in circle mark. $145.00 – 185.00.

Exceptionally well-made handcrafted solid chain and ball bracelet which opens up into a photo album, made by Miguel Melendez. Melendez "m" in a circle mark. $250.00 – 350.00.

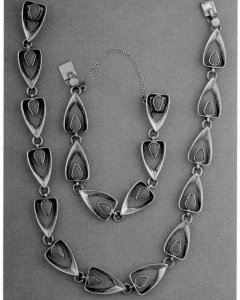

Matching necklace and bracelet made of silver and natural turquoise, marked Miguel, Rancho Alegre, and "GVE." $250.00 – 350.00.

Inlaid silver and turquoise bracelet by Miguel Melendez with his "m" in a circle mark. $250.00 – 350.00.

Sterling silver bat bolo, marked Miguel, made for Rancho Alegre. $250.00 – 350.00.

Wonderful brooch in multi-tone silver, marked "JMP," for Jose Maria Pineda, initially with Los Castillo, later with Antonio Pineda. $200.00 – 300.00. *John Christopher collection.*

Variety of silver and abalone shell jewelry, all marked "MR." $40.00 – 100.00.

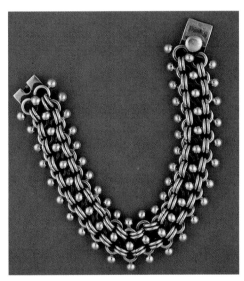

Solid silver bracelet, marked 925 Mexico and with the maker's initials "PAL" in lozenge shaped cartouche. $50.00 – 75.00.

Large sterling silver brooch with the maker's mark "RAG." $40.00 – 60.00.

Solid sterling silver bracelet made by Salvador Teran and marked Salvador. $375.00 – 475.00. *John Christopher collection.*

Pair of gold plated sterling silver cuff links, marked Salvador. $70.00 – 100.00.

Two pairs of screwback earrings marked "Sigi.Tasco" Plain set, $60.00 – 95.00; pair with Mexican "jade" $100.00 – 140.00.

Wide silver bracelets, marked Diaz Santoyo, $100.00 – 150.00; bracelet in somewhat similar style without the maker's mark, $45.00 – 65.00.

Sterling silver brooch, marked Sigi Tasco. $150.00 – 200.00.

Oxidized sterling silver necklace by Sigi Pineda and marked Sigi Tasco. $350.00 – 450.00 *John Christopher collection.*

William Spratling coil silver and amethyst earrings. Marked Spratling with his "WS" logo. $250.00 – 350.00. *John Christopher collection.*

William Spratling silver and lapis pendant. Marked Spratling with his "WS" logo. $300.00 – 400.00.

William Spratling wide silver bracelet. Marked Spratling with his "WS" logo. $1,200.00 – 1,800.00. *John Christopher collection.*

Exquisite William Spratling necklace. Marked Spratling with his "WS" logo. $1,800.00 – 2,500.00. *Photo courtesy of Kile Farese.*

Sterling silver clip earrings and pill box, marked TD-91. Box, $20.00 – 25.00; earrings $18.00 – 22.00.

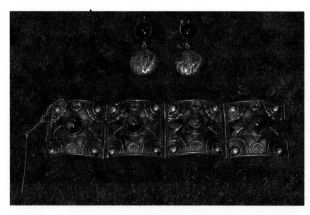

Marked William Spratling silver and amethyst bracelet and earrings. Bracelet, $2,000.00 – 2,500.00; earrings, $250.00 – 350.00. *Robin Allison collection.*

Wonderful bracelet by Victoria. Marked 322 Victoria Mexico Taxco Sterling. $450.00 – 600.00. *John Christopher collection.*

Late 1930s bracelet set with Mexican "jade" (colored onyx) stones. No stone missing, the blank space is an intentional part of the design. Marked with an open-winged bird and Mexico Silver. Possibly a Mexico City piece. $80.00 – 135.00.

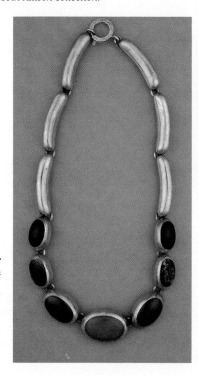

Sterling silver necklace set with semi-precious stones. Marked TC-11. $60.00 – 90.00.

Two sterling silver bracelets, $20.00 – 25.00; and a wonderful seal pendant with well defined motifs on both sides with eagle #38 and illegible initials of the maker, $50.00 – 80.00.

Sterling silver enameled bracelet. No maker's mark. $60.00 – 95.00.
John Christopher collection.

Sterling silver choker and cuff bracelet set with black onyx and marked "TV-99." Choker, $50.00 – 75.00, bracelet, $20.00 – 25.00.

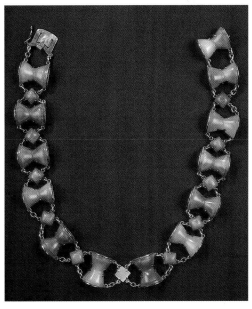

1940s sterling silver necklace with Mexican "jade" (colored onyx) and marked Sterling Mexico. Possibly from Mexico City. $175.00 – 250.00.

1950s sterling silver and abalone shell necklace. No maker's mark. $50.00 – 85.00.

Sterling silver cuff bracelet with illegible maker's mark. $30.00 – 50.00.

Silver, abalone shell, and onyx necklace, marked Hecho en Mexico 925. $60.00 – 90.00.

Silver and abalone shell necklace. No maker's mark. $50.00 – 70.00.

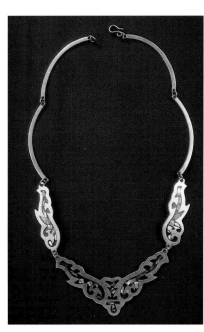

Finely crafted sterling silver and turquoise bracelet. No maker's mark. $175.00 – 250.00. John Christopher collection.

Well crafted sterling silver and natural turquoise bracelet with a carved central "scarab" stone. No maker's mark. $150.00 – 200.00.

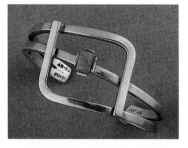

Sterling silver "Hecho en Mexico" bracelet. No maker's mark. $30.00 – 45.00.

Sterling silver cuff bracelet with abstract design and natural turquoise. No maker's mark. $40.00 – 60.00.

Two large 1940s figural brooches, marked Mexico Silver, set with Mexican "jade" (colored onyx), possibly of Mexico City origin. No maker's mark. $50.00 – 80.00 each.

Variety of Mexican sterling silver pins circa 1950s – 1960s. $10.00 – 22.00.

Variety of Mexican sterling silver jewelry circa 1940s – 1960s. $12.00 – 20.00 each or pair.

Sterling silver and obsidian brooch and matching screwback earrings. No maker's mark. $85.00 – 135.00.

Sterling silver Mexican cuff bracelet. No maker's mark. $70.00 – 100.00.

Large Iguala silver filigree brooch. $30.00 – 45.00; earrings, $5.00 – 10.00.

Mexican sterling silver grape necklace, brooch, and earrings. No maker's mark. $75.00 – 100.00.

Two Mexican silver cuff bracelets. $30.00 – 45.00 each.

All finely crafted Mexican 980 silver jewelry without the maker's mark. Necklace and matching screwback earrings, $100.00 – 150.00; screwback bird earrings, $25.00 – 35.00; other two screwback earrings, $20.00 – 30.00 each.

Variety of Mexican silver sombrero jewelry. Bracelet, pendant, and cuff links, $20.00 – 30.00 each; pins $15.00 – 20.00 each.

Variety of sterling silver Mexican jewelry. Earrings, $20.00 – 25.00, large pin, $20.00 – 30.00; small pin, $15.00 – 20.00.

Variety of low quality Mexican silver jewelry which were made in both sterling silver and Alpaca. $20.00 – 25.00.

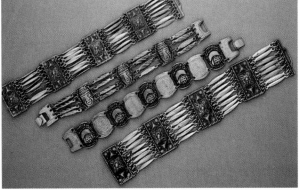

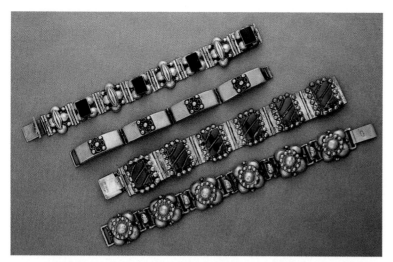

Variety of sterling silver Mexican bracelets. $25.00 – 40.00.

1960s – 1970s sterling silver bracelet, $20.00 – 25.00; rings, $15.00 – 20.00 each.

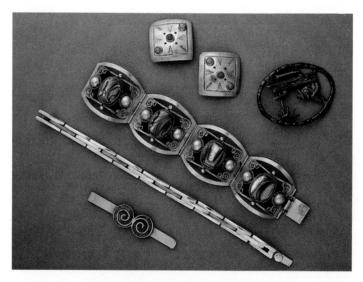

Variety of sterling silver Mexican jewelry. $20.00 – 35.00.

Unidentified Marks

Peru

Peruvian Silver Jewelry

The territory now known as Peru was once home to one of the major civilizations of the New World. Over the course of several thousand years, different people and cultures evolved in this area, each leaving behind a legacy and contributing to the development of a social formation that was eventually and tragically destroyed by the Spaniards' invasion led by Francisco Pizarro in 1532.

But the new culture imposed by the conquerors on the native population was itself eventually influenced by their rich heritage, leading to the merger of the new with the remnants of the old in such a fusion that today's society, in many ways, reflects both its more recent as well as its distant past.

Among these is its rich tradition of metalwork dating back to the second millennium B.C. and sophisticated techniques such as those developed by the Mocha culture during the first to seventh centuries, revealing stunning beauty, craftsmanship, and a high level of creative capacity and artistic accomplishment. These included the fusion of metals and gilding, repousse and embossing, wirework and false filigree, beads and inlay work. After the invasion, much of the Inca gold and silver booty was melted down by the Spaniards and sent back to Spain along with massive raw extractions from the gold and silver mines worked with slave labor which caused the death of a large number of the natives. But the legacy of this poignant past is retained in modern Peruvian silver work, rich with multitudes of historical motifs and proud displays of the Inca and national symbols.

The modern silver metal work was built into an industry by the Spanish and Italian metalworkers during the colonial period which initially supplied the churches and the elite with ecclesiastical, personal, and household items. The Spanish preference for silver and its old silver working tradition brought from Spain strongly influenced the development of the industry. Hence, modern Peruvian silver jewelry strongly reflects the influences of both cultures, their skills and ingenuity.

Among the famous Peruvian centers of gold and silver manufacture are Calacaos near the northern desert town of Piura long known for its filigree gold jewelry; San Jeronimo in the central highland territory; and the cities of Cuzco and Lima. Lima, the capital city, is the main commercial center, attracting silver products made throughout Peru which are sold in hundreds of boutiques or exported abroad. Among the silver jewelry offered for sale, there is an ample supply of melted down coin silver jewelry with the heavy concentration of outlets in and near Plaza San Martin. Plaza de Armas in Cuzco also serves as a distribution center. This type of jewelry, much of which is crudely made, has also found its way into the U.S. collectible market. High quality handcrafted silver jewelry is also made in Huancayo, Peru, an example of which is displayed here.

Some of the higher quality Peruvian silver jewelry displays competent enamel work along with engraved, stamped or embossed motifs which make up the design. Others are enhanced with small high karat gold pieces, sometimes made separately and attached to the silver base in order to highlight the central motifs. The better quality pieces also show good weight and better fasteners. Due to variations in quality, the prices may vary drastically, depending on the experience and the knowledge of the seller.

Generally, lack of knowledge in this field provides frequent opportunities for buyers to purchase quality pieces for bargain prices. For example, while a regular silver piece may be sold for $30 to $40, another of about as much value just for the gold it contains can be purchased for that same price. Use of a national silver standard mark on the silver jewelry is not required, but the jewelry often is marked with the silver fineness though it may or may not be marked "Peru," or "Made in Peru."

Round silver brooch, marked Peru 925 and with the maker's mark. $35.00 – 45.00.

Round silver brooch with enameled ring of Peruvian historic motifs surrounding a riveted 18k gold llama. $75.00 – 100.00.

High quality sterling silver enameled brooch. $40.00 – 65.00.

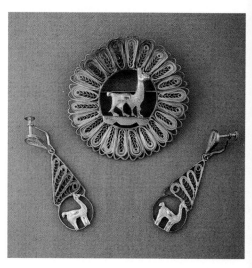

Large sterling filigree brooch and matching earrings. $40.00 – 60.00.

High quality llama pin, marked 925, $40.00 – 60.00; and a pair of screwback llama earrings, $20.00 – 35.00.

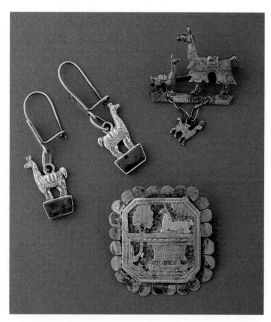

Sterling silver wide bracelet with typical Peruvian motifs. $75.00 – 100.00.

Sterling pin in two layers giving the illusion of depth and carved motif, $25.00 – 35.00; small sterling llama pin; 20.00 – 25.00; sterling earrings, $20.00 – 25.00.

High quality sterling bracelet handcrafted in Huancayo, Peru. The mask-like figures are the heads of the Tumi, the sacred offering knife of the Chimu and several other Pre-Colombian cultures. $100.00 – 150.00.

Sterling silver bracelet with enameled ancient Peruvian motifs and applied 18K gold plaques. $125.00 – 175.00.

Scandinavia

Because of the people's oral tradition, Scandinavian history, particularly that of the Viking age (approximately ninth through eleventh centuries) was largely written by foreigners in which the natives are depicted as bands of "uncivilized" and "barbaric pagans" bent on looting and destruction. But the critical and objective reading of the historical accounts, available not only in Latin, but also left behind by the Arab, Persian, and Ottoman historians, reveals that the Viking traders and explorers were, at worst, no more prone to violence than the British, Portuguese or Spaniards who several centuries later set out on their own world explorations and conquests. Ironically, the nations that were once considered and portrayed as the scourge of Europe evolved to become the most peaceful, prosperous, democratic, literate, and civilized in the world. In the bosom of these frozen northern lands also developed a highly distinguished culture marked by artistic and scientific accomplishments, of which metalworks and design are only a few facets in a multitude of dimensions.

The Scandinavians have a long tradition of quality metalwork, especially in gold, silver, bronze, and pewter. In addition to jewelry with modern designs, two other types of jewelry are still being manufactured: reproductions of ancient pieces such as the Viking jewelry discovered in archaeological finds or inspired by it; and folk jewelry such as those worn by the Lapplanders (Sami) or other regional groups which are also popular among the Scandinavian general public and silver collectors. Modern twentieth century Scandinavian jewelry has a strong arts and crafts tradition dating back to the late nineteenth century and early 1900s, a tradition that continued in many ways and in many small workshops even after the decline of the movement internationally. While the Scandinavian countries were influenced by the arts and crafts movement and ideas of William Morris, the craft associations and societies established in Sweden and Finland predate the movement and the founding of similar organizations in England. The world's oldest arts and crafts society, Slöjdföreningen, was founded in Sweden in 1845, and two similar societies, the Finnish Society of Crafts and Design (Suomen Taideteollisuusyhdistys) and Friends of Finnish Handicraft (Suomen Käsityon ystävät) were founded in Finland in the 1870s. In Finland,

the first craft school was also established in 1875, later becoming the Institute of Industrial Arts, an institution where many later Finnish designers and silversmiths received their training.

In Denmark, the Society of Arts and Crafts and Industry was established in 1906, and the Society of Applied Arts, Foreningen Brukskunst, was founded in Norway in 1918. These institutions and societies played an important role in educating, training, and in general establishing support for and development of handcrafted products, including silver products and jewelry.

Scandinavian jewelry has its unique look which can be distinguished from other silver jewelry with relative ease. It was generally produced in limited quantities in small workshops and strongly reflects the artistic expression of the jeweler/designer. With the exception of several major manufacturers that produced large quantities of jewelry for the export market, many of the Scandinavian producers can be classified as small shop silversmiths or studio artists. Accordingly, aside from the jewelry of some of the major manufacturers, only a limited volume of other Scandinavian jewelry was imported into the United States, and the author's research and inquiries suggest that a significant portion of the older Scandinavian jewelry found in the collectible market was perhaps brought into the country by the tourist traffic, Scandinavian immigrants, or sold through small ethnic retail outlets since no records of sizable imports or evidence of large distribution by jobbers could be located. This is not an unlikely hypothesis considering the fact that more people of Norwegian descent reside in the U.S. than in Norway or that out of a population of approximately 4 million, over 1.5 million Swedes immigrated to the U.S. during the 1846 – 1868 period. Of course, the recent rapid rise in domestic demand for vintage Scandinavian silver jewelry has also caused a flood of silver jewelry brought from abroad.

Until recently, collecting Scandinavian jewelry itself was also limited to a relatively small segment of the collectible jewelry market and aside from advanced collectors in this field, the general collectors' knowledge about this type of jewelry did not go beyond recognizing some of the important names, such as Georg Jensen and Anderson. This was partly due to the lack of information on Scandinavian jewelry in the English language and though several books on collectible jewelry, particularly in the last decade, have displayed and identified Scandinavian jewelry and manufacturers, there is still a dire need for a specialized book on the subject, particularly on the twentieth century silver jewelry of Norway and Sweden. Several outstanding books on the silver jewelry of Denmark and Finland have been published in recent years, both in English and native languages, which were used in writing this section and the biographies of the silversmiths of the respective countries. These sources were supplemented by translations of some of the relevant and available literature in native languages, correspondence with and information provided by several museums and experts in the respective countries, and the generous assistance and information provided by several manufacturers such as Lapponia. What follows is merely an introduction limited by space and the author's knowledge. In-depth research in this field and a systematic treatment of the subject which would include the trademarks and facilitate identification are still needed.

For connoisseurs and students of Danish jewelry, the best and most comprehensive book to date is Jacob Thage's *Danske Smykker (Danish Jewelry)* with text in both Danish and English, while there are several in-depth works focusing on a particular company or silversmith, also available in both languages. Two excellent books on Finnish silver are the main general references on that country's silver products and jewelry in the English language: John Haycraft, *Finnish Jewellery and Silverware;* and Tuula Poutasuo (ed.), *Finnish Silver*. Several other books and pamphlets focus on individual designers and/or companies such as Kaj Kalin's work, *Lapponia Jewelry,* used in this section. Unfortunately, the primary sources on Swedish and Norwegian silver jewelry are in native languages which were heavily supplemented by the information provided by several museums, the individual companies, and silversmiths. Interested readers are directed to the bibliography where many primary and secondary sources are listed. It should also be noted that several additional Scandinavian silversmiths are featured in the chapter on Current and Upcoming Silversmiths.

Danish National Silver Standard Marks

Modern Danish silver may be marked just "Sterling Denmark" or "DENMARK" accompanied by the silver fineness with or without the maker's name or initials. This is the most common mark and the national hallmark was used rather infrequently on silver jewelry. The twentieth century silver jewelry was required to have the minimum fineness of 826 which is stamped on the piece followed by the letter "S;" the letter "S" stands for "sølv" which means silver. The piece may also be stamped with the assay mark which guaranteed this fineness and consists of the three towers of Copenhagen above wave lines within an oval frame. The last two digits of the year in which the assay was made are within the wave

lines. Two towers instead of three indicate that the piece is silver plated.

Since 1961, the three towers of Copenhagen have not been used, and the absence of this mark does not necessarily date the jewelry to the post-1961 era. Also the common silver fineness marks are 830S and 925S. However, readers should note that marking Danish jewelry was optional, and only a few firms such as Jensen followed a consistent method of marking their jewelry and some preferred their own trademarks rather than the national hallmark. The list and biographies of many major Danish silversmiths of this century follow, in many cases accompanied by their trademark and/or sample images of their jewelry.

Danish Silversmiths, Designers, and Manufacturers

Ad Design

Ad Design was founded circa 1971 and was in operation until 1979. The firm manufactured well-designed jewelry, some of which was apparently exported to the U.S. Most of the jewelry is made of base metal with heavy silver plating. The jewelry is sometimes marked with the designer's name, among which was Erik Dennung.

Albertus, Gundroph (1887 – 1970)

Trained as a chaser and silversmith in both Denmark and France and one of the early graduates of the Royal Academy of Fine Arts in 1915. He worked for Georg Jensen as early as 1911 until the late 1940s.

Anderson, Just (1884 – 1943)

A highly talented and skilled silversmith, Just Anderson was actually born in Greenland and moved with his family to Denmark in the mid 1890s. Anderson received his early training as a painter and sculptor which influenced his jewelry designs executed in both gold and silver. With his wife, Alba, a silversmith and chaser by training, the couple opened their first workshop in 1918. For a period in the late twenties through the early thirties, Anderson relocated to Sweden and in collaborative efforts with Guldsmed Aktiebolaget, successfully introduced a new line of jewelry with ancient Nordic influences. By the time of his death in 1943, Anderson was a well recognized designer in Europe and recipient of many awards. He was also quite influential in leading the breakaway from *skønvirke* of the early 1900s in Denmark.

Bjorn-Anderson, Mogens (b. 1911)

Contemporary Danish silversmith who has designed silver hollowware for several major Danish companies, including Jensen. His designs are a mix of traditional and modern.

Anderson, Jens

Contemporary Danish silversmiths. The mark shown here is speculated on the collectible market to be the mark of Jens Anderson, but as of this writing, this is doubtful and unconfirmed.

Bahner, Volmer (b. 1912)

Danish silversmith known for his enameled silver jewelry manufactured after WWII. The jewelry designs are drawn from nature with flowers, plants, fish, and animal motifs. Bahner usually marked his jewelry with his initials VB. This mark was first registered in 1962 in Copenhagen and active through 1987.

Ballin, Morgan (1871 – 1914)

Born in Copenhagen in 1871, and trained as an artist in Paris, Ballin renounced his Jewish faith and converted to Catholicism and for a time lived as a Franciscan monk. Artistically, Ballin was influenced by the nascent Arts and Crafts movement, and his jewelry which often demonstrates visible hammer marks is reflective of the ideas and practices popularized by this school. Ballin is considered among the founding fathers of the new school of Danish design, combining silver and semi-precious stones, creating what came to be recognized as the distinct and internationally identifiable "Danish look."

Bang, Arne (1901 – 1983)

Designer of primarily functional and decorative items for A. Michelsen.

Bernadotte, Sigvard (b. 1907)

Born in Sweden, Bernadotte was already an accomplished designer before joining Georg Jensen in the 1930s, but much of Bernadotte's work was in the area of flatware although he also made some silver jewelry with simple, modern designs. His long association with Jensen spanned three decades.

Bisgaard, Palle

Contemporary Danish silversmith with high quality pieces featuring inlaid work. A few pieces seen by the author appear to have been made circa the late 1950s to the 1970s.

Bjorklund

Workshop Brdr. Bjorklund was founded around 1961 in Copenhagen and was in operation for only a short time, ceasing production in 1971. The firm must have been a prolific producer or exporter of silver jewelry based on the number of pieces seen in the U.S. collectible market. The jewelry is usually marked "Brdr. B," sometimes in script.

Christensen, Allan

Silver workshop established in Dragor, Denmark, by Allan Christensen around 1969 and ceasing operation in 1973. Allan Christensen silver jewelry is of high quality with well-balanced designs and skillful construction. The jewelry is marked "AC."

Christiensen & Son

This silver workshop was founded circa 1967 in Herlev, Denmark, by Hemmer Christiensen and was in operation until 1971. The jewelry was marked with a conjoined "HC. S." The jewelry shown here and the mark reproduced is attributed to Christiensen, but since these pieces are not marked Denmark, this attribution is not definite.

Cohr, Carl M.

A major Danish silver manufacturer adopting *skønvirke* and responsible for its widespread exposure and popularity at the turn of the century. The firm was founded in 1860 by Ditlev Cohr (1821 – 1883) in Frederica who was later succeeded by his son Carl. By 1918 the firm was employing several hundred people and well known for its flatware, much of which was exported. Many major silversmiths and designers were trained at Cohr, including Sigfred Wegner, H.P. Jacobsen, Hans Hansen, Eduard Eggelin, and Bent Knudsen. The common marks are

Cohr   CMC

Ditzel, Nanna (b. 1923) & Jørgen (1921 – 1961)

Having both graduated from the School of Arts, Crafts, and Design, the couple began designing jewelry in the early 1950s. Some of the jewelry was made at G. Jensen and A. Michelsen which exhibits beautiful, simple, modern designs that characterized 1950s and 1960s Danish silver jewelry. An example of their work is shown under Georg Jensen in this section. Their Jensen jewelry is sometimes marked with their initials "NJ" or just "ND" for Nanna.

Dragsted, A.

A major Danish company and jewelers to the Royal Courts of Denmark, Greece, and Russia. The firm was founded by Arent Nicolaj Dragsted (1821 – 1896). Its major designer in the early twentieth century was Aage Dragsted (1886 – 1942). The firm is responsible for launching and marketing the jewelry of many important Danish designers, including Johan Rohde, Anton Rosen, Thyra Marie Vieth, Jais Nielsen, Arno Malinouski, and Karen Strand.

Engle, Gertrud

Designer with works appearing to have been made in the late 1940s to 1960.

Exner, Bent

Designer and silversmith with works appearing to have been made in the 1950s to the 1970s.

Fogh, S. Christian

This silver workshop was founded by S. Christian Fogh in Copenhagen and was in operation from 1947 to 1973. The jewelry is usually marked **SCF**.

From, Niels Erik (1908 – 1986)

From was among the most prolific Danish designers and manufacturers of silver jewelry. He was born in Fyn and trained as a silversmith before opening his own workshop which also served as a retail outlet, selling the jewelry designed by himself and other Danish designers.

The business continued to expand and after WWII, in a newly built factory a large volume of jewelry was manufactured for the export markets in Europe and America. N. E. From has not been sufficiently credited in the literature on jewelry partly because his jewelry was mass produced. But in the author's view, N.E. From jewelry is among the finest made in Denmark during the 1960s – 1970s. The jewelry exhibits fine craftsmanship with soft stylized floral and geometric designs, sometimes enhanced with semi-precious stones. Because of a significant volume exported to the U.S., his jewelry is easier to find at affordable prices in the collectible market, but these prices are expected to rise in the near future. The jewelry is always marked N.E FROM and Denmark in slightly varied arrangements.

Frydenberg, Carl Ove

Carl Ove Frydenberg established his workshop in Copenhagen just after WWII. The COF mark found on his silver jewelry was first registered in 1949 and active until 1982.

Grann & Laglye (1906 – 1955)

A sizable turn of the century Danish company in Copenhagen founded by Johannes Laglye and Johannes Grann which also produced jewelry designed by Laglye or other designers such as Georg Thylstrup. The common mark is shown here.

Griegst, Marje (b. 1938)

Trained by Just Anderson, Griegst opened his own workshop circa 1960 and introduced a series of innovative modern designs.

Gross, H.F.

Jewelry designer. Premier designer for Hans Hansen in the 1920s and A. Michelsen in the 1940s.

Gundlack-Pedersen, Oscar (1896 – 1960)

As with several other Danish designers, Gundlack-Pedersen was educated and trained as an architect before joining G. Jensen in the early 1920s. His work during this period, as was Jensen's, was among the leading Art Deco influences in Denmark.

Hansen, Frederik Kastor (1871 – 1918)

Trained as a painter and sculptor, Kastor Hansen ventured into the field of jewelry design and production during the first decade of the twentieth century. Much of the jewelry depicts stylized birds and animals which show a faint resemblance to the works of A. Malinowski produced a few decades later.

Hansen, Hans (1884 – 1940)

Silver manufacturing firm founded by Hans Hansen in 1906 in Kolding, Denmark. Trained at C.M. Cohr, Hans Hansen gradually became a major silverware and jewelry firm in the country.

Initially Hansen was the only designer at his workshop, later joined by H.F. Gross, while Karl Gustav Hansen and Bent Gabrielsen were the primary designers in the 1930s and 1950s, respectively. Over many decades, Hansen manufactured a broad range of jewelry reflecting the prominent art and market trends. With numerous exhibitions and recipient of many awards and prizes, the firm was acquired by Royal Copenhagen in 1991. The early jewelry is marked with a superimposed double "H" and the later pieces with Hans Hansen in script which seem to have been in use since the early 1930s. The designers' names usually do not appear as part of the mark.

Hansen, Karl Gustav (b. 1914)

Son of Hans Hansen and an able and visionary designer as well as an acute businessman. A pioneer in the development of modern hollowware, flatware, and jewelry production for the company. Karl Gustav Hansen designed the successful futurist line of jewelry for Hans Hansen in 1932 and was responsible for the growth and expansion of the firm in the following decades. The mark below is found on his "Future" line of jewelry manufactured by Hans Hansen during the 1932 – 1948 period.

HaH

Herlow, Erik (1913 – 1991)

Danish designer responsible for the popular post WWII enamel and other silver jewelry made at A. Michelsen. Beginning his work as a designer during the war, Herlow's successful lines of jewelry catapulted him into a prominent position as a designer and a major influence in the post-war jewelry design in Denmark. Also well recognized for his hollowware which was designed for A. Michelsen.

Hertz, Bernard (1834 – 1909)

A major Danish jewelry manufacturer. One of several members of the Hertz family involved in the production, wholesale, and retail facets of silver jewelry and responsible for popularizing the *skønvirke* at the turn of the century. **B H**

Hingelberg, Frantz (b. circa 1870)

Hingelberg was a silver workshop founded by Frantz Hingelberg in Arhus, circa 1928, which rapidly grew into a prominent Danish workshop in the 1930s. Instrumental in the firm's early success was the designer Svend Weibrauch who created many of the popular designs. Most of the jewelry is in solid silver with floral and naturalistic designs. **F.H. 925S DENMARK**

Holmstrup, Ole

Danish silversmith with works appearing to have been made in the 1950s through the 1970s.

Jacobsen, Ole

Danish silversmith with works appearing to have been made in the 1950s through the 1970s.

Jensen, Søren Georg (1917 – 1982)

Son of Georg Jensen, trained as a sculptor and silversmith, Søren Jensen's career followed a path similar to his father, but reflected the more contemporary and modern post-war designs. His work is marked with vertically conjoined "GJ" or his full initials "S.G.J."

Jensen, Jørgen (1895 – 1966)

Son of Georg Jensen and not to be confused with another Danish designer with a similar name whose works are primarily in pewter. Jørgen Jensen received his training in Munich and worked at his father's workshop for near a decade before relocating to Sweden and opening his own workshop in Stockholm sometime around 1923. He rejoined the Jensen workshop before the outbreak of the war in the late 1930s.

Jensen, Eigil (b. 1917)

A major post-war Danish silversmith and designer. Responsible for some of the popular lines at A. Michelsen during the 1940s and 1950s. Prior to joining A. Michelsen, Eigil Jensen was associated with the Hansen silversmiths where he also received his training. Eigil Jensen also designed decorative silver products during his long association with A. Michelsen. His jewelry is marked with his initials "EJ." (See A. Michelsen.)

Jensen, Georg (1866 – 1935)

The best known Danish silversmith, Georg Jensen was originally trained as a sculptor but unable to make a living in that field, he began experimenting and exploring other fields such as the decorative arts of silver and goldsmithing which eventually led to the establishment of his workshop in 1904. Jensen was influenced by Mogens Ballin for whom he worked as a foreman for a short period and Johan Rohde whom he met through Ballin. His first silver jewelry was made in collaboration with Ballin in 1901 using amber and semi-precious stones.

From the beginning, Jensen designs were unique and distinct, not following any popular and set trends. The jewelry was manufactured for the middle class without fancy ornamentation and precious stones, and sold at affordable prices. His jewelry incorporated primarily semi-precious stones such as amber, moonstone, malachite, carnelian, lapis, coral, and opal, used sparsely to complement the silver which was masterfully designed and created with a sculptured look.

Over the years Jensen rose to became a major Danish manufacturer and exporter of silver products and jewelry with a marketing network and branches in many major cities around the world. The firm was incorporated as Georg Jensen's Silver-

smith in 1916, but by the early 1920s Georg Jensen no longer held majority control and his role and influence within the firm thereafter were marginalized by the board of directors.

The recipient of numerous international awards, Jensen products and jewelry are known for high quality workmanship and wonderful unique designs. Aside from his sons, Søren and Jørgen Jensen, the firm employed many renowned Danish and other Scandinavian designers, some of whom are listed in this chapter. Jensen is still in business but is now owned by the Royal Copenhagen (Scandinavia) Company. A suit against Royal Scandinavia brought by the Jensen family for the use of Georg Jensen's signature and trademark was pending as of this writing.

During WWII because of shortages and the disruption of trade, Jensen designs were reputedly brought to the U.S. and Frederik Lunning manufactured some of the silver jewelry under the Georg Jensen USA, a mark which was later disavowed by the company. Others were designed by Alphonse La Paglia, Joan Polsdorfer (unconfirmed name for JoPoL mark found on the jewelry) and apparently, Madeleine Turner. George Jensen USA production was discontinued in 1950. These pieces are shown in this chapter and usually sell at lower prices than the Danish pieces.

1.   *2.*   *3.*   *4.*   *5.*   *6.*   *7.*   *8.*   *9.*

1) Georg Jensen, circa 1904 – 1908. 2) Georg Jensen, circa 1909 – 1914 with Georg Jensen Copenhagen. The mark G.j. was also used during this period. This mark by itself was first registered in the U.S. in 1940, renewed in 1981, claiming first use in 1923. 3) Georg Jensen circa 1915 – 1930. May be with or without 925S within or without the dotted circle or oval. 4) Georg Jensen mark. A similar mark was used circa 1915 – 1927. This mark was first registered with the U.S. Patent and Trademark

Office on 01/07/41 and renewed in 1981, claiming first commercial use in 1923. 5) "Georg Jensen USA" mark used circa 1940 – 1945. 6) Georg Jensen mark used after 1946. This mark was registered in the U.S. by Royal Copenhagen in 1998. 7) Two examples of full Georg Jensen marks. 8) Currently active Jensen silversmiths mark registered with the U.S. Patent and Trademark Office. 9) Two examples of La Paglia marks found on Georg Jensen USA silver jewelry.

The Jensen jewelry may also be marked by the designer's initials, some of which are given below.

Gundroph Albertus	GA	Gudmund Hentze	GH	Lene Munthe	LM
Sigvard Bernadotte	Sigvard or SB	Annette Howdle	AH	Kim Naver	KN
Ib Dahlquist	ID	Ole Ishoj	OI	Harald Nielsen	HN
Agnete Dinesen	AD	Axel Jensen	AJ	Henry Pilstrup	HP
Flemming Eskildsen	FE	Jørgen Jensen	JJ	Allan Scharf	ASCH
Kay Fisker	FK	Søren Georg Jensen	SGJ	Anne Schiang	ASch
Astid Fog	AF	Ole Kortzau	OK	Gail Spence	GS
Kirsten Fournais	KF	Peter Kristiansen	PK	Mette Stengaard	MS
Bent Gabrielsen	BG	Hugo Liisbergh	HL	Ove Wendt	OW
Paul Hansen	PH	Inger Møller	INGER MØLLER		

Kindt-Larsen, Edward (1901 – 1982) and Tove (b. 1906)

Both received their training in architecture at the Royal Academy of Fine Arts and married in 1937. The couple began designing silver hollowware, jewelry, and accessories such as toiletries for both A. Michelsen and Georg Jensen in the 1940s. These exhibited innovative modern and abstract forms employ-ing enamelwork. The couple played an important role in the development of modern Danish jewelry during the post-war decades.

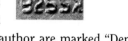

Knudsen, Anni (b. 1926) and Bent (b. 1924)

Bent Knudsen received his training at C.M. Cohr and worked for Hans Hansen for several years before establishing his own workshop with his wife, Anni, in 1956. The couple working together designed some of the earliest post-war silver jewelry emphasizing simple designs enhanced by semi-precious stones. Without making a distinction, the work of the couple is usually marked "Bent K."

Koppel, Henning (1918 – 1982)

After graduating from the Royal Academy of Art, Koppel received further training in Paris before settling in Stockholm and only returned to Denmark at the termination of WWII in 1945 where he began designing silver jewelry for Jensen and assumed a prominent position among the top post-war Danish designers. Koppel's jewelry exhibits mod-ern and abstract designs derived from nature, sometimes enhanced with enamelwork. He was the recipient of many awards and perhaps the most influential post-war designer shaping modern Danish silver jewelry.

Kunsthandvaerk, Salamander

This firm was established in Rodovre, Denmark, around 1971, and was in operation for several years, ceasing operation around 1974. The jewelry is usually marked "925SK" with the letter "K" reversed and a facing "S." The jewelry displayed here and the mark reproduced is attributed to Salamander Kunsthandvaerk, but since none of the pieces seen by the author are marked "Denmark," this attribution is not definite.

Kyster, Holger

Founder of a major silver workshop in Kolding, circa 1900. Holger Kyster produced the jewelry designed by some of the major twentieth century Danish designers such as Thorvald Bindesboll, and painter Svend Hammershoi. Hammershoi's mark is also reproduced here.

Lunding, Ib (1895 – 1983)

An architect by training, Lunding began designing jewelry and accessories such as toiletries for A. Michelsen as early as 1930. Much of his work was enamel jewelry with floral motifs. As a chief designer for A. Michelsen for some time, Ib Lunding was responsible for the development of mass produced enamel jewelry which became the specialty of A. Michelsen and a major influence in the post-war development of the now well-established and recognized Danish enamel jewelry.

Lyngaard (Aps), Ole

Danish silver designer receiving national recognition in 1954 by capturing an award in the annual competition organized by the Danish Jewelers' Association. Ole Lyngaard Aps opened a workshop in Hellerup, Denmark, in 1957 and is still in business. The jewelry is marked "OLE L."

Magnussen, Erik (1884 – 1960)

Among the most creative and original Danish designers, Magnussen was a self-taught artisan and pioneer in the Art Nouveau school. He established his first workshop in 1901 after his first exhibition in Copenhagen. But Magnussen did not remain in Denmark. He spent nearly two years in Berlin and in 1920 immigrated to the U.S. and was hired as the artistic director of the Gorham Silver Company. Although Magnussen designed a series of items for Gorham, his stay with the company was not a happy one, and he left the company around 1930 to establish his own workshop in New York. But this venture taking place at the depth of the Great Depression proved unsuccessful, resulting in bankruptcy. In 1933, Magnussen opened a workshop in Los Angeles, launching modern designs which met with relative financial success and attracted several Hollywood clients; these pieces are also marked California. However, Magnussen returned to Denmark in 1939 and began the last phase of his productive life, creating silver jewelry in the Nordic style perhaps inspired by the contemporary nationalist environment of WWII. In the author's view, Magnussen should be considered among the greatest Danish silversmiths and one of the best twentieth century designers.

Malinowski, Arno (1899 – 1976)

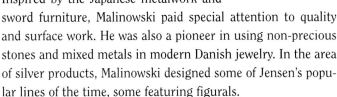

Trained as a silversmith, Malinowski became one of the most renowned designers for Georg Jensen. Beginning his association with Jensen in 1936, Malinowski was influential in the abandoning of the traditional motifs. However, his most popular jewelry was a series of silver jewelry with naturalistic motifs designed for Georg Jensen in the 1930s and early 1940s. Another quite popular and successful piece was the "King's badge," made in both gold and silver in 1940. Inspired by the Japanese metalwork and sword furniture, Malinowski paid special attention to quality and surface work. He was also a pioneer in using non-precious stones and mixed metals in modern Danish jewelry. In the area of silver products, Malinowski designed some of Jensen's popular lines of the time, some featuring figurals.

Michelsen, A.

A major Danish firm and jewelers to the royal court founded by Anton Michelsen (1809 – 1877) in 1841. Anton was succeeded by his son Carl under whose direction the firm changed course, employing some of the best Danish designers such as Bindesboll, Georg Jensen, and Georg Thylstrup. That tradition has continued at A. Michelsen with many renowned designers joining its ranks, including Ib Lunding, Eigil Jensen, Erik Herlow, Karen Strand, Gertrude Engle, and Nanna and Jørgen Ditzel. A. Michelsen was famous for its enamel work and instrumental in popularizing Danish enamel jewelry. Most common marks are the crown with initials "A.M." in slightly varied form. (See Sweden for more Michelsen jewelry.)

Møller, Inger (1886 – 1979)

Among the first Danish women silversmiths and designers known for her high quality jewelry. Worked for Georg Jensen for two decades (1901 – 1921) before opening her own workshop circa 1922.

Musse, Peder

Contemporary Danish silversmith and designer with silver jewelry in both modern and semi-traditional designs.

Nielsen, Evald (1879 – 1958)

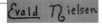

A major designer first apprenticing as a chaser and engraver and finally opening his workshop in 1907. Highly influential in the popularizing of *skønvirke* with works similar to that of Georg Jensen.

Nielsen, Harald (1892 – 1977)

Trained as a silversmith and chaser at Georg Jensen, Harald Nielsen was among the first Danish designers employed by Jensen to break away from the traditional and design jewelry in what is often referred to as the "functional" style. Nielsen, along with a number of other Danish designers, was responsible for introducing the simple modern forms in the industry. He must also be included among a select number of Danish silversmiths who experimented with non-precious and mixed metals, particularly during and after WWII.

Nielsen was Georg Jensen's brother-in-law and for a period served as the artistic director of the firm, exerting considerable influence on its artistic direction.

Nielson, Jais (1885 – 1961)

A Danish designer noted for his jewelry incorporating porcelain. Much of the jewelry was produced at A. Dragsted, a leading Danish manufacturer and a pioneer in the production of jewelry combining silver with natural and manmade products such as amber, glass, and porcelain.

Rasmussen, Carla

Among prominent Danish designers and silversmiths in the 1920s and 1930s (active circa mid 1920s to 1960) and notable for her innovative mixed metal jewelry often combining silver with copper and bronze.

Rasmussen, Bent (b. 1931)

Contemporary Danish silversmith.

Ring, Anders (1900 – 1948)

A Danish silversmith who operated his own workshop circa 1930s and is noted for his high quality silver jewelry and accessories. The jewelry is usually marked with "Ring" or "A. Ring."

Rohde, John (1856 – 1935)

A major Danish designer who worked in a variety of fields including jewelry. Educated and trained as a painter, Rohde became a major influence in Danish decorative arts and development of *skønvirke* school as well as the transitional period in the 1920s. Rohde began designing for Georg Jensen in 1906, and his work is considered by some as comparable to the work of the master himself. Much of his jewelry was executed in gold though there are a limited number of silver pieces.

Siersbol, Hermann

A manufacturer of silver products and jewelry founded in Kostrup, Denmark, in 1948. The firm is still in business and must have been a prolific manufacturer or exporter of silver jewelry since its jewelry is frequently encountered in the U.S. collectible market. The jewelry is marked with Hermann Siersbol's initials, "HS" and "H.S."

Thylstrup, Georg (1884 – 1930)

Thylstrup designed primarily silver hollowware and products, including some jewelry for Georg Jensen, A. Michelsen, and Grann & Laglye.

Warmind, Poul

Danish silversmith and designer known for his wonderful enamel jewelry made during the 1960s. Poul Warmind changed his interest to wine making and discontinued making jewelry. His mark was first registered in 1949 and active through 1984.

Unidentified Danish mark

Large floral sterling silver brooch made by Aarre & Krogh. Marked "A & K," encircled by STERLING DENMARK. $65.00 – 95.00.

Silver and enamel leaf brooch, marked Sterling Denmark and "VB," the initials of Volmar Bahner. $80.00 – 120.00.

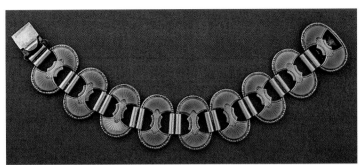

Silver and enamel bracelet marked only with conjoined "JA" and "925S." Believed to be Danish and attributed to Jens Anderson. $125.00 – 160.00.

Wonderful sterling silver brooch, possibly made by Allan Christensen. Marked AC STERLING DENMARK. $250.00 – 300.00. *John Christopher collection.*

Silver and enamel bracelet, marked with conjoined "JA" and "925S" in a circle. Believed to be Danish and possibly the mark of Jens Anderson. $75.00 – 100.00.

Wonderful singing bird pendant by Carl M. Cohr. Marked 830 and with Cohr's "CMC" (last C reversed) trademark. $300.00 – 400. *John Christopher collection.*

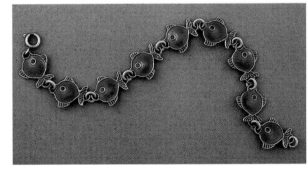

Silver and enamel bracelet with swimming fish, marked Export Christian Sterling Denmark and with "VB" for Volmar Bahner. $90.00 – 135.00.

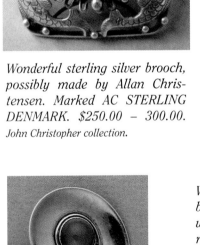

Silver and chalcedony paisley shaped brooch made by Brdr. Bjorklund, marked Brdr. B and 925S Sterling Denmark. $90.00 – 135.00. *John Christopher collection.*

Sterling silver and amethyst bracelet with a matching ring made by Brdr. Bjorklund. Marked in script Brdr. B and HANDMADE. $200.00 – 300.00 set. *John Christopher collection.*

Sterling silver brooch with stylized floral design made by Hemmer Christiensen & Son. Marked with conjoined "HC. S" and "830S" believed to be, but not definitely confirmed, as the company's mark used in the late 1960s. $75.00 – 100.00.

Sterling silver screwback earrings, marked "ED" and Sterling Denmark. Unidentified maker. $40.00 – 60.00.

Sterling silver and lapis Danish ring by N. E. From. Marked FROM 925S. $50.00 – 85.00.

Silver pendant with modern abstract design, marked AD DESIGN and Made in Denmark. $125.00 – 175.00. John Christopher collection.

Sterling silver vermeil brooch, marked Flora Dancia Sterling 925 Eggert Denmark. In the original Flora Dancia box. $35.00 – 55.00.

Sterling silver floral brooch made by S. Christian Fogh. Marked "S.C.F." surrounded by Sterling Denmark on an applied oval plaque. $65.00 – 95.00.

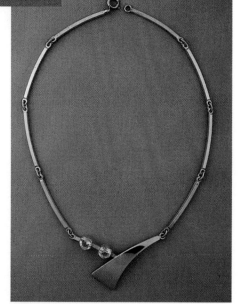

Modern abstract Danish sterling silver and onyx brooch. Marked in script N. E. FROM. $85.00 – 125.00.

Sterling silver Danish ring with a concave surface set with a glass stone. Marked N.E. FROM. $60.00 – 85.00.

Sterling bracelet and screwback earrings by Niels Erik From. Marked N.E. FROM and Sterling Denmark 925S. Bracelet, $100.00 – 150.00; earrings, $50.00 – 75.00. John Christopher collection.

Sterling silver Danish necklace set with two crystal stones. Marked N.E. FROM. $135.00 – 185.00. The author purchased this piece and a few other N. E. From pieces indirectly from the From family when new and unsold 1970s stock was being liquidated. The asking and auction prices for these pieces vary significantly, with some pieces going for less than these listed prices.

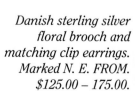

Sterling silver square tiger's eye bracelet. Marked N. E. FROM. $100.00 – 150.00.

Danish sterling silver floral brooch and matching clip earrings. Marked N. E. FROM. $125.00 – 175.00.

Sterling silver and polished amber cuff links made by Carl Ove Frydenburg. Marked "COF" encircled by Sterling Denmark. $90.00 – 145.00.

Marked N. E. FROM, Danish sterling silver and black onyx cuff bracelet. $150.00 – 200.00.

Matching set of sterling silver bracelet and earrings with stylized floral design. Marked N. E. FROM. $125.00 – 175.00.

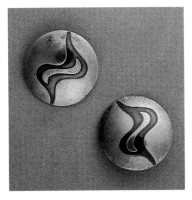

Pair of 1960s or 1970s earrings made by Niels Erik From. $30.00 – 50.00.

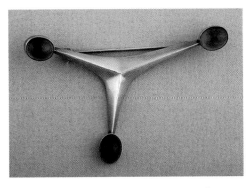

Sterling silver and amethyst abstract brooch. Hans Hansen script mark. $350.00 – 450.00. *John Christopher collection.*

Two Sterling silver Danish rings by N. E. From, both marked FROM 925S. $40.00 – 65.00 each.

Sterling silver brooch, marked in script Hans Hansen. $100.00 – 175.00. *John Christopher collection.*

Silver and cat's eye quartz pendant designed by Jacob Hull and made by Buch and Deichman. Most of Jacob Hull's jewelry was made in heavy silver plate as is this piece. Unless the piece is marked sterling or with other silver fineness marks, it is most likely silverplated. $100.00 – 150.00. *John Christopher collection.*

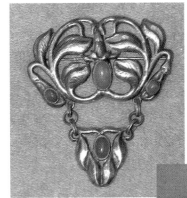

Wonderful example of skønvirke by Bernard Hertz. Marked "BH" and possibly "828." $650.00 – 900.00. *Robin Allison collection.*

An old Hansen sterling bangle, marked with the firm's old H within H trademark. $75.00 – 100.00.

Sterling silver and cat's eye quartz bracelet. Hans Hansen script mark. $300.00 – 400.00 *John Christopher collection.*

Modern abstract sterling silver brooch by Hans Hansen, marked with the company's old H within H trademark. $300.00 – 400.00.

Georg Jensen sterling vermeil floral brooch set with Labradorite. Early Jensen mark circa 1915 – 30, 925S silver and #107. $2,500.00 – 3,500.00. Robin Allison collection.

Georg Jensen sterling vermeil flower basket set with Labradorite. Early Jensen mark circa 1915 – 27, 830S silver, #67 and with tube catch. $2,000.00 – 3,000.00. Jensen brooch with similar construction and of the same period, $1,600.00 – 2,200.00. Robin Allison collection.

Post 1945 marked Jensen sterling silver floral drop earrings. $200.00 – 300.00.

George Jensen silver and enamel "Kingmark" designed by Arno Malinowski and manufactured during WWII, 1940 – 45. Marked with the Jensen "GJ" in square logo. This emblem was produced on King Christian X's 70th birthday and became a patriotic rallying symbol, selling over one million. The same emblem produced between 1945 – 47 has the 1945 date on the face. $75.00 – 125.00.

Georg Jensen sterling silver dove pin designed by Mohl-Hansen for Jensen in 1904, and a copied pin by an unknown manufacturer below it. Marked with the Jensen "GJ" in a dotted oval logo. The second piece is marked only "sterling." Jensen bird and animal figural pins were very popular and copied by a variety of manufacturers including Coro in the U.S. Jensen pin, $225.00 – 275.00; second pin, $45.00 – 65.00.

Georg Jensen abstract brooch designed by Nanna and Jørgen Ditzel. $400.00 – 500.00. Vicki Fulton collection.

Georg Jensen sterling silver bracelet made in the USA primarily during WWII years. Marked with La Puglia logo and GEORG JENSEN USA HANDWROUGHT. $250.00 – 350.00. John Christopher collection.

Sterling silver Georg Jensen USA tulip brooch. Marked Georg Jensen Inc. USA HAND WROUGHT. $150.00 – 225.00.

Hand wrought sterling silver Georg Jensen USA floral brooch. $150.00 – 200.00.

Georg Jensen abstract "double finger" ring designed by Swedish designer Ibe Dahlquist and produced by Jensen in 1970. Marked with Georg Jensen in dotted oval and #161. $300.00 – 500.00.

Sterling silver and glass neckring by Bent Knudsen. Marked BENI K and Sterling Denmark. $450.00 – 600.00. *John Christopher collection.*

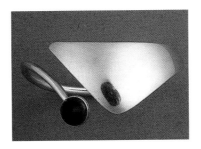

Sterling silver and amethyst bracelet by Anni and Bent Knudsen. Marked BENI K and HANDMADE DENMARK STERLING. $450.00 – 650.00. *John Christopher collection.*

Sterling silver enameled daisy brooch created by A. Michelsen in 1940 commemorating Princess Marguerethe's birthday. This line of jewelry by Michelsen was very popular and was probably inspired by the French word for daisy, "marguerite." $85.00 – 125.00.

Sterling silver and enamel Viking ship brooch, possibly made by Salamander Kunsthandvaerk. Marked only "925S" followed by the reversed letter "K." Since there is no country mark, the attribution is not certain. $40.00 – 65.00.

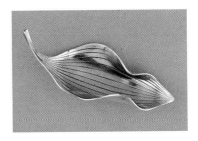

Handcrafted sterling silver leaf brooch made by A. Michelsen. Michelsen "AM" below crown mark and also marked in script "rengel." The latter mark is seen on both Danish and 1950s Swedish A. Michelsen silver jewelry. $90.00 – 125.00.

Silver and malachite skønvirke brooch made by Evald Nielsen. Marked with Evald Nielsen signature and CJØBENhAVN 830 SØCV. $450.00 – 600.00 *John Christopher collection.*

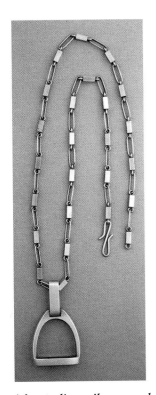

Danish sterling silver pendant and chain made by Ole Lyngaard Aps. Marked OLE L and 925S DENMARK. $200.00 – 300.00. *John Christopher collection.*

Sterling silver pendant and matching ring set with porcelain rose. Marked with the Danish three tower hallmark, 925S, "RCP," and what may be superimposed "WH." $65.00 – 95.00.

Wonderful sterling silver and enamel brooch designed by Eigil Jensen for A. Michelsen. $250.00 – 350.00.

Danish sterling silver brooch made by Erik Magnussen. Marked with Magnussen "EM" logo and Sterling Made in Denmark. $350.00 – 450.00. *John Christopher collection.*

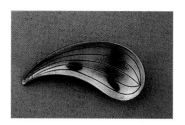

Sterling silver paisley shaped brooch made by Hermann Siersbol. Marked "HS" surrounded by STERLING DENMARK on an applied oval plaque and believed to be, but not definitely confirmed, the Siersbol mark. $60.00 – 85.00.

Sterling silver Danish heart brooch made by Anders Ring. Marked A RING 925S DENMARK. $85.00 – 125.00.

Sterling silver tie tack with innovative fastener, marked W & S SORENSEN DENMARK. $40.00 – 70.00.

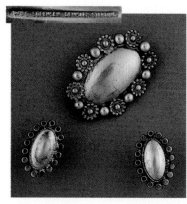

Silver brooch and matching screw-back earrings. Marked "HS 830S" believed to be the mark of Hermann Siersbol. $75.00 – 100.00.

Two sterling silver pins both marked "HS" surrounded by Sterling Denmark on an applied oval plaque, believed to be the mark of Hermann Siersbol. $50.00 – 75.00 each.

Large sterling silver brooch, marked "925" surrounded by STERLING DENMARK H.S. believed to be the mark used by Hermann Siersbol. Sterling silver pendant locket with floral motif marked "Chr. V" and 830/S or 835/S, possibly a Danish piece but not yet identified. $50.00 – 75.00.

Wonderful round sterling silver brooch by Poul Warmind. Marked POUL WARMIND DENMARK STERLING. $350.00 – 450.00. *Photo courtesy of Pop Beads to Platinum.*

Danish silver bangle bracelet with blue enamel over Nordic motif. Marked 830S and illegible maker's mark. $40.00 – 65.00.

Sterling silver abstract ring by Poul Warmind. $175.00 – 250.00. *John Christopher collection.*

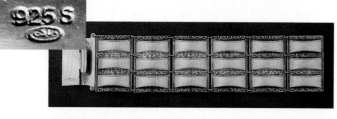

High quality wide sterling silver and enamel bracelet. Marked 925S and with an unidentified "V" mark, possibly that of a Danish silversmith. $175.00 – 250.00.

Finnish Silver Jewelry

Although Finland is often classified as a Scandinavian country, it should be noted that the Finnish language is not related to the Scandinavian family of languages. It in fact belongs to the family of Finno-Ugric languages which includes the Estonian, Hungarian, Lappic, Permic, and Volgaic languages. The linguistic studies suggest that the original historic homeland of the Finno-Ugric languages was perhaps situated in the forest area stretching from the Baltic region to Western Siberia. Accordingly, the Finns' regional habitation can be traced to the earliest periods with a long history of resisting subjugation and eviction.

For centuries, Finland was part of Sweden which deeply influenced its history and culture, and it became a suffering prize in the eighteenth century conflict and war between Sweden and Russia. As a result, it was ceded to Russia in 1809 after the Russo-Swedish war of 1808 – 1809 and did not gain its independence until the Russian Revolution and fall of the Tsar Nicholas in 1917. Hence its history and location also gave it Russian cultural influences.

Interestingly, the Finnish silversmiths accomplished international fame and recognition first in Russia.  Under the patronage of the Russian aristocracy, many Finnish artists and artisans found employment in Russia and according to several sources, they accounted for a significant portion of the active silversmiths in nineteenth century St. Petersburg. Master Finnish gold and silversmiths worked for many top Russian manufacturers of luxuries and decorative arts, including Faberge, catering to the upper class and nobility.

When Finland acquired its independence, large scale repatriation of the people had a significant impact on industry and commerce, including the Finnish arts and crafts. By this time, the modern styles influenced by the Arts and Crafts movement had already established roots in Finland which in conjunction with a deep sense of nationalism, recent inflow of highly skilled craftsmen, and the necessity of relying on domestic raw material such as silver and native semi-precious stones, merged to shape the course of development of Finnish jewelry and decorative arts. Several firms founded during this period and after WWII laid the foundation of the distinct, modern Finnish jewelry avidly sought by the collectors today. Expanding post-WWII export markets provided a strong impetus for further development of the silver working industry.

Among the early Finnish firms was A. Tillander, which was actually founded in Russia in 1860 and continued to manufacture traditional types of jewelry after the independence. But Tillander's major contribution to the development of modern Finnish silver industry was perhaps its zealous training of many young and upcoming silversmiths and continued support in this field through the establishment of national competitions. One of the prize winners at the 1948 Tillander sponsored competition was Tapio Wirkkala who was later to receive international recognition. Another major pre-war manufacturer was Kalevala Koru, founded in 1935, which is still in operation. This firm specializes in the production of historic jewelry.

Before WWII, Finnish jewelry consisted of primarily traditional designs or those reflective of the Finnish historic past with designs inspired by ancient Finnish motifs. But it did not take long for the nation to reveal the depth of its genius and independent artistic expression through the development of modern and distinctly Finnish arts and crafts, including silver jewelry. While the pre-WWII jewelry production was primarily traditional and ornamental with little export potential, the post-war jewelry exhibited simple and imaginative designs which gradually received world recognition and has now become among the most collectible silver jewelry internationally.

Because of the war-related shortages and the disruption in international commerce, Finnish jewelers turned to silver and available semi-precious domestic stones such as diopsid, spectrolite, rose and smokey quartz, garnets, and other readily available material and creatively combined them with silver in innovative designs which have come to characterize modern Finnish silver jewelry.

Nearly all modern Finnish silver jewelry exhibits simple designs, such as massive silver rings and bangles displaying large semi-precious stones or set with cabochons to highlight and complement the design. Some of the jewelry may involve simple silver wire-work which make up many necklaces enhanced and completed with dangling marble size glass or semi-precious cabochons. The patterns are simple, the lines and curves smooth, distinct and well defined, lacking ornamentation and reflecting the reductionist approach which employs what is minimal and necessary, but functional and beautiful, and creates the maximum effect.

Among the successful post WWII firms was Kupittaan Kulta founded in 1945. One of the founders, Elis Kauppi (b. 1921), catapulted the firm into national prominence by designing a series of modern silver jewelry featuring the native Finnish stone, spectrolite. Building on this success, Kupittaan continued to expand production with new modern designs and should be considered one of the early post-war firms which gave definition to what evolved as modern Finnish silver jewelry.

Another firm, Kaunis Koru, founded by Martta Ritvanen in 1954, provided an opportunity for a group of flourishing Finnish silversmiths and designers such as Eero Rislakki, Paula Haivaoja, Björn Weckström, Jan Salakoai, Kaija Aarikka, and Jan Salminen, who carried the 1950s momentum into the 1960s and 1970s. Another firm which was the manufacturer of primarily fine jewelry, Ossian

Hopea, also marketed beautiful and distinctive silver jewelry designed by Saara Hopea. Several other firms whose jewelry is also occasionally encountered in the U.S. market are Aarika, Kultakeskus, and Granit. Limited space does not permit an extensive and in-depth treatment of the subject, but the brief biographies of the major Finnish silversmiths and firms are listed below, in many cases along with the image of their trademark and a sample of their jewelry production.

However, a firm founded in 1960s evolved to have the greatest impact on modern Finnish jewelry and the highest and most widespread international recognition. It is hence apt to begin this brief survey with the story of Lapponia.

Lapponia

Lapponia was founded in Helsinki, Finland, by Pekka Valdemar Anttila (b. 1931), one of seven children born to a family of farmers in rural Finland. As a boy growing up during the harsh war years, Anttila had to struggle to earn a living by selling produce in the Helsinki market. After the war, he enrolled at the Goldsmith School and upon the completion of his studies and apprenticeship in 1953, received several awards in national competition, including the first prize in 1954.

It was also during these years that Anttila began his long association with his schoolmate, Björn Weckström. For the next six years, Anttila worked for Westerback Oy, under contract to produce bracelets and as a result acquired practical experience in both production as well as business. It was not until 1960 when Pekka had saved enough money, supplemented by the financial backing of his siblings, that he could open his very small workshop, Toiminimi Pekka Anttila, manufacturing gold bracelets. Gradually, the business grew as Finland found larger export markets, but Anttila's vision reached more distant horizons than being a mere manufacturer of "ordinary" products, a vision that he shared with his old classmate, Weckström, a vision of carving a new path in the field of jewelry and design, of creating unsurpassed jewelry of par excellence, recognized and appreciated internationally. Today, Lapponia is the realization of those hopes and dreams, a credit to the genius and efforts of these two men who added a new dimension to jewelry design internationally and redefined what is, and what can be expected of jewelry.

Lapponia's trademark and two Lapponia marks, one with Weckstrom's "BW" initials.

Björn Weckström (b. 1935), also a graduate of the Goldsmith School (1956), established a small workshop making jewelry models for other manufacturers under contract. The business was gradually expanded to include a retail section selling the jewelry Weckström produced as well as jewelry made by his friends such as Bertel Gardberg. Weckström also began his association with the recently established Kaunis Koru, making jewelry with modern designs for them.

A dramatic breakthrough and shift in focus occurred in 1961 when Björn Weckström was commissioned to design and make jewelry using gold nuggets. The jewelry he created employed the gold nuggets in their natural state in unconventional designs that went against the traditional luster and finish expected from gold jewelry. The finished pieces looked "unfinished," reminding the observer of nature and the earth; what better land to give birth to such sensitive pieces than the romantic Laplands. Thus was created the successful gold nugget jewelry which Weckström called the "Lapland jewelry" and the beginning of his venture with Anttila to chart a course for Finnish jewelry and Lapponia.

Pekka Anttila helped in exhibiting and marketing the new Lapland jewelry and in 1963 employed Weckström as the designer for his company which now changed its name to Kruunukoru Oy. The company proceeded to launch many lines of Lapland jewelry with romantic names and titles which glorified the unbridled and pristine northern lands where man and nature, not yet shackled by the necessities of commerce and industry, were still in harmony. Each piece emphasized the natural, warm, matte glow of gold as found in nature rather than the finished brilliance which Weckström considered cold and artificial. The firm, now successful in its first major venture and enjoying a growing export market, also changed its name to Kruunkoru Oy/Lapponia Jewelry Oy in 1969, later to become Lapponia Jewelry in 1974.

In his vast geography of imagination and creativity, Weckström's designs and creations traversed both earth and space. Many creative new lines were introduced and are still being created which have helped to maintain Lapponia's well-recognized international reputation. These include the Kinetic Jewelry where the movement gives each piece a life of its own; and the Space Jewelry or silver/acrylic pieces using contemporary modern themes and material in creating miniature sculptures. The latter received world-wide attention with close-up shots of a piece worn by Yoko Ono on the Dick Cavett TV show and another piece some years later adorned Princess Leia in the Star Wars movie. Each piece not only exhibits outstanding detailed craftsmanship, but is also the manifestation of Weckström's expressive and aesthetic formulations which defy the conventional forms and structures, in a free and flowing collection of shapes which assume a multitude of versatile and ever-changing dimensions. Weckström is not just Finland's best, but also one of the world's most creative contemporary designers.

Poul Havgaard (b. 1936), a Danish blacksmith and jewelry designer, was trained as a smith in Denmark but also ventured into other fields by working as a restorer of murals and frescos in medieval churches, a pottery designer for Rörstrand in Sweden, and as a ceramist running his own workshop in Faborg, Denmark. Havgaard's interest in jewelry did not begin until the early 1960s when he made jewelry and sculpture using iron and steel. For this type of work which he still occasionally manufactures, Havgaard received recognition as an able and creative jewelry designer, particularly after his sculptural metal belt buckles were selected as accessories by Pierre Cardin in the late 1960s. Poul Havgaard joined Lapponia in 1971 and within a year created a new line of three-dimensional sculptured-like collection of jewelry for the firm. A collection created in 1974 showed ample use of spectrolite, a native

stone which has become identifiable with Finnish jewelry. The 1982 – 1983 collection combined silver jewelry with lead while the 1988 collection combined gold with silver in innovative designs which emphasized the contrast and balance between the two metals.

Like Weckström, the nature metaphor also runs deep in Havgaard's work with an erotic and sensual emphasis since in his view, one of the uses of jewelry is to impress the opposite sex. Hence each piece of jewelry, becomes "part of the body language of sensuality, important tools in influencing the other sex."

Zoltan Popovits (b. 1940), the Hungarian born sculpture and designer, completed his studies in architecture in the U.S., spending an additional year at the Finnish Academy of Art in 1965 – 1966.

Popovits spent a few years designing ceramics for the Finnish firm, Arabia, before joining Lapponia in 1975. His first work for the firm consisted of a sterling silver chess set followed by a collection of jewelry introduced in 1978 and a wonderful collection of mixed silver and ebony jewelry in 1981. Popovits's designs also relate to nature in the same manner that jewelry made of simple, organic materials served as expressive means in Native American and African cultures, reflecting a bond between the wearer and the jewelry and their affinity for nature and the surrounding environment. Jewelry, in his view, "has unique significance for its wearers, connecting them to a certain person, time and place."

Christophe Burger (b. 1950) is one of the newer members of the Lapponia design team, joining the firm in 1989. Originally pursuing a career in teaching English literature and philosophy, Burger changed emphasis and went on to study design and goldsmithery at the Strasboug School of Applied Arts. Subsequently, he established his workshop in his native country, France, in 1977, and began designing jewelry and decorative arts.

At Lapponia, the jewelry designed by Burger reflects a combination of Finnish craftsmanship and French avant-garde concepts skillfully expressed in geometric forms, sometimes in asymmetrical arrangements, and often enhanced by gemstones. The unique graphic shapes are expressive, for in Burger's view, jewelry serves as a means of communication and conveying individualism, part of the language of human social interaction. Much of the jewelry Burger designed for Lapponia is executed in gold.

Uniqueness of designs and outstanding craftsmanship characterize the Lapponia jewelry. Today, the firm has over 100 employees with 85% of the jewelry exported to more than 20 different countries. The jewelry is distributed through an effective network of representatives and the company has subsidiaries in Germany, Sweden, and Norway. Its jewelry is linked to man's most primitive roots, his vast imagination of the future, and harmony with nature. It has been the recipient of many awards and is included in the collection of several major museums, such as the Pforzheim Jewelry Museum in Germany and the Royal Scottish Museum in Edinburgh.

Finnish National Silver Standard Marks

Finnish silver jewelry is usually stamped with the national silver standard mark and the maker's mark. Newer pieces may just be marked "made in Finland." Marks encountered on vintage Finnish silver jewelry include the Finnish assay mark, a crown within a heart; the fineness of silver, usually 813H, 830H, and 925H (or without the H if it is a post 1973 piece); the city mark in the form of various symbols; and the date mark.

National Mark: A crown in a heart for domestic production and in an oval for imports.

Date Mark: The date mark employs the letters of the alphabet, except J and W, along with a number in a pattern repeated using higher numbers.

A5 through Z5	1906 – 1929
A6 through Z6	1930 – 1953
A7 through Z7	1954 – 1977

City Mark: The city marks consist of a figure or a letter; those of the major centers are given below.

 Forssa

 Helsinki

 Hämeenlinna

 Iisalmi

 Lohja & Lieksa

 Nurmes

 Provo

 Turku

 Varkaus

Maker's Mark: A figure, the name, or initials of the manufacturer. Some of these are included in the following entries.

Finnish Silversmiths, Designers, and Manufacturers

Aarikka, Kaija (b. 1929)

Initially trained in textile and fashion design, Kaija began experimenting with jewelry in the late 1950s. The transition into the field of jewelry first began with the design and production of wooden buttons which were well received by the public. These were later combined with silver to make jewelry in simple forms and designs, but it was this simplicity of the wood and metal jewelry that began to shape and define the firm's character and the "Aarikka look" which is now well recognized internationally. The jewelry is exported in large quantities.

Burger, Christophe

See Lapponia.

Gardberg, Bertel (b. 1916)

Major Finnish silversmith who received his training in Denmark working for A. Michelsen in the 1940s. Upon returning to Finland in 1949, Gardberg established his own workshop and had a revolutionary impact on Finnish design. Gardberg's modern designs were innovative and imaginative as well as of superb craftsmanship. The turning point for modern Finnish silver jewelry is marked by an exhibition at Galerie Artek in Helsinki in 1958 where Gardberg, along with colleagues Kauppi, Rajalin, and Rislakki, first displayed their innovative modern silver products and jewelry. Winner of many awards and prizes, Gardberg should be considered a pioneer in the introduction of modern designs in the 1950s and its offshoot, abstract design, in the late 1950s and 1960s. His jewelry is extremely scarce in the U.S. and commands high prices. It is usually marked with his last name.

Granit

A Finnish manufacturer of silver jewelry founded by Erik Granit in Helsinki in the 1950s. Some of the earliest silver jewelry had stylized modern designs based on nature, but most of Granit's silver jewelry has highly stylized and abstract modern designs, including  rings of substantial proportions. The silver jewelry is of high quality and is usually marked with a stylized EG or E. GRANIT. The former, seen less frequently, may have been the mark used only on the early jewelry.

Havgaard, Paul

See Lapponia.

Häiväoja, Paula (b. 1929)

Häiväoja was among an early group of artists and silversmiths attracted by Martta Ritvanen after the establishment of Kaunis Koru in 1954. Trained in textile and fashion design, Häiväoja began experimenting with jewelry and designing for Kaunis Koru in the late 1950s, eventually becoming one of the chief designers for the company. Her jewelry at this time consisted of modern geometric designs with large unfaceted domestic stones. In the 1960s after moving to Kalevala, Häiväoja changed course, abandoning the geometric designs for the more dynamic abstract designs, but this transition reached its apex after Paula opened her own small shop, Studio Paula, which featured her now exceptionally large and modern jewelry. Häiväoja's jewelry was another phase and dimension in the evolution and development of the distinctly Finnish look which is now recognized internationally.

Hopea-Untracht, Saara (1925 – 1984)

A well-traveled and versatile artist, Hopea-Untracht came from a family of jewelers dating back several generations. She began her long artistic career as a furniture designer in the late 1940s then turned her attention in the 1950s to art glass which is avidly sought and collected today. Next she turned to jewelry executed both in gold and silver and manufactured by the family business, Ossian Hopea. Her jewelry is usually in exceptionally large sizes. These pieces usually date back to the 1960s and 1970s. Hopea-Untracht also ventured into the field of textile design where her work was well received by the public internationally. Her husband, Oppi Untracht, an exceptionally erudite scholar and an expert in the field, is the author of the most authoritative technical work on jewelry which should be included in the library of any serious student or connoisseur of jewel making. He also authored a book on the life and works of Saara Hopea-Untracht which is the most authoritative source on her creations in a variety of mediums.

Ilvessalo, Kristi

Finnish designer receiving prominence as the result of winning the 1947 design competition held by Kalevala Koru for her hedgehog pins later manufactured by the company. She continued a long collaboration with Kalevala, designing a variety of jewelry, executed in both gold and silver, incorporating modern with traditional Finnish motifs such as an extensive line of wedding rings manufactured and marketed by Kalevala.

Kalevala

Founded in 1935, initially Kalevala Koru specialized in the production of historic jewelry pieces which were quality reproductions of ancient jewelry discovered on many archaeological sites. The name of the firm itself, Kalevala, is based on the Finnish national epic recounting the exploits of three legendary brothers in a mythical land. The legendary epic was a collection of folk verses gathered and published by Elias Lönnrot in 1835 and had a significant impact on the Finnish national consciousness and the arts and interestingly on the American poet, Longfellow, in composing his "Hiawatha."

Kalevala still manufactures this type of jewelry though it also became a pioneer in designing and manufacturing modern silver jewelry. Many major Finnish silversmiths and designers worked for or collaborated with Kalevala, including Börje Rajalin, Kristi Ilves-

salo, Eero Rislakki, and Paula Häiväoja. But even today, the bulk of their jewelry is of the historic type, and the modern designs are marketed under the name Kaunis Koru. The motifs on the Kalevala jewelry date back as far as the Iron Age (pre 400 AD), though a majority is of the prosperous Viking Age (800 – 1025), and some even as late as the nineteenth century. The early pieces were designed by the artist Germund Paaer (1881 – 1950), some of which the firm still manufactures. Kalevala's latest collection is Luistani, named after one of the most important archaeological discoveries in Finland which has yielded thousands of pieces since it was first excavated in 1969. Currently, there are approximately 400 models offered by Kalevala which are manufactured in bronze, silver, and gold. The prices of the current silver jewelry range from approximately $45 to around $400. (See Appendix.)

Kaunis Koru

Established in 1954 by Martta Ritvanen in Helsinki. Ritvanen was the managing director of Kalevala Koru and by founding Kaunis Koru became a pioneer in introducing modern designs and concepts by attracting many avant-garde designers such as Eero Rislakki, Paula Häivaoja, Björn Weckström, Kaj Blomqvist, and Jan Salakari.

The firm's jewelry had modern designs with an emphasis on geometric forms and motifs popular in Finland at the time. Kaunis Koru was apparently acquired by Kalevala and its production constitutes the modern line of jewelry marketed by Kalevala.

Kultaseppä

Auran Kultaseppä is among the oldest manufacturers of silver products in Finland. These are known for quality workmanship and cover a broad range from silverware to jewelry and gift items and novelties. Included among designers for the firm are Börje Rajalin and Pekka Piekäinen. The firm's jewelry is usually marked with its eagle head trademark.

Kultaseppä Salovaara

This firm was founded in Turku in the early 1950s, changing its name to Kultaseppä Salovaara Ky in 1970. The polar bear mark was first registered in 1955 and has been used consistently thereafter even though the firm has reorganized and/or changed ownership several times since 1988. The succeeding firms were Kaarinan Kulta (1988 – 1990); Perring Oy (1990 – 1997); Perkko Oy in Helsinki (1966 – 1997); and currently Heimo-Koru Oy in Turku.

Kultakeskus

A relatively major Finnish firm, the Kultakeskus Oy, Hämeenlinna, was originally founded as Hopeakeskus circa 1918. The name was apparently changed sometime in the 1960s though the author is not certain of the date. The firm manufactured and marketed jewelry and silver products designed by many major Finnish designers and artists including Gardberg, Wirkkala, Vitali, Juvonen, Palonen, and Still-McKinney. The company mark is a seated lion in a hexagonal reserve.

Kultateullisuus Ky

A major Finnish manufacturer of jewelry and decorative products.

Kupitaan Kulta

Founded by Elis Kauppi (b. 1921) and friends in 1945. Kauppi was a well-trained silversmith and engraver, and in the 1950s he designed a modern line of jewelry featuring spectrolite which met with great success. This established Kauppi as one of the major designers and Kupittaan Kulta Turku as one of the major manufacturers of silver jewelry in Finland. The firm's kinetic jewelry is very popular with collectors. Kupitaan Kulta's jewelry is usually marked with the anvil symbol.

Lehtonen, Liisa

Contemporary Finnish designer with primarily wirework and crocheted metal jewelry combined with semi-precious stones and glass stones or beads.

Lindholm, Inger (b. 1929)

Educated and trained at the Institute of Industrial Arts under the supervision of master silversmith and teacher Bertel Gardberg. Her jewelry and designs began to be noticed in the late 1950s, but Lindholm has always worked as an independent silversmith, manufacturing a limited number of pieces.

Her jewelry is carefully handcrafted with heavy emphasis on the form and motifs executed in silver without the use of stones or other material.

Lindholm, Berndt (b. 1946)

Contemporary Finnish goldsmith with some works in silver. Educated and trained in Sweden and Denmark, Lindholm established his workshop in Provo upon returning to Finland.

Mattson, Matti (b. 1950)

Contemporary gold and silversmith with ultra modern jewelry designs combining rubbish with precious metals. Known for his miniature sculpture silver jewelry.

Minkkinen, Eila (b. 1945)

Educated and trained as a silversmith, Minkkinen's jewelry is unique and beyond ordinary classifications. Her designs exhibit a combination of influences such as the primitive, ethnic, pastoral, and abstract, sometimes all simultaneously captured in one piece. Some of the jewelry is sculpture-like figurals.

Oy Sterling Silver Ltd.

This company was founded in 1983 and was still in operation in the late 1990s. The examples of the jewelry seen by the author suggest that the firm is primarily a manufacturer of silver jewelry with modern abstract designs. The jewelry displayed here and the mark reproduced are attributed to Oy Sterling 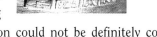 Silver Ltd., but this designation could not be definitely confirmed as of this writing.

Paaer, Germuned (1881 – 1950)

Finnish artist who designed jewelry based on the ancient archaeological finds in the 1940s and whose designs were manufactured by Kalevala which popularized this type of historic jewelry. Her famous "Bear" bracelet is still manufactured by Kalevala.

Palonen, Taisto

Contemporary Finnish designer with works manufactured by the Kultakeskus Company.

Piekäinen, Pekka (b. 1945)

Among the well-known contemporary Finnish silversmiths, Piekäinen began his career designing jewelry for Kaunis Koru in the 1960s and since the 1970s continues as a designer at Auran Kultaseppä, one of the oldest manufacturers of silver products in Finland.

Popovits, Zoltan

See Lapponia.

Rajalin, Börje (b. 1933)

Known for his designs in silverware and decorative arts as well as silver jewelry. Rajalin served as the chief designer at Kalevala Koru in the late 1950s. In the 1960s he began to receive international recognition after winning the 1963 Lunning prize which led to many more exhibitions and awards. Rajalin's designs, which were manufactured by Kalevala, not only influenced the expansion of modern lines at Kalevala, but also the development of modern Finnish design.

Rehnström, Helmer

Contemporary Finnish designer noted for filigree designs manufactured by Kalevala Koru.

Rislakki, Eero (b. 1924)

Trained as an artist, Rislakki began his career as a designer at Kalevala in 1951. Like Wirkkala, Rislakki relied heavily on domestic semi-precious stones combined with silver which were becoming so popular in Finland at the time. In the late 1950s, Rislakki was employed as the chief designer by Westerback, but much of the jewelry manufactured at this time was executed in gold and this too slowly diminished in time as he shifted interest to industrial and art exhibition layout and design.

Saastamoinen, Reino

Contemporary Finnish designer noted for jewelry combining natural semi precious stones and geodes with silver.

Salminen, Mirjam (b. 1918)

An employee of Kaunis Koru who began designing jewelry for the company and receiving warm public reception. She eventually rose to become the major designer for the company. Her jewelry is in the same manner and exhibits similar simple and minimalist designs that characterize Finnish jewelry.

Still-McKinney, Nanny

Contemporary Finnish designer noted for her stylized depiction of nature such as a fruit line designed for and manufactured by Kultakeskus Company.

Tamminen, Olli (b. 1944)

Contemporary Finnish silversmith known for his silver hollowware, who also designed some jewelry with post-modern abstract designs.

Tilander

The oldest Finnish jewelry manufacturer originally founded in St. Petersburg, Russia, catering to the royal house and nobility. Tilander was killed in Russia at the time of the revolution, and his son who escaped established the firm in Finland after the Independence. Manufacturer of a variety of jewelry, medals, and other silver products. Several major Finnish designers such as Mauno Honkanen, Anita Sarlin, and Kristi Ilvessalo worked for the firm.

Turn Hopea

Major Finnish manufacturer founded in the city of Turku. The silver jewelry is inspired by Finnish themes and motifs. The jewelry is usually marked with a T inside an H.

Martti Viikinniemi

Martti Viikinniemi & Co. was founded in Heinola, Finland, by Martti Viikinniemi and was in operation during the 1946 – 1968 period, changing its name to Martti Viikinniemi & Co. in 1969 and continued operation until 1974. Much of the jewelry made by this company and seen by the author is of average quality and is usually marked with the initials "MV." Apparently, Martti Viikinniemi was the sole designer until 1968 when the company changed its name while the later post-1968 jewelry may have also been designed by others.

Wirkkala, Tapio (1915 – 1985)

The well-known Finnish designer worked in a variety of media and was known internationally, particularly for his designs accomplished in glass, porcelain, and silver. Tapio Wirkkala began designing for Kultakeskus, a collaboration which lasted for over three decades. A recipient of many awards, Wirkkala was among a handful of leading Finnish designers who were instrumental in popularizing modern Finnish designs, leading to their world-wide recognition.

Weckström, Björn

See Lapponia.

Westerback Oy

A manufacturer of silver products.

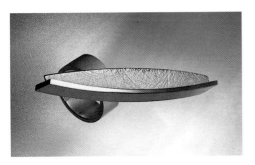

Lapponia sterling silver ring, "Strand," designed by Christophe Burger. Lapponia trademark. $200.00 – 350.00. Photo by W. Zakowski and courtesy of Lapponia Jewelry Oy.

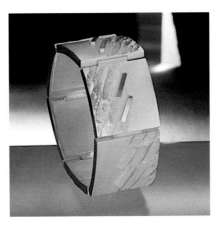

Lapponia sterling silver bracelet, "Wrist Watchers," designed by Christophe Burger. Lapponia trademark. $350.00 – 500.00. Photo by W. Zakowski and courtesy of Lapponia Jewelry Oy.

Sterling silver necklace, "Two Together," designed by Poul Havgaard and produced by Lapponia Jewelry Oy. Lapponia trademark. $350.00 – 500.00. Photo by W. Zakowski and courtesy of Lapponia Jewelry Oy.

Outstanding sterling silver and ebony necklace with soft satin finish titled "Tuareg," designed by Zoltan Popovits and produced by Lapponia. $350.00 – 500.00. Photo by W. Zakowski and courtesy of Lapponia Jewelry Oy.

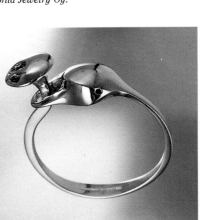

Masterfully created piece titled "Strange Days," designed by Poul Havgaard and produced by Lapponia. $350.00 – 500.00. Photo by W. Zakowski and courtesy of Lapponia Jewelry Oy.

Wonderful sterling silver earrings, "Lilia Tigris," designed by Zoltan Popovits and produced by Lapponia. $175.00 – 250.00. Photo by W. Zakowski and courtesy of Lapponia Jewelry Oy.

Lapponia sterling silver and acrylic ring, "Cool and Calm," designed by Poul Havgaard. $200.00 – 300.00.

Lapponia sterling silver and acrylic necklace, "Tribu," designed by master designer Björn Weckström. $1,500.00 – 2,500.00. *Photo by W. Zakowski and courtesy of Lapponia Jewelry Oy.*

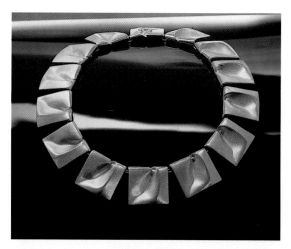

Sterling silver necklace, "Planetoid Valley," featured in the movie "Star Wars," one of the original and innovative designs introduced by Björd Weckstörm. This piece was produced by Lapponia in limited quantities during the 1969 – 1981 period. $2,500.00 – 3,500.00. *Photo by W. Zakowski and courtesy of Lapponia Jewelry Oy.*

Sterling silver and acrylic pendant, "Kilimanjaro," designed by Björn Weckström and produced by Lapponia. $2,000.00 – 3,000.00. *Photo by W. Zakowski and courtesy of Lapponia Jewelry Oy.*

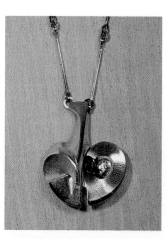

Sterling silver necklace, "Space Apple," designed by Björn Weckström and produced by Lapponia Jewelry. $1,800.00 – 2,500.00.

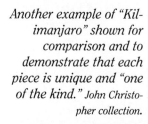

Another example of "Kilimanjaro" shown for comparison and to demonstrate that each piece is unique and "one of the kind." *John Christopher collection.*

Lapponia sterling silver pendant designed by Björn Weckström. $1,000.00 – 1,800.00. *John Christopher collection.*

Silver bangle by Erik Granit. Marked E. GRANIT & Co 925 MADE IN FINLAND and "U7" for 1973. $150.00 – 200.00.

Silver brooch by Kalevala Koru with modern design. Kalevala trademark. $150.00 – 225.00.

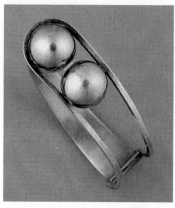

Wonderful silver bracelet by Kaunis Koru shop, marked with back-to-back "KK" mark of the company. $150.00 – 225.00.

Aarikka pendant and matching earrings. Marked Aarikka. Aarikka jewelry was made in both silver and silver plated metal and frequently combined with wood. Similar pieces in silver, $100.00 – 150.00; non-silver, $65.00 – 90.00.

Typical and early Kalevala Koru silver jewelry with an historic motif based on archaeological digs in Finland. With C clasp, marked only with the Kalevala trademark. $150.00 – 200.00.

Silver brooch with palmette motif based on a 13th century piece found at Suotniemi in Käkisalmi, Finland. Kalevala trademark, crown in the heart Finnish silver standard mark, a boat as Helsinki city mark, 916H, date letter "L7" for 1964, and partially legible initials of the designer, possibly superimposed HT, or back to back and conjoined letters "KK." $150.00 – 225.00.

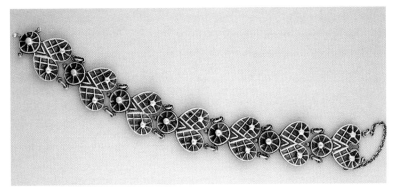

Silver bracelet made by Kalevala Koru and marked with the company trademark, crown in a heart for Finland, a boat as the Helsinki city mark, 916H, the initials of the designer "HGL," and date letter "M7" for 1965. $150.00 – 225.00.

Wonderful silver bracelet set with a flat rectangular stone and innovative tension-based fastening, marked 925 STERLING and Design Raimo Keskinen, Swedish import mark. Believed to have been made in Finland. $200.00 – 300.00.

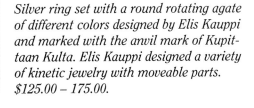

Silver ring set with a round rotating agate of different colors designed by Elis Kauppi and marked with the anvil mark of Kupittaan Kulta. Elis Kauppi designed a variety of kinetic jewelry with moveable parts. $125.00 – 175.00.

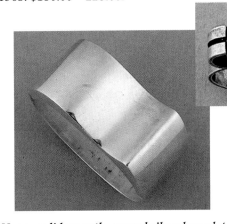

Heavy solid smooth, curved silver bracelet with innovative tension-based fastening, marked Design Raimo Keskinen, Swedish import mark along with 925 Sterling. Believed to have been made in Finland. $180.00 – 250.00.

Sterling and cat's eye quartz ring marked 925S with the anvil mark of Kupittaan Kulta. $150.00 – 225.00.

Silver pendant with modern cube design made by Kupittaan Kulta and marked with the company's anvil trademark. $150.00 – 225.00. John Christopher collection.

Silver leaf brooch set with cabochon amethyst stone made in 813H silver by Kupittaan Kulta. Kupittaan anvil mark, Finnish hallmark, Turku city mark, and "K7" for 1963. $75.00 – 100.00.

Silver brooch set with chrysoprase cabochons, marked STERLING FINLAND and Kultaseppa Salovaara Ky's mark, the side profile of a walking polar bear. $175.00 – 250.00. *John Christopher collection.*

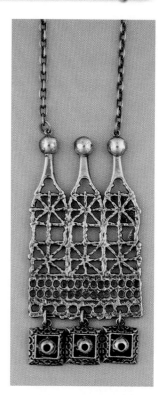

Wonderful silver and amethyst pendant with a modern design made by Kultaseppa Salovaara Ky. Marked FINLAND, 830H, with the Kultaseppa's trademark, the side profile of a polar bear walking facing right. $250.00 – 350.00. *John Christopher collection.*

Large silver pendant made by Hopea Turn. Marked FINLAND, with Turku city mark, Turn's superimposed "HT" mark, and "HOCB." $150.00 – 225.00.

Two-tone silver shield type pin marked with the Finnish hallmark, 813H, and "MV" standing for Martti Viikinniemi & Co. $45.00 – 65.00.

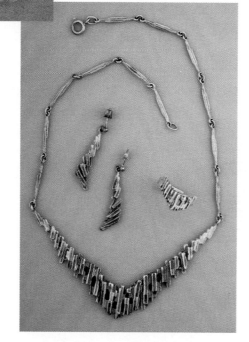

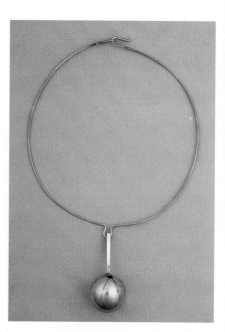

Modern coiled-top cuff bracelet, marked with crown in a heart for Finland, walking lion as Heinola city mark, 830H, date letter "S7" for 1971, and initials "MV" standing for Martti Viikinniemi & Co. $100.00 – 150.00.

Silver necklace and matching ring and earrings in modern textured and folded design stamped with 925, Turku city mark, date letter "K8" for 1987, and trademark of possibly Oy Sterling Silver Ltd. $125.00 – 175.00.

Silver necklace with a hollow ball pendant, marked 830H and with the Swedish import mark. $150.00 – 225.00.

Norwegian Silver Jewelry

The name Norway, Norge in Norwegian, is derived from Norvegar which approximately means "way north" or "the way to the north," a reference to the northern sea route followed by the **Vikings**. breathtaking Geography and climate, the landscape of snow covered mountain peaks adjacent to deep and jagged fjords, the coexistence of modern with pastoral, and proud reverence for tradition and customs, all have had a role in defining and influencing the development of Norwegian arts and crafts. Although perhaps better known for its traditional crafts such as weaving, embroidery, and woodcarving, the country also has a long tradition in manufacturing silver jewelry; folk silver jewelry; the enamel silver jewelry; semi-traditional and modern silver jewelry, some of which were inspired by historic themes and motifs.

For many centuries, the Norwegian political economy was dominated by Denmark and Sweden and the nation did not achieve its full independence until the declaration of independence by the Norwegian parliament in 1905. The capital city, Oslo, was founded in the mid eleventh century. The city burned down and was rebuilt several times and was named Christiania after it was rebuilt by the Danish ruler, Chris-

tian IV. The name of the city remained Christiania until it was officially changed back to Oslo in 1924. Some of the nineteenth century and early turn of the century silver jewelry pieces are marked Christiania.

Although there were some concentrated efforts to export silver jewelry and other Norwegian crafts to the U.S., a large volume was already brought in by many Norwegian immigrants. This is not surprising given the fact that today there are approximately over five million Americans of the Norwegian decent, more than the population of Norway itself.

Not all of the Norwegian jewelry carries the manufacturer's mark. Many pieces may just be marked "Norway" or "Made in Norway." The silver jewelry, however, must have a fineness of at least 830 which is stamped on the piece followed by the letter "S." Thus the jewelry of sterling grade is marked "925S." The letter "S" stands for *sølje* or silver in Norwegian. Assaying is optional and does not appear on most of the jewelry found in the U.S. collectible market. The official assay mark is a crowned standing lion within a circle. The manufacturers' marks are shown following along with their brief history and images of their jewelry.

Norwegian Silversmiths, Designers, and Manufacturers

Andersen & Scheinpflug

Andersen & Scheinpflug was founded in Oslo at least in the early 1940s. The firm was a manufacturer of traditional Norwegian folk silver jewelry, including *sølje*, and high quality enamel jewelry. All of the pieces seen by the author date back to the mid 1940s to 1950s. Unlike many other Norwegian enamel jewelry pieces of the same period which emphasized floral designs, modern and stylized geometric motifs are more prevalent

among Andersen and Scheinpflug's enamel jewelry. Some of the *søljes* were large, with a Norge inscription on the face, sometimes with the name of the person for herself or for presentation. The firm's jewelry is usually marked with the stylized jointed "TYA" letters.

Andersen, David

A major Norwegian retailer and manufacturer of silver jewelry and silver products founded by David Andersen (d. 1901) in Oslo (Christiania) in 1876. His son Arthur Andersen assumed the leadership of the company and changed the name to the hyphenated David-Andersen. Subsequently, Arthur's son and later grandson joined him as directors of the company. The firm began experimenting with enamel jewelry in the late nineteenth century, and beautiful pieces were created under the direction

of Gustav Gaudernack (1865 – 1914), a Bohemian employee trained in the Viennese school. However, it was under the son's leadership that the now well-recognized Andersen enamel pieces of silver jewelry were developed. The helm was passed to Ivar David Andersen in 1952 and from him to the next generation of Andersens.

Aside from the Andersens, such as Arthur who was an excellent designer, many major Norwegian designers such as Harry

Andersen, David (cont.)

Sørby, Thor Lie-Jorgensen, and Bjøorn Sigurd Østern worked for David-Andersen company, but Andersen jewelry is seldom marked with the designer's name and initials. The firm established an international marketing and distribution network with a significant portion of its jewelry exported abroad, and perhaps for this reason the firm's jewelry is comparatively easier to find in the U.S. market. Several Andersen marks are reproduced below. The earliest mark is the Christiana mark dating back to the nineteenth century followed by the D-A mark in the early twentieth century. These are marked with 830S silver fineness mark and may also include the firm's official forging tongs and a hammer mark. The scale mark was introduced circa 1940, and it was at this time that the sterling standard of 925S was also adopted.

An early Andersen mark found on silver jewelry and accessories with no other markings.

Early David-Andersen marks with dates and the company's bench tools trademark.

Two Andersen marks, one with the designer's initials, and the other with the common D-A and the scale mark.

Christophersen, Erling (b. 1932)

Erling Christophersen, led the Plus silver workshop in Fredrikstad, Norway, where several Norwegian designers/silversmiths, including Tone Vigeland, apprenticed. Christophersen also designed silver jewelry for Plus which carries his stylized "EC" mark along with the Norway Designs and PLUS mark. (See also Norway Designs.)

Eker, Anna Greta (b. 1928)

Originally from Finland, Anna Greta Eker established her own workshop in Fredrikstad in 1959. Married to Erling Christophersen, who designed for and managed the Plus silver shop, Eker also designed silver jewelry for Plus. These are marked with her name and the trademark of Plus Norway Designs. Some of the jewelry also carries the full name, including "Christophersen."

Eriksen, Sigurd Alf (b. 1899)

Began his training at J. Tostrup and abroad in Vienna and Paris. Eriksen studied at various institutions in Norway and eventually became a teacher and taught in Denmark, the U.S., and Norway. During the 1950s – 1960s period he was active in traveling, and exhibitions, and received several awards. He produced some jewelry with miniature enamel of exceptional quality. The jewelry is extremely rare and he is suspected to have produced silver jewelry but none has been seen by the author.

Hammer, Marius (1847 – 1927)

This firm was founded by Marius Hammer in the late nineteenth century in the city of Bergen located in western Norway. Marius Hammer, along with Anderson and Tostrup, was a pioneer in the development of enamel jewelry, both basse-taille and plique-à-jour. The firm manufactured a variety of silver products and its silver souvenir spoons and jewelry are occasionally encountered in the U.S. collectible market. It is not clear whether there ever was a direct export of Marius Hammer jewelry to the U.S., and the author suspects that much of what is found in the market was brought back by tourists or Norwegian immigrants. The jewelry is marked with a hammer superimposed on the letter "M."

Holmsen, Aksel

Major manufacturer of enamel silver jewelry in Sandefjord, Norway. The jewelry exhibits beautiful designs worked in enamel with outstanding craftsmanship. The mark is a set of bench tools which is similar to and frequently mistaken for a pair of letters, "W," arranged back to back on their sides. The post-1970 pieces are marked with the initials for Aksel Holmsen Slag.

Juhls, Regine & Frank

This couple operates their own workshop, Sølvsmie Regine & Frank Juhls, in Kautokeino, Norway. Situated above the Arctic Circle in the Norwegian Laplands, it is apt that Lapp and traditional folk silver jewelry are products of this enterprise. However, the firm also manufactures contemporary silver jewelry with modern designs which are created by Regine Juhls. Among these, the reticulated, folded, and textured pieces, some similar to natural silver nuggets or in free forms, which are displayed in this chapter are good representations of her creations. Juhls jewelry is handmade and of high quality and artistic merit not yet fully recognized and appreciated in America. This is partly due to its scarcity in the U.S. market and the lack of public familiarity with the Juhls jewelry. To the best of the author's knowledge, the couple was first introduced to English language readers in Oppi Untracht's 1988 encyclopedic work, *Jewelry Concepts and Technology,* a source of enlightenment for many connoisseurs of jewelry and a factor in motivating the author to seek and collect their jewelry. The jewelry is usually marked JUHLS, sometimes buried in hard-to-see places within the textures and folds.

Lie-Jorgensen, Thor (d. 1961)

A designer for David-Andersen.

Meldah, Bernard

Post-WWII Norwegian designer and silversmith in Oslo noted for his Norwegian style silver jewelry with enamel work. The enamel pieces have delicate stylized floral forms and designs accomplished skillfully and similar to the enamel works also manufactured by David-Andersen. The jewelry is marked with the superimposed script MB mark.

Modahl, Einar

The jewelry marked with the conjoined letters "E" and "M" where the letter M is reversed and resting on its side was manufactured by Einar Mohdal. Mohdal's shop was located in Oslo and this mark was first registered in 1965, but the author suspects it may have been used prior to 1965. The mark may be with or without "NORWAY" and is found primarily on two types of silver jewelry: traditional *sølje* and enamel jewelry. Examples of these are shown in this chapter.

Nordlie, Arne

Arne Nordlie A/S, founded in Oslo, is a manufacturer of silver jewelry, including enamel jewelry. Most of the jewelry seen in the U.S. collectible market appears to have been made in the 1960s to 1970s.

Norway Designs

Some of the jewelry by major Norwegian designers wasfirst created for Norway Design Center at Plus in Fredrikstad. Norway Design was a large shop in Oslo with a branch also in Trondheim. The company was established by Per Tannum who also in 1958 founded the center in Fredrikstad, a non-profit organization consisting of many workshops in arts and crafts and design. The aim of this center was to preserve and utilize traditional Norwegian arts and crafts to created distinctive designs and quality products as inspiration for production and future development. According to the archives at Kunstindustrimuseet in Oslo, the objective was "to promote systematic co-operation between designers, craftsmen, and industry enterprises to achieve better prototypes and patterns for production series." In the field of jewelry, new concepts with simple modern designs were introduced at Plus executed in gold, silver, and pewter. The silver workshop was led by Erling Christoffersen and the jewelry designed by him and others such as Tone Vigeland, Anna Greta Eker, Ragnar Hansen, Hein Hoogstad, and Odvar Pettersen was conceived and produced at Plus. The common mark for Plus is superimposed letters "ND" which appear as a thick letter "N" on the jewelry along with the "+" sign. This mark is accompanied by the designer's name or initials. (See also Tone Vigeland, Christoffersen, and Eker.)

N   **[+]**

Østern, Bjørn Sigurd

Among the notable postwar designers for David-Andersen. The jewelry designed by Østern may be marked with his initials in a rectangle.

Prytz, Grete (b. 1917)

Notable Norwegian designer for J. Tostrup. Studied at the State School of Arts and Crafts in Oslo and at Chicago's Institute of Design. Apprenticed as a goldsmith and established her own workshop. She won many awards, including the 1953 Lunning Prize and 1954 Milan Triennale gold medal, for her distinctive enamel jewelry and silver jewelry combined with glass. The family's association with J. Tostrup dates back to the nineteenth century when Grete's grandfather made enamel jewelry for the same firm. Early pieces are signed with her maiden name while later pieces also include her married name.

1. Grete Prytz   2. Grete Prytz-Korsmo   3. Grete Prytz-Kittelsen

Scharning, Albert

Post-WWII Norwegian designer and silversmith in Oslo noted for Scandinavian style silver jewelry with enamel work. The jewelry is marked with his script initials "ASch."

Sorby, Harry

Designer for David-Andersen during the post-war decades. The jewelry is inspired by historic themes and motifs rendered in modern designs, frequently set with semi-precious stones. His initials as a designer may appear on the jewelry

Tostrup, J.

A major Norwegian manufacturing and retail firm founded in 1832 by Jacob Tostrup. The firm is well known for its decorative art products and enamel jewelry. Much of its nineteenth century products were in decorative arts, but the firm is responsible for introducing the Norwegian folk filigree silver jewelry to the international market in the late nineteenth century which also rejuvenated the domestic production. Also in that time period, Oluf Tostrup pioneered the development of plique-à-jour enamel jewelry which is considered the best example of this type of jewelry manufactured in Norway. At the turn of the twentieth century, Torolf Prytz, an architect by training, served as the production manager and also designed outstanding pieces such as boxes and cups which received world-wide praise in international exhibitions. Torolf married Jacob's granddaughter Hilda Tostrup and their son Jacob Prytz became the firm's proprietor sometime around 1918. Post-WWII silver jewelry were designed by Torolf Prytz's granddaughter, Grete Prytz (later Kittelsen), continuing a long tradition of superb jewelry designs and fine craftsmanship. (See Grete Prytz.)

Vigeland, Tone (b. 1938)

A major Norwegian designer whose jewelry was manufactured by various firms, mainly, the Norway Designs at Plus in Fredrikstad. She established her own workshop at Plus in 1961 after apprenticing in the late 1950s and completing her studies at the State School of Arts and Crafts in Oslo. She created several lines of jewelry in the late 1950s while still an apprentice at the Plus silver shop, work which exhibits innovative modern designs and construction for which she received widespread recognition. An important aspect of her jewelry was the lack of fasteners. Her jewelry is included in the collection of various museums. The VT mark is the early mark, not used after 1979.

Aside from Norwegian silversmiths and designers who are identified in this chapter, the marked jewelry of several other Norwegian manufacturers and designers is also found frequently in the U.S. collectible market. Unfortunately, as of this writing, these marks were not yet identified, but a sample of their jewelry along with their marks is displayed with a hope that such exposure will lead to eventual identification. Among these are many sølje pieces made by a Norwegian manufacturer whose mark was the letter H in a circle. The examples seen by the author may date back to the 1930s or perhaps even earlier while others are post-WWII specimens circa 1940s and 1950s.

The enamel jewelry of another Norwegian manufacturer carries the mark which appears to be a reversed letter "C" embracing a reversed letter "A" lying on its side or just a symbol similar to it. The examples seen by the author are all made in silver with typical enamel decoration similar to other Norwegian enamel jewelry and roughly date back to the 1940s and 1950s. Additional unidentified marks primarily on søljes are: H.O.; H.B.; and V. Olsen.

Two gilded silver sølje brooches, both marked "830S" and with the maker's mark, "H" in a circle. $60.00 – 90.00 each.

Late 19th century to early 20th century sølje with hand engravings on both sides, marked 830S and with the maker's mark, V. Olsen. $95.00 – 135.00.

Beautiful 5" long vermeil sølje brooch from the early 1900s, marked with an interwoven double oval and 830S. $125.00 – 175.00.

Late 19th century handcrafted and engraved sølje by David-Andersen, one of the early works by that company. Marked 830 D. ANDERSEN 1882 CHRISTIANIA. $200.00 – 300.00.

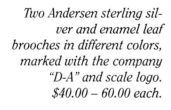

Two Andersen sterling silver and enamel leaf brooches in different colors, marked with the company "D-A" and scale logo. $40.00 – 60.00 each.

Silver sølje brooch, marked H.O. 830S. $45.00 – 70.00.

Andersen sterling silver enamel leaf pin and matching earrings. Marked with the company "D-A" and scale logo. $75.00 – 100.00.

Large gilded silver brooch/ pendant, marked K.B. 830S. $85.00 – 135.00.

Two Andersen sterling silver and enamel butterfly pins in different colors, marked with the company "D-A" and scale logo. $40.00 – 55.00.

Wonderful turn of century sølje by David-Andersen. $300.00 – 450.00. Photo courtesy of Pop Beads to Platinum.

Marked DAVID ANDERSEN, sterling silver pendant and matching screwback earrings. $150.00 – 200.00.

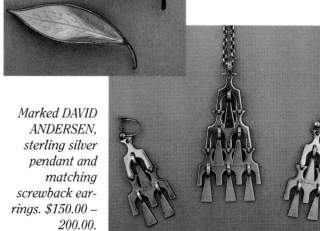

125

Silver bookmark with early David Andersen mark, $35.00 – 50.00.

Marked DAVID ANDERSEN, sterling silver necklace. $150.00 – 200.00. *John Christopher collection.*

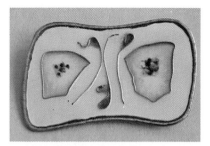

Marked David Andersen sterling silver and enamel brooch with modern design. Marked with the designer's initials not fully legible. $350.00 – 450.00. Photo courtesy of Pop Beads to Platinum.

Art Deco sterling silver and enamel bracelet, marked with Andersen & Sheinpflug's trademark, conjoined "TYA." $75.00 – 100.00.

Sterling silver and enamel leaf necklace, marked with Aksel Holmsen's trademark. $100.00 – 160.00; and a leaf sterling silver and enamel brooch, marked "ASch" in script, the mark of Albert Scharning in Oslo. $50.00 – 70.00.

Sterling silver Viking ship with textured surface, marked with Aksel Holmsen's trademark. $35.00 – 50.00.

Andersen & Sheinpflug's sterling silver and enamel bracelet with traditional Norwegian motifs. Conjoined "TYA" and "925S" mark. $150.00 – 200.00; and marked David-Andersen sterling silver and enamel brooch with modern abstract motif. $85.00 – 120.00. *John Christopher collection.*

Wonderful sterling silver and enamel brooch, marked 925S MADE IN NORWAY and with Aksel Holmsen's trademark. $90.00 – 135.00. *John Christopher collection.*

Large gilded sølje brooch, marked "830S" and with the maker's mark, conjoined "TYA," a registered trademark of Andersen & Sheinpflug in Oslo. The face is marked Hilsen Norge 48 and most likely was brought to America by Norwegian immigrants. The author has seen similar pieces by the producer marked only Norge or Norge with a date. $150.00 – 200.00.

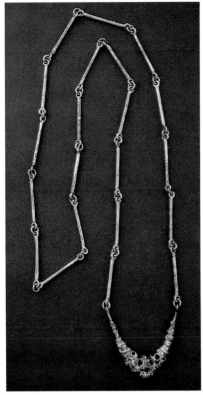

Modern abstract sterling silver necklace with typical Juhls design. Marked JUHLS. $250.00 – 350.00. John Christopher collection.

Two silver søljes, marked 830S and "J" which may be the mark used by Juhls. $40.00 – 55.00 each.

Sterling silver necklace with modern abstract design, marked NORWAY STERLING 925S and with the script signature Ostern, the mark of Bjorn Sigurd Ostern. $250.00 – 350.00. John Christopher collection.

Modern abstract sterling silver necklace with textured and folded body, marked JUHLS. $250.00 – 350.00.

An exceptional and rare Marius Hammer silver and chrysoprase brooch. Marked with the "M" and superimposed hammer. $1,000.00 – 1,500.00. Robin Allison collection.

Wonderful silver and enamel Marius Hammer necklace, marked with the master enameler's "M" and superimposed hammer. $800.00 – 1,400.00. Robin Allison collection.

Large sterling silver and enamel bird brooch marked with Bernard Meldahl's logo. $100.00 – 135.00 when in very good condition.

Beautiful Marius Hammer silver and enamel necklace. Marked with the "M" and superimposed hammer. $500.00 – 700.00. Photo courtesy of Pop Beads to Platinum.

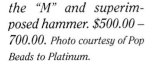

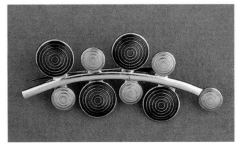

Sterling silver and enamel brooch, marked JT 925S for J. Tostrup. $175.00 – 225.00. John Christopher collection.

Sterling silver and enamel floral brooch, marked with Meldahl's logo, $40.00 – 60.00; and a pair of sterling silver and enamel leaf earrings, marked NORWAY 925S and with maker's mark, possibly letter "A" on its side within inverse "C," not yet identified. $40.00 – 60.00.

Large sterling silver and enamel brooch, marked NORWAY 925S, same maker's mark as at left and not yet identified. $50.00 – 75.00.

Sterling silver and enamel necklace, marked with the script superimposed "MB," mark of Bernard Meldahl in Oslo. $90.00 – 135.00. Sterling silver and enamel leaf clip earrings marked with the Meldahl logo. $35.00 – 50.00.

Modern pendant with amethyst stones. Marked with Norway Designs' "ANA" mark. $125.00 – 165.00.

An outstanding cloisonne type enamel piece by J. Tostrup, marked JT 925S. $750.00 – 1,000.00. *Photo courtesy of Pop Beads to Platinum.*

Sterling silver and enamel insect pin with Einar Mohdal's logo. $40.00 – 55.00. Sterling silver and enamel scarf pin and a pair of clip earrings marked 925S and with Arne Nordlie's "ANA" logo. Scarf pin, $25.00 – 35.00; earrings, $30.00 – 40.00.

Very large gilded sølje, marked 830S, with Einar Mohdal's "EM" logo. $165.00 – 235.00.

Two silver rings with modern designs, stamped with the Norway Design and Plus trademarks and the initials "AGE" for Anna Greta Eker. $100.00 – 150.00 each. *John Christopher collection.*

Sterling silver and enamel brooch marked TOSTRUP. $350.00 – 450.00. *John Christopher collection.*

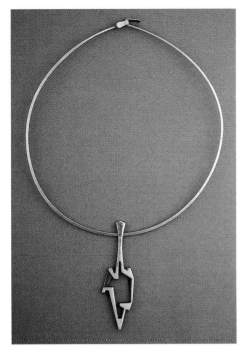

Sterling silver necklace with modern abstract design. Marked STERLING TOSTRUP NORWAY. $225.00 – 300.00. John Christopher collection.

Pair of sterling silver earrings stamped with the Norway Design and Plus trademark and the initials "T" within "V" standing for Tone Vigeland. $65.00 – 95.00.

Sterling silver and onyx brooch stamped with the Norway Design and Plus trademark and the initials "T" within "V" standing for Tone Vigeland. $175.00 – 250.00.

Outstanding silver and enameled Russian wolfhounds brooch, marked G.G. 925S N.M., possibly the mark for Gustav Gaudernack. Insufficient information to price. Photo courtesy of Pop Beads to Platinum.

Marked sterling silver neckring with polished semi-precious stones. Possibly Norwegian. $150.00 – 250.00.

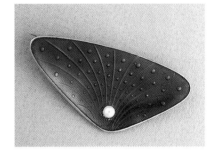

Sterling silver and enamel brooch set with a pearl, marked S925S. $80.00 – 120.00.

Swedish Silver Jewelry

The first mention of Swedes in extant historical texts was made by Tacitus (56 – 120 AD), the Roman historian who refers to a Germanic tribe as Svear. Svear or Sverige eventually became Sweden, a powerful kingdom which dominated the region for centuries and is now a prosperous country and one of the oldest continuous states in the world.

Although a major manufacturer of gold and silver jewelry, Sweden's jewelry has not received the same attention as other Scandinavian countries. This may be because there is very little information on Swedish silver jewelry and manufacturers in the English language and to the best of the author's knowledge, there is also no book in Swedish which catalogues and records the history and marks of twentieth century Swedish silversmiths. A difficult to find and indispensable book by the Statens Provningsanstalt, *Stämplar*, which includes the names and initials of Swedish gold and silversmiths operating during the 1913 – 1987 period, is of great value in identifying many of the silversmiths. Among the best works on the subject is Ann-Marie Ericsson's

book, *Svensk Smychekonst-från jugend to postmodernism (Swedish Jewelry Art from Art Nouveau to Postmodernism)* which was used for the biographies of two of the silversmiths discussed here. Others were acquired directly from the individual silversmiths and firms or through the kind assistance of Birgitta Martinius, curator of the Nordiska Museet in Stockholm.

The advent of modern designs began early in Sweden which also affected the jewelry designs. There is a similarity between Swedish and other Scandinavian silver jewelry, but the Swedish pieces are more subtle and conservative when compared to Danish and Finnish designs. Moreover, Sweden itself was a major importing country, and much of the post-war Swedish silver jewelry found in Sweden or even in the U.S. has the Swedish import mark. These pieces were primarily imported from Finland as well as other countries. The imported pieces are marked with the Swedish three crowns in an oval. The appendix includes a list of additional names and marks of silversmiths not covered in this section.

Swedish National Silver Standard Marks

Swedish jewelry may be marked by the manufacturer in addition to the mark "Sweden," but it normally carries the Swedish hallmark of three crowns in a triangular arrangement within a clover cartouche. The shape of the cartouche which frames the crowns distinguishes imports from domestic silver products. Additional marks are 830S for silver fineness; city mark which is the first letter of the name within a geometric symbol such as a square or circle; and the date mark. The date marks are similar to

the Finnish practice described previously, using the letters of the alphabet, except J and W, combined with a number.

A7 through Z7	1903 through 1926
A8 through Z8	1927 through 1950
A9 through Z9	1951 through 1974
A10 through Z10	1975 through 1998

Swedish triple crown hallmark found on most Swedish silver jewelry.

Swedish triple crown hallmark in an oval stamped on imported silver jewelry.

City Marks:

 Dalsjöfors

 Falköping. Similar mark in a square is for Falun.

 Götberg

 Helsingberg

 Kalmar

 Köping. Similar mark in a triangle is for Karlsköga.

 Malmö. Similar mark in a circle is for Malmköping.

 Nora. Similar to city mark for Nordingrä.

Swedish Silversmiths, Designers, and Manufacturers

Alton

Alton Guldvaru AB is a major manufacturer of silver jewelry in Falköping, Sweden. Much of the jewelry manufactured by Alton is of high quality with wonderful and interesting designs. The firm's jewelry was designed by several major Swedish designers, including that of the principal, K. E. Palmberg. The

ALTON mark was first registered in 1946 by Alton Guldvaru AB and by Ekström Sweden AB since 1985. Karl-Erik Palmberg used the mark "KP" first registered in 1945, and this mark was used by Alton beginning in 1946 and thereafter.

Bylow-Hybe, Viviana Torun (b. 1927)

Viviana Torun Bylow-Hybe (Bulow-Hube) is among the top Swedish designers and had a workshop in Stockholm during the 1948 – 1956 period and also established workshops in Denmark and France. Later Bylow-Hybe moved to Indonesia where she

currently resides, and the Swedish Goldsmiths' Directory provides no address in Sweden. According to the Sämpler, the trademark "TORUN" was registered by Torun Bylow-Hybe Guld & Silversmide during the 1951 – 1978 period.

Carlson, K & E

K & E Carlson was founded in Göteborg, Sweden, in 1918. It used the registered trademark "K & E C" in a rectangle and K & E CARLSON until 1948. The firm later changed its name to Cesons Guldvaru AB in 1955 and continued to use the K&EC

mark as well as CESON and CESONS until 1983 and was finally acquired by Alton in Falköping, Sweden.

Dahlquist, Ibe (b. 1924, see Georg Jensen)

Ingra Britt (Ibe) Dahlquist completed her studies at the School of Arts, Crafts, and Design in Stockholm. She designed jewelry for Georg Jensen beginning in 1965, and a "double fingers ring" designed in 1970 for Jensen is among several interesting and innovative pieces she designed for the firm. Aside from collaborating with Georg Jensen, Dahlquist also established her own workshop in Stockholm. Her jewelry is in many public collections including several museums in Sweden and the Goldsmiths' Hall in London. The jewelry manufactured in Sweden is marked with her name or initials. The ABD mark was first

registered by Ide-Silver, Inga-Britt Dahlquist, in 1955 which operated in Arboga, later relocating to Malmö. In 1959 the firm Debe-Form, Smyckesmederna I-B Dahlquist & Olov Barve was established which continued to use the same mark as well as the mark "SMY." The company was reorganized into Silversmederna Ibe Dahlquist & Olov Barve in Visby in 1970 when the IBE DAHLQUIST mark was also registered and used thereafter. Jewelry designed by Olov Barve, is marked OLOV BARVE, first registered in 1970. The company also used the mark "OBA."

Fleming, Erik (1894 – 1954)

Trained and educated as an architect in Germany, Fleming was attracted to designing jewelry as were many other Scandinavian artists and architects, and upon returning to Sweden, he established Atelier Borgila in Stockholm which expanded into a major concern in the 1940s. Several other major Swedish silver-

smiths such as Rey Urban, Giertta, Bringer Haglund , and Fleming's own son, Lars, were trained by Fleming while others such as Sigurd Persson and Stig Engelbert designed for the firm. The BORGILA mark was first registered in 1921 and the FLEMING mark in 1934. Both marks have been used consistently.

Ge-Kå, Kaplan

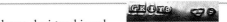

Ge-Kå Smycken was a major Swedish manufacturer in Stockholm founded by G. Kaplan circa 1945. The firm produced both gold and silver jewelry and used the registered trademark, "GK." The firm came under the leadership of Rolf Kaplan which continued to use the same mark. Some of the major designers

such as Olle Ohlsson designed jewelry for the firm. The company is still in business in Stockholm and reorganized in 1981 under the name Safir AB, Guldsmedssaffären, retaining the same trademark.

Giertta, Cläes (b. 1926)

Cläes Erik Giertta is among the foremost Swedish designers. Giertta was a student of Erik Fleming (Atelier Borgila) and has been designing and making jewelry since the 1950s. He established his first workshop in Stockholm in 1956, and his works began to attract public attention immediately. Among the early dramatic and powerful pieces was a "back necklace" exhibited in Hantverket in 1961. He and Rey Urban (b. 1929) held another exhibition in this city which also received public accolade.

In 1966, Giertta along with Rey Urban and Lars Flemming (b. 1928) founded the group, "Three Smiths" (Tre Smeader), launch-

ing an exhibition tour across the country. Their success led to the expansion of the silver shop, employing 25 gold and silversmiths. Giertta jewelry is unique, emphasizing reticulated, chiseled, textured, and fused metal forms combined and shaped into modern contemporary designs. Others display smooth texture with modern and abstract designs.

The jewelry is marked GIERTTA in block or script letters. This mark was first registered in 1954. Also used are the initials "GIE," first registered in 1954.

Hedbergs

Hedbergs Guld Company was founded by Nya Hedbergs in Stockholm in 1961, relocating to Dalsjöfors in 1964. The firm changed its name to Hedbergs Guld & Silver AB in 1982. From the beginning the company used the registered trademark

"HSG" and was still in business as of this writing. However, the family history may date back to an earlier period in connection to Hedbergs Guld & Boettverkstad which used the mark "HGB" during the 1946 – 1961 period.

Högberg, Sven-Erik & Anders

Sven-Erik (b. 1924) Högberg designed and manufactured silver jewelry in Göteborg using the trademark S HÖGBERG and SEHG, first registered in 1951. Around 1957 he formed a partnership with his brother Anders Högberg (b. 1921) and manufactured silver jewelry in Göteborg which is marked SEH. This mark was registered by Sven-Erik Högberg in 1963 – 1973 and Margareta Högberg after 1973. The S HÖGBERG mark was also used throughout this period. Anders used the mark A. Högberg during

the 1963 – 1982 period. Although much of the jewelry marked SEH has the Göteborg city mark, Sven-Erik Högberg appears to have also worked in Helsingborg as there is some jewelry with his initials which carry this city's mark. The Helsingborg mark was registered by Stilsmychen Per Ericsson and used from 1949 to 1957. The Högbergs manufactured some jewelry designed by the Finnish designer, Berndt Lindholm.

Janusch, Berind

Contemporary Swedish designer and silversmith noted for modern designs with highly stylized floral motifs executed by

employing shaped metal forms fused to reticulated textured bases.

Johansson, Owe

Contemporary Swedish designer with a workshop in Verberg. Collaborated with Kultakeskus Oy, Hämeenlinna, Finland, which manufactured the jewelry designed by Johansson. Owe

Johansson relocated several times, but consistently used the mark "OJN," first registered in 1965.

Keskinen, Raimo

Jewelry of Raimo Keskinen is difficult to classify. Some of the jewelry with this mark has no country designation, other pieces are believed to have been made in Finland, but have only the Swedish import mark, while another category made in Swe-

den has the "RK" mark. The latter mark was registered in Sweden, operating in Luleå from 1984 through 1986. A few Keskinen pieces believed to have been made in Finland are shown in the section on Finland.

Lindgren, Märta

Silver & Guld, Märta Lindgren company was founded in Nora, Sweden, in the early 1950s. The jewelry is usually marked

MVL in a rectangular box. This trademark was registered by the firm in 1955 and was active through 1966.

Liedholm

Swedish designer and silversmith with contemporary silver jewelry that is usually with modern abstract designs. Liedholm's marks on the silver jewelry are in cursive script punched deep into the metal and very difficult to read as well as impossible to photograph. This mark may be related to Äldelsmed Magnus G:son Liedholm which operated under various names and used the registered marks "MGJ" (since 1964) and "TSKB" (since 1975), but no relationship could be confirmed as of this writing.

A. Michelsen (Stockholm)

The Danish company A. Michelsen manufactured jewelry in Stockholm which are found with the Swedish domestic triple crown hallmark. These pieces are marked MIC which was the A. Michelsen's trademark used in Sweden. The MIC mark was reg- istered for the 1946 – 1963 period. The mark MICHELSEN was also used during the same period.

Nilsson, Wiwen (1897 – 1974)

Born in Lund, Sweden, Wiwen Nilsson was trained at his father's workshop with later studies in Hanau, Copenhagen, and Paris. While studying in Paris, Nilsson also worked for the Georg Jensen studio in that city. Returning to Lund, he established his own workshop in 1927 which at one time employed around 30 people. All of the jewelry was handmade, shown in many national and international exhibitions and recipient of numerous awards. Wiwen Nilsson was a leading figure in popularizing geometric designs pioneered in the 1920s – 1930s as a part of the functionalist movement. He is credited with establishing functionalism in Sweden with his 1930 exhibition in Stockholm which is also considered a turning point in his career. But he also made naturalistic jewelry influenced by Oriental, particularly Japanese, motifs in the 1950s. His jewelry is extremely rare even in Sweden and is usually marked Wiwen Nilsson in fancy script. A NILSSON in block letters was also used during the 1929 – 1974 period.

Noko

In the collectible market, the mark NOKO is believed to be the abbreviated mark for Nordiska Kompaniet, an old and prominent department store in Stockholm, incorporating the first two letters of each word. Nordiska held exhibitions on the premises displaying the jewelry of various designers over the years. However, according to the *Stämplar*, the mark NOKO was the registered trademark of Nordisk Kokusai AB operating in Sundbyberg and active during the 1974 – 1979 period. As of this writing, the author could not determine whether there is a link between the two concerns. Based on the jewelry seen by the author, the names of the designers usually appear with the NOKO mark, such as Giertta pieces shown in the following section. Sigurd Persson, Etsuko, and Olle Ohlsson (b. 1928) are a few other designers who collaborated with Noko.

Öberg, Per

The Swedish silver shop Ädelsmide, Per Öberg was founded in Kalmar sometime in the mid to late 1960s. The firm's ÄPÖ mark was registered in 1969 and the firm was still active in Ljungbyholm as of the early 1990s.

Persson, Sigurd (b. 1914)

Born in Hälsingborg, Sigurd Persson was trained by his father who was a silversmith. Subsequently, Persson went to Munich and studied at the Academy of Fine Arts and also in Sweden at the School of Arts, Crafts, and Design. Opening his own workshop in Stockholm in 1943, Sigurd Persson proceeded to design some of the most impressive and creative pieces in gold, silver, and glass (produced by Kosta), during the next three decades which had a significant impact on the development of contemporary Swedish design. His work was seen in many exhibitions and was winner of numerous awards, including the Golden Ring of Honor from the German Goldsmiths Society and Milan's Triennale gold medal in 1960. His works are in major private and public collections including several Swedish museums. Persson's jewelry is rare and when found, commands high prices.

Robbert

Robbert was founded in Stockholm and used the trademark "ROBB" which was registered in 1951. Apparently, due to a change in name or reorganization in 1965, the same trademark was registered by Silversmedjan Trosa Kvarn, Inger Robbert which was active until 1997.

Söderman, Nils-Eric

Nils-Erik Söderman founded the NSE company in Köping, Sweden. He used the trademark "NSE" from 1963 to 1965. The firm became NSE Guldvaru AB in 1965 and continued to use the same trademark. It is still in business with a large building complex in Köping, Sweden.

Sporrong

Sporrong AB was founded in Danderyd, Sweden, and used the trademark SPORR, registered in 1971. The mark SPORRONG is also found on its jewelry. The firm apparently also imported jewelry, usually marked with its trademark and the Swedish triple crown in oval import mark. Some of these pieces appear to have been made in Finland and may include the designer's initials. Readers should note that the first "R" in the trademark is not always fully legible and may be read as an "H." The last available address for Sporrong AB was in Norrtälje.

Taikon, Rosa

Contemporary Swedish silversmith and designer whose work is frequently inspired by ancient jewelry often featuring granulation and filigree work. Rosa Taikon established her workshop in Trollbäcken sometime in the early 1960s and has been using the registered trademark "TAI" since 1965. In 1973 this mark was re-registerd by Rosa Janusch Taikon, operating in the city of Ytterhogdal.

Urban, Rey (b. 1929)

Contemporary Swedish silversmith and designer working in Stockholm and receiving increased recognition abroad. Urban's jewelry is marked with his initials and was first registered in 1951.

Widenberg, Nils

Nils Widenberg was founded in Helsingborg, Sweden, in the late 1940s. The firm manufactured handcrafted silver jewelry and used the trademark "NHW." This registered mark was used from 1948 through 1974. The examples of the jewelry seen by the author are all circa late 1940s to 1950s and are usually stamped HANDARBETE (handmade).

Silver pin with oval cabochon agate stone, marked with the Swedish national silver standard mark, "F" in a circle for the city of Falkoping, letter date I9 for 1959, and ALTON. $50.00 – 75.00.

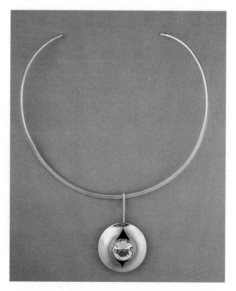

Silver and crystal necklace, marked with the Swedish hallmark and ALTON with the designer's name, Palmberg. $150.00 – 200.00.

Silver and rose quartz pendant, marked with the Swedish hallmark and the maker's mark "A&D." $45.00 – 65.00.

Sterling silver ring, marked with the Swedish hallmark and ALTON. $65.00 – 95.00. John Christopher collection.

Pair of silver cuff links by Carlson. Marked K& E C, Swedish silver standard mark, "G" below crown for the city of Goteborg, and date letter L9 for 1961. $30.00 – 50.00.

Silver perfumer pin, marked with the Swedish hallmark, date mark X8 for 1948, and the maker's mark "GK" for Kaplan Ge-Kå Company. $65.00 – 95.00.

Silver ring with floral motif, marked with the Swedish hallmark, date letter K8 for 1936, and the maker's mark "GK" for Kaplan Ge-Kå. $65.00 – 95.00.

Silver bracelet with the Swedish hallmark, date mark Y8 for 1949, and the maker's "GK" for Kaplan Ge-Kå. $125.00 – 165.00.

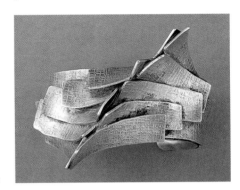

Silver cuff links with textured and fused surface typical of Giertta jewelry. Marked with date letter, X9 for 1972 and Giertta in block letters. $75.00 – 100.00.

Marked Giertta, gilded sterling silver wide bracelet with the Swedish hallmark and R9 for 1967. $175.00 – 250.00. *John Christopher collection.*

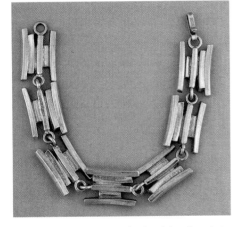

Silver bracelet, marked with the date letter A10 for 1975, "925", NOKO, and the designer's script mark, Giertta. $150.00 – 225.00.

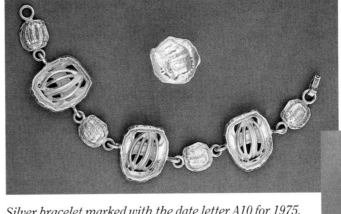

Silver bracelet marked with the date letter A10 for 1975, "925", NOKO, and the designer's script mark, Giertta. $150.00 – 200.00 Sterling silver ring marked NOKO and Giertta. $50.00 – 75.00.

Marked Giertta, silver cuff links with date letter "M9" for 1962. $65.00 – 95.00.

Modern silver ring marked "925", with the Göteborg city mark and "SEH" for Sven-Erik Högberg. $45.00 – 60.00.

Silver glob ring marked with the Swedish hallmark, city mark "D" for Dalsjöfors, date letter, Z9 for 1974, and "HSG," the mark of Hedberg Guld Company. $35.00 – 50.00; silver and crystal ring with the Swedish hallmark, $35.00 – 50.00.

Silver rings with flat crystal and chrysoprase, one marked with the Swedish hallmark, date letter K9 for 1960, "HGB,"
standing for Hedbergs Guld & Boettverk-
stand, the other with the mark "GVH,"
standing for Guldvaruhuset AB in Stockholm. Crystal ring, $35.00 – 45.00; and the
chrysoprase ring, $40.00 – 55.00. Silver pill
box with the Swedish import mark.
$30.00 – 45.00.

Silver bracelet marked with the Swedish hallmark,
city mark script "H" for Halsingborg, date letter A9
for 1951, and maker's mark "SEH" standing for Sven-
Erik Högberg. $50.00 – 75.00.

Sterling silver modern
abstract ring, marked
Sterling Sweden and
Geor. Liedholm. $75.00
– 100.00.

Contemporary folded and textured silver and rose quartz pendant, marked 830 and "BAK" or
"PAK." Most likely Swedish.
$50.00 – 70.00.

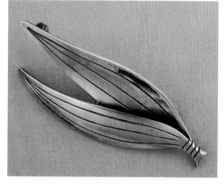

Double leaf brooch, marked with the
Swedish hallmark date letter D9 for
1954, and the maker's initials "MIC" for
A. Michelsen in Stockholm, Sweden.
$75.00 – 100.00.

Two pairs of silver earrings. Bottom: Screwback earrings by A. Michelsen in Sweden,
marked Sweden, with the Swedish hallmark, "MIC," "rengel" for Michelsen, and
date letter "C9" for 1953. $30.00 – 50.00
Top: Modern stylized floral clip earrings
marked with the Swedish import mark and
TSR 925 STERLING. $33.00 – 50.00.

Silver floral pin with the Swedish hallmark, date mark "T8" for 1945, and the
maker's stamp A/B NM, standing for
Nometa Metallindustri, active circa
1944 – 1974. $40.00 – 65.00.

Handcrafted silver bracelet with the
Swedish hallmark, city mark "K" for
Kalmar, date mark D10 for 1978, and
benchmark "APO," standing for Per
Öberg. $45.00 – 70.00.

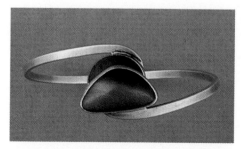

Modern cuff bracelet with the Swedish
hallmark, date letter K9 for 1960, and the
maker's mark, "MLV" standing for Märta
Lindgren. $125.00 – 175.00.

Silver pendant with Swedish hallmark, and maker's mark ROBB, trademark of Robbert in Stockholm. $80.00 – 120.00.

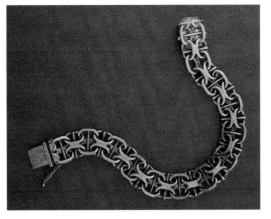

Silver bracelet with the Swedish hallmark, city mark "k" for Köping, date letter Y9 for 1973, and "NSE" standing for Nils-Eric Söderman and NSE guldvaru aktiebolag. $75.00 – 100.00.

Marked sterling silver and amethyst glass necklace and matching earrings, marked SPORR. $145.00 – 185.00.

Large handcrafted silver leaf pin with the Swedish hallmark, city mark "H" for Helsingborg, date letter C9 for 1953, and the initials "NHW" for Nils Widenberg. $45.00 – 60.00. Small leaf pin marked with the Swedish silver import mark. $20.00 – 25.00.

Silver Celtic brooch with Swedish hallmark, remaining marks are illegible. $50.00 – 75.00.

Silver floral pin with the inscription KOOPERATIVA KVINNOGILLSEFORBUNDET, Swedish Women's Cooperative on the front central rim. The cooperative movement was widespread in Sweden with the women's group opening many stores throughout Sweden. $45.00 – 65.00.

Swedish silver and amethyst cuff bracelet. $60.00 – 95.00.

Swedish ring with maker's mark "W." $30.00 – 40.00.

19th century handcrafted silver pin with repousse and engraved work. Partially visible Swedish national silver standard mark. $90.00 – 140.00.

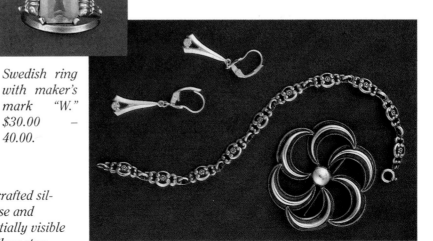

Group of silver jewelry with the Swedish silver hallmark. $18.00 – 25.00 each.

Large silver brooch. $40.00 – 65.00.

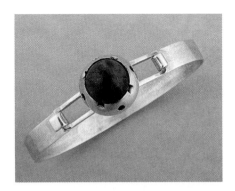

Silver amethyst bracelet, marked 830 SILVER, possibly Swedish. $75.00 – 100.00.

Two 830 silver pins with Swedish import mark. Larger pin also marked with the maker's mark of conjoined "MP." $45.00 – 60.00. Small pin, $30.00 – 50.00.

Modern 830 silver and amber ring, marked with the Swedish import mark, possibly from Finland. $80.00 – 120.00.

High quality 830 silver bracelet with the Swedish import mark. $75.00 – 100.00.

Two 830 silver rings with the Swedish import mark. $25.00 – 40.00.

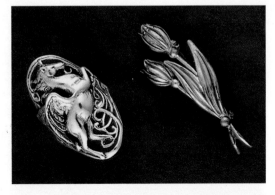

An exceptional, well-made unicorn 925 ring with Swedish import mark. $80.00 – 120.00. Floral pin, marked TEKA, with the Swedish import mark. $20.00 – 30.00.

Sterling silver cuff bracelet, marked RK290, believed to be that of Raimo Keskinen. $145.00 – 195.00.

Other European Countries

Because of their significance, the Scandinavian countries were covered in a separate chapter while the silver jewelry of 10 other European countries is displayed and discussed in this chapter. An extensive and in-depth treatment of European silver jewelry is beyond the scope of a single volume, but sufficient information and examples are provided in this chapter to familiarize the readers with the type of silver jewelry manufactured in these countries and frequently found in the collectible market, and to enable collectors to identify and date the jewelry.

The focus in this chapter will be on the typical jewelry found in the U.S. collectible market which may not necessarily be the typical or popular jewelry sold or worn in the respective countries. An exception is made in a few cases because of the author's admitted bias. Additionally, less space is devoted to the silver jewelry of those countries which had very limited exports to the U.S., such as Portugal, Spain, France, and most eastern European countries; after the dissolution of the Soviet Union, there has been a flood of both old and new merchandise, including silver jewelry, into the U.S. No biographies are provided in this chapter, but the description of the jewelry includes brief background information on the marks of the silversmiths and manufacturers that are identified. The readers should note that several European manufacturers and silversmiths such as Ola Gorie and Zebra are specially featured in the chapter on Current Silver Jewelry.

British and Scottish National Silver Standard Marks

The English silver ordinarily carries several marks. These may include two or more of the following:

Town mark: A symbol which identifies the region of production or where the piece was assayed (assay office).

Date mark: Letters of the alphabet in a cartouche that were repeated after each cycle by changing the font and usually the shape of the cartouche.

Duty mark: Sovereign's head, discontinued in 1890.

Manufacturer's mark: Usually initials and/or a symbol.

Commemorative and Jubilee marks: Optional mark such as the monarch's head appearing on 1934 – 1935, 1952 – 1953, and 1977 products.

These marks, used randomly over the years, constitute a massive and confusing maze of information which is difficult to master without extensive study and experience. For example, the town marks over the years, even when essentially the same symbol is used, underwent slight to drastic variations. Moreover, the date letters in some cases such as those of Birmingham consist of the letters of the alphabet, "A" through "Z," except the letter J, constituting a 25-year cycle before being repeated by a change in the font; while in other cases such as that of London, the dating is based on a 20-year cycle consisting of the letters "A" through "U," excluding the letter J. Furthermore, some of these cycles end abruptly before reaching the last letter in a normal cycle. An additionally complicating factor is that the shape of the cartouche that frames the letters may not be uniform and in some cases more than one type was used within the same cycle. Accordingly, in order to identify and date a piece of English jewelry, one must consult a long list of marks about which there are many excellent books written in the past several decades (see Bibliography). However, by referring to these tables, one is usually able to date a piece of hallmarked jewelry with relative accuracy — an advantage which only the British silver and that of a few other countries have.

Fortunately, the knowledge of all of this material is not absolutely necessary if one is satisfied with approximate identification and dating. Once this mass of material is reduced to the bare essentials, the task of learning and remembering the hallmarks becomes much easier and quite manageable. Careful examination of the hallmarks reveals that there are only two distinguishing features about the English hallmarks that differentiate among them: town marks and letter marks with changing fonts and cartouches. Both of these are relatively easy to master in a relatively short time, particularly when organized and systematically presented as shown here. In the following table the full hallmark for each area is given first, followed by the essentials, consisting of the town mark, the alphabetical cycle, and an example of the font and cartouche used during that particular cycle. During some cycles where the cartouche had more than one uniform shape, only the particular shape which was used frequently and predominantly within that cycle is shown, while in a few cases, where more than one shape equally predominates and is used frequently, examples of each are given. Moreover, minor variations in the marks are ignored since they do not alter basic identification and approximate dating.

Mark: *London*	Date Letters	Sample Letter	Yr. of Sample
	A through U 1876 – 1895	T	1894
	A through U 1896 – 1915	e	1906
	A through U 1916 – 1935	n	1928
	A through U 1936 – 1955	E	1941
	A through T 1956 – 1974	f	1961
	A through U 1975 – 1994	A	1975

Mark: *Glasgow*	Date Letters	Sample Letter	Yr. of Sample
	A through Z 1897 – 1922	g	1903
	A through Z 1923 – 1948	t	1942
	A through Z 1949– 1963	b	1956

The letter "J" is excluded in the alphabetical cycles for both London and Birmingham.

Mark: *Birmingham*	Date Letters	Sample Letter	Yr. of Sample
	A through Z 1875 – 1899	Z	1899
	A through Z 1900 – 1924	O	1913
	A through Z 1925 – 1949	E	1929
	A through Z 1950 – 1974	K	1959
	A through Z 1975 – 1994	L	1985

Mark: *Edinburgh*	Date Letters	Sample Letter	Yr. of Sample
	A through Z 1882 – 1905	r	1898
	A through Z 1906 – 1930	P	1920
	A through Z 1931 – 1955	G	1944
	A through Z 1956 – 1974	C	1960
	A through Z 1975 – 1999	D	1978

English Registry Marks: The registry marks provide information on the type, day, month, and year of manufacture. Two types of registry marks were used. In Type I, the letter on the top portion of the lozenge, in this case "Q," gives the date year while in Type II, the year of manufacture is given by the letter in the middle right portion of the lozenge, in this case "E." The tables below provide the actual dates for these letter codes, according to which Q=1866 and E=1881.

Type I

1842=X	1851=P	1860=Z
1843=H	1852=D	1861=R
1844=C	1853=Y	1862=O
1845=A	1854=J	1863=G
1846=I	1855=E	1864=N
1847=F	1856=L	1865=W
1848=U	1857=K	1866=Q
1849=S	1858=B	1867=T
1850=V	1859=M	

Type II

1868=X	1876=V
1869=H	1877=P
1870=C	1878=D
1871=A	1879=V
1872=I	1880=J
1873=F	1881=E
1874=U	1882=L
1875=S	1883=K

Sterling silver Victorian cherub belt. Initials "WC" the mark of William Comyns. $500.00 – 700.00. William Comyns was a manufacturer of silver jewelry and accessories and produced Art Nouveau jewelry at the turn of the century which is highly collectible. The Comyns Company was actually founded in 1948 and was still in business as of the 1990s. *Robin Allison collection.*

English floral pendant attributed to George Hunt. George Hunt (1892 – 1960) was trained in the arts and crafts tradition and had his own workshop in Birmingham. He marked his jewelry as "G. Hunt," but not all his jewelry was marked. $850.00 – 1,200.00. *Robin Allison collection.*

Wonderful sterling silver and enamel "Proserpine" cigarette case made in Birmingham. Marks not fully legible: Birmingham mark of possibly 1911 and "J. CL co" in a cartouche. $500.00 – 750.00.

Silver and mother-of-pearl pin, 1923 Birmingham mark, and "ALL." $40.00 – 50.00.

19th century unmarked English pin. $40.00 – 50.00.

Two 19th century English repousse pins. $35.00 – 45.00 each.

Large Scottish Viking ship pin. 1900 Glasgow hallmark and initials "RA," standing for Robert Arthur. $75.00 – 100.00.

English pin with the 1888 Chester hallmark and partially legible maker's mark. $60.00 – 85.00.

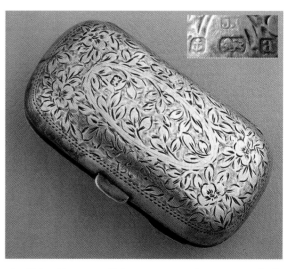

English silver snuff box. Birmingham 1900 hallmark and marked "J.G.," the initials of an unascribed silversmith working as early as the 1860s. $150.00 – 200.00.

141

Pair of 1870 Victorian silver, turquoise, pearls, garnet and mother-of-pearl pins. $250.00 – 300.00. John Christopher collection.

English arts & craft sterling enamel brooch. English Registry number for 1904 and the maker's initials, "RH" or "CRH." $200.00 – 250.00. John Christopher collection.

The mark on the pocket watch below.

Sterling silver pocket watch manufactured by J.G. Graves. Case with 1897 Chester hallmark and the maker's initials "TPH." $175.00 – 235.00.

Scottish silver, cairnogorm, and amethyst brooch. English Registry mark date for 1866. $275.00 – 350.00.

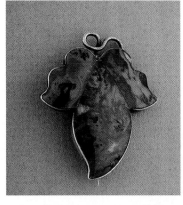

Unmarked Victorian Scottish silver and agate leaf brooch. $200.00 – 275.00.

English silver coin jewelry. Brooch, $60.00 – 90.00; bracelet, $35.00 – 45.00.

Scottish sterling pin with 1961 Edinburgh hallmark, and the maker's initials "T.E." $30.00 – 45.00.

Marked "sterling" Scottish agate pin. $75.00 – 100.00.

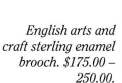

Scottish sterling pin with 1956 Edinburgh hallmark and the maker's initials "W. Bs." $30.00 – 40.00.

Scottish silver and citrine pin. $40.00 – 60.00.

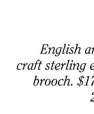

English arts and craft sterling enamel brooch. $175.00 – 250.00.

Handcrafted Scottish abstract pendant. Illegible hallmark. Maker's mark "P.D." $150.00 – 200.00.

Jewelry from Scotland: Silver figural fob inset with carnelian stone, hallmark illegible, $300.00 – 375.00; unmarked silver, agate, and cairnogorm brooch, $225.00 – 275.00; and unmarked silver and cairnogorm earrings, $75.00 – 100.00. Robin Allison collection.

Handcrafted sterling and moonstones brooch with Celtic motif. Marked "GHG." or "CHG." $175.00 – 250.00.

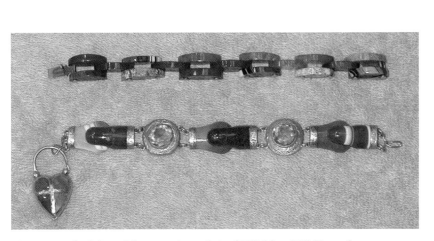

Two unmarked Scottish agate bracelets. $250.00 – 375.00 each. Robin Allison collection.

Unmarked English or Scottish Victorian citrine pendant with a matching cross. $450.00 – 650.00. Robin Allison collection.

Unmarked Scottish silver and cairnogorm buckle type bracelet. $300.00 – 400.00. Robin Allison collection.

Unmarked Scottish hoof brooch. $100.00 – 150.00. Robin Allison collection.

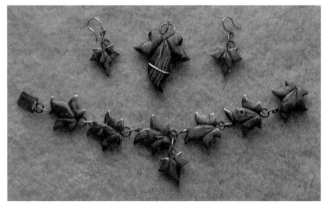

Unmarked Scottish silver and malachite set. $500.00 – 700.00. Robin Allison collection.

German and Austrian National Standard Silver Marks

Since the nineteenth century, Germany has been a major exporter of products to the U.S. In terms of volume, jewelry accounted for a very insignificant portion despite the fact that beautiful and high quality handcrafted silver jewelry was manufactured in Germany during the pre-WWII era, but much of the German silver jewelry found in the collectible market is mass produced silver jewelry especially of the post-WWII vintage. Among the pre-war manufacturers whose works are avidly sought are Theodor Fahrner, Heinrich Levinger, George Kleeman, Meyle & Mayer, Albert Holbein, Herman Wilm, Perli, Rodi & Wienenberger, and Herman Bender. The early twentieth century pieces are usually marked DEPOSE 900, 950, 835, and 800, sometimes with no other markings

to indicate the country of origin. The French word *depose* is the English equivalent of copyright or patent and was used on French, German, and Austrian jewelry. Due to this problem of attribution, some potentially German silver jewelry is shown among the unidentified or unmarked jewelry in separate chapters.

The post-war jewelry is usually marked "sterling" or "800" along with the name of the country, Germany or West Germany. The West Germany mark dates the jewelry to the post-war period while the Germany mark does not guarantee that it is necessarily of pre-war vintage. Older pieces may also show the German national silver mark, a crown and crescent symbol introduced in 1888. The readers should also refer to the chapter on current silversmiths where the jewelry by the German firm, Zebra, is featured.

Germany

The German "crown and moon" mark adopted in 1888 accompanied by various silver fineness of 800 and higher. Not found on most German silver jewelry which may be only marked "Germany" or "West Germany" along with "Sterling" or silver fineness; or DEPOSE with silver fineness.

Austria

The Austrian mark found infrequently on silver accessories and used circa 1886 – 1922.

The national standard mark used beginning in early 1920s. This mark appears on cartouches of various shapes and a number which indicated silver fineness such as 1 for 935, 2 for 900, and 3 for 835. The manufacturer's mark and the silver fineness of 800 or higher were also punched next to the national standard mark beginning in the mid 1920s.

German Art Deco marcasite necklace. Marked Germany and with the maker's mark "JMP," $175.00 – 225.00.

German hand-crafted pin, marked hand-arbeit and 835. $35.00 – 50.00.

German shell cameo pin, marked 800. $60.00 – 85.00.

Handcrafted German pin, marked handarbeit and 800. $35.00 – 50.00.

Handcrafted German pin marked handarbeit and 835. $40.00 – 65.00.

Wonderful and masterfully created plique-à-jour Art Nouveau brooch set with chrysoprase. Marked Depose 900. $2,000.00 – 3,000.00.

German silver bracelet, clasp not original. German national silver standard mark. $50.00 – 75.00.

German enamel bar pin. German national standard mark. $130.00 – 160.00. John Christopher collection.

Silver and chrysoprase brooch, probably Vienna Secessionist. $300.00 – 350.00. John Christopher collection.

Silver filigree pendant with seed pearls and synthetic rubies circa 1890. Austro-Hungarian or German. $165.00 – 200.00. John Christopher collection.

Handcrafted German silver and smokey quartz necklace, bracelet, and matching ring. Late 1930s. Erna Zarges-Dürr trademark. $250.00 – 350.00.

Handcrafted German cuff bracelet, marked on the face with the German national silver standard and partially visible maker's mark. $65.00 – 95.00.

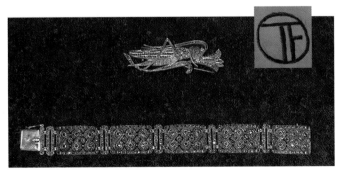

Theodor Fahrner silver grasshopper pin, jointed "TF" in circle mark, $450.00 – 600.00; and Fahrner silver bracelet, jointed "TF" in circle mark, $600.00 – 900.00 Robin Allison collection.

145

German sterling enamel bow brooch, marked Perli. $100.00 – 150.00. John Christopher collection.

Art Deco German marcasite pendant and matching screwback earrings, marked Sterling Germany with manufacturer's mark "JMP." $150.00 – 200.00.

Levinger enamel notepad case, marked Henrich Levinger, $600.00 – 850.00. Enamel locket, no maker's mark, $200.00 – 300.00. Robin Allison collection.

Austrian Art Nouveau enameled iris heart locket, $350.00 – 500.00; enameled locket depicting a lady with the spider web background, marked 900. $350.00 – 500.00. Robin Allison collection.

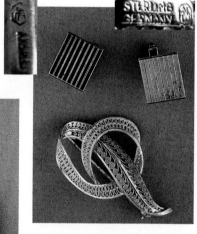

German silver pendant, marked 800 on the face. $50.00 – 75.00.

Pair of silver cuff links, marked Sterling with the maker's mark, conjoined letters FA in a lozenge. $30.00 – 40.00. Bow pin, marked Sterling Germany with the maker's trademark N within W in an oval. $25.00 – 35.00.

Pendant set with black onyx, marked Germany and Sterling. $35.00 – 50.00.

West German abstract sterling bangle bracelet. Circa 1960. Marked "F.S" in an oval. $85.00 – 125.00.

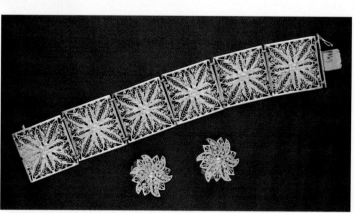

Pin, marked Sterling Germany with same maker's mark as bow pin at center right. $30.00 – 40.00.

Sterling bracelet, marked Germany, $35.00 – 45.00; and a pair of sterling silver clip earrings, marked Germany, $15.00 – 20.00.

Sterling German butterfly pin with moving wings, decorated with chrysoprase stones and plique-à-jour enamel work. Marked E.B in rectangle; in original U.S. distributor box. $50.00 – 85.00.

Possibly German modern pendant. Marked "835" with an unidentified maker's mark consisting of the letter "F" or "LF" in a vase or bottle. $100.00 – 125.00.

Pair of silver earrings, marked with "R" and "W" flanking an anchor, the registered trademark of Rodi Wienenberger. $40.00 – 60.00; and a pendant with the Wienenberger mark, $60.00 – 90.00.

Modernist silver and amazonite brooch with the maker's mark of "W" under a crown, possibly the mark of Herman Wilm. $185.00 – 245.00.

Silver pendant with modern abstract design marked "sterling" and with the superimposed "VW" trademark which appears to be that of Vereinigte Werkstatten fur Kunst im Handwerk. $100.00 – 150.00.

Italian Silver Jewelry

Unlike many other European countries, Italy maintained its long tradition of working in gold throughout the twentieth century. This preference was reinforced with the development of new techniques employed in creating modern and abstract gold jewelry in cities such as Padua which under the influence of Mario Pinton and Giampaolo Babetto became a center of modern gold jewelry. For this reason, until recently, the amount of Italian silver jewelry imported into the U.S. was quite limited both in range and volume.

Silver jewelry currently imported from Italy accounts for a sizeable portion of the supply in the U.S. domestic market, but the old Italian silver jewelry imported into the U.S. and found today in the collectible market is quite different from the current Italian and vermeil silver jewelry. These can be classified into three broad categories: filigree; shell cameo; and so-called "designer" jewelry. Italian filigree jewelry usually has floral designs and is marked 800, often with no other identifying marks. There has been a long tradition of filigree work on the Ligurian coast of Italy which still serves as a major center of production. Since filigree jewelry was also produced in many other countries, some also using the 800 mark, the identification and attribution are not always easy tasks and require at least some familiari-

ty with the construction, findings, and the type of filigree jewelry manufactured in Italy. Those that are displayed in this section were selected based on the author's knowledge and experience, but not all can be guaranteed with full certainty to be of Italian origin.

Shell cameo jewelry became exceptionally popular during the Victorian era with the British and American fancy for classical themes and Italian arts which led to a large volume of this type of jewelry exported abroad. Those imported into the U.S. are of the late nineteenth to early twentieth century vintage, though the imports continued unabated with the exception of a brief disruption during WWII. The center for shell cameo production is the city of Torre de Greco, and much of the cameo jewelry found in the U.S. market originates there. The cameos which often depict the profile of a woman were originally hand carved but many of the twentieth century pieces, especially after WWII, are carved by machinery. They were mounted on both gold and silver, and the quality varies drastically depending on the carving and workmanship. Italian silver cameo jewelry is usually marked 800 or sterling, sometimes accompanied with an "Italy" or "made in Italy" mark.

To a much lesser extent, other types of Italian silver jewelry are also found in the collectible market, including well-designed pieces with the manufacturer's mark. Among these, the most common and also highly collectible pieces are those made by Peruzzi which may also carry the Florence or Boston mark. But readers should note that many of the so called "designer" pieces are new or recent silver jewelry imported in massive quantities, including those designed and manufactured under contract, such as the Tiffany silver jewelry.

Both older and more recent Peruzzi silver jewelry is of high quality exhibiting a broad range of designs. Many of the older pieces are inspired by nature and use stylized floral designs. These are also, in the author's view, of better quality and superior casting.

Fratelli Peruzzi Argentieri has been manufacturing silver products, accessories, and jewelry for over a century. The Peruzzi shop is located at the famed Ponte Vecchio in Florence, a historic location consisting of a number of jewelry shops on a bridge constructed in 1565. The Peruzzi family began producing silver products and jewelry at the end of the nineteenth century, employing local artisans, and is currently under its fourth generation of management.

The Italian laws did not require the hallmarking of exported silver jewelry and much of the older silver jewelry exported abroad is marked 800 or sterling. The hallmarking used for jewelry in the domestic market involves a number assigned to each registered gold or silversmith shown along with the abbreviated name of the province, all arranged in a cartouche. However, lack of such a mark does not indicate that the piece was made for export. According to several Italian silversmiths, as related to the author, with the exception of established houses in the jewelry industry, many silversmiths operate without a legal and assigned registration number because of the cumbersome Italian bureaucracy, including dealings with the local police department, in order to comply with the regulations.

The Italian national silver standard mark adopted in 1934 and consisting of a cartouche which contains an identification number followed by the two letter initials signifying the Italian province where the mark was registered. Found on Italian gold jewelry, infrequently on silver jewelry, and seldom fully legible.

Most common type of mark found on Italian silver jewelry with or without the manufacturer's mark. The older pieces are simply marked 800. The post-WWII pieces may also have the name "Italy."

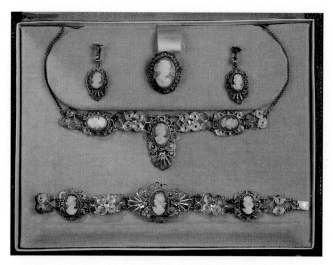

Parure consisting of silver and shell cameo necklace, bracelet, pin, and earrings in original box giving the name of the manufacturer, "Lopez" of Naples. $400.00 – 500.00.

Late 19th century Italian silver and shell cameo. $150.00 – 225.00.

Italian shell cameo pendant and matching earrings, marked "BA 800." $95.00 – $145.00.

Italian shell cameo ring, marked "800," with the maker's registration mark "27-GE" following the post-1935 Italian national silver marks. $35.00 – 50.00; and a variety of Italian shell cameos, marked "800." $40.00 – 65.00 each.

Italian filigree jewelry, all marked "800." Large pin, $20.00 – 30.00; small pin, $10.00 – 15.00; and two pairs of earrings, $15.00 – 18.00 each.

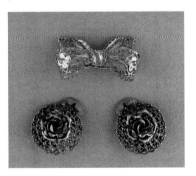

Italian filigree vermeil bow pin, $15.00 – 20.00; and marked "800," Italian clip earrings, $12.00 – 18.00.

Italian filigree pin, $16.00 – 22.00; and filigree bracelets, $20.00 – 30.00 each.

Italian pin set with glass "stone," marked "800." $25.00 – 35.00.

Italian filigree necklace and matching bracelet. $35.00 – 50.00.

High quality Italian filigree brooch set with carnelian, marked "800." $40.00 – 60.00.

Italian silver pin in shape of shell, set with a carnelian. $35.00 – 50.00.

Italian bracelet and earrings set with semi-precious stones. $75.00 – 100.00.

Italian bangle with floral motif, $18.00 – 25.00; and multi-strand bangle with a dangling silver vessel set with carnelian stones. $35.00 – 50.00.

Italian silver cross set with chrysoprase, marked Sterling Italy. $60.00 – 95.00.

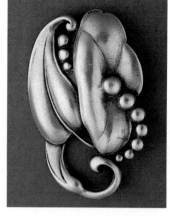

Sterling silver brooch, marked Peruzzi. $85.00 – 135.00.

Atypical marked Peruzzi sterling silver brooch. $90.00 – 145.00. Photo courtesy of Pop Beads to Platinum.

Two Peruzzi marks of 800 silver with Florence and Boston.

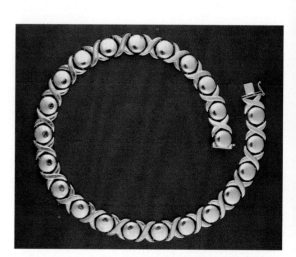

Silver bracelet, marked PERUZZI FLORENCE 800 SILVER. $95.00 – 145.00. John Christopher collection.

Pair of 800 silver brooches, marked PERUZZI. $85.00 – 125.00 each.

An exceptional and very large brooch, marked PERUZZI BOSTON. $200.00 – 250.00. John Christopher collection.

Italian gold plated sterling silver pendant. Three-dimensional, shows good definition. $75.00 – 100.00.

Gold plated modern necklace, marked 925 ITALY, with the maker's mark "SU" in an oval. $85.00 – 125.00.

150

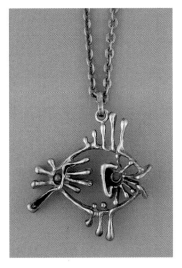

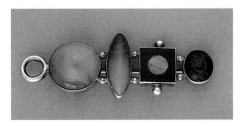

Large Italian brooch set with geometric semi-precious stones and inlaid wood. $125.00 – 175.00.

Modern Italian pendant in the form of a stylized fish with enamel accent. Marked with post-1935 Italian registered manufacturer mark, "134-AR." $100.00 – 145.00.

Sterling silver clip with superimposed "CI," possibly the Chain Italia Ltd. trademark, as well as Nieman Marcus inscription. $20.00 – 35.00.

Dutch Silver Jewelry

There is very little Dutch silver jewelry in the U.S. collectible market and much of what is found consists of delft and silver jewelry. The European craze over Chinese porcelain motivated many countries and manufacturers to discover the formula and develop the technology to replicate the highly priced pieces (eventually accomplished by Meissen in Germany). The Dutch, with colonies and bases in the Far East, were the major importers of Chinese porcelain and with disruptions in trade, serious attempts were made to reproduce the blue and white Chinese porcelain. This attempt, with the assistance of Italian immigrants who were experienced in the production of pottery, resulted in the making of delft, named after the city of Delft, Holland. The result was an exceptionally poor reproduction of the Chinese blue and white, but delft pottery became a permanent Dutch export product which is still produced and exported, though only one of the original companies has survived.

A natural outgrowth of making delft pottery was its application to jewelry production, a practice followed by other major porcelain manufacturing countries, Germany, Britain, and Denmark. Nearly all delft jewelry pieces depict provincial Dutch scenery and themes. The delft pieces are frequently mounted on silver, creating different types of traditional jewelry such as necklaces, bracelets, pins, and earrings.

The silver is usually marked sterling or with silver fineness, and there are usually no other markings. Some old stocks of new pieces purchased by the author in the past also carried a tag marked sterling and Holland or with the name of the U.S. distributor or retail outlet. These tags were most likely added later. The ceramic delft pieces are usually not marked, but occasionally marked pieces can be found which carry the trademark of one of the many Dutch delft manufacturers. Such pieces usually command higher prices. Readers should note that this type of jewelry is still being made and exported to the U.S. and can usually be purchased in specialty and gift shops.

The Dutch "sword" mark which is the most common found on Dutch silver though seldom fully visible or legible, often escaping detection. The mark was used since the early nineteenth century, indicating the silver fineness of 833 or higher, which beginning in 1953, was written on the blade.

The delft mark found sometimes on the back of the Dutch delft silver jewelry.

Necklace with applied filigree on solid silver base. Dutch sword mark and the date letter "C" for 1921, and unidentified maker's mark. $75.00 – 100.00.

Dutch delft bracelet and screwback earrings. $40.00 – 60.00.

Dutch pin depicting typical genre Dutch theme. Dutch sword national silver standard mark. $50.00 – 75.00.

Two pairs of silver and delft earrings. $18.00 – 25.00 each.

Dutch delft bracelet and clip earrings. Ceramic marked delft, and the silver marked with the Dutch sword national silver standard mark. $50.00 – 75.00.

Eastern European Silver Jewelry

Much of the Russian, Polish, and even Hungarian silver jewelry found in the collectible market has been brought into the country after the dissolution of the Soviet Union. These include both antique and recently manufactured jewelry from the region. The national standard marks for these countries are shown on the next page.

Czechoslovakia, formed in 1918 after WWI and several years ago divided into two separate countries, Slovakia and the Czech Republic, was a major exporter of jewelry and decorative arts to the U.S. between the two world wars. An overwhelming majority of the jewelry is made of non-precious material consisting primarily of multi-color rhinestones, glass beads, and other jewelry. But limited amounts of silver jewelry were also imported from Czechoslovakia which are occasionally found in the collectible market. These consist of sterling silver or vermeil set with garnets in either classic or Art Deco style and marcasite and other silver jewelry and accessories. The jewelry is usually hallmarked according to the country's national silver standards which consisted of a woman's profile with scarf for most of the early years and a rabbit or a goat head after 1955. Assay marks were also introduced in 1955. Among the five (initially six) assay marks used, one that is frequently encountered is the letter "J" in a square standing for Jablonec, a major center of production.

Czechoslovakia

 Used circa 1922 – 1929 and found on cigarette cases and accessories. The shape of the cartouche varies and the number gives the silver fineness: 1 for 950; 2 for 900; 3 for 800; and 4 for 750.

 Used in the 1920s signifying 800 silver fineness.

 Used in the 1920s signifying 900 silver fineness and reintroduced in various shapes after the mid 1950s indicating silver fineness of 900 or lower.

 The goat mark used since 1941 and the most common mark found on Czech silver jewelry. The size and shape of the cartouche varies, and the number indicates the silver fineness, 1 standing for 950 or higher; and 2 for 925. An assay mark may also appear. The most common assay city marks are the letter "J" for Joblonec (varied spelling) and "P" for Praha.

Hungary

Despite national standards marks, most post-WWII pieces are marked "MADE IN HUNGARY." For early Austro-Hungarian marks, see the section on Germany and Austria in this chapter.

Poland

 The Polish silver standard mark used within various cartouches since 1920. The number indicates silver fineness: 1 for 940; 2 for 875; and 3 for 800. The letter "W," when legible, is the most important feature differentiating the Polish mark from somewhat similar marks used in other countries such as Russia. Since 1963 the lady's profile is facing to the right.

Russia

 The pre-revolution imperial Russian mark used within various cartouches circa 1896 – 1908. The distinguishing feature is the number "84" which differentiates this mark from somewhat similar marks used by other countries. The Russian measure of fineness was in Zolotniks with 84 being the approximate equivalent of 875 fineness.

 The right facing profile used circa 1908 – 1917. This mark with 84 along with the city names Tabriz or Van in Persian, Armenian, or Latin script is also found on Persian and Ottoman silver.

 The profile of a worker with or without the hammer visible and within varied cartouches, and often with Cyrillic characters which indicated the district, used circa 1927 – 1958.

  The Soviet hammer and sickle mark within various cartouches used after 1958.

Czech marcasite brooch. $60.00 – 95.00.

Two silver rings, marked "835," possibly from Czechoslovakia. $25.00 – 35.00 each.

Czech garnet bangles, $95.00 – 140.00 each; garnet earrings, $40.00 – 50.00.

Art Deco silver Czech bracelet. $30.00 – 40.00.

Silver and garnet necklace, pin, and earrings. $300.00 – 400.00.

Silver marcasite cameo necklace. $75.00 – 100.00.

Polish silver and agate bracelet. Polish national silver standard mark, and the maker's mark: "EG" and "Rvr." $100.00 – 140.00.

Renaissance Revival sterling, pearl, glass, and enamel bracelet, marked MADE IN HUNGARY. $200.00 – 300.00.

Polish abstract silver pendant. Polish national silver standard mark. $85.00 – 125.00.

Czech silver and gilded necklace with glass citrine stone. $75.00 – 100.00.

Russian silver ring and matching earrings. Soviet national standard mark. $50.00 – 75.00.

Polish silver pendant with a large cherry amber containing an insect. Polish national silver standard mark. $125.00 – 160.00.

Silver and malachite ring and matching earrings. Soviet silver standard mark. $60.00 – 85.00.

Polish silver cigarette case, marked with the Polish national silver standard mark. $75.00 – 100.00.

Silver and jade bracelet, marked with Soviet silver standard mark. $45.00 – 70.00.

Matching set of silver and turquoise bracelet, ring, and earrings. Soviet silver standard mark. $100.00 – 160.00.

Russian Orthodox Byzantine style pendant with color glass. $65.00 – 95.00.

Russian traditional silver and inlay glass pendant. $65.00 – 95.00.

Russian two-tone silver bracelet, $30.00 – 40.00; owl ring, $18.00 – 22.00; and silver band with mother-of-pearl, $15.00 – 18.00.

Russian silver and lapis pendant with matching bracelet. Soviet national standard mark. $75.00 – 100.00.

Russian silver and citrine ring and matching earrings. Soviet national standard mark. $75.00 – 100.00.

Russian silver and hematite ring with matching earrings. Soviet national standard mark. $50.00 – 70.00.

Russian silver and jade ring and matching earrings. Soviet national standard mark. $60.00 – 95.00.

Spanish, Portuguese, French, and Swiss Silver Jewelry

Despite a long and historical tradition in silver works, particularly in Spain, there is very little Spanish and Portuguese silver jewelry that can be found in the U.S. collectible market. So far as Spain is concerned, the collectors are more likely to encounter non-silver Spanish jewelry, especially what is known in the market as Toledo jewelry, rather than sterling silver pieces. The silver pieces encountered occasionally consist of high quality designer pieces or others which depict Spanish national symbols and themes. Spanish silver jewelry is usually marked Spain in addition to sterling or silver fineness.

The same can be said about the Portuguese silver jewelry. Much of what is encountered in the market consists of enamel or filigree work or a combination of both. There is a long tradition of filigree work in Portugal, made in both gold and silver and associated with Portuguese peasant jewelry. Old nineteenth century pieces made in Portugal can be occasionally found on the market, particularly in the New England area. These can be identified and dated because of the minute punch marks with Portuguese national silver standards. These marks are often missed by the seller since they are nearly always extremely small and placed inconspicuously and when discovered, may not be fully visible or legible. Many of the pieces also include the maker's mark. Twentieth century pieces are usually in vermeil

and post-WWII pieces generally are marked Portugal.

Although France was a center for fashion for several centuries and beautiful jewelry made by highly skilled craftsmen was manufactured in different parts of the country, a very limited volume of silver jewelry was imported into the U.S. French jewelry, when found, is most likely to be gold rather than silver. Few examples of the silver jewelry are shown on the next two pages.

The bulk of imported jewelry from Switzerland consisted of pocket and wrist watches and to a lesser extent fine jewelry in gold with gemstones. A limited amount of silver jewelry is occasionally encountered in the market with ladies' silver watch pins and jewelry made by firms such as Bucherer, among the most prominent names. The company was founded by Carl-Friedrick Bucherer in 1888 which expanded into a group of companies in the watch, clock, and jewelry industries in Lucerne, Switzerland. The firm is currently led by the third generation Bucherer, Jorg Bucherer. The products are distributed through Bucherer retail stores in Switzerland, Berlin, and Vienna, and through select authorized stores in other parts of the world. Over the years Bucherer has manufactured many watch pins and necklaces with innovative designs, some executed in sterling silver. The watches are normally marked Bucherer while the jewelry is ordinarily marked with the company initials: C.B. The Bucherer trademark was registered with the U.S. Patent and Trademark Office in July 1965.

Portugal

The most common Portuguese national silver standard mark consisting of a bird's head within various shapes of cartouches used circa 1886 to 1938. The number indicated the silver fineness: I for 916 and II for 833.

The more common mark with "Sterling" and "Portugal" in addition to the manufacturer's mark found on Portuguese silver jewelry produced circa the 1960s.

The Portuguese national standard silver mark found on silver jewelry and used since 1938. The Portuguese silver jewelry made before circa 1970 frequently has several marks in addition to the silver standard mark, but these are exceptionally minute punch marks which are not fully legible and often escape detection.

France

Number of marks were used on the French silver. The most common twentieth century marks on silver jewelry are the crab and boar's head marks, standing for 900 and 800 fineness.

Switzerland

The Swiss duck mark in an octagon signifying sterling quality and found mostly on silver watches and accessories. Also in a hexagon frame found on silver jewelry. Used since 1935.

The Swiss grouse mark indicating 800 fineness and used within various cartouches since the 1880s.

Turn of century Portuguese filigree bracelet. Portuguese national standard mark and 935; illegible maker's mark. $40.00 – 60.00.

Silver money clip with an 1899 silver coin. Portuguese national standard mark and 935, two additional illegible marks, and W.A. SARMENTO. $60.00 – 85.00.

Outstanding sterling repousse bracelet, marked with the national standard mark, 935, and the maker's mark Safir. $200.00 – 275.00.

Lacy vermeil brooch with enameled central flower, marked MADE IN PORTUGAL and DAVID. $35.00 – 50.00.

Three vermeil floral pins, all marked STERLING PORTUGAL, and with the maker's mark, superimposed "VG." $20.00 – 25.00 each.

Two sterling enameled pins of women in traditional Portuguese dress, both marked 925 PORTUGAL TOPAZIO. Large pin, $40.00 – 60.00; small pin, $35.00 – 45.00.

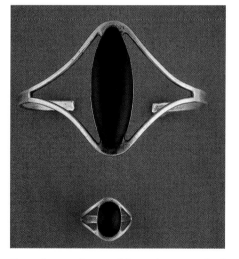

Bracelet and matching ring, marked Sterling Spain. Bracelet, $40.00 – 65.00; ring, $20.00 – 30.00.

Heavy solid modern bracelet with tiger's eye, marked SPAIN and S'PALIU. $175.00 – 250.00.

Large saddle ring with a semi-polished agate stone, marked SPAIN and S'PALIU. $125.00 – 165.00.

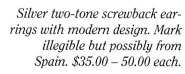

Silver two-tone screwback earrings with modern design. Mark illegible but possibly from Spain. $35.00 – 50.00 each.

Round textured concave pendant featuring an applied bull. Marked "935" and an illegible maker's mark. $35.00 – 50.00.

1940s French enamel souvenir bracelet. $40.00 – 60.00.

Abstract 1960s pin, marked with the French silver standard mark. $250.00 – 350.00. John Christopher collection.

Vermeil cicada pin. French hallmark and GUIRAND. $200.00 – 300.00. The earrings are in gold by the same maker. Robin Allison collection.

Swiss lady's gold plated sterling silver pin watch. Marked Pronto. $40.00 – 60.00.

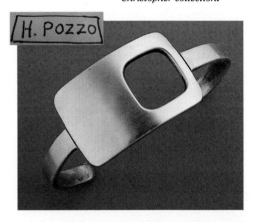

French modernist sterling cuff bracelet marked with French standard silver mark and 925 MADE IN FRANCE and H. POZZO. $95.00 – 145.00. John Christopher collection.

Victorian French snake bracelet. $350.00 – 500.00.

Bucherer round sterling marcasite pin set with cultured pearls, and sterling silver marcasite screwback earrings, marked "C.B." $40.00 – 65.00 each.

Bucherer sterling silver marcasite and chrysoprase clip earrings. Marked "C.B." $75.00 – 100.00.

Bucherer sterling silver marcasite watch pin. Watch marked Bucherer and with the Swiss National Standard mark. Pin section marked "C.B." $200.00 – 300.00.

Persian Silver Jewelry

Middle Eastern silver jewelry can be classified into three broad categories: modern with the classic look of fine jewelry, many indistinguishable from their counterparts made in Europe unless closely inspected; traditional silver jewelry with motifs and designs derived from the region's rich history; and tribal jewelry which reflects the centuries-old motifs and techniques, often peculiar to a particular tribal group, but not easily discerned by the average collector. The first two categories are usually the product of urban silversmiths, while the tribal jewelry is usually manufactured in the rural areas and provinces by either settled or nomadic silversmiths. The Central Asian and Afghan jewelry in many ways falls within these same broad categories, though the jewelry show much greater similarity and affinity with the Persian and Turkish silver jewelry.

Since the regions covered in this chapter are comprised of over 20 countries, detailed background information on each country along with a sample of its jewelry is beyond the scope of one chapter or even a full volume, but by way of example, relatively more space is devoted to the Persian and Turkish jewelry, including a select list of Persian and Turkish gold and silversmiths' names and marks, many of which to the author's best knowledge are being published for the first time. However, it should be noted that much of what follows in describing the Persian silver jewelry, particularly tribal jewelry, motifs, and techniques, applies to Afghan and Central Asian jewelry, and perhaps to a lesser extent to other Middle Eastern and Persian Gulf jewelry.

As in many parts of the Middle East, the Persian silver jewelry dates back to ancient times with archaeological finds estimated to be over 4,000 years old. But the bulk of ancient gold and silver jewelry was produced during the Achaemenid (Hakhamanesh, 559 – 330 B.C.), Parthian (Ashkanian, 247 B.C. – 224 A.D.), and Sassanid (Sassanian, 224 – 651 A.D.) dynasties, and many of the techniques currently used were first developed during those periods. These ancient gold and silver objects, including jewelry, preserved in various museums indicate a well-developed metalwork tradition and skilled craftsmanship highlighted by the frequent use of various real or mythical animals and birds as part of the motifs. The figural motifs and terminals later came to influence jewelry forms and designs in Europe among which Celtic jewelry is one of the examples. Also popular were the naturalistic motifs among which the Sassanid silver plates and vessels with hunting scenes were the most prominent.

The Persian arts experienced a serious decline after the Arab invasion of Iran in the seventh century, but within a few centuries there was a widespread recovery in many fields, including metalwork which incorporated the ancient legacy (animal heads and figures, plants, natural motifs, and geometric forms) with the Islamic influences that culminated in the development of a distinctly Persian style which continued to exert worldwide influences in various fields up to the late nineteenth century. The development of Persian arts and literature is best manifested in the emergence of new schools of miniature paintings in the eleventh century which embellished a large volume of manuscripts and books of poetry and literature written at the time. Hunting and polo scenes and natural themes which were favored during the Sassanid dynasty are among the recurring themes of Persian miniature paintings. These developments along with the ancient motifs of the Achaemenid and Parthian jewelry helped to establish a lasting tradition in jewelry designs and motifs which have served as a source of inspiration for both urban and tribal Persian jewelry in modern times.

Among these are Persian jewelry with miniature paintings which depict many traditional themes, filigree and granulated jewelry, enamel and niello or fretwork, and tribal jewelry. The miniature paintings are usually on small ivory, bone or mother-of-pearl panels, which are drawn under a magnifying glass using a single hair brush. The panels are then put in silver frame cases, creating bracelets and pendants. The quality varies and those which were made before WWII exhibit exceptional craftsmanship. Some of the pieces may be signed by both the silversmith and the artist. Readers should also note that somewhat similar miniature paintings were also made by the Ottomans and in the Mogul style in colonial India, pieces which are also highly collectible. The latter are usually in gold rather than silver.

The major silver smithing centers in Iran were Zanjan, Tabriz, Ispahan, Shiraz, and

Tehran. Ispahan, the previous seat of the government from 1599 to 1722, was the major source of miniature jewelry followed by Tehran, the subsequent and current capital city. Today Ispahan is still the largest center of silver jewelry manufacturing which is primarily handcrafted. Over the years, Tehran has attracted a large number of gold and silversmiths from various parts of the country, especially Zanjan and Ispahan, and is now itself a major center for silver jewelry and hollowware production. Zanjan and Tabriz are located in the northwest and historically served as a major source of Persian metalware, including the highly collectible Persian swords, armor, and utilitarian wares. Shiraz, located in the southern part of the country, was long a source of chased and embossed silver vases and vessels, some several feet tall weighing many pounds, with historic and naturalistic motifs and also a major outlet for tribal silver jewelry made along the Persian Gulf coast. However, the production of silver products has declined significantly in Shiraz. The majority of the collectible silver jewelry found in the U.S. market originates from Tehran and Ispahan, while the tribal jewelry is primarily from the provinces of Khurasan (Turkoman) and Kurdistan (Kurdish).

It is not clear when Persian jewelry began being imported into the U.S., but sufficient pieces found in the collectible market are of late nineteenth to early twentieth century vintage, leading the author to suspect the early Armenian and Persian Jewish rug merchants as the earliest conduits since historical records indicate well-established export enterprises in the Persian cities of Ispahan and Tabriz with heavy Armenian involvement and organized export of Persian textile and other merchandise to Europe and later to America. The Armenians, known historically for their metalwork, were a major influence on the Persian silver production originating in Ispahan and Tabriz which were home to the largest Armenian communities, and also on the American jewelry designs with a long list of accomplished American gold and silversmiths claiming Armenian descent. They still account for a significant portion of renowned Persian silversmiths creating outstanding decorative silver pieces which unfortunately are not jewelry.

Although Persian silver vessels and decorative products of the highest quality and massive weights and sizes were imported into the U.S., the quality of the imported silver jewelry was quite inferior and appears to have been manufactured under contract, often lacking the special features and artistic touch and individuality of the Persian craftsmen normally found on their handmade silver jewelry. This is also evident in the fact that most large silver pieces are marked, a practice reserved only for quality products, while the majority of the jewelry is unmarked.

The list that follows includes some of the prominent Persian silversmiths with a copy or transliteration of their marks. Unfortunately, the author was able to contact only a few living individuals and although their jewelry and particularly decorative silver products are found in the U.S. market, the information on them is quite sparse. The nineteenth and very early twentieth century marks usually begin with the Persian word, "amal," meaning "made by" or "work of," followed by the maker's name, a practice of marking that dates back to the Middle Ages and is also found in other parts of Middle East and Central Asia, but seldom after WWII. Another term, Tejarati (commercial), was frequently used on products which were made for export and can be found on silver jewelry dating back to the early twentieth century, gradually declining in use by the 1940s.

Persian Silversmiths

Edik Nazarians (b. 1926)

Born in Baku, Azarbaijan, then a Soviet Republic, Nazarians emigrated to Iran in 1938 and apprenticed at the age of 12 in the city of Maku in the Tabriz district. Later moving to Tabriz, Nazarians founded the "Vige" silver workshop in partnership with Gargin Nazarian, manufacturing silver decorative arts and giftware. Relocated to Tehran around 1986, Nazarians owns and operates the "Vige Nazarians" shop which is still in business as of this writing. He has works in Persian, Armenian, and Russian museum collections. The mark above was used by Nazarians. The "VIGE" ("Special") marks are the earliest marks used in the Tabriz district. The other two marks, consisting of his name written in Armenian script, were used later while he was working in the Tehran district.

Vahab

Active circa mid to late nineteenth century in Tehran. Mark is seldom fully legible. Reads "Amal (work of) Vahab."

Ostad Vahab

Active circa 1950s to 1970s. Primarily carved and chased decorative arts.

Mohammad Hassan

Active circa late nineteenth century. Mark reads "Amal (work of) Mohammad Hassan."

Abdol Hassan

Active 1920s – 1950s in Ispahan. Shown here is his mark above the Tejarati (commercial) mark. Found on enameled sil- ver jewelry made in the Ispahan district circa 1920s – 1950s.

Avodis Hakopian (b. 1934)

Active in Tabriz and later Tehran. Primarily carved silver decorative arts with many pieces in museums and private collections. Only the best pieces are marked and the earliest pieces are in Armenian initials. The mark shown at far right has the upside-down "84" mark.

Parvaresh

Family of silversmiths in Ispahan dating back to the mid nineteenth century. The workshop was founded by Jafar Sadegh Parvaresh, manufacturing utilitarian and decorative silver objects and passed on to his descendants who still operate workshops in Ispahan and Tehran.

Reza

Active circa late 1920s to late 1950s in Ispahan. Manufacturer of miniature enamel jewelry primarily for the export market. Most pieces are marked with his name and the word "commercial" as shown here.

Ardokhanian

A family of silversmiths dating back to the nineteenth century with a well-established workshop in Tehran since at least the 1930s and manufacturers of silver products and decorative arts with apparently a sizeable volume of exports to the U.S. A signifi- cant portion of marked twentieth century Persian silver found in the U.S. collectible market carries the firm's mark and commands high prices when correctly identified.

Mahapak Irandoost (b. 1920)

Active 1940s – 1970s in Tabriz.

Javad Vafadar (1922 – 1993)

Primarily silver decorative arts in Ispahan. His son, Jafar, has workshops both in Ispahan and Tehran.

Robert Tarodian

Contemporary silversmith in Tehran.

Sob'he

Family of gold and silversmiths in the city of Ahavaz on the Persian Gulf known for their niello work on silver, a type of jewelry which gradually diminished after WWII and is no longer being made. The earliest pieces are marked with the name, but post-war pieces are marked with the image of a bridge, caravan or palm trees.

Gregory (b. 1924)

Active circa late 1940s – 1970s, thereafter in Armenia.

Serges (1892 – 1974)

Active circa late 1920s – 1960s.

Agassi (1909 – 1969)

Active circa 1940s – 1960s.

G. P. Van

Active nineteenth century with one of the largest workshops in Tabriz, employing over 70 people. Many later silversmiths from this area apprenticed at Van's workshop.

Mozafarian

A family of gold and silversmiths dating back to nineteenth century with the master goldsmith Mohammad Mozafarian Javaheri. A major silver workshop was established by Morteza Mozafarian in Ispahan circa late 1930s later relocating to Tehran. The firm also became a major exporter of Persian turquoise and is still a notable manufacturer with several retail outlets.

Amir Sa'ei (b. 1945)

Beginning his apprenticeship at a young age in Ispahan, Amir Sa'ei established his own workshop manufacturing hand-crafted silver decorative arts, giftware, and accessories featuring open fretwork. Works in Persian, German, and other European museum collections. The mark shown here is found on silver decorative arts and gift ware. The oldest pieces are marked with his name in Persian.

Partially legible mark, possibly Iraj Darabi, along with "84" fineness, found on silver products and accessories, early twentieth century.

Mark of an unidentified Persian silversmith found on a variety of silver products in the U.S. antique market, early twentieth century.

Ottoman/Turkish Silver Jewelry

Ottoman and Turkish silver jewelry exhibits Byzantine, Persian, and Central Asian influences, and during the zenith of the Ottoman empire in the sixteenth and seventeenth centuries, magnificent pieces were produced to satisfy the appetite of the Turkish aristocracy; pieces preserved in the museums or captured in images and drawings of the period reflect outstanding craftsmanship and superior designs.

Unlike Turkish textiles, little Ottoman jewelry was imported into the U.S. and antique pieces are seldom encountered in the collectible market. Some of those that are found were perhaps brought in by Balkan and East European immigrants. These, among which are many medals, often carry the Imperial Tughra (see page 165) silver mark. For several centuries, the Tughra and Farman (the Imperial Seal) were the symbols of the Ottoman sultans' rule over their domains, and although they may all appear similar, each is a distinct calligraphic rendition of the reigning sultan's name and mark. Each mark, unless a forgery, actually dates the jewelry. The use of the Tughra ceased after the reign of the last Ottoman sultan, coinciding with the Ottoman defeat in WWI and the founding of modern Turkey under the leadership of Ataturk. Hence, any piece that carries the Tughra mark cannot be later than the early twentieth century.

The post-WWII Turkish silver jewelry pieces are much easier to find, and it appears that after the 1960s, a much larger volume was systematically imported. Prominent among these are the mesh or filigree type of silver jewelry or other pieces set with semi-precious stones. The latter, now mass manufactured frequently with European designs, constitutes the bulk of currently imported Turkish jewelry.

Following are some of the prominent nineteenth and early twentieth century Turkish silversmiths with their marks.

Ottoman/Turkish Silversmiths

Ahmad

Early nineteenth century silversmith. Mark reads "Amal (work of) Ahmad."

Avedis

Early twentieth century silversmith. Mark is found on silver accessories made in the Erzincan district, circa early twentieth century.

Missag Torosyan

The Missag marks is found on works by this Armenian silversmith working in the city of Izmid in the early twentieth century. The modern Turkish transliteration is Misak.

Zayghran

Early twentieth century silversmith.

Karim

Early twentieth century silversmith.

Ghazarusyan

Silversmith working circa mid nineteenth century, possibly early twentieth century.

Ghaghon

Mid nineteenth century silversmith whose mark is found along with the Ottoman Tughra on silver jewelry and accessories.

Kushian Akhavan

The mark of Akhavan is found on nineteenth century hollowware and accessories, made possibly in Damascus.

Unidentified Marks

 The *"N.S. 900"* found on silver jewelry and accessories, possibly made in Damascus.

 The *"Nu-Nu 900"* mark, possibly that of a Turkish silversmith, found on silver jewelry circa 1930 – 1940s.

Tribal, Nomadic, and Central Asian Silver Jewelry

As with Oriental rugs, there is a great variation in the tribal jewelry, and these subtle differences are not always apparent to the average collector. In general, the tribal jewelry of Iran, Turkey, and central Asia consists mainly of flat, geometrical pieces displaying various techniques such as filigree and fretwork, or with surfaces punched, chased, engraved, and embossed with various geometric and floral designs, frequently enhanced by many dangling silver pieces in the form of balls, fish, circles, hearts, and other shapes. Actual silver coins may be used as in the Kurdish jewelry of Iran, Iraq, and Turkey. Often the jewelry is set with semi-precious stones such as carnelian (or blown glass), turquoise, and lapis lazuli. The jewelry contains a lower silver content (coin silver) of about 60 to 80 percent.

A tremendous amount of silver jewelry is worn, particularly on special occasions, by the younger married nomadic women such as the Turkoman of northeastern Iran and central Asia.

These include headbands; cap crowns, some with chain veil; various hair ornaments, including elaborate beads for braids (four vs. two strands of braids distinguishes a maiden from a married woman); talisman pendants or boxes; exceptionally wide cuff bracelets and rings, necklaces, and earrings. The same is true of the Kurdish women of Iran and Turkey with elaborate gilded silver head pieces consisting of granulated and filigree crescents and discs supplemented by dozens of coins and dangles.

Since many methods employed are traditional techniques using material employed over

163

many centuries, the dating of the nomadic jewelry of Iran, Turkey, and the Central Asian countries is rather difficult. Though there are some signed and dated pieces, the jewelry is seldom marked, not even for the silver content. While Afghan and Persian tribal jewelry could always be found in the collectible market, particularly offered for sale by dealers in antiquities, the bulk of tribal jewelry made in central Asia, both old and new, began to appear in the market after the dissolution of the Soviet Union, and the establishment of the new republics of Turkmanistan, Uzbekistan, Kazakhstan, and Tajikistan. Moreover, the tribal and ethnic jewelry of this region has received special attention and was featured in several publications, such as the superb and informative article by Kate Fitz Gibbon on Turkoman jewelry in the Spring 1999 issue of *Ornament*.

There is a striking similarity in the appearance of the tribal jewelry originating from various parts of Turkey, Iran, Afghanistan, and Central Asia. This is largely due to the shared historic, cultural, and inter-cultural heritage of the people which populate these areas, primarily descendants of the ancient Indo-Iranian and Turkic speaking groups which at one time or another roamed the Central Asian steppes with some branches migrating south and to the southwest. While some of the Indo-Iranian speaking branches, such as the Sythians, Sarmatians, and Alans, pressured by the Turkic tribes and Huns, migrated toward Eastern and central Europe, several branches had already moved south and southwest circa 2000 BC and later founded the Persian Empire. Centuries later, the Turkic speaking tribes followed suit and founded the Saljuk dynasty in Iran; other branches found their way to Anatolia and Europe, establishing the Ottoman Empire. These deep-rooted intercultural ties were reinforced by a common religion, Islam, prevalent throughout the region.

Israeli and Palestinian Silver Jewelry

Another type of Middle Eastern jewelry found in much larger volume is from the Jerusalem region which has been a source of conflict since ancient times and was occupied by the Ottomans for a long time before being ceded to the British after WWI, later carved by them as part of Jordan, and finally lost to Israel in the 1967 war. As an historic center of the world's three major religions, the area was always a source of supply of holy relics, and from the time of the Crusaders, there has been a steady flow of such articles to Europe, brought back by the Christian pilgrims or directly imported. Among these are a large volume of silver crosses and other religious relics which are usually offered for sale by dealers in antiquities and often referred to as the Holy Land Relics. An overwhelming majority of such jewelry is unmarked and despite the claims by many dealers of antiquities and ethnographic galleries, is of nineteenth and early twentieth century vintage. Also from the same region is silver jewelry, often filigree set with semi-precious stones, which is marked "Jerusalem," but some post-WWII pieces may also bear the mark "Israel" or "Jordan." However, if a piece is marked only Jerusalem, it is not necessarily of pre-WWII vintage. Some pieces may be marked "Palestine," and these could also be of pre- or post-WWII period. In addition to this type of jewelry, there are also other types of silver jewelry made in Israel reflecting a broad spectrum of quality and designs, some modern and post modern, that would enhance any collection. Among well-known Israeli silversmiths and designers during the past few decades are Avi Soffer, Hanna Bechar-Paneth, Malka Cohavi, V. Kaminski, and Rachel Shraiber. The modern and highly accomplished silver pieces by Avi Soffer, a few examples of which are shown in this chapter, are finding an expanding circle of devoted collectors in America. In general, all modern silver jewelry by renowned Israeli silversmiths which can be purchased at reasonable prices is expected to rise in price.

Related to religious jewelry are the talismans which are manufactured throughout the Middle East and Central Asia. These are usually in flat, geometric forms or in the shape of the palm of a hand, fish or fowl, with Hebrew, Arabic, or Persian inscriptions that are supposed to ward off evil. They are sewn into garments, such as in the sleeves, or worn as a pendant. Most of the inscriptions contain biblical or Islamic phrases or the secret wishes of the owner. The latter, since it is to be kept secret and unknown to others, may be expressed in a numerical code, utilizing an ancient numerical code system known as the Abjad. Corollary to these are prayer or talisman silver boxes which are worn independently or incorporated as part of a more elaborate necklace and contain rolls of paper with similar inscriptions.

Much of the religious and tribal jewelry discussed above can be found at U.S. collectible jewelry and antique shows and markets, but such pieces were often supplied by the dealers in ethnic jewelry or antiquities; with the advent of online marketing and auctions, they are now being offered in relative abundance from a variety of sources.

Identification and Dating of Middle Eastern and Central Asian Jewelry

Prominent Arab, Persian, and Turkish silversmiths usually signed and dated their products, sometimes including the name of the client who had ordered the piece — a practice dating back to the Middle Ages. But this practice was seldom extended to the marking of silver jewelry. In fact, much of the Middle Eastern jewelry is not marked at all, particularly those pieces which are of lower silver fineness. When marked, they may be in either romanized, Arabic or Persian script. Minimal familiarity with these characters and numbers will enable readers to determine at least the silver fineness and the country or region where the jewelry was manufactured. It should also be noted that the marks are not necessarily in conventional locations found on U.S.-made jewelry. As in some European countries, they are most likely to be found on the O rings of bracelets and pendants, rims of the jewelry or its parts, and both inner and outer ring shanks. Sometimes the mark may be on the face of the piece itself or incorporated as part of the design. Once the mark is found, it is important to be able to read the numbers which indicate the fineness and the date, and some basic familiarity with the standard silver marks may also help to identify the country of origin. Few master smiths signed their jewelry, but reading the manufacturer's marks, if not in English, requires familiarity with both Arabic and Persian, while modern Turkish pieces are in romanized Turkish; familiarity with the transliteration of a few letters would enable the dealer/collector to read the name. Brief descriptions of the marks and some of the manufacturers' marks, particularly the Persian and Turkish marks, are provided in relevant sections of this chapter.

Numbers

Learning the numbers on Middle Eastern silver jewelry is quite easy since the convention and positioning of figures are similar and basic familiarity with only the first ten numbers, 0 through 9, is sufficient to read multiple digit figures. Below is a list of equivalents:

1	2	3	4	5	6	7	8	9	0
١	٢	٣	٤	٥	٦	٧	٨	٩	٠

The standard silver fineness figures are usually expressed in two digits.

$$٦٠ = 60 \qquad ٨٤ = 84$$
$$٨٠ = 80 \qquad ٩٠ = 90$$

The same method can be used to read the dates in cases where numbers instead of letters are used to date a piece of jewelry. For example, ١٣٤٥ = 1345, however, the dates are based on the Islamic calendar and these figures have to be converted in order to determine the actual date in our calendar. Two such calendars are used and these with their approximate equivalents are given below, but a rough method of converting these dates is to simply add 582 to the Arabic and 621 to the Persian figure in order to find its equivalent in our calendar. It should also be noted that pre-WWII figures found on the Persian pieces most likely adhere to the Arabic calendar.

Arabic		USA		Persian
١٣٠٨	=	1890	=	
١٣١٨	=	1900	=	
١٣٢٨	=	1910	=	
١٣٣٩	=	1920	=	
١٣٤٩	=	1930	=	١٣٠٩
١٣٥٩	=	1940	=	١٣١٩
١٣٦٩	=	1950	=	١٣٢٩
١٣٨٠	=	1960	=	١٣٣٩
١٣٩٠	=	1970	=	١٣٤٩

National Silver Standards and Symbols

The national silver standards given below are primarily twentieth century silver marks used in various Middle Eastern countries. These may be accompanied by other marks or writings such as the silver fineness. Only rough sketches of the major marks without the details are provided, but readers should be able to easily recognize them in case they appear on the jewelry they own.

Ottoman

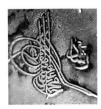

The common Ottoman Tughra (Tuğra) or the sultan's seal found on gold and silver Ottoman products including jewelry. Each Tughra is the calligraphic rendition of the reigning sultan's name, difficult to decipher, particularly when the punch mark is not complete. This mark, also found on silver coins, included the sultan's name, Reshad, or Mehmed V (1844 – 1918) whose reign was during the 1909 – 1918 period. For over four centuries, the official written language of the Ottoman court was Persian before the adoption of Latin characters in 1928. The Tughra mark is also found on silver manufactured in Ottoman-occupied territories, such as old Egyptian silver.

165

The "star and crescent" mark, introduced circa 1923, and found in various forms with a much smaller star within and outside the crescent, or the letters "T.C." within the crescent (circa 1939 – 1943). The fineness of either 800 or 900 may also appear on the body of the crescent. The mark with the word "SAH" within a circle was used during the 1930s.

Egypt

The oldest silver pieces are marked with the Ottoman Tughra (see page 165).

The Egyptian cat mark, used circa 1916 – 1946 along with the silver fineness marks.

The Egyptian palm tree mark, used after 1946 along with the silver fineness marks.

Various silver fineness marks: 60, 80, and 90. The silver fineness mark may be the only mark on Egyptian silver jewelry. The Arabic letter above each number identifies the assay office: Alexandria, Bani Suff, and Tanta respectively.

An 800 silver fineness mark with the Cairo assay mark found with or without other marks on Egyptian silver jewelry.

Persia

Persian "84" silver fineness which may be the only mark on the silver jewelry. For a brief period, beginning in 1967, a standard mark consisting of a lion's head holding a sword was adopted which was largely ignored and used *only by the licensed silversmiths. Some silver jewelry and products made circa early 1970s may also have the shah's crown mark which is quite rare and seldom encountered.*

Israel, Jerusalem, Palestine

"Jerusalem Israel" mark. The Israeli silver jewelry is usually marked "ISRAEL" or "Made in Israel." The "Jerusalem" mark by itself may predate the founding of Israel and is also found on the jewelry of a much later date. It is also seen with the "Jordan" mark.

Made in Palestine mark found on both pre- and post-WWII silver jewelry.

Morocco

Two examples of numerous nineteenth and twentieth century Moroccan marks with actual dates which in the Islamic or Christian calendars may be combined with the Arabic script. The approximate converted dates are 1902 and 1916.

Mark without a date used circa 1900.

Mark without a date used circa early 1920s.

Ram's head mark adopted in 1925.

Front profile of a vulture resting on a branch punched on imported Turkish silver jewelry.

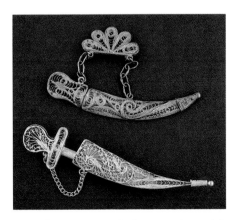

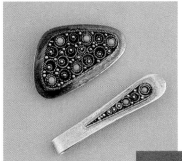

Silver and turquoise pin and a tie tack, both marked Handmade Jerusalem Israel. Pin, $25.00 – 35.00; tie tack, $20.00 – 25.00.

Two filigree curved dagger pins with small solid dagger insert. One marked Jerusalem. This type of jewelry was made throughout the Middle East as well as in Victorian Europe, but many pieces seen by the author are marked Jerusalem or Palestine. $30.00 – 45.00 each.

Silver hand pin set with polished quartz stone, frequently referred to as Fatima's hand with religious significance for Moslems, particularly, the Shi'a sect. $25.00 – 30.00.

Silver brooch featuring a cross, marked Jerusalem Silver 900. $40.00 – 60.00.

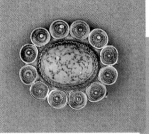

Silver pin with faux turquoise, marked made in Israel. $20.00 – 25.00.

Silver and carved mother-of-pearl pin, marked Jerusalem 950. $35.00 – 45.00.

Handcrafted silver necklace set with semi-precious stones. Marked Made in Israel Sterling Silver 935. $75.00 – 100.00.

Pair of silver cross earrings set with garnet, marked Jerusalem 900. $35.00 – 50.00.

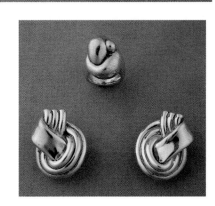

Bracelet, marked Israel Sterling Silver 925 and maker's mark in Hebrew. $40.00 – 50.00. Pin marked Israel 935. $30.00 – 40.00.

Silver dagger set with an amber stone. Dagger marked Sterling Made in Palestine. $30.00 – 40.00.

Israeli modern ring and matching earrings, marked 925. $45.00 – 65.00.

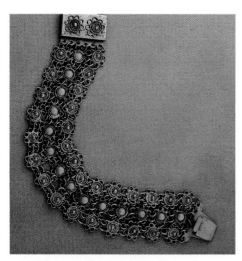

Modern ring set with semi-precious stones, marked Israel. $40.00 – 50.00.

Silver bracelet with ornamental Arabesque pattern. Egyptian silver standard mark. $50.00 – 75.00.

Gilded bracelet set with natural turquoise, marked Israel silver 925. $40.00 – 60.00.

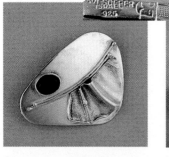

1920s Turkish bracelet. Turkish standard silver mark. $50.00 – 75.00.

Pin with textured and creased surface typical of Soffer silverwork. Marked Avi Soffer Israel. $125.00 – 175.00.

Marked Avi Soffer pin. $250.00 – 300.00. Photo courtesy of Pop Beads to Platinum.

Modern pin with abstract enameled motif, marked Israel 925. $40.00 – 60.00.

Two Egyptian pendants with ancient Egyptian pharaonic motifs. Egyptian silver standard mark. Smaller, newer piece with applied motifs on both sides, $30.00 – 40.00; larger pendant circa 1950s, $35.00 – 45.00. Asking prices vary drastically ranging from $15.00 to $75.00.

Saudi silver and garnet ring and matching earrings. $60.00 – 90.00.

Unmarked late nineteenth century Arab Bedouin silver cuff band. $125.00 – 175.00. Old silver bracelet turned into an ashtray in Lebanon circa 1950s. $40.00 – 50.00. Christine Kehely collection.

Filigree silver bracelet with applied historic Egyptian motifs. Egyptian silver standard mark. $35.00 – 50.00.

Arab hollow repousse Bedouin ankle bangle made throughout the Arab Middle East, depicting different motifs. This piece was made in Egypt with the Egyptian silver standard mark, $150.00 – 200.00. Old bangle was turned into an ashtray, a common practice for recycling damaged and dented pieces. $40.00 – 50.00. Christine Kehely collection.

Handcrafted silver necklace set with semi-precious stones, most likely of North African origin, possibly Morocco. $60.00 – 95.00.

Niello pendant from the Persian Gulf area, possibly an Ahvaz piece. $30.00 – 45.00.

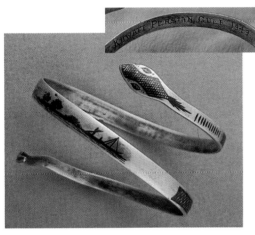

Coiled serpent arm band decorated in niello with shore landscape and Arab fishing boats, marked Kuwait Persian Gulf, 1949. $65.00 – 95.00.

Well-crafted leaf pin, marked Made in Palestine 800. $25.00 – 35.00.

Silver fibula from North Africa. $75.00 – 100.00. Photo courtesy of Dale Davis.

Silver pendant known as Fatima with religious significance particularly for the Shi'a branch of Moslems. North Africa, most likely Morocco. $100.00 – 150.00. Photo courtesy of Dale Davis.

Silver pendant, known as Khamsa, from North Africa, most likely Morocco. $125.00 – 160.00. Photo courtesy of Dale Davis.

Silver pendant, known as Khamsa, from North Africa, most likely Morocco. $150.00 – 200.00. Photo courtesy of Dale Davis.

Silver pendant, known as Tuareg, from North Africa, most likely Morocco. $100.00 – 150.00. Photo courtesy of Dale Davis.

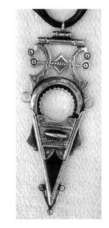

Silver pendant, known as Tuareg from North Africa, most likely Morocco. $100.00 – 150.00. Photo courtesy of Dale Davis.

169

Turkish bracelet featuring "Tunis" (Tunisia), flanked by crescents. Turkish hallmark, unidentified maker's mark, and Moroccan "vulture" import mark. $60.00 – 95.00.

Turkish bracelet with turn of century Ottoman coins and large moonstones. $60.00 – 90.00.

Silver pin with Arabic calligraphy and small Persian turquoise stones. The Arabic script reads "Mashallah" a common expression in Arabic, Turkish, and Persian, meaning "God Bless" and a good luck gesture as the biblical word "Mizpah" found on American and some European jewelry discussed in Chapter 2. Marked "NU-NU 900." $40.00 – 60.00.

Heavy nineteenth century handcrafted Ottoman wide cuff bracelet. Ottoman marks and Ghaghon. $250.00 – 300.00.

Turkish nomadic pendant with a central agate stone. $50.00 – 75.00.

Possibly Turkish pin with filigree work on flat base and set with ceramic stones. Marked Y.T. 900. $35.00 – 50.00.

Turkish round pin with fancy Arabic calligraphy, decorative turquoise, and filigree work. The script reads "Mashallah" (God bless). $45.00 – 60.00.

Large convex oval silver pendant with enamel paintings on both sides. Circa 1960s. $35.00 – 45.00.

Turkish silver necklace, bracelet, and earrings. $60.00 – 95.00.

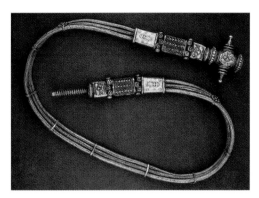

Persian silver belt with gilded decorative sections. Circa 18th – early 19th century. Faint engraved mark on the fastener section, possibly "Kharazm" or "Kharazmi" in Persian which was most likely the name of the owner rather than the maker. $500.00 – 750.00.

Persian silver jewelry box with the scene of the Persepolis ruins, made by Ardokhanian. Marked 84 and with Ardokhanian stamp. $250.00 – 350.00.

Small silver pillbox with Persian miniature painting of polo players, the ancient Persian sport. $40.00 – 65.00.

Persian bracelet with miniature paintings on mother-of-pearl inserts. Circa 1920 – 1930s. Stamped with the maker's mark Abdolhassan, and the word Tejarati (commercial). $100.00 – 125.00. Prices vary based on age and quality.

Persian pins with miniature paintings on ivory. Circa early 1900s. Frequently these were blocks from damaged jewelry made into pins and buttons. $15.00 – 25.00 each.

Persian bracelet with miniature paintings on mother-of-pearl inserts. Circa 1920s – 1930s. Stamped with the maker's mark Reza and the word Tejarati (commercial). $100.00 – 125.00.

Persian bracelet with miniature painting on ivory inserts. Circa 1940s – 1950s. $65.00 – 95.00. Low quality Persian bracelet with miniature paintings on bone. Circa 1950s. $30.00 – 45.00.

Persian silver necklace made of silver crescents displaying enamel floral and fowl paintings, enhanced by silver heart dangles. Circa early 1920s. $80.00 – 120.00.

Convex silver pendant with floral enamel paintings on both sides, $25.00 – 35.00; and enameled silver clip earrings, $15.00 – 20.00.

Persian pin with applied filigree work and a central silver dome with enamel painting of a floral motif. $30.00 – 40.00.

Small pendant and earrings set with miniature paintings on mother-of-pearl. $20.00 – 30.00.

Custom-made sweetheart niello pin with the U.S. Marine insignia sent to Violet by a GI named Tony. Also marked Iran and 1943. Purchased from a dealer who had bought it at an auction in New Mexico. $100.00 – 125.00.

Silver bracelet with niello work depicting Persian Gulf scenery motifs and IRAN, 1944. Despite declaring neutrality at the onset of WWII, Iran was occupied by the American, British, and Russian forces deposing the king, Reza Shah, and crowning his son who became a close American ally during the next several decades. Many of the sweetheart and other souvenir jewelry brought back by the American GIs were silver niello work made in the southern city of Ahvaz, depicting local and Persian Gulf scenery largely made by a family of silversmiths named Sob'he. Prices vary based on the subject and quality. $45.00 – 60.00.

Silver pendant with chained filigree work. $30.00 – 45.00.

Pendant with miniature paintings on mother-of-pearl depicting a dancing girl on one side and polo players on the other side. Circa 1940s. $40.00 – 50.00 Persian silver bracelet with enamel paintings on metal inserts. $30.00 – 40.00.

Silver niello depicting Persian Gulf scenery, with the name IRAQ, and 1945. Most likely made in the Iranian city of Ahvaz. $40.00 – 50.00.

Silver niello depicting Persian Gulf scenery, with the name IRAN and 1943. Maker's mark: Sob'he. $60.00 – 85.00.

Triangular pin with faux turquoise, marked Israel Jerusalem 925. $15.00 – 18.00. Undoubtedly Siamese motif on a pair of earrings, undoubtedly marked IRAN. $12.00 – 15.00.

Persian poison ring and matching earrings set with Persian turquoise. Marked Mozafarian and 84 in Persian. $40.00 – 60.00.

Persian nomadic necklace set with semi-precious stones. This type of jewelry was imported by the European countries as well as the U.S. The author once bought a piece in Copenhagen. Those seen in the U.S. market vary in age and quality. $50.00 – 85.00.

Persian silver necklace about 6" long in the center when worn. Earrings are not original and were shortened because of damage and missing parts. This type of jewelry was made in Turkey as well as in Europe. $150.00 – 200.00.

Silver necklace. Possibly Persian. $45.00 – 65.00.

Persian nomadic silver necklace. $40.00 – 65.00.

Silver necklace set with lapis lazuli. This type of jewelry was made in northwest Iran, Afghanistan, and Central Asia. This piece has the Persian 84 silver standard mark. $30.00 – 45.00.

Persian silver heart pendant with lapis stone. $20.00 – 25.00.

Three Persian men's rings set with polished carnelian. All marked "84" on the outer shank and one marked Mozafarian. $20.00 – 30.00 each.

Two Persian rings, both marked "84" in Persian. $18.00 – 22.00.

Pair of silver Persian earrings. $18.00 – 25.00.

Handcrafted Persian silver cigarette case. $200.00 – 250.00. Photo courtesy of Saman Shams.

Early 18th century Persian silver bangle. $250.00 – 350.00. Photo courtesy of Shamsi Shamlou.

Persian silver necklace, matching bracelet and earrings. $50.00 – 70.00. Pair of round earrings made in similar fashion. $10.00 – 12.00.

Central Asian necklace made of silver set with lapis lazuli and malachite. Most likely from Turkomanstan or Kazakhstan. $60.00 – 90.00.

Afghan or Turkoman silver necklace set with lapis lazuli. $40.00 – 65.00.

Central Asian cuff bracelet with three finger rings. This type of jewelry is frequently made in gold. $85.00 – 135.00.

Central Asian or Afghan necklace with a central prayer box set with lapis lazuli. $65.00 – 95.00.

Turkoman or Kazak necklace set with lapis lazuli. $50.00 – 75.00. Pair of silver earrings. $12.00 – 18.00.

Central Asian pendant with prayer box. $50.00 – 80.00.

Central Asian cuff bracelet with three finger rings. The rings may have been added later and the pattern does not match the cuff bracelet which shows Transcaucasian and Russian influence. $85.00 – 135.00.

Central Asian cuff bracelet set with lapis lazuli. $60.00 – 85.00.

Two Central Asian pendants with triangular prayer boxes. $35.00 – 50.00 each.

Afghan style wide cuff bracelet, made by Afghan refugees. $40.00 – 65.00.

Turkoman or Kazak wide cuff bracelet with gilded section. $75.00 – 100.00.

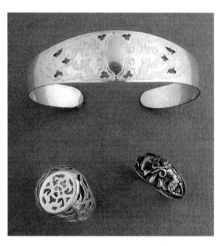

Kazak or Russian silver cuff bracelet and two silver rings, all marked with the Soviet national silver mark. Bracelet, $30.00 – 45.00; rings, $20.00 – 35.00.

Siamese Silver Jewelry

One type of silver jewelry that collectors frequently encounter at antiques shops and shows is Siamese silver jewelry. Siam (presently Thailand), the enchanted land depicted in the fantasy movie *The King and I*, has a long tradition of fine metal and silver works. In fact, according to several renowned archaeologists, based on finds in an ancient village in Ban Chiang which happened to include bronze bracelets, the Bronze Age may have originated in Thailand rather than Mesopotamia as previously thought. Although this conclusion has been disputed by many, there is no doubt of a very early civilization in Thailand and a long tradition in metalwork, including silver jewelry, dating back to ancient times.

Siamese silver jewelry found today in the collectible market provides a contrast of colors between the black field and highlighted silver design. This contrast of polished silver against a black field, accentuated by the figural design of a Thai woman dancer in traditional costume, gives Siamese silver jewelry its unique and distinctive look.

The popular technical term for this type of jewelry is niello, in Latin *nigellum*, derived from *niger*, meaning black, and possibly borrowed from Spanish by the English speaking Americans. The technology dates back several thousand years and was used by the Egyptians, Persians, Greeks, Celts, Romans, and Byzantines, as well as the Transcaucasian tribes. The first reference to the technology is made by Pliny where he briefly mentions a method used by the Egyptians to blacken silver. But until the Middle Ages, both the technology and compound used were different than modern times, involving primarily engraved channels filled with inlay work. During the Renaissance, the Italians perfected the method and the famous sixteenth century Italian goldsmith, Benvenuto Cellini, wrote a treatise on the preparation of the niello compound and the method of its application to silver. Many of the Italian religious and church ornaments of the period were niello metalwork and the improved technology spread to other parts of Europe and throughout the world.

The Siamese niello is a metallic sulphide compound traditionally prepared in a formula of one part fine silver, five parts each copper and lead, and sulphur. The compound, which melts at a temperature several hundred degrees below that of silver, is brought to a melting point, filling all the channels and cavities of the designed silver base. The result is a permanent fusion of the niello and the silver base. Once polished, the reflective contrast of black and silver colors highlight the design. The amount of sulphur added at the time of melting determines the shade of the black color. Low levels of sulphur create a dark gray tone while high levels of application render a deep and dark black shade.

Today, Bangkok is the center of production with many workshops producing Siamese silver jewelry for the export market. The jewelry found in the U.S. market could date back to the pre-WWII era, but most black pieces were imported in the 1940s and 1950s. There are some variations, with fields other than black, or translucent enamel designs, primarily blue, but these are of a later date. Bracelets, earrings, and cuff links abound, but very large bangles and arm bands are rare.

Readers should note that not all collectible niello jewelry is made in Thailand, nor is it all executed in silver. Several other types of collectible jewelry using somewhat similar technology are also found in the market, among which Toledo jewelry from Spain and Japanese damascene jewelry are common, while the antique European pieces are quite rare. But the Siamese silver jewelry can be easily identified by its unique ethnic motifs, aside from technical differences and/or different metal base, and cannot be mistaken with other jewelry.

Siam silver jewelry is usually marked Siam; Siam Silver; or Siam 925. Bracelets are normally marked on the back of the clasp while necklaces and earrings are frequently marked on the back of the piece rather than on the findings such as chain, clips or screws. There is a noticeable variation in the asking prices, even when it is sold by experienced dealers in antique shops, malls, shows, and flea markets. Few of the pieces are marked with the manufacturer's mark; those known are identified in this chapter and shown along with the jewelry.

Several common marks found on imported Siamese and Thai silver jewelry.

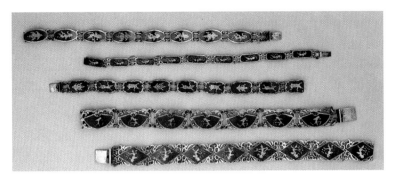

A group of Siam link bracelets. $35.00 – 50.00.

Three sets of matching pins and earrings, all marked SIAM STERLING. $45.00 – 65.00 set.

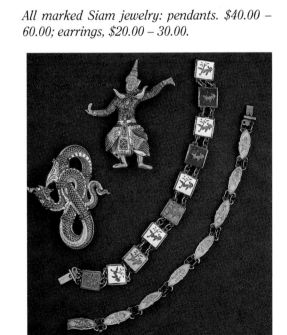

All marked Siam jewelry: pendants. $40.00 – 60.00; earrings, $20.00 – 30.00.

Multicolor bracelet, $30.00 – 45.00; gold enamel Siam bracelet, $30.00 – 40.00; two multicolor Siam pins, $40.00 – 65.00 each.

Marked SIAM jewelry: wide bracelet, $50.00 – 75, bracelet, $40.00 – 60.00; large square brooch, $30.00 – 45, and earrings, $30.00 – 40.00.

Large brooch with movable parts, $35.00 – 45.00; fan earrings, $18.00 – 22.00.

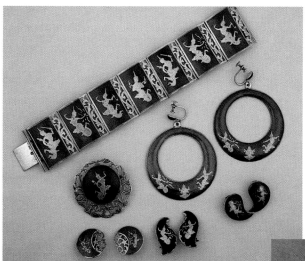

Men's Siam jewelry: Belt buckle, $30.00 – 45.00; two pairs of cuff links, $35.00 – 45.00; tie bars, $20.00 – 25.00.

Siam wide bracelet, $50.00 – 75.00; matching pin and earrings, $45.00 – 60.00; large earrings, $35.00 – 50.00; small earrings, $15.00 – 25.00.

Marked Siam wide bracelet. $60.00 – 90.00.

Marked SIAM, sterling cuff bracelet. $65.00 – 95.00.

Large Siam sweater guard, $85.00 – 125.00; sterling picture pin, $35.00 – 45.00; 1970s heavy sterling silver gold nugget bracelet, $35.00 – 50.00.

Rare large white enamel Siam necklace, marked AMFARCO, $100.00 – 140.00.

Bracelet, $35.00 – 50.00, earrings, $20.00 – 25.00; locket pendant, $50.00 – 65.00.

Siam blue field cuff links. $25.00 – 30.00.

Siam pendant and near matching earrings, $50.00 – 70.00; two bracelets, $35.00 – 50.00 each; earrings, $20.00 – 28.00.

Marked Siam jewelry: bangle bracelet, $40.00 – 55.00; large oval ring, $30.00 – 45.00; small ring, $20.00 – 30.00; two screwback earrings, $20.00 – 25.00.

Chinese and Japanese Silver Jewelry

Trade with the Far East, specifically China, dates back to the colonial period and the connoisseurs of Chinese export porcelain are aware of Martha Washington's elaborate set of Chinese dishes on which the visitors and dignitaries were served some of the first official American meals. During the first decades of the nineteenth century, trade with China increased, came to a near halt during the Civil War, and resumed again with full force during the last decades of the century.

Much of this trade did not involve silver products or jewelry, but silver certainly played an important role in influencing domestic monetary policy in order to take advantage of trade opportunities in the Far East. The event involved the minting of U.S. silver coins and though the subject is only marginally related to the import of silver jewelry, the readers may find it of interest since it involves the silver fineness of U.S. coins and how it affected trade with China.

With the expanding trade with China and Japan in the late nineteenth century, American businesses soon realized that the Spanish peso was preferred to the U.S. dollar in Far Eastern trade transactions. A petition by the California legislature to the Congress stressed that the Mexican 418 grain peso compared with the 412.5 grain U.S. dollar was diverting business and working against the U.S. trade interests. As the result a heavier commercial or trade dollar of 420 grains of 900 fine silver was struck in 1873. But this effort failed because even though the U.S. dollar was heavier, it contained less pure silver compared to the lighter Mexican peso of 960 fineness. This resulted in the flood of trade dollars in the domestic market and the excess supply of silver dollars led to its market value falling below the face value, usually accepted at 90 to 95 cents by the merchants. An 1887 act finally prohibited further minting and dropped the trade dollar as a legal tender.

Whether paid for by U.S. or Mexican silver, Chinese silver artifacts began to find their way to America, particularly the West Coast where there was an increasing concentration of Chinese immigrants. This trade approached much higher proportions during the 1880s – 1930s period and much of the antique jewelry found in the U.S. collectible market was imported during this period. Imports from China ceased after WWII due to the Chinese civil war and the establishment of Communist rule in 1949 and did not resume until after President Nixon's trip to China in 1973 and the gradual negotiations and normalization of trade relations which are still continuing.

Metalwork in China dates back to ancient times and elaborate large bronze pieces that reveal advanced artistic and metallurgical accomplishments. This is not surprising since the ancient Chinese were perhaps responsible for more inventions and innovations than the Greeks and Romans combined, a claim that is finding more credence thanks to the modern translations of Chinese historical texts and the laborious works of contemporary scholars such as Professor Needham. These talents and skills are also reflected in jewelry manufacture, much of which was executed in gold with a special preference for jade and frequently depicting Chinese folklore and traditional themes. The Chinese reverence for the past has carried this tradition unabated into present-day manufacturing of decorative arts where historic and traditional themes, both floral or figural, still dominate. However, the modern pieces made during at least the past hundred years are far inferior to the older pieces.

Filigree or solid pieces which are often stamped or engraved, combined with enameling, both champleve and cloisonne types, and carved semiprecious stones or organic materials, made into designs inspired by traditional themes best characterize Chinese silver jewelry. Jade, frequently carved, amethyst, turquoise, lapis, and agates are the favorite stones. Ivory and coral, also usually carved, amber, Peking glass, and a variety of beads make up the other preferred materials. Another common type of silver jewelry highlights the ivory or bone pieces decorated with miniature paintings, normally depicting traditional floral or figural motifs, some recalling the ancient folklore. Sometimes these paintings are combined with shallow carvings and engravings. The old, quality pieces were sometimes signed by the artist/carver. Frequently encountered are also solid silver pieces, cast, carved or engraved, showing some type of good fortune statement in Chinese characters or depicting traditional Chinese scenery.

Collectors should be warned that there is an abundance of reproductions of old Chinese pieces with paste jade and corals, plastic or composition ivory, amber, and turquoise. These are mounted on sterling silver or even gold bases. The plastic pieces can be discovered with a hot needle test in an inconspicuous place; the heat will not affect genuine stones and ivory. In the case of amber, the needle will penetrate and release a pine smell, but this method is not foolproof since resin/amber compositions may also pass this test. Also bone pieces should not be confused with ivory. Bone pieces have a different and rougher grain which can be easily distinguished under a magnifying glass, and some experience in handling both types will enable the collector/dealer to see the difference.

Japanese culture shunned the wearing of jewelry, particularly by men, and specifically elaborate and ornamental pieces. This tradition which is deeply rooted in the Japanese culture and probably stems from the Shinto religious/philosophical beliefs continues to this day in modern Japan, and the younger generation of Japanese teenagers receive ample advice from their traditional elders not to wear necklaces and bracelets or jewelry that displays flamboyance or calls for attention. This practice also applied to women with the exception of certain hair and dress ornaments or toiletry. The author's careful study of over 600 seventeenth and eighteenth century Japanese paintings and woodblock prints, many including the images of the nobility and courtesans, revealed near total lack of traditional jewelry and ornamentations such as finger rings, necklaces, bracelets, and earrings. Wearing of jewelry and accessories gradually became more acceptable after the Japanese efforts at modernization and especially after WWII, but this social and cultural transformation did not raise the place of jewelry in the society and fashion to the same level as in many other cultures, particularly for men.

For centuries, Japan was essentially a closed economy with an isolationist policy which restricted trade and contact with the rest of the world except a few Dutch and Chinese ships landing annually at the isolated port in Nagasaki. With Admiral Perry's visit to Japan and its subsequent opening of trade, the nation underwent major revolutionary changes. The Japanese cognizance of their economic, military, and technological inferiority relative to the Western powers ushered in a new era of modernization.

The Meiji Restoration of 1868 ended the power of the shogunate, and the subsequent changes transformed Japan in nearly all cultural fields. Although Japan had a long tradition of high quality metalwork, famed for its superb swords and sword furniture, the end of the age of shogunate and samurai, motivated a shift of emphasis in metalwork, from military hardware to decorative and utilitarian metal works. Some of the renowned families of swordsmiths and makers of sword furniture who were engaged in this profession for many generations turned increasingly to the manufacturing of utilitarian and decorative metal products. But because of lack of domestic demand, very little jewelry was manufactured, though this Japanese tradition of metalwork with uncluttered, free, simple designs, motivated many European gold and silversmiths, particularly the Scandinavian school.

One category of metal products, including jewelry, that was a result of this transition came to be known as the Komai Jewelry named after a Kyoto family of swordsmiths which successfully transferred the art of inlay (zooan) used in making sword furniture to metal vessels and jewelry. This type of jewelry with gold and silver inlays and its imitations which are known as damascene or Kyoto jewelry gradually became one of the Japanese exports to the Western world. A major manufacturer and exporter of this type of jewelry was Amita, which to the author's best knowledge is still in business.

Silver jewelry decorated with pearls was also made by Amita Corporation, jewelry of very high quality, normally with modern designs. But for a century, Mikimoto has been the king of pearls and pearl jewelry, some of which is mounted on silver. As with Ming jewelry made in Hawaii, Mikimoto silver jewelry has a devoted circle of collectors and is usually found in the higher price range. Old pieces are extremely rare. The jewelry is marked Mikimoto, but it is the author's unconfirmed understanding that some of the early pieces were not marked.

Within the Japanese society with the rapid adoption of Western attire, simple accessories such as cuffs, tie clips, belt buckles, watches and chains, cigarette cases, match boxes and lighters, and other similar objects found common use and were manufactured gilded using precious metals such as silver. In the case of women, simple pearl jewelry set on silver and gold, hair ornaments, and other accessories found favor. Some of this early twentieth century silver jewelry found its way to the U.S. and is occasionally encountered in the collectible market.

Although there was no strong domestic demand for jewelry in Japan, the country became a major exporter of costume jewelry after WWII. These, rarely in silver, were imitations of fashionable Western jewelry made particularly for the American taste and market. Some silver jewelry was also manufactured for the export market, while others, including sweetheart silver jewelry, was made to order, and then sent or brought back by American GIs and increasing numbers of American tourists.

As in Japanese decorative arts, uncluttered simplicity and harmony defines Japanese silver jewelry regardless of whether they are decorated with pearls and stones or carved and engraved. Nature and some traditional Japanese themes are the sources of inspiration. Unlike the costume jewelry of the same period, the silver jewelry is of exceptionally high quality, often of 950 fineness, exhibiting good craftsmanship and usually at least partly handmade.

Both Chinese and Japanese silver many be marked only "silver" along with the name of the country. The silver fineness varies with the Japanese pieces usually containing a higher silver content. Sterling, 925, or 950 marks are also found on the silver jewelry. The 950 silver mark was frequently used in Japan. Some of the jewelry may also carry the maker's mark.

Chinese enamel champleve brooch with an Oriental motif. Circa 1930s – 1950. $90.00 – 120.00.

Early twentieth century Chinese silver bracelet, set with ivory. $80.00 – 120.00.

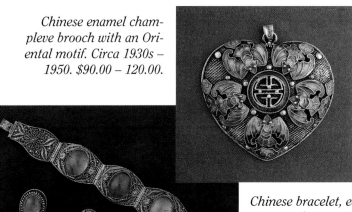

Chinese bracelet, earrings, and ring with lacy filigree motif and natural amethyst stones. $150.00 – 200.00.

Chinese brooch with miniature painting on ivory. $40.00 – 60.00.

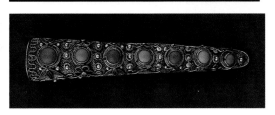

Chinese gilded filigree pin, set with turquoise and coral stones. Circa 1950. $90.00 – 120.00.

Marked sterling pin, with the maker's mark in nearly illegible Japanese characters which are most likely not Japanese. This piece may be of Western origin, but the mark does not match any of the known Western silversmiths which used Japanese characters as their trademark. Auction purchase price $35.00.

Large brooch set with carved colored stone, possibly colored soapstone. $45.00 – 65.00.

Set consisting of bracelet, pin, earrings, and finger ring in lacy filigree silverwork combined with hand painted ivory insets. Circa 1930s – 1950s. $200.00 – 300.00 Prices vary based on age and quality.

Enameled silver ring. $30.00 – 45.00.

Chinese cloisonne bracelet. $30.00 – 45.00.

Chinese brooch featuring carved cinnabar inset with typical Chinese floral motif. Circa 1920s – 1930s. $65.00 – 95.00.

Well-made vermeil Chinese floral pin, set with natural coral and turquoise stones. Circa 1930s. $50.00 – 75.00.

Handcrafted Oriental belt buckle. $30.00 – 45.00.

Chinese silver cinnabar ring, $35.00 – 50.00; Chinese silver and carved jade ring, $50.00 – 75.00.

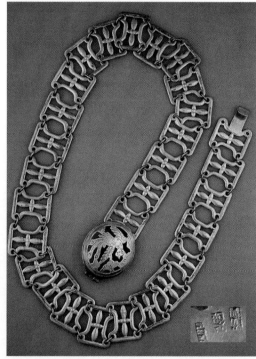

Marked Chinese silver belt. Maker's mark and several other marks. $125.00 – 175.00.

Hollow Chinese three-dimensional bull with a natural coral bead. $60.00 – 90.00.

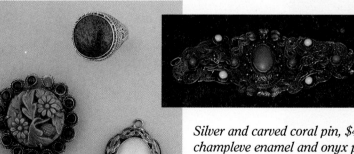

Chinese vermeil bracelet with turquoise and coral stones. $200.00 – 300.00. *Robin Allison collection.*

Silver and carved coral pin, $40.00 – 60.00; silver champleve enamel and onyx pendant, $50.00 – 80.00; quality silver ring with punched pattern and Chinese characters on the shank and round cabochon stone. Marked SILVER BEE. $65.00 – 95.00.

Oriental silver and enamel dragon face belt buckle. $150.00 – 225.00. Robin Allison collection.

Japanese floral silver and enamel belt marked TOKIO. $250.00 – 350.00. Robin Allison collection.

Pair of Oriental silver earrings. $12.00 – 15.00.

Silver and natural opal ring made in Hong Kong. Circa 1960s. $40.00 – 60.00.

Two Chinese character silver dress pins. $12.00 – 18.00 each.

Early twentieth century pin set with genuine pearls and marked silver. Possibly Japanese. $90.00 – 120.00.

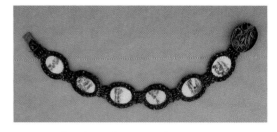

Japanese silver bracelet set with miniature paintings of conventional Japanese motifs on bone. $60.00 – 85.00. Prices vary based on age and quality.

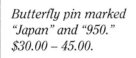

Butterfly pin marked "Japan" and "950." $30.00 – 45.00.

Large, heavy cast silver Oriental brooch. $40.00 – 65.00.

Outstanding porcelain bracelet and matching screwback earrings. This type of Japanese jewelry is extremely rare. Quality and age vary. The relatively flat relief pieces cased in silver usually bring lower prices. $300.00 – 400.00.

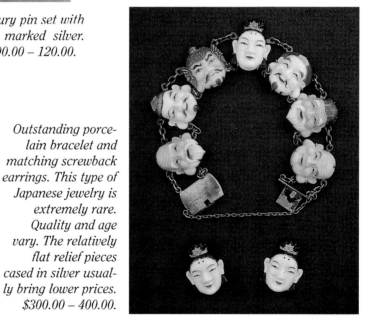

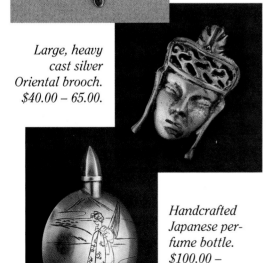

Handcrafted Japanese perfume bottle. $100.00 – 150.00.

1930s Japanese bracelet with bone insets of miniature paintings. $65.00 – 90.00.

183

Floral silver pin set with cultured pearls. Unmarked but came in a Mikimoto box. $80.00 – 140.00. A marked piece would double in price.

Japanese damascene pin. Marked Japan and 950. $25.00 – 35.00.

Marked Amita and silver, damascene cuff links. $18.00 – 25.00.

Silver ring with a 1945 date and a name in Japanese characters. Approximate transliteration, La Bâné, and most likely made specially for an American GI. Inconclusive maker's marks. $30.00 – 45.00.

A tie tack with Japanese motif employing the well-known Japanese technique of color contrast in metalwork to create and highlight a design. $25.00 – 40.00.

Sterling silver bracelet and matching screwback earrings, set with cultured pearls. Marked Amita and in marked Amita original box. $75.00 – 100.00.

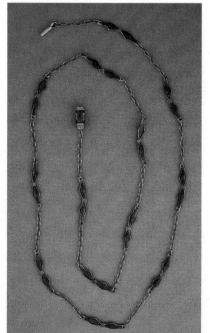

Silver and enamel fish necklace, marked silver. $40.00 – 60.00.

Handcrafted, carved, and engraved Japanese belt buckle. Marked 950. $35.00 – 50.00.

Japanese barrette. Marked Japan and silver. $18.00 – 25.00.

Japanese sterling silver cigarette lighter with an applied three-dimensional image of Buddha. $35.00 – 45.00.

Silver, enameled, coral, and seed pearl earrings, possibly from India. $200.00 – 350.00.

Pin depicting a pair of Japanese children. Marked Japan and 950. $35.00 – 50.00.

Low quality wide Japanese silver damascene cuff bracelet. $20.00 – 25.00.

The jewelry shown in this chapter is all marked silver jewelry. However, the marks were either not identified as of this writing or were not clearly and fully legible to make definite and certain attribution. On some of the marked pieces listed here as unidentified, the author has scattered information and near certain attribution, but they were nevertheless included in this chapter because of lack of certainty and verification. In the case of illegible or not fully visible marks, some of the marks could be identified but only based on speculation and again because of lack of certainty were included in this chapter. It is the author's hope that further research, perhaps aided by the readers, will eventually lead to full identification and certain attribution for many of the pieces shown in this chapter.

Sterling silver pin, marked PCC and SORGE. $45.00 – 60.00.

Sterling silver, possibly Scandinavian pendant. Marked 925 and with the maker's stamp. This motif may be a Wiccan Coven symbol of collective mind. $75.00 – 100.00.

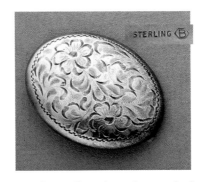

Sterling silver brooch, marked sterling and letter "B" framed in a hexagon. $30.00 – 45.00.

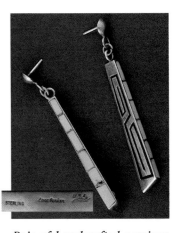

Pair of handcrafted earrings set with natural turquoise, marked Leon Parker and sterling below a feather symbol. $65.00 – 95.00.

Large handcrafted belt buckle marked 925, possibly a clover-shaped stamp, and BENEDIC or BENEDICT. $45.00 – 65.00.

Large silver pendant with green agate with an inconclusive mark. $35.00 – 50.00.

Well-made brooch, marked ALUPE STER. $60.00 – 95.00.

Bracelet marked sterling and with the maker's mark "BA.S." $60.00 – 95.00.

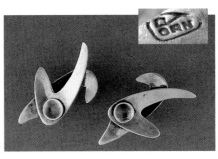

Pair of sterling silver earrings, possibly marked ORN. $35.00 – 60.00.

Silver match box with an inconclusive mark. $65.00 – 95.00.

Large figural brooch marked HAND-WRAGHT STERLING and with inconclusive maker's superimposed, AT or AR stamp. $75.00 – 100.00.

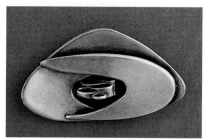

1950s handmade abstract brooch, marked sterling and with inconclusive maker's mark of rDr or TDT. $75.00 – 100.00.

Handwrought silver and agate pendant, marked WRG. $35.00 – 50.00.

Pin fob, marked sterling and with maker's fleur-de-lis stamp. $40.00 – 60.00.

Handcrafted earrings, marked sterling and with maker's inconclusive mark of T.S. on one and possibly L.C. on the other. $35.00 – 65.00.

Silver cuff bracelet with floral motif and the maker's mark of possibly conjoined VAD or VHD. $30.00 – 45.00.

Sterling silver pin with inconclusive maker's mark of possibly IJ or TJ. $20.00 – 25.00.

Sterling silver pin with an unidentified maker's mark of letter "F" in a diamond frame. Various domestic and foreign possibilities. $30.00 – 50.00.

Sterling silver cuff bracelet with an unidentified partly legible maker's mark. $35.00 – 50.00.

Well-made sterling silver floral brooch with an illegible maker's mark. $25.00 – 40.00.

Sterling silver cuff bracelet with inconclusive partially legible mark of possibly J. MUESELER. $125.00 – 175.00.

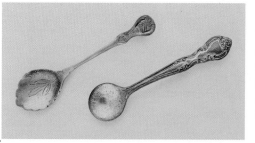

Two spoon pins, both with illegible hallmarks. $15.00 – 20.00 each.

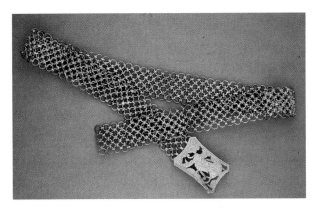

Silver belt, marked sterling and inconclusive maker's mark of possibly J.B. $75.00 – 100.00.

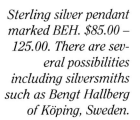

Sterling silver pendant marked BEH. $85.00 – 125.00. There are several possibilities including silversmiths such as Bengt Hallberg of Köping, Sweden.

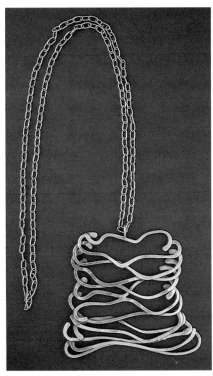

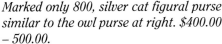

Marked only 800, silver cat figural purse similar to the owl purse at right. $400.00 – 500.00.

Outstanding silver owl figural purse. Marked 900 and possibly LQ. $400.00 – 500.00.

Well-made figural horse head pin. Mark not completely visible and appears to be similar to Yeffeth mark. $30.00 – 45.00.

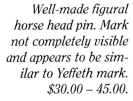

Thick silver bracelet, hollow construction, with floral motif. Marked 900 VA and a partially legible mark, possibly script letter "z" in a triangle. $80.00 – 120.00.

All of the jewelry shown in this chapter is unmarked silver jewelry with only the word "sterling" or "silver fineness" stamped on it. Many of these pieces were made in the U.S. but there are others which are definitely imported silver jewelry, primarily from Europe, where the country of origin could not be determined with great certainty. With some exceptions, the marks are primarily sterling or 925 for silver fineness which are not very helpful in identifying the country of origin. The only clues we have are the designs, motifs, and methods of construction as guiding principles in identifying and distinguishing the origin. However, this is a rather speculative exercise and in classifying the jewelry in this book, only those unmarked pieces where the origin could be guessed with relative certainty are shown in other chapters, while the remainder are displayed in this section. In some cases, a mention of their possible origin is made in the descriptions.

Large sterling Art Nouveau lady brooch. $200.00 – 275.00. Robin Allison collection.

Arts and Crafts sterling floral necklace. $450.00 – 600.00. Robin Allison collection.

A group of sterling silver owl jewelry. $125.00 – 275.00 each, depending on size and condition. Robin Allison collection.

Art Nouveau vermeil sterling purse with a lady and serpent. $200.00 – 300.00. Robin Allison collection.

Marked 900, silver blue plique-à-jour jewelry. This type of jewelry in good condition is very rare. The lower piece is a locket which also came with an interesting beetle chain shown on page 189. Pin, $400.00 – 550.00; pendant, $650.00 – 900.00; locket, $750.00 – 1,000.00. Robin Allison collection.

Silver enamel hearts necklace. Put together by Robin Allison. $350.00 – 500.00. Robin Allison collection.

Marked Sterling, owl locket and slide. $300.00 – 400.00. *Robin Allison collection.*

Silver enamel hearts bracelet. Charm bracelets are usually put together by adding favorite charms. This piece was put together by Robin Allison. $200.00 – 250.00. Robin Allison collection.

An outstanding and rare marked "900" silver enameled serpent bracelet. This piece shows the finest craftsmanship and was certainly created by a master. $750.00 – 1,000.00. Robin Allison collection.

Marked 900, silver blue plique-à-jour locket with a chain of enamel beetles. $1,000.00 – 1,300.00. Robin Allison collection.

Sterling and enameled grape brooches. $250.00 – 400 depending on quality and workmanship. *Robin Allison collection.*

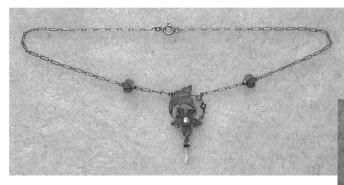

Plique-à-jour green and blue paste necklace. $350.00 – 450.00. Robin Allison collection.

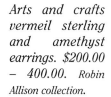

Arts and crafts vermeil sterling and amethyst earrings. $200.00 – 400.00. Robin Allison collection.

Victorian silver insects decorated with paste rhinestones. $85.00 – 135.00. *Robin Allison collection.*

Marked Sterling, enamel orchid brooch. $350.00 – 500.00. Robin Allison collection.

Marked 900, pansy and iris slip lockets. $175.00 – 250.00. Robin Allison collection.

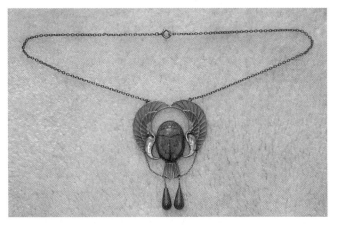

Sterling silver plique-à-jour scarab and peacock pendant. $850.00 – 1,200.00. *Robin Allison collection.*

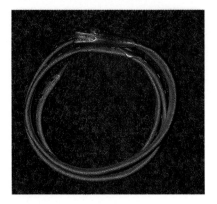

Victorian silver snake bracelet. $200.00 – 300.00. *Robin Allison collection.*

Victorian silver and enameled birds brooch. Unmarked yet attributed to several manufacturers, but no confirmed identification. $400.00 – 600.00. *Robin Allison collection.*

Sterling silver and enamel compacts. $200.00 – 300.00. *Robin Allison collection.*

European 900 silver enamel and turquoise festoon necklace. $600.00 – 900.00. *Robin Allison collection.*

Early nineteenth century continental floral brooch made of 18k gold with silver overlay set with genuine diamonds. $2,500.00 – 3,500.00 The seller of this piece had originally purchased it at a garage sale for $10.00. After turning over several times, the last sale price was $2,000.00.

Unmarked Art Nouveau pin. $100.00 – 130.00.

Handcrafted money clip set with a large stone on the front and a silver U.S. coin on the back. $100.00 – 150.00. *John Christopher collection.*

Art Nouveau pin, possibly by Unger. $125.00 – 150.00.

Large silver and faceted foilless rhinestones brooch, $40.00 – 50.00; and handcrafted pin with genuine carnelian stones, marked Handbuilt Sterling. $40.00 – 60.00.

The back side of the money clip with the silver coin.

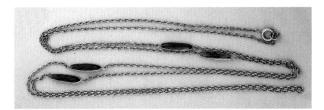

Late nineteenth century silver and genuine amethyst necklace. $90.00 – 130.00.

Turn of century enamel brooch, marked sterling. $70.00 – 95.00.

Pair of horse earrings and a marcasite pin, both marked sterling and possibly foreign imports. Earrings, $25.00 – 30.00; pin, $45.00 – 60.00.

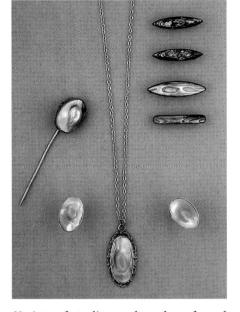

Variety of sterling and mother-of-pearl negligee pins and other jewelry. All circa late nineteenth century to early twentieth. Necklace and earrings set, $35.00 – 45.00; and others $10.00 – 20.00 each.

Sterling silver and vermeil floral brooches. $30.00 – 45.00, based on size and quality.

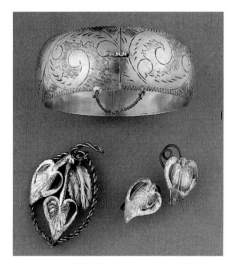

Cuff bracelet, $30.00 – 40.00; and handcrafted mixed silver and copper matching pin and earrings. $40.00 – 50.00.

Enamel hearts necklace, marked sterling. $85.00 – 125.00.

Large mesh purse, marked silver. $125.00 – 175.00.

Two sterling brooches. $30.00 – 50.00.

Two very large, well-made brooches set with rhinestones. Both marked sterling. $35.00 – 50.00 each.

191

Unmarked sterling bow pin with multicolor rhinestones. $70.00 – 95.00.

Chatelaine pin, marked sterling. $95.00 – 135.00.

Sterling necklace and matching earrings. $40.00 – 65.00.

Variety of screwback earrings, all marked sterling. $10.00 – 18.00 each.

Lady's sterling silver compact, marked sterling. $65.00 – 95.00.

High quality handcrafted bracelet marked "sterling." $50.00 – 75.00.

Monogram rhinestone pins, $25.00 – 35.00 each; and heart locket "Mother" pin, $25.00 – 35.00.

Large floral brooch with foilless topaz stone, $35.00 – 45.00; rhinestone bracelet, $35.00 – 50.00; and a modern bracelet, $30.00 – 40.00.

Group of rings set with artificial stones. $20.00 – 25.00 each.

High quality two-color sterling rope knot bracelet, $40.00 – 50.00; pair of enamel insect earrings, $20.00 – 25.00; and figural pin, $25.00 – 35.00.

1930s bracelet, marked sterling, $35.00 – 50.00; two floral brooches, $30.00 – 35.00 each; and sterling earrings, $12.00 – 15.00.

Modern sterling necklace, $30.00 – 50.00; barrette, $15.00 – 20.00; and earrings, $12.00 – 15.00.

Handcrafted sterling necklace and matching bracelet. $70.00 – 95.00.

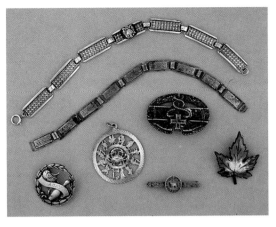

Two early 1900s mother's bracelets, frequently found with the children's names and birth dates. $40.00 – 60.00 each. Variety of specialty pins. $20.00 – 40.00. Prices generally depend on the fraternal organization, association, and the subject.

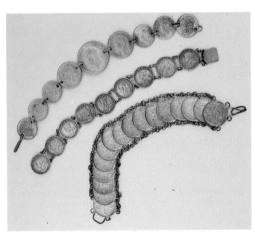

Three silver coin bracelets. Bottom piece made of old Canadian coins, $50.00 – 70.00; others, $30.00 – 45.00.

Variety of organizational pins. $12.00 – 30.00 each. Military, associations, and advertising jewelry are generally higher priced than religious jewelry.

Sterling silver bracelet, $30.00 – 45.00; and four screwback earrings, $15.00 – 20.00 pair.

Variety of rhinestone rings, one set with moss agate. $20.00 – 30.00 each.

Large ring with emerald glass stone, marked sterling. $35.00 – 50.00.

Sterling silver ring with an agate stone and gold-tone accent. $35.00 – 60.00.

Sterling rings. The band has a fitted rotating central ring with a cross. $20.00 – 40.00.

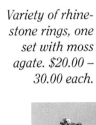

Large unmarked and partially handcrafted silver ring with a genuine cabochon stone. $35.00 – 60.00.

Sterling ring with cast top and enamel accent. $50.00 – 80.00.

Very large bird brooch, marked Sterling. $40.00 – 60.00.

Dutch dancing children pin and matching earrings. $40.00 – 60.00.

Exceptionally large, well-executed eagle brooch. $40.00 – 60.00.

1940 U.S. coin ring with textured band. $35.00 – 50.00. Sculptured three-dimensional bull-head pin, marked sterling. $35.00 – 50.00.

Enamel bracelet, possibly of European origin, marked sterling. $35.00 – 50.00.

Lady's repousse belt furniture. $30.00 – 45.00.

Bracelet, possibly of European origin, marked sterling. $30.00 – 40.00. Goose family brooch with rhinestone eyes, $20.00 – 30.00; and a ship wheel pin, $15.00 – 20.00.

Exceptionally large floral brooch with carved stones, marked sterling. $40.00 – 65.00.

Large crown brooch, $30.00 – 45.00; vermeil crown pin with a rhinestone accent, $25.00 – 35.00; two late Victorian pins, $35.00 – 45.00 each.

Quality Jensen style pin, marked sterling. $40.00 – 60.00. Quality bracelet, marked sterling, possibly of Mexican or European origin. $50.00 – 75.00.
Susan Whealler collection.

Victorian gilded scimitar pin, $25.00 – 35.00; and pair of scimitar screwback earrings, marked Sterling, $20.00 – 25.00.

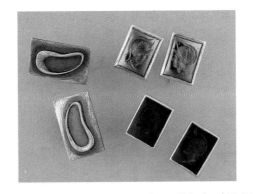

Two pairs of hematite intaglio cuff links, $20.00 – 30.00 each; and a pair of cuff links with 1940s – 1950s modern design. $20.00 – 35.00.

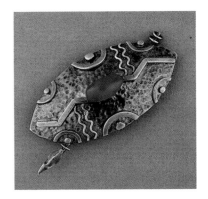

Handcrafted belt buckle, marked sterling. $40.00 – 65.00. *John Christopher collection.*

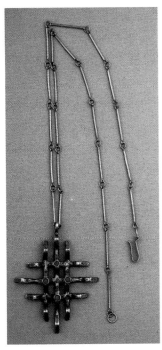

Necklace, marked sterling and most likely of Scandinavian origin. $125.00 – 175.00. *John Christopher collection.*

Marked sterling, pin with rough spectrolite stones, possibly of European origin. $50.00 – 75.00. *John Christopher collection.*

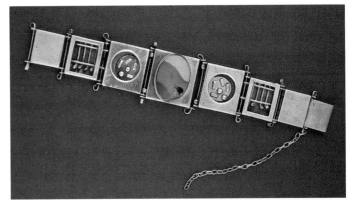

High quality silver bracelet with modern motifs and a large agate stone. Marked 925 and most likely of European origin. $100.00 – 150.00. *John Christopher collection.*

An exceptional modern bracelet, most likely of European origin. $100.00 – 150.00. *John Christopher collection.*

Two sterling brooches; top, $30.00 – 45.00; bottom, $20.00 – 30.00.

Charm bracelet, $35.00 – 50.00; butterfly pin; $15.00 – 20.00; and a "folk story" figural pin, $30.00 – 40.00.

Large equestrian brooch, marked sterling. $40.00 – 65.00.

Well-designed sterling figural brooch. $40.00 – 55.00.

An exceptional handcrafted curved vinaigrette (pendant) with different floral motifs on both sides. Also engraved with a heart, fancy script initials of the presenter and recipient, and 12-29-91 date mark. $175.00 – 225.00.

Two cat pins, marked 925. The smaller cat most likely of recent vintage. $15.00 – 20.00; large cat, $30.00 – 40.00.

Two heart bracelets, both marked sterling of pre- and post-WWII vintage. $20.00 – 30.00 each.

Charm bracelet. $40.00 – 60.00.

Family of ducks brooch, marked sterling. $30.00 – 45.00.

Two spoon rings. There is an abundance of old sterling spoons turned into rings and bracelets displaying the Victorian and Art Nouveau patterns. $10.00 – 15.00 each.

Marked sterling, large floral brooch. $50.00 – 70.00.

Arts and Crafts period enameled sterling pendant. $250.00 – 350.00. Photo courtesy of Pop Beads to Platinum.

Current Silver Jewelry

Current and Upcoming Silversmiths

There are thousands of silversmiths in the U.S. and abroad working in relatively small workshops, and manufacturing a variety of jewelry in multitudes of designs, from the traditional and classical to the ultra-modern and unusual. Some are fully handcrafted while others are only partly handmade. This section provides a very small sampling of some of the jewelry currently being made by what the author considers the current and upcoming silversmiths whose jewelry is already collectible or will become collectibles of tomorrow. Some of the featured firms and silversmiths such as Ola Gorie or Lee Epperson are well recognized and established enterprises with several decades of continued operation, while several others are relatively new in the field, beginning to draw national and international recognition, but all are specially featured in this section to provide the readers with a very small sample of the varied range of quality silver jewelry being manufactured today. Of course, the selection is based on the author's familiarity with the individual silversmiths or their jewelry and at best represents a very limited sampling of what is available on the market. Many examples of art jewelry by renowned as well as less known silversmiths are featured in the author's forthcoming book about studio and art jewelry.

Sabine Amtsberg

Sabine Amtsberg (b. 1969) was born in Varel, Germany, and studied design at the Fachhochschule Hildersheim/Holzminden, later specializing in metal design. She also received practical training in restoring antiques as well as goldsmithing. Her jewelry reflects simple forms and uncluttered designs executed in both gold and silver. Sabine draws her inspiration from a variety of sources, industrial or pastoral, history and cultures, especially the megalithic culture and men's early artworks. Her focus is primarily rings which are designed to serve independently as a sign or symbol; or incorporate signs in subtle ways that are initially nearly invisible and gradually noticed as the piece is worn. Good examples of this approach are the black Stone Age series ring and the signet rings displayed in the following pages. The jewelry also exhibits an interest in form and material. While the sculptured look is emphasized, sometimes assuming non-traditional forms, the rings are often combined with non-precious natural and organic materials such as bone, alabaster, steel or copper. The driving concept is to make jewelry in shapes and forms or with materials which are different than established and traditional expectations.

Sabine Amtsberg's jewelry is marked with a stylized letter "S" over "A." Pieces range in price from 570 to 1360 German marks ($250.00 – 600.00). Her jewelry is distributed through various galleries and her website (see Appendix).

Emanuela Aureli

Emanuela Aureli (b. 1960) was born in Savona, Italy. She began experimenting with making jewelry as a young girl while living in Germany where her father was working at the time and sold her work at flea markets, rock concerts, and in the streets of Munich. Upon returning to Italy, she completed a two-year apprenticeship with the master goldsmiths Vincenzo Quattrocchi and Gianna Usai in Rome before moving to California and completing her education in sculpture and experimental art at the California College of Arts and Crafts. Aureli also acquired additional training as the bench assistant jeweler with Sandra Enterline in San Francisco and through an internship with Louis McGuines in Oakland. Emanuela's jewelry has been featured in many shows, art and metalsmiths exhibitions, throughout the U.S. and in Europe. It has also been featured in many articles such as in the winter 1998 issue of the *Ornament* or in trade journals and publications in the English, German, and Italian languages.

Emanuela's jewelry is exceptionally unique, challenging the traditional western definition of jewelry and ornaments, and attempting to push the limits of the pre-conceived ideas of what is wearable. Unlike most jewelry, it is not the material or fancy and colorful ornamentations, but the simple forms and unconventional configurations which dominate the jewelry. The somewhat minimalist designs in unconventional forms constitute the main theme which convey loud and irresistible messages difficult to ignore. Each piece of Emanuela's jewelry is a work of art, the solid realization of abstract and thought-provoking concepts, beckoning for a reaction and challenging the viewer's perceptions. If one of the objectives of art is to provoke a reaction, Aureli ably succeeds. Whether the jewelry

Aureli (cont.)

is functional or not, you cannot resist to wonder. She states: "In jewelry, I am mostly intrigued by shifting and requestioning the boundaries of the wearable. I want the wearer to 'feel' the work on their skin."

But Aureli's message through her art is not merely limited to the preponderance of forms and designs, it is also conveyed through fine craftsmanship and an innovative approach to using different materials. The handcrafted jewelry exudes and flaunts her skills, the careful attention to texture and patina, the contrast of colors, shades, and shapes or the mix of metals.

Aureli jewelry is marketed through various galleries and museum shops throughout the country (see Appendix). The prices range from $500 to $1,000. The jewelry is marked directly on the finished piece with her name or initials.

Emanuela Aureli © or EA ©

Laura Evans Bowers

Laura Evans Bowers' life changed after she attended her first Scottish festival where she purchased a sterling silver knotwork band and George Bain's book, *Methods of Construction*. After several semesters of training in metalsmithing at Georgia State University in Atlanta, Bowers (b. 1953) was on her way to making her first Celtic jewelry. With more training and experience and having become a regular at the Scottish and Celtic festivals around the country, Bowers began selling her jewelry with great success. Bowers tries to remain faithful to the old Celtic designs, some of which are especially designed and made for the Highland gear. Until recently, the silver jewelry was made at her workshop at home before setting up a separate studio. The jewelry is primarily handcrafted using the lost wax method with great detail by cutting, piecing, and hand finishing the pieces to create the intricate and detailed designs on Claddagh rings and knotwork on the pins and necklaces. The average price is approximately $65 with small pieces selling for as low as $20 while the larger and more elaborate pieces such as the plaid brooches or ornate necklaces are priced at $400 (see Appendix). The early pieces were marked "Legend," but the current pieces are marked with the letter "L." and .925.

Sandra Buchholz

Sandra Buchholz was actually educated and trained as a psychologist with a Ph.D. in the field and many years of practice in psychotherapy. Her interest in jewelry and metalwork began over a decade ago, and she studied at the Jewelry Arts Institute in New York with Bessie Jamieson (formerly Kuhlick-Strack); Touchstone Center for Crafts with John Cogswell; and at the C. Bauer Studio with Cecelia Bauer. Her jewelry has been exhibited at many galleries on the East Coast and at the time of this writing was on display at the 10+ Gallery in Manhasset, New York, and at the Metaphors in New York City.

Sandra's jewelry is produced at her workshop, Elegant Insects, using the lost wax method for the main body with many smaller individual pieces fabricated separately, and the final product put together and finished by hand. The jewelry is sometimes enhanced with the use of gemstones. She specializes in manufacturing insects and butterflies and her collection over the years includes a wide assortment of insects such as dragonflies, unicorn beetle, cicadas, cockchafers, bees, and butterflies. Sandra's use of insects and butterflies is because of her interest in form and the decorative sculptural aspect of the subjects which offer a unique complexity of structure and dimensionality. According to her: "In their incredible variety of form and decoration, insects are truly among the most unusual creatures and are an inescapable part of our environment. By translating them into esthetic objects that can be handled and worn as jewelry, I hope to help demystify them so that their unusual beauty and charm can be appreciated."

Sandra Buchholz's jewelry is marked with her initials "SB." The prices of her jewelry range from approximately $85 for small pieces to $400 for more elaborate and larger pieces (see Appendix).

Kelly Drake

Kelly Drake studied art and design at the Parsons School of Design and Wayne State University, focusing on painting and metals. Although she also makes solid silver jewelry, her interest is in textile techniques with wire such as weaving, crocheting, and knitting which she calls wearable arts. Her metalwork is influenced by the designs, patterns, colors, and textures in the fashion industry. Among her works are many privately commissioned pieces. Kelly makes her jewelry in her workshop at home and sells it exclusively through her website gallery on the internet, the Lounge Gallery of Art (see Appendix).

Lee Epperson

Lee Epperson is one of the major contemporary silversmiths in North America working in the Southwestern style. His sterling silver jewelry and pottery are unique in design and fabrication, demonstrating a deep three-dimensional look with great detail, sharpness, and clarity. As a native Cherokee American from Arizona, Epperson draws his inspiration from the cultural and artistic heritage of the Southwest, a heritage which is celebrated and honored in his silver jewelry and other silver objects.

Originally trained and educated as a mechanical engineer, Epperson's artistic career began with painting and watercolor before experimenting with sculpture, and the captivating effect of sculpting in metal was the motivating factor in his taking the next step to making jewelry in 1973 and later other silver products such as his sterling miniature art pottery. His exquisite art pottery, boxes, and containers will always surprise collectors and connoisseurs by revealing inlaid designs of semi-precious stones adorning the inside, the bottom, or underneath the lid, in formations of signs and symbols which not only communi-

cate with you, but also put you in touch and in communication with the distant past and the creative ancestors of the culture he celebrates.

Epperson's jewelry reflects his skills as a silversmith and a lapidarist in innovative designs and artistic interpretations which skillfully and creatively integrate the metal with semi-precious stones and materials such as turquoise, coral, lapis, and sugilite. He produces a broad range of jewelry and accessories, including earrings, bracelets, necklaces, pins and pendants, belts and belt buckles, tie tacks and bolos. His work is collected internationally, and he has been a recipient of numerous awards and featured in several publications such as the *Lapidary Journal.* He was also featured in several articles in *Rock & Gem Magazine,* which credited him with discovering the "revolutionary technique of completely eliminating" firescale, a reddish or black scale formed on the surface when sterling silver is heated and cooled.

J. Erik

J. Erik (b. 1936) began his career as a furniture designer with custom-made pieces for international celebrities and royalty such as Prince Rainier of Monaco. His designs were influenced by the Scandinavian heritage passed down by his grandparents who were from Norway and Sweden.

J. Erik's venture into designing silver jewelry began in 1994 with the encouragement of Antonio Castillo while he was visiting the Castillo "ranch" in Mexico. Erik's silver jewelry reflects the Scandinavian influence of clean, simple, and uncluttered approach to design and the strong influence of his natural surroundings in the northern Wisconsin woodlands. Native north-

ern natural subjects such as wildlife and exotic flora and fauna, are the dominant themes of his silver jewelry. The simplicity in design and execution, without the detractions of details and ornamentations, the emphasis on form reflecting the nature, best define Erik's silver jewelry.

J. Erik's jewelry is usually marked with his mark, "J.E." It may also be marked "Mexico" where the jewelry is actually manufactured by contracted silversmiths in Taxco, Gro., Mexico, using the prototypes created by Erik. The jewelry is distributed in the U.S. through exclusive arrangements with the Silver Artisans located in Presque Isle, Wisconsin (see Appendix).

Susan Gifford-Knopp

Susan Knopp (b. 1955) received her training and education in art at the California State University with additional training at the California College of Arts and Crafts and Mendicino Art Center where she attended many workshops by renowned metalsmiths and enamelists. Susan considers herself first and foremost a painter and enamelist, rather than a silversmith and a jeweler. She finds her inspiration in works by Tiffany or Lalique's art jewelry where precious masterpieces were created often with non-precious materials. According to Susan, "Their works were always new, sometimes experimental, but always celebrating life, always fantastic color and design, and miniature art unto itself." In her jewelry, she strives to achieve a similar level of craftsmanship, of uniqueness, and of uplifting spiritual content. Susan's work has been featured in many

juried national and international shows and she is the recipient of several awards for her enamel jewelry. She has also been featured in trade magazines such as the October 1997 and 1998 issues of the *Lapidary Journal* and was recently selected as the Niche Award Finalist.

All of Knopp's enamel jewelry is cloisonne executed on fine silver. Frequently, the enameling is done over etched patterns on silver, attempting to create a greater illusion of depth. Although her jewelry features her miniature enamel paintings, it is always complemented by fine silverwork and semi-precious stones. She does her own lapidary work and many of the freeform stones are specifically selected to enhance and complement the art work. The jewelry portrays a variety of subjects, but fantasy figures such as fairies are her favorite subjects. Her

Gifford-Knopp (cont.)

jewelry is always marked on the back of each piece with either stamped or engraved initials, "SGK" and sterling. The jewelry is marketed through many fine galleries and shops throughout the country (see Appendix).

Deb Karash

Deb Karash has been making jewelry for two decades. Her interest in making jewelry actually began by taking classes with a local jeweler, a captivating experience which motivated her to pursue a bachelor's degree in metalsmithing and a master of arts degree. Karash's designs are unique and personal, largely concerned with the abstract representation of figures and executed primarily in silver and mix metals, sometimes combined with semi-precious stones. They suggest a similarity with the American Studio Jewelry recalling some of the forms and themes they made popular in the 1950s, but Karash credits her circle of artist friends and their paintings and sculptures that incorporate assemblage of mixed materials with direct influence on her work and designs. Karash's interest in jewelry is focused on its intimate nature as an art form and its role in the society as a cultural and social symbol, denoting status or indicating particular relationships. For many years she handcrafted the jewelry in her own workshop at home before establishing a studio in Rockford, Illinois. The jewelry is marketed through various galleries and shops (see Appendix). The price range for most of her brooches is $175 to $250.

Marly Malone Company

The Marly Malone Company was established in 1992 by Francesca Malloy in Brooklyn, New York. Her interest in jewelry began in her childhood as she watched her mother make jewelry. Later Francesca and a woman caster and maker of fine jewelry joined to manufacture jewelry designed by Francesca in the style of her mother. As the firm grew, the designs were also contracted out. The Marly Malone Company specializes in producing contemporary jewelry inspired by historic jewelry. Much of the jewelry is based on old Celtic jewelry and the company promotes its collection as Irish jewelry. A broad range of sterling silver jewelry and gift items are manufactured which are sold exclusively from the Grafton Shop in New York City or through its website (see Appendix). Special pieces are marked "E.I.R.E." The prices range from $30 to $300.

Charlotte Modig

Charlotte Modig received her training by spending five years as an apprentice to Sven Roos in Vasteras and an additional year at the art school, Nychelviksskolan, before opening her own workshop in the craft village, Nykvarn. Since the mid 1980s, Charlotte had many shows and exhibitions in Sweden and the jewelry shown on the following pages are from her collection of silver jewelry and decorative arts at Crossroads, an exhibition which focused on the materials and inspirations brought home by the Vikings from their journeys and sea explorations.

All of Charlotte's jewelry and other silver products are handmade, employing traditional methods. The jewelry reflects the influence of historic Scandinavian traditions and designs.

Pat Moses-Caudel

Pat works under the name Wild Poppy Designs, specializing in wirework often decorated with semi-precious stones such as jade, tourmaline, citrine, and garnet. Pat has been creating wirework jewelry made of fine gold and silver for almost two decades and her crocheted jewelry is beautiful and quite interesting. Crocheted and woven wire jewelry have a long history and in recent years they have enjoyed renewed interest and a rise in their popularity. Pat's jewelry and accessories combine her love of crochet with skills in wirework and design, producing fine pieces that clearly display her talents. Much of the silver crochet work is in gauges of 26, 28, and 30 wire. Her jewelry is worn and collected nationally by those who appreciate this type of work and include several prominent personalities. It has also been featured several times in the *Lapidary Journal*. For obvious reasons, the jewelry is not marked but comes with a tag featuring her "Wild Poppy" logo (see Appendix).

Carrie Nunes

Carrie A. Nunes was born in Nashville, Tennessee, where she began studying the art and craft of metalworking at the University of Tennessee, continuing her training at the Appalachian Center for Arts and Crafts where she learned casting, blacksmithing, hollowware, and jewelry fabrication. Carrie designs and manufactures her jewelry in her home workshop, The Metal Petals. Her jewelry is handcrafted using traditional and basic jewelers' tools and techniques where each piece is designed and fabricated individually.

Carrie's jewelry is inspired by nature, and it is her love for nature and her long interest in gardening that provide her with an abundance of subjects for her silver jewelry. Much of her work is in small pieces portraying insects and flowers.

Her jewelry is marked "Carrie Nunes" engraved in script and may also include the date it was made. The silver jewelry has a price range of $50 to $250. The butterflies generally sell for $50 and brooches for $65 – 120.

Amy O'Connell

Amy O'Connell is a self-taught jewelry artist currently working in San Francisco. She was born in Northampton, Massachusetts, and began designing and handcrafting jewelry in 1992 after establishing a body jewelry workshop in Iowa City, Iowa. Drawing upon her training in the visual arts, including design and sculpture, she made the transition from steel to sterling and began making jewelry. All of Amy's jewelry is handcrafted, including chains, findings, and the lapidary work. She learned lapidary work specifically in order to remove the design constraints of commercially cut stones and have complete control over her designs.

Each piece is hand forged, carved, and shaped, with an emphasis on pattern and textures, often highlighted and enhanced with 14k gold, and complemented by unusual gemstones. The designs and metalwork are a combination of traditional with contemporary, creating quality solid pieces with a sense of strength and vitality. As O'Connell states: "I work intuitively from a primal aesthetic integrating the images of our modern world."

O'Connell's jewelry is always hand signed with her name "Amy O'CONNELL" or with her initials "AOC." The jewelry is sold through galleries and stores, particularly in the Bay area, and on her website (see Appendix).

Ola Gorie (b. 1937)

Ola Gorie was the first graduate of jewelry making from Gray's School of Art in Aberdeen in 1959 and upon returning to her native Orkney, she began designing and fabricating jewelry inspired by the islands' rich cultural heritage. North of the mainland, Orkney was populated by the Norse for many centuries and that language was spoken there as late as the eighteenth century. Ola Gorie is credited with establishing the first jewelry enterprise in Orkney since the time of the Norse which evolved into a major concern employing more than 50 people on this small island. In recognition of her creativity and contributions to the jewelry industry, in 1999 Ola was awarded an MBE (Member of the British Empire) issued by the Queen in Edinburgh.

Ola Gorie first began manufacturing her jewelry in her garden shed and her talents combined with the keen marketing and business skills of her husband, Arnold Tailed (b. 1935), led to their successful business venture. As a result, the company of Ola Gorie has developed into an internationally recognized manufacturer of quality jewelry. Since that time, the firm has produced specially commissioned pieces for the Queen and other members of the Royal family, the British Museum, the Royal Shakespeare Company, and other firms such as Liberties of London.

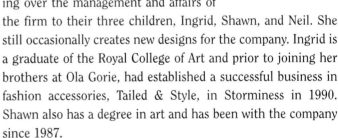

Ola and Arnold retired in 1997, turning over the management and affairs of the firm to their three children, Ingrid, Shawn, and Neil. She still occasionally creates new designs for the company. Ingrid is a graduate of the Royal College of Art and prior to joining her brothers at Ola Gorie, had established a successful business in fashion accessories, Tailed & Style, in Storminess in 1990. Shawn also has a degree in art and has been with the company since 1987.

Both Ingrid and Shawn are involved in the design and manufacturing of the jewelry while Neil works on marketing and retail. Ola's son-in-law, Duncan McLean, recently assumed the position of master designer and works closely with the master patternmaker, Colin Watson. An employee of the firm for the past 20 years, Watson worked with Ola interpreting her designs and paying particular attention to the three-dimensional aspects of her creations and is credited for contributing to the quality of the jewelry. Anne Crackdown serves as design and marketing manager.

Ola's designs are inspired by the islands' rich historical and cultural heritage. One of her popular designs is based on the consecration cross near the altar at the Charcoal Cathedral, an

Ola Gorie *(cont.)*

old building not far from her residence and workshop. Much of the jewelry is based on historic Norse and Celtic objects, some excavated at Orkney, others in Scotland and Scandinavia. Each piece came with a small provenance card giving the historical source for the design.

The new Ola Gorie jewelry is sold throughout the United Kingdom in jewelry stores and gift shops, several department stores, and major museums in London, Edinburgh, and Glasgow. The older jewelry is occasionally encountered in the U.S. collectible market and is highly collectible. The prices of the new jewelry range from $40 for small pins to $140 for bangles while the vintage pins found infrequently are usually marked from $50 to $120 (see Appendix).

Oliva

Oliva Rød (b. 1942) lives and works on Aukra, an island of 2,900 inhabitants on the northwest coast of Norway surrounded by the roaring ocean. She turned to silversmithing late in life after her hearing disability forced her to explore other career avenues. After attending Plytechnical College in Telemark studying metallurgy and folk arts, she opened her own workshop in 1996 and since then has been making silver and gold jewelry in the traditional Norwegian filigree style. In 1999 her skill and talent were recognized by her receiving the first prize from the Norwegian Handcraft Association (Norges Husflidslag) and the "Excellence in Craftsmanship" award exhibiting at the Norwegian Autumn Celebration (Norsk Høstfest) in Minot, North Dakota. This occasion also marked the introduction of her jewelry to the American public. Oliva

was also featured in the trade magazine, *Gullsmedkunst (Goldsmith Art),* as the "Cinderella of the goldsmith trade" while the David-Andersen Company held an exhibition of her work in Oslo.

Oliva's jewelry is inspired by Norwegian history, and the folk jewelry which she reproduces in filigree. It is frequently complemented with pearls and semi-precious stones. All of her jewelry is handcrafted and made in limited quantity. Her exquisite bridal jewelry made in the traditional Norwegian style, has found a market not only among young Norwegian brides, but also the general public as regular jewelry and hair ornaments. Oliva's jewelry is beautiful and will continue to receive wider international public recognition.

Bernard Rosenberg

From a family with a long history in the jewelry industry, Bernard Rosenberg began to learn about and appreciate jewelry at an early age, but not until recently did he begin to make and sell the jewelry himself. Bernard's father began his career making and peddling costume jewelry in Cuba before coming to the U.S. His uncle was a jeweler in New York City and his aunt worked for many years for Tiffany & Company.

Having successfully experimented with making jewelry and finding the signs of a receptive market, Bernard established Le Count Designs, in Brewster, New York, and began marketing

his jewelry. In his jewelry, Rosenberg attempts to create three-dimensional effects by employing various techniques with the objective of expressing a sense of energy and movement. His designs are simple, yet elegant, and that is precisely the impression Rosenberg aims to achieve with his jewelry. The jewelry is marked Le Count and can be directly purchased from the firm's website (see Appendix). Most of the jewelry is within the $90 to $250 price range with the exception of some pieces such as the Sun, Moon and Star pin/pendant shown on page 209.

Dave Stephens

Dave Stephens was educated and trained as a graphic designer and his career in jewelry began with his interest in rock cutting and polishing. After silver smithing classes, he combined his talents as a designer with his interest and skills in lapidary and smithing to create unique jewelry. He also designed one of the first art jewelry websites on the Internet, selected as one of the top five sites by Yahoo's *Internet Life Magazine.* He was also featured in the September 1999 issue of the *Lapidary Journal.*

David's basic love of stones and interest in their energy

effects on the human body drive his somewhat mystical designs which  appeal to collectors. Each of his pieces is given a name, such as "Queen's Ankh," "Azteca," or "Ibis," which connects his jewelry to Egyptian archaeological digs and the ancient beliefs in the mystical powers of stones and real or mythical subjects. Although he is primarily self-taught, his jewelry exhibits fine craftsmanship with particular attention to details that highlight his specially

Stephens (cont.)

selected and shaped handcut stones. His jewelry is rapidly finding a wider circle of collectors. The silver jewelry ranges in price from $50 to $400 depending on the size and stones (see Appendix).

Bryna Tracy

Bryna Tracy studied art jewelry at George Brown College and began making and showing her jewelry while still a student. She now works from her studio in Ontario, Canada, and her jewelry is displayed and sold through various galleries such as the Art Gallery of Ontario and the Guild Shop in Toronto. Her jewelry is worn by some of Canada's celebrities and media personalties.

Bryna draws her inspiration from many sources, sometimes conceptualizing designs based on the materials, such as the stones and beads she discovers in her travels, hand-blown glass beads from Santa Barbara or handmade silver beads from Santorini, Greece. All of her jewelry is fabricated by hand using traditional techniques, rendering each piece one-of-a-kind with her special touch and signature. "Every piece is one in its own, for I believe that a piece of jewelry is an emotion felt by the maker, the buyer, and the person whom it adorns."

The jewelry is not marked but is tagged with her shop logo: "METALOGIC BY BRYNA TRACY." The prices range from $150 for rings, $350 – 450 for bracelets, and $600 – 850 for necklaces.

Randall Wilson

Randall S. Wilson has been a designer and manufacturer of handcrafted jewelry since the 1970s. He specializes in inlaid and overlaid silver jewelry with a Southwestern look. Each piece is completely handcrafted by Wilson in his workshop. All the metals and material are cut, soldered, assembled, and finished by him, including the inlay or overlay which is cut, shaped, and fitted one piece at a time. Produced by a highly skilled and experienced craftsman, Wilson's jewelry reflects meticulous attention paid to details and creation of quality products.

Each piece uniquely displays his talents and skill. His jewelry had been exhibited in many juried arts and crafts shows and he is featured in the *Goodfellow's Catalog of Wonderful Things,* a national publication of America's finest crafts. It is distributed through shops and galleries primarily in the Southwestern region and was recently made available on the Internet. The jewelry is carded with Wilson's RSW logo.

Zebra

Zebra is one of the rapidly expanding manufacturers of jewelry in Germany with an international distribution network covering Europe and North America. Zebra Design GmbH was founded by Helmut Klysch (b. 1957) in 1986 who is also the company's designer. His first collection consisted of only 30 pieces which has now evolved into two annual collections comprised of many pieces. According to Klysch whose playful exploration led him from philosophy through art history to jewelry design, his main challenge is "to guide the interplay between material, form and colour, surfaces, and structures."

Zebra jewelry is manufactured in both gold and silver, some set with precious and semi-precious stones. Special attention is paid to details, superior handwork, and finishing. Quality products and craftsmanship are the guiding principles. According to Klysch: "Hand-made objects have their own 'aura' that cannot be recreated by machine… my designs are at first glance identical. A closer look reveals fine variations, turning each piece into a one-of-a-kind item. An item with its own soul."

Zebra jewelry itself is not marked but comes in marked packaging. The firm has a pending trademark application with the German Patent and Trademark office. The prices range from $70 to $500 for rings and $200 to $600 for bracelets.

Amtsberg: Signet rings with moveable bone sections, one marked "925" and the artist's mark. *Courtesy of Sabine Amtsberg. Photo by Jürgen Voss.*

Amtsberg: Sterling silver signet rings with moveable steel cylinders, inspired by Egyptian signet cylinders combined with modern industrial roller bearings. *Courtesy of Sabine Amtsberg. Photo by Jürgen Voss.*

Amtsberg: Two sterling silver rings from Amtsberg's "Stone Age" series. Each ring has a unique hidden mark or characteristic, such as raised signs on inner shank, which become visible and known to the wearer over time. *Courtesy of Sabine Amtsberg. Photo by Jürgen Voss.*

Aureli: Pair of hollow construction brooches made of sterling silver and copper. *Photo courtesy of Emanuela Aureli.*

Aureli: Rings with gesticulating hands and trapped ball made of sterling silver and copper. *Photo courtesy of Emanuela Aureli.*

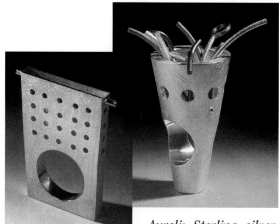

Aureli: Sterling silver and copper brooch of hollow construction with hanging oxidized sterling chain. *Photo courtesy of Emanuela Aureli.*

Aureli: Trapped ring of hollow construction made of sterling silver and 18K gold by Aureli. *Photo courtesy of Emanuela Aureli.*

Aureli: Sterling silver, 18K gold, and copper ring in hollow construction with heat and black patina. *Photo courtesy of Emanuela Aureli.*

Bowers: Large brooch with Celtic motif.

Bowers: Silver bracelet with a typical motif inspired by historic Scottish themes.

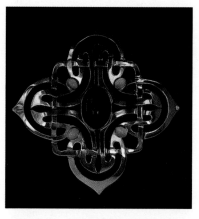

Bowers: Sterling silver brooch.

Buchholz: Elegant silver insect by the Elegant Insects. *Photo courtesy of Sandra Buchholz.*

Buchholz: Delicate and finely crafted silver insect, Praying Mantis. Photo courtesy of Sandra Buckholz.

Buchholz: Sterling silver Swallowtail typical of Sandra Buchholz's work. Photo courtesy of Sandra Buchholz.

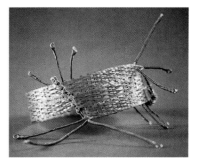

Drake: Woven sterling silver and copper wire bracelet. Photo courtesy Kelly Drake.

Drake: Sterling silver crochet bracelet with garnets. Photo courtesy Kelly Drake.

J. Erik: Sterling silver moose brooch typical of naturalistic pieces.

J. Erik: Sterling silver sailboat.

Karash: Primitive, industrial, and modern influences characterize Karash's jewelry. Courtesy of Deb Karash. Photo by Larry Sanders.

Karash: Mixed metal brooch with great sense of balance. Courtesy of Deb Karash. Photo by Larry Sanders.

Karash: Large brooch made of silver and semi-precious stones. Courtesy of Deb Karash. Photo by Larry Sanders.

Karash: Silver and semi-precious stones in select shapes are combined to create a brooch typical of Karash's jewelry. Courtesy of Deb Karash. Photo by Larry Sanders.

Epperson: Two silver inlay bolos and a matching set of silver and inlay brooch and cuff links. Photo courtesy of Lee Epperson.

Epperson: A group of pots from 2" to 7" high with variety of relief and sculptured Native American motifs complemented with inlay work. Photo courtesy of Lee Epperson.

Epperson: Variety of silver jewelry. Note the miniature pots in the bottom row, ranging in size from 1" to 2". Photo courtesy of Lee Epperson.

Epperson: Various silver pieces representative of Epperson's jewelry and silver pots. The large box, approximately 6½" high, has a removable lid in shape of a mountain sheep kachina mask. The bottom of the lid and the base of the pottery are inlaid with stone mosaics and the edge and the top inlaid with turquoise and lapis. Photo courtesy of Lee Epperson.

Epperson: Silver and inlay belt furniture. The third lower buckle shows the prayer line and the sun symbol inlaid with coral and turquoise dots. Photo courtesy of Lee Epperson.

Knopp: Silver and enamel pendant and brooch by Susan Knopp. Photo courtesy of Susan Knopp.

Knopp: Wonderful and well executed bracelet and earrings displaying Knopp's talent and skills. Photo courtesy of Susan Knopp.

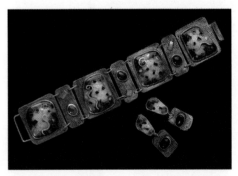

Knopp: Silver pendant, with enamel painting on silver base. Photo courtesy of Susan Knopp.

Knopp: Silver and enamel pendant with a typical Knopp theme, usually angels and fairies. Photo courtesy of Susan Knopp.

Malone: Solid sterling silver "Joan of Arc" letter opener with mother-of-pearl. Photo courtesy of Marly Malone Company.

Malone: Sterling silver brooch with carved coral roses; and sterling silver lapel or tie tack in shape of a pruner. Photo courtesy of Marly Malone Company.

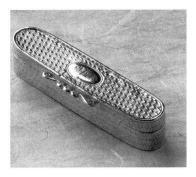

Malone: Handwrought sterling silver box. Photo courtesy of Marly Malone Company.

Malone: Sterling silver lyre stick pin. Photo courtesy of Marly Malone Company.

Modig: One-piece solid silver necklace in Celtic motif, decorated with tourmaline. Photo courtesy of Charlotte Modig.

Modig: Bracelet made of silver and gold threads with crosses of oxidated silver. Photo courtesy of Charlotte Modig.

Modig: Silver and amethyst ring with the contrast of gold-plated sections. Photo courtesy of Charlotte Modig.

Moses-Caudel: Wonderful "flapper" woven purse.

Nunes: Sterling silver brooch. Courtesy of Carrie Nunes. Photo by Marianne Leach.

O'Connell: Sterling silver and jasper necklace with 14k detail specially constructed and arranged to give the impression of landscape picture frames. Photo courtesy of Amy O'Connell.

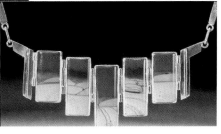

Nunes: Three silver insects with applied wire and silver balls. Courtesy of Carrie Nunes. Photo by Marianne Leach.

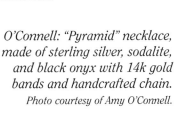

O'Connell: "Pyramid" necklace, made of sterling silver, sodalite, and black onyx with 14k gold bands and handcrafted chain. Photo courtesy of Amy O'Connell.

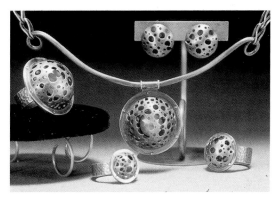

O'Connell: "Moon Series" consisting of a group of oxidized sterling silver jewelry made of sheet silver and wire with 14k gold rivets, pierced domes, and apricot moonstones on the larger pieces and sun stones on the smaller rings. Photo courtesy of Amy O'Connell.

O'Connell: Oxidized sterling silver "Palm" brooch, with petrified palmwood, spectrolite, and punched and hammered textured surface. *Photo courtesy of Amy O'Connell.*

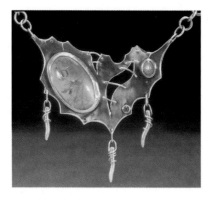

O'Connell: Sterling silver necklace with large amber and sun stones complemented by riveted sterling "stitches" and 14k gold accent. *Photo courtesy of Amy O'Connell.*

Ola Gorie: Silver brooch inspired by an ancient saddle found at Alskog in Gotland, Sweden, circa 1000 – 1050 AD.

Ola Gorie: Silver brooch depicting a dragon based on the carvings in Maeshowe, the neolithic chambered tomb at Stenness, Orkney, which was broken into by the Norse. The "Jerusalem farers" who were Earl Rongnvald's companion on his pilgrimage in 1142 are reputed to have been responsible for the carving.

Ola Gorie: Silver brooch with a Celtic design based on a penannular brooch found in the grave of a 9th century woman at Wetness, Rousay, Orkney, and presumed to have been acquired through barter or pillage in Ireland.

Ola Gorie: Brooch with typical scroll motif popular during the Tudor times.

Ola Gorie: Matching silver set with beautiful and highly stylized design based on the motif found on an ancient sword hilt in Suontaka, Finland, dating from circa 850.

Ola Gorie: Silver brooch inspired by The Book of Kells, a richly illuminated Gospel manuscript from Iona, but taken to Kells in Ireland around 806 to protect it from the Vikings.

Oliva Rød: Silver and gilt offering locket. Such trinkets were originally worn by primarily Northwestern Norwegian women in which they kept the money to pay the priest for the wedding ceremony. *Photo courtesy of Oliva Rød Design.*

Oliva Rød: A bridal hair ornament made of oxidized and gilt silver, 18 and 23k gold, and cultured pearls which can also be used as a brooch. *Photo courtesy of Oliva Rød Design.*

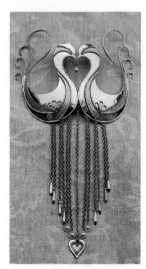

Oliva Rød: Brooch and matching earrings made of sterling and gilt silver. Photo courtesy of Oliva Rød Design.

Rosenberg: Wonderful silver and gold composition, titled Sun, Moon and Star. Photo courtesy of Bernard Rosenberg.

Oliva Rød: Filigree silver and gilt brooch, inspired by historic Norwegian themes. Photo courtesy of Oliva Rød Design.

Rosenberg: A pair of silver and turquoise earrings. Photo courtesy of Bernard Rosenberg.

Oliva Rød: Perfume locket, made of oxidized silver, 18 and 23k gold and cultured pearl. For centuries such lockets filled with fragrance were worn by women in Norway. Photo courtesy of Oliva Rød Design.

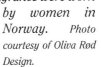

Stephens: Asymmetrical pendant with specially cut stones. Photo courtesy of Dave Stephens.

Stephens: "Ibis" pendant displaying Stephens's good sense of design. Photo courtesy of Dave Stephens.

Stephens: Silver and specially cut semi-precious stones showing a combination of ancient and modern influences. Photo courtesy of Dave Stephens.

Stephens: Silver pendant titled "Purpled Flame." Photo courtesy of Dave Stephens.

Stephens: A special feature of Stephens's jewelry is the irregular shaped stones planned and cut as part of the design. Photo courtesy of Dave Stephens.

Tracy: Silver acid-etched pendant with green tourmaline. Photo courtesy of Bryna Tracy.

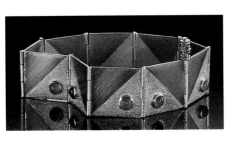

Tracy: Married metal, copper and silver, bracelet with blue and green cabochon onyx stones. Photo courtesy of Bryna Tracy.

Tracy: Silver nugget domes with assortment of natural cabochon stones. *Photo courtesy of Bryna Tracy.*

Tracy: Silver and enamel hieroglyphic animals necklace. *Photo courtesy of Bryna Tracy.*

Tracy: Silver hinged ring with assortment of stones. *Photo courtesy of Bryna Tracy.*

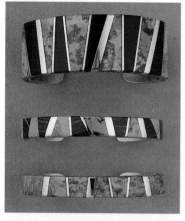

Wilson: Variety of silver and inlay cuff bracelets.

Wilson: Wide silver and inlay cuff bracelet.

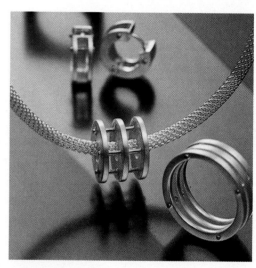

Zebra: Pendant, ring, and earrings in modern form and designs.

Zebra: Silver jewelry from a large collection offered semi-annually by Zebra.

Zebra: Several examples of rings set with precious and semi-precious stones.

Zebra: Contemporary silver and gold jewelry designed by Helmut Klysch.

Current Mass Produced Silver Jewelry

The following pages provide a very small sample of mass produced and mass marketed current jewelry found primarily in jewelry and department stores. Undoubtedly some of these will become the prized collectibles of the next generation. Much of the jewelry displayed in this section is imported jewelry sold by weight.

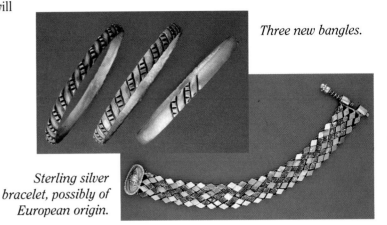

Three new bangles.

Sterling silver necklace and bracelet, marked Zanfled.

Sterling silver bracelet, possibly of European origin.

Ring made by Zina. Typical of Zina jewelry.

High quality sterling silver and large genuine carnelian stone.

Variety of 1990s marcasite and filigree pins, usually made in Thailand.

Variety of marcasite jewelry set with semi-precious stones, imported from both Italy and Thailand.

Bangles, usually imported from Mexico.

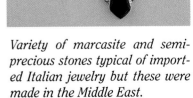

Sterling silver and garnet necklace from Thailand, and bracelet set with genuine semi-precious stones from Italy.

Sterling silver and genuine garnet, imported from Thailand.

Variety of marcasite and semi-precious stones typical of imported Italian jewelry but these were made in the Middle East.

Sterling silver jewelry, imported from Thailand and the Middle East.

Typical sterling silver jewelry found in major department stores, usually imported from Thailand.

Imported marcasite and silver jewelry, usually from Italy or Thailand.

Sterling silver bangle, imported from India.

Ethnic sterling silver sari jewelry and two anklets from India.

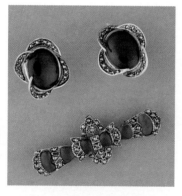

Marcasite and carnelian jewelry, usually imported from Italy and the Middle East.

Early 1990s marcasite motorcycle pin with moveable parts from Thailand. This type of jewelry began to appear in the market in the 1980s.

Figural pin, imported from Thailand.

Large brooch, imported from Mexico.

Group of modern bracelets imported from Mexico.

A group of enamel pill boxes, usually imported from India and China.

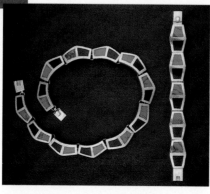

Matching Mexican sterling silver necklace and bracelet.

Wide cuff bracelet, imported from Mexico.

Appendix

This appendix was organized to serve as a resource base for collectors of silver jewelry as well as providing pertinent information relative to the material covered in the book.

Addresses and Websites of Featured Silversmiths and Manufacturers

(In a few cases, the author's letters were returned and the listed address is the last known address.)

A & Z Hayward Co.
655 Waterman Avenue
East Providence, RI 02914

Alton
e-mail: gunnar.ekstrom@alton.se

Sabine Amtsberg
e-mail: sabine@amtsberg.de
http://www.sabinea.com

Emanuela Aureli
ema@sirius.com

James Avery Craftsman Inc.
P.O. Box 1367
Kerrville, TX 78029

Ballou, B.A. & Co. Inc.
800 Waterman Avenue
East Providence, RI 02914

Los Ballesteros
Av. de los Plateros No. 68, C.P.
40200
Taxco, Gro.
Phone: (7)622-1076, 6224235
Fax: 622-0370
e-mail: Balleste@taxco.net

Beaucraft Inc.
215 Georgia Avenue
Providence, RI 02905

Binder Bros. Inc.
663 Grand Avenue
P.O. Box 711
Ridgefield, NJ 07657

Black Hills Jewelry Mfg. Co.
405 Canal
Rapid City, SD 57701

Laura G. Evans Bowers
legendsilver@pipeline.com

Sandra Buchholz
ElegantBee@aol.com

Cellini Inc.
215 Jefferson Boulevard
Warwick, RI 02888

Ciner Mfg. Co.
20 W 37th
New York, NY 10018

Clark & Coombs Co.
162 Clifford Street
Providence, RI 02903

Curtis Jewelry Mfg. Co.
1284 Plainfield
Johnston, RI 02919

Curtman
623 Atwls Avenue
Providence, RI 02909

Danecraft Inc.
1 Baker Street
Providence, RI 02905

Leonore Doskow
1 Doskow Road
Montrose, NY 10548

Kelly Drake
kdrake@the-lounge.com
http://www.the-lounge.com

Eisenberg Jewelry
350 North Orleans Street
Chicago, IL 60654

J. Erik
http://www.silverartisan.com

Espo-Flex MFG CO Inc
225 Dupont Drive
Providence, RI 02907

Hand & Hammer Silversmiths
2610 Morse Lane
Woodbridge, VA 22192
e-mail: deChip@handhammer.
com.
http://www.hand-hammer.com.

Hobe
http://www.hobe-ltd.com

Kabana Inc.
616 Indian School Road
Northwest
Albuquerque, NM 87102

Kalevala Koru
Arinatie 17, 00370
Helsinki, Finland
http://www.kalevala.com

Deb Karash
kjewelry@aol.com

Susan Knopp
knopp@directcon.net

Plateria La Fuente
Miguel Hidalgo No. 9
C.P. 40200, Taxco, Gro
Phone: (7) 622-3152
Fax: (7) 622-5339
e-mail: lafuente@taxco.net

Lapponia Jewelry
P.O. Box 72
FIN-00511 Helsinki
Finland
Phone: +358-9-2293 440
Fax: +358-9-2293 4411
e-mail: info@lapponia.fi
http://www.lapponia.com

Ledesma Plateros Silverworks
Miguel Hidalgo No. 54-B,
C.P.40200
Taxco, Gro.
Phone: (7) 622-4493
Fax: (7) 622-1969
e-mail: ledeplat@taxco.net

Los Castillo Silverworks
Carretera Federal Mexico-
Acapulco, Km. 175-A
Taxco, Gro.
Phone: (7) 622-1988
Fax: (7) 6622-5048
e-mail: Castillo@taxco.net

Marly Malone
marlymalone@irishjewelry.com

Monet Group Inc.
3400 Pawtucket Avenue
Riverside, RI 02915

Monet Inc.
2 Lonsdale Avenue
Pawtucket, RI 02860

Pat Moses Caudel
e-mail: patmcaudel@aol.com
http://members.aol.com/wild
    poppy1/index.html

Napier Co.
530 5 Avenue
New York, NY 10036

Carrie Nunes
e-mail: tnunes@usit.net

Stuart Nye
http://www.stuartnye.com

NS Co. Inc.
2125 La Vista Executive Park Dr.
Tucker, GA 30084

NSE
http://www.nseguld.se
e-mail: nilserik@nseguld.se

Amy O'Connell
e-mail: amy@ezmo.com
http://www.ezmo.com/amy

Ola Gorie
11 Broad Street Charcoal
Orkney, Scotland
http://www.orkneyislands.com
    /olagorie/index.html
e-mail: info@olagorie.com.

Cläes E. Giertta
Box 450 57, 104 30
Stockholm, Sweden
Phone: 08-102112; 20 28 84

Oliva Rød
e-mail: info@oliva.no (Info
    Oliva Rød Design)

Orb Gold/Silversmiths
127-A South Main Street
New Hope, PA 18938

Rogers, Lunt & Bowlen Co.
298 Federal
Greenfield, MA 01301

Rolyn Inc.
189 Macklin
Cranston, RI 02903

Bernard Rosenberg
e-mail: lecount@bestweb.net.
http://www.bestweb.net/~lecount

Silver Cloud Inc.
2417 Baylor Drive Southeast
Albuquerque, NM 87106

Dave Stephens
StephensDesign@opendoor.com
http://www.opendoor.com/
    stephensdesign/crystalguy.html

To_o Silver Shop
Av. De Los Plateros No. 97
Taxco, Gro.
Phone: (7) 622-0228
Fax: (7) 622-4220

Torun Bülow-Hübe
P.O. Box 2331
JKT Jakarta, Indonesia

Bryna Tracy
e-mail: smartdog1@msn.com
http://www.geocities.com/heartland
    /ranch/8539/jewellery.html

Uncas Mfg. Co.
623 Atwells Avenue
Providence, RI 02909

Rey Urban
Sibyllegatan 49
114 42 Stockholm, Sweden
Phone: 08-662 5989
    662 55 66

Van Dell
100 Niantic Avenue
Providence, RI 02907

Victoria
Plateria Cony, Plata Victoria
http://www.silver.net.mx/brilanti
e-mail: brilanti@silver.net.mex

Randall Wilson
e-mail: RSWilson@webtv.net
    (Randall S. Wilson)

Zebra
http://www.zebra-design.com

Addresses and Websites with Information on National Standard and Manufacturer's Marks

General
http://home.wxs.nl/~luijt005/
    hallm.htm

USA

General Information Services
    Division
U.S. Patent Trademark Office
Crystal Plaza 3, Room 2CO2
Washington, DC 20231
http://www.uspto.gov

The Encyclopedia of American
    Silver Marks
http://www.silvercollecting.co
    m/silvermarks.html

Costume Jewelry Designers
    and Manufacturers
http://www.illusionjewels.com
    /list.html

Austria
http://www.klammer.com/Fra-
    gen/Punzierung e.htm

Holland
Waarborg Platina, Goud en Zilver
http://www.waarborg.nl/

Portugal
Imprensa Nacional Casa da
    Moeda
http://www.incm.pt/index.html

Sweden
Swedish Assay Office, SP
Box 857
SE-50115 Borås, Sweden

Phone: +46 33 165000
Fax: +46 33 135502
http://www.sp.se/kattfoten/eng/

United Kingdom
The UK Assay Offices
http://www.teg.co.uk/teg/assay.htm

The Assay Office
Goldsmiths' Hall
Foster Lane
London EC2V 6BN UK

The Assay Office
137 Portobello Street
Sheffield S1 4DR UK

The Assay Office
Newhall Street
Birmingham B3 1SB UK

The Assay Office
9 Granton Road
Edinburgh EH5 3QJ UK

UK Patent Office
http://www.patent.gov.uk
e-mail:
    enquiries@patent.gov.uk

The Goldsmiths' Company
http://thegoldsmiths.co.uk

British Horological Institute
http://www.bhi.co.uk/hints/
    hmarks.htm

Collectiques' Hallmark Database
http://www.collectiques.net/
    hallmarks/mkdecode.html

ROM Silver
http://romlx6.rom.on.ca/art-
    design/silver/silver-hall-
    marks.html

Antiques UK
http://www.antiques-
    uk.co.uk/buy in britain/hall-
    marks2.htm#top

Sources with Information on Silver Products and Jewelry

Silvermine
http://freespace.virgin.net/a.da
    ta/worldindex.htm

Silver Hawk
http://www.silverhawk.com/cr
    afts/welcome.html

Spratling Silver
http://www.spratlingsilver.com

Silver Forum
http://www.mschon.com/
    SilverForum.html

Modern Silver Magazine
http://www.modernsilver.com

The ArtMetal Project
http://wuarchive.wustl.edu/ed
    u/arts/metal/ArtMetal.html

Metal Arts Guild
http://ptolemy.eecs.berkeley.e
    du/~mag/

Metal Arts Society of
    Southern California
http://members.aol.com/mass-
    cnews

The Silver Institute
http://www.silverinstitute.org/
    frames.htm

Antique Jewelry Times
http://www.antiquejewelry-
    times.com/

The Society of American
    Silversmiths
http://www.silversmithing.com

Ganoksin
http://ganoksin.com

Gulsmedsforbundet (Organi-
    zation for silver-goldsmiths)
http://www.guldsmedsforbu-
    undet.se
E-mail: info@guldsmedsfor-
    bundet.se

Silversmedjan
http://www.silversmedjan.se

Dansk Design/Jewelry
http://www.jewelry.dk/jewel
    da.htm

Costume Jewelry Resource
    Page
http://www.efn.org/~jabrams/
    jewelry.htm

The National Museum of
    Women in Arts (Biographies
    of women silversmiths)
http://www.nmwa.org/legacy/
    bios/bsilver.htm

Crafts Denmark (Second site
    given is devoted to jewelry)
http://www.craftsdk.com/
http://www.craftsdk.com/crafts
    dk-craftsm.html

The Nordic Pages (Arts and
    Culture)
http://www.markovits.com/
    nordic/culture.shtml

Major Magazines and Publications

Jewelers Circular Keystone
    Magazine
Chilton Way
Radnor, PA 19019
(610) 964-4470
JCK Publications
http://www.jckgroup.com/

Silver Magazine
http://www.silvermag.com/
    SILVER.HTM

Modern Jeweler Magazine
19 W 44th St. 9th Floor
New York, NY 10036
(212) 921-1901

National Jeweler Magazine
One Penn Plaza
New York, NY 10119
(212) 615-2380
http://www.national-jeweler.com

The Estate Jeweler Magazine
849 Almar Ave.
Santa Cruz, CA 95060
(415) 834-0718

The Vintage Fashion & Costume Jewelry Newsletter
P.O. Box 265
Glen Oaks, NY 11004
(718) 939-7988

The Metalsmith
Society of North American
   Goldsmiths
5009 Londonderry Drive
Tampa, FL 33647

Antique Collectors' Club
   (Publications on Antiques &
   Collectibles)
Market Street Industrial Park,
Wappingers Falls, NY 12590

Lapidary Journal
Circulation Department
P.O. Box 124
Devon, PA 19333

Eden Sterling Company
   (Reproduction of old catalogs)
http://www.edensterling.com

Arlington Book Company, Inc.
2706 Elsmore Street
Fairfax, VA 22031 USA
Phone: 703-280-2005
Fax: 703-280-5300
e-mail: info@arlingtonbooks.com
http://www.info@arlington-
   books.com/

Collector Books (Publica-
   tions on antiques & collectibles, including jewelry)
Paducah, KY 42002-3009
http://www.collectorbooks.com

American Style Magazine
http://www.americanstyle.com

Auction Market Resource
   (Quarterly published data
   on jewelry auction sales)
(718) 897-7305

Ornament
P.O. Box 452
Mount Morris, IL 61054

Schiffer Publishing Ltd. (Publications on antiques & collectibles, including jewelry)
77 Lower Valley Road
Atglen, PA 19310

Auction Catalog Co. (Clearing
   house for post-auction catalogs)
503 Live Oak St.
Miami, AZ 85539

Organizations and Associations

American Craft Council
72 Spring St.
New York, NY 10012
(212) 274-0630
fax: (212) 274-0650

American Gem Society
8881 W Sahara Ave
Las Vegas, NV 89117
(702) 255-6500
http://www.ags.org

The American Society of
   Jewelry Historians
Box 103, 1B Quaker Ridge Rd.
New Rochelle, NY 10804
(212) 744-3691

American Society of Appraisers
Box 17265
Washington, D.C. 20041
(800) ASA-Valu
fax: (703) 742-8471

Appraisers Association of
   America Inc.
386 Park Ave. South, Suite
   2000
New York, NY 10016
 (212) 889-5404
fax: (212) 889-5503
e-mail: AppraisersAssn@com-
   puserve.com.

Canadian Jewellers Association
27 Queen St. E, Suite 600
Toronto, Ont. M5C 2M6
(416) 368-7616
fax: (416) 368-1986

Canadian Jewellers Institute
27 Queen St. E., Suite 600
Toronto, Ont. M5C 2M6
(416) 368-7616
fax: (416) 368- 1986

CIBJO International Confedera-
   tion of Jewellery, Silverware,
   Diamonds, Pearls and Stones
78-A Luke St.
London EC2A 4PY, United
   Kingdom
+44 171-613-4243
fax: +44 171-613-4450
e-mail: nag@easynet.co.uk

Estate Jewelers Association of
   America
209 Post Street Suite 718
San Francisco, CA 94108
(415) 834-0718
e-mail: estatejaa@aol.com

Fashion Jewelry Association
   of America Inc.
3 Davol Sq., #135
Providence, RI 02903

Indian Arts & Crafts
   Association Inc.
122 La Veta Dr., NE, Suite B
Albuquerque, NM 87108
(505) 265-9149
fax: (505) 265-8251

International Society of
   Appraisers
16040 Christensen Rd #320
Seattle, WA 98188-2929
(206) 241-0359
http://www.isa-appraisers.org

Jewelers of America Inc.
1185 Ave. of the Americas
   30th floor
New York, NY 10036
(212) 768-8777
fax: (212) 768-8087
e-mail: info@jewelers.org.

National Association of
  Jewelry Appraisers
P.O. Box 6558
Annapolis, MD 21401-0558
(301) 261-8270

The National Cufflink Society
Box 5700
Vernon Hills, IL 60001

Silver Institute
1112 16 St. N.W., Suite 240
Washington, D.C. 20036
 (202) 835-0185
fax: (202) 835-0155
e-mail: info@silverinstitute.org.

Silver Users Association
1730 M St. N.W., #911
Washington, D.C. 20036
(202) 785-3050

Society of American
  Silversmiths
P.O. Box 3599,
Cranston, RI 02910
(401) 461-3156
fax: (401) 461-3196,
e-mail: jherman@silver-
  smithing.com.
http://www.silversmithing.com

Women's Jewelry Association
333B Route 46 West, Suite B-
  201
Fairfield, NJ 07004
(973) 575-7190
fax: (973) 575-1445

Online Vintage Jewelry Outlets

The author's select list of Internet outlets for purchasing vintage jewelry. A few new jewelry sites are given for information.

Soren Jensen
http://jensensilver.com

Tijeras Traders
http://www.allrep.com/

Arts & Artifacts
http://www.arts-artifacts.com/

Cleora's Vintage and Estate
  Jewelry
http://www.q-tiques.com/cleo-
  rasjewelry/

Jewelry Mall (new jewelry)
http://www.jewelrymall.com/

Modern Silver Jewelry
http://www.mschon.com

Buck a Gram (New "American
  Indian Style" silver jewelry
  produced in the Far East)
http://www.buckagram.com/

Granat (New silver jewelry
  sold from Czech Republic)
http://www.granat-
  cz.com/default.html

Native Hands Gallery (Indian Jewelry)
http://www.nativehands.com/h
  tml/catalog/index.html

For Your Ears Only
http://www.oldjewels.com/
  index.html

Liz Collectible Costume Jewelry
http://www.lizjewel.com/

The Glitter Box
http://www.glitterbox.com

Retro Gallery
http://www.retrogallery.co.uk

Eureka I Found It
http://www.eureka-i-found-
  it.com/

A Link to the Past
http://www.alinkto.com/

All Vintage Jewelry
http://www.tias.com/stores/all
  vintagejewelry/

Hillary's Antique Jewelry Store
http://pacificws.com/jewelry/vi
  ctoria.phtml

Lace Wing Jewelry (interesting designs by Lisa Youell)
http://www.lacewing.com

Mad Jewelry
http://www.madjewelry.com

Auction Houses

These are both major on-site and online auction houses. The area of specialization or additional information is given in brackets. Readers not familiar with auctions, particularly online auctions, are urged to read the section on auctions in Chapter 1.

Antiquorum (Antiques, collectibles, jewelry)
609 Fifth Ave.
New York, NY 10017
(212) 750-1103
http://www.antiquorum.com

Beverly Hills Auctioneers
  (Recent and vintage jewelry)
9454 Wilshire Boulevard
Suite 202
Beverly Hills, CA 90212
(310) 278-8115

Butterfield & Butterfield
  (Antiques, including
  jewelry)
220 San Bruno Avenue
San Francisco, CA 94103
(415) 861-7500 and
7601 Sunset Boulevard
Los Angeles, CA 94103
(213) 850-7500

Christie's (Antiques, including
  jewelry)
502 Park Avenue
New York, NY 10022
(212) 546-1000 and
360 North Camden Drive
Beverly Hills, CA 90120
(310) 385-2600
http://www.christies.com

Dupuis (Jewelry)
94 Cumberland Street,
   Suite 908
Toronto, ON M5R, 1A3 Canada
(416) 968-7500
http://www.dupuisauctions.com

G. G. Sloan & Co. (Mixed
   merchandise, including
   occasional jewelry)
4920 Wyaconda Rd. N.
Bethesda, MD 20852
(301) 468-4911

Grogan & Company (Jewelry)
22 Harris St.
Dedham, MA 02026
(617) 569-1502

Jones & Horan Auction Team
   (Watches and jewelry)
Goffstown, NH
(603) 623-5314
http://www.jones-horan.com

Joseph Dumouchelle Fine
   Estate Jewelry Auctions
   (Jewelry)
199 N. Main St., Suite 204
Plymouth, MI 48170
(734) 455-4555

Phillips (British &
   Continental)
406 E. 79th St.
New York, NY 10021
(800) 825-2781
http://www.phillipsauctions.com

Skinner Gallery (Antiques & collectibles, including jewelry)
Park Plaza
Boston, MA 02116
(617) 350-5400
http://www.skinnerinc.com

Sotheby's (Antiques & collectibles, including jewelry)
1334 York Ave
New York, NY 10021
(212) 606-7000
http://www.sothebys.com

Weschler's
905-9 E Street, N.W.
Washington, D.C.
(800) 331-1430

William Doyle Gallery
175 E. 87th St.,
New York, NY 10138
(212) 427-2730
http://www.doylegalleries.com

Online Auctions

Amazon Auctions (extensive
   jewelry section with light to
   medium traffic)
http://www.amazon.com

Auction Universe (jewelry section
   with light to medium traffic)
http://www.auctionuniverse.com

Ehammer
http://www.ehammer

eBay (extensive jewelry section with heavy traffic)
http://www.ebay.com

Icollector
http://www.nmwa.org/legacy/b
ios/bsilver.htm

Jewelcollect Auction (site specializing in jewelry)
http://playle.com/jewels

Ubuy2 Inc
http://www.mschon.com./msj.
html

YahooAuctions (free auctions
   with extensive jewelry section
   with light to medium traffic)
http://auctions.yahoo.com

Major Art Museums and Galleries

Only institutions with major collections of silver products, jewelry, or significant relevant historical and cultural material are listed.

United States
Alaska
Homer: Miller Comb Museum

Arizona
Phoenix: Phoenix Art Muse-
   um; The Heard Museum
Tucson: Tucson Museum of
   Art
Flagstaff: Museum of North-
   ern Arizona

California
Los Angeles: Armand Ham-
   mer Museum of Art and
   Cultural Center; Fisher
   Gallery of Art; The LA
   County Museum of Art; The
   Southwest Museum
Oakland: The Oakland Museum
San Francisco: Asian Art
   Museum of San Francisco;
   Museum of Modern Art
Santa Ana: Bowers Museum of
   Cultural Art
Sacramento: Crocker Art
   Museum

San Diego: Museum of Con-
   temporary Art
Berkeley: University of California Art Museum

Colorado
Denver Art Museum

Connecticut
The New Britain Museum of
   American Art

Delaware
Wilmington: Delaware Art
   Museum

District of Columbia
Freer Gallery of Art
National Gallery of Art
National Museum of American
   Art
The Smithsonian Institution

Florida
Coral Gables: Museum of His-
   panic and Latin American
   Art; Lowe Art Museum
West Palm Beach: Norton
   Gallery and School of Art

Indiana
Bloomington: Indiana University Museum

Illinois
Chicago: The Art Institute of Chicago; The Museum of Architecture and Design; Museum of Contemporary Art; The Oriental Institute Museum; Field Museum of Natural History
Elmhurst: Lizzadro Museum of Lapidary Arts

Maryland
Baltimore: The Walters Art Gallery

Massachusetts
Andover: Addison Gallery of American Art
Cambridge: Harvard University Art Museums
North Adams: Massachusetts Museum of Contemporary Art
Boston: Museum of Fine Arts

Michigan
Detroit: The Detroit Institute of Arts
Ann Arbor: The Kelsey Museum of Archaeology; University of Michigan Museum of Art
East Lansing: University of Michigan Museum of Art

Minnesota
Minneapolis: The Minneapolis Institute of Arts; Weisman Art Museum
St. Paul: Minnesota Museum of American Art

Missouri
Kansas City: Kemper Museum of Contemporary Art and Design; The Nelson-Atkins Museum of Art

New Hampshire
Conway: The Cuff Link Museum

New Mexico
Santa Fe: Museum of International Folk Art; Wheelwright Museum of the American Indian
Taos: Millicent Rogers Museum

New Jersey
The Art Museum (Princeton University)

New York
New York City: American Craft Museum; Brooklyn Art Museum; Cooper-Hewitt National Design Museum; The Guggenheim Museum; The Metropolitan Museum of Art; Museum of Modern Art; New Museum of Contemporary Art; National Museum of the American Indian

Ohio
Cleveland: Cleveland Institute of Art; The Cleveland Museum of Art
Cincinnati: Contemporary Arts Center

Pennsylvania
Pittsburgh: Carnegie Museum of Art
Philadelphia: Pennsylvania Academy of the Fine Arts Museum; Philadelphia Museum of Art; The University of Pennsylvania Museum

Rhode Island
Providence: Providence Jewelry Museum; Rhode Island School of Design Museum of Art

Texas
Houston: Contemporary Arts Museum of Houston
Fort Worth: The Modern Art Museum of Fort Worth

China
Beijing Art Museum

Czech Republic
Joblanc: Glass and Costume Jewelry Museum
Prague: Museum of Decorative Arts

Denmark
Copenhagen: Georg Jensen Museum; Danske Kunstindustrimuseum (Danish Museum of Decorative Arts)
Kolding: Museet på Koldinghus

Egypt
Cairo: Egyptian Museum (Ancient jewelry)

Finland
Helsinki: Museum of Applied Arts; National Museum of Finland

France
Paris: Musée des Arts Décoratifs; Musée des arts et métiers (Museum of Arts and Crafts); Conservatoire National de Arts et Métiers

Germany
German National Musuem/ LGA Museum of Applied Arts and Design
Pforzheim: Schmuck Museum
Hohenhof: Museum des Hagener Impulses (Jugendstil)

Greece
Athens: National Museum; Benaki Museum (Extensive ancient jewelry collection)

Ireland
Dublin: National Museum of Ireland

Israel
Tel Aviv Museum of Art

Italy
Rome: Museo Nazionale delle Arti e Tradizioni Popolari (National Museum of Popular Arts and Traditions)
Firenze: Museo degli Argenti

Japan
Kyoto National Museum (Metalwork)

Mexico
There is no substitute for visiting Taxco.
Musfo Franz Mayer (Colonial silver collection)

Morocco
Marrakech: Dar Si Said Museum (Berber Jewelry Collection)
Fez: Bert Flint Museum (Costumes & jewelry collection)

Norway
Oslo: The Oslo Museum of Applied Art; Norskfolk

Peru
Lima: Museo Arqueologico (Pre-Colombian gold); Museo de Arte de Lima; Museo de la Nación

Portugal
Lisbon: Calouste Gulbenkian Museum

Sweden
Stockholm: The National
Museum; Nordiska Museet
(Historical on the island of
Djurgårde); Arjeplog: Silver
Museet (extensive Saami/
Lapps collection); Malmö
Museet; Göteborg Museum
of Art

Turkey
Istanbul: Topkapi Palace
Museum (Extensive metal-
work collection)

United Kingdom
London: The British Museum;
Victoria and Albert Museum
Birmingham: Birmingham
Museum
Cambridge: Fitzwilliam
Museum

Supplies

Sources listed are suppliers of material for silversmiths, dealers, and collectors.

ABI Precious Metals (silver and related
supplies for silversmiths)
P.O. Box 11509
Carson, CA 90749
Phone: 800-878-2242
Fax: 310-768-1566

Ace's Gems & Minerals, Inc. (variety of
lapidary and related supplies)
300 Westport Rd
Kansas City, MO 64111
Phone: 816-561-2004
Fax: 816-561-2043

Alpha Supply, Inc. (variety of jewelry
making supplies)
1225 Hollis St.
Bremerton, WA
http://www.alpha-supply.com
e-mail: two@alpha-supply.com

Indian Jewelers Supply Co.
P.O. Box 1774
601 E. Coal Ave
Gallup, NM 87305

Jewelry Display Service (display boxes
and stands)
10218 Georgibelle Dr, #300
Houston, TX 77043
http://www.jewelry-display.com
e-mail: jds300@nol.net

Kiefer (variety of supplies for antique
dealers and collectors)
417 West Stanton Ave
Fergus Falls, MN 56537
Phone: 888-543-3377
Fax: 218-736-7474

Invention and Design Patent Numbers

The following table provides the approximate dates for the U.S. invention and design patent numbers which can be used to date jewelry which is marked with a patent number.

Patent Numbers	*Patent Dates*	*Design Patent Numbers*
1 – 7,000	1836 – 1850	
7,000 – 29,000	1850 – 1860	260 – 1,180
29,000 – 98,000	1860 – 1870	1,180 – 3,810
98,000 – 158,000	1870 – 1875	3,810 – 7,970
158,000 – 223,000	1875 – 1880	7,970 – 11,570
223,000 – 310,000	1880 – 1885	11,570 – 15,680
310,000 – 419,000	1885 – 1890	15,680 – 19,550
419,000 – 532,000	1890 – 1895	19,550 – 23,900
532,000 – 640,000	1895 – 1900	23,900 – 32,000
640,000 – 778,000	1900 – 1905	32,000 – 37,280
778,000 – 945,000	1905 – 1910	37,280 – 40,400
945,000 – 1,123,000	1910 – 1915	40,400 – 46,800
1,123,000 – 1,327,000	1915 – 1920	46,800 – 54,360
1,327,000 – 1,522,000	1920 – 1925	54,360 – 66,350
1,522,000 – 1,172,000	1925 – 1930	66,350 – 80,250
1,172,000 – 1,986,000	1930 – 1935	80,250 – 94,200
1,986,000 – 2,185,000	1935 – 1940	94,200 – 118,360
2,185,000 – 2,366,000	1940 – 1945	118,360 – 140,000
2,366,000 – 2,493,000	1945 – 1950	140,000 – 156,700
2,493,000 – 2,919,000	1950 – 1960	156,700 – 187,000
2,919,000 – 3,487,000	1960 – 1970	187,000 – 216,400
3,487,000 – 4,181,000	1970 – 1980	216,400 – 253,800
4,181,000 – 4,891,000	1980 – 1990	253,800 – 305,280

Bookstores

GIA Bookstore
5355 Armada Drive, Suite 300
Carlsbad, CA
92008 (800) 421-8161

J.M. Cohen, Rare Books
2 Karin Court
New Paltz, NY 12561
New titles as well as large selection of
out-of-print books. Catalog.

Joslin Hall Rare Books
P.O. Box 516
Concord, MA 01742
(508) 371-3101
http://www.joslinhall.com
e-mail: jhall@tiac.net
A treasure trove of rare and out-of-print
books. Ordering one or two books per
year is worth it to receive their highly
entertaining catalog!

Rocks of Ages
P.O. Box 3503
Tustin, CA 92781
(714) 730-8948
Used and out-of-print books about
gemology, mineralogy, and jewelry.
Catalog.

Twelfth Street Booksellers
P.O. Box 3103
Santa Monica, CA 90408
(310) 822-1505
Used and out-of-print titles on gemology,
precious stones, and jewelry. Catalog.

National Authorized Assay Offices

As of the 1972 convention, designated under the hallmarking convention.

Austria
Hauptpunzierungs und
    Probieramt
Gumpendorferstrasse 63-B
A-1060 VIENNA

Czech Republic
Puncovni Urad
Kozí 4
CZ-110 00 PRAHA 1

Denmark
FORCE Institutes
Dantest - Aedelmetalkontrollen
Park Allé 345
DK-2605 BRONDBY

Finland
Technical Inspection Center
Technical Department
P.O. Box 108
Vilhonvuorenkatu, 11 C
FIN-00181 HELSINKI

Ireland
Ireland Assay Office
Dublin Castle
IRL - Dublin 2NorwayEdel-
    metallkontrollen
Postboks 2608
St. Hanshaugen
N-0131 OSLO 1

Portugal
Imprensa Nacional
Casa da Moeda
Av. Antonio José de Almeida
P-1092 LISBON CODEX
Contrastaria do Porto
Rua Visconde de Bobeda
P - 4000 Porto

Sweden
Swedish National Testing and
    Research Institute
P.O. Box 857
S-501 15 BORÅS

Switzerland
SwitzerlandOberzolldirektion
Zentralamt für
Edelmetalkontrolle
CH-3001 BERNE

Other Swedish Silver Manufacturers

Mark(s)	Company/Silversmith	City	Active Period
AAS	Agne Allvin Silversmedjan	Vetlanda	1971-
AB MN	Nometa Metallindustri AB	Stockholm	1944-1970s
ACP	Carl Silversmed/Anna Påhlman	Ystad	1956-1961
AGM	Anna-Greta Mossbäck	Lindesberg	1951-
AGSs	Andrens Guld & Silversmedja	Trelleborg	1951-
AHÅ	Astrid Håkansson Silversmedja	Uppsala	1973-
AHÖ; A HÖGBERGS	Anders Högbergs Silversmedja	Göteborg	1963-1982
ALG	Axel Lindberg*	Söderhamn	1942-1977
A&R	Arvidson & Reutner	Falköping	1945-1946
ASA	ASA-Silver/H Olsson, T Linde, P Block	Falkenberg	1928-
ASN; ASÅ	Anna-Stina Åberg*	Nyköping	1972-
ÅML	Åke Landström	Kalmar	1969-
ÄLB	Ädelsmide, Lars Bostrand	Gävle	1957-1969
BBKB	Bengt Bellander	Stockholm	1972-
BJÖ	Lena Björkman	Stockholm	1977-
BO	Bror Onnela*	Haparanda+	1938-1980
BOL	Lennart Oehmke	Stockholm	1963-1979
BRU	Jan Brunk	Stockholm	1976-
CASI	Carl Nyströmer*	Stockholm	1956-1962

CFC; CFS SAB	C F Carlman*	Stockholm	1913-1961
C I ENG; CIENG; ENG	Carl Ingvar Eng*	Stockholm+	1935-1978
CPO	Paul Ollson	Sunne	1959-1987
EDEN	Edensvärds Guld & Silversmide	Göteborg	1962-1980
EKS; SES	Erik Ströms*	Stockholm+	1936-1970s
GC	Christiansilver/S Christiansson*	Stockholm	1944-1959
GÖ	Gösta Andersson	Linköping	1970-
GÖL	G Lindelöfs	Malmö	1973-1977
HBD	Hans Gjörklund	Stockholm	1956-1970s
HELMER	Helmer Åstrand	Skruv	1966-1979
HGC	Hans G Claesson	Gävle	1961-1969
ILS	Inga Lagervall	Lidingö	1970-
IWP	Ivar Wremp	Ljungby	1951-1966
JEAS	Jan Eve Stengårds	Visby	1974-
JED	Jörgen Dock*	Laholm+	1955-1982
JFD	Jörgen Fruergaard	Norrköping	1969-1980
JLSF	S Fryklunds	Sundbyberg	1958-1987
KERO	Sven & Bertil Silversmide/Roos & Kempe	Västerås	1965-1971
KGW	Kjell Gidlöw	Bonässund	1972-1987
KSL	K Lindbloms	Jönköping	1974-
KÖ	Krestin Öhlin	Östersund	1962-
LANTZ	Roland Lantz	Stockholm	1960-
LCW	Lars Christer Wenngrens	Gävle	1970-
LGL	Laver-Carlsson*	Stockholm	1950-
LGN	L Nilssons Silversmedja	Söderköping+	1948-1970s
LHM	Lena Mellander	Göteborg	1965-
LKS	Lars Kaj Rinman	Stockholm	1965-1987
LS	Lindbergs Silversmide AB	Stockholm	1950-1958
LSS	Leif Söderlund	Malung	1974-
MBN	Bruno Nilsson*	Östersund+	1966-
MFS	Mats Fridmark	Älvsjö	1964-1978
MÅ	Georg Ströde	Göteborg	1973-1983
NAL	Silversmedja Nils Lindkvist	Helsingborg	1934-1980
N&D	Nyberg & Dahlin	Göteborg	1948-1951
OJN	Owe Johansson*	Landskrona+	1965-
OOS	Olle Ohlsson	Stockholm	1961-
PWF	Ådelsmedjan Apollo/ Peter W Fielder*	Järna	1972-
RU	Ray Urban	Stockholm	1952-
SAJ	Annie Jägbeck	Lund	1976-
SET	Einar Telander	Lidingö	1961-
SIK	Sivert Källden*	Noraström+	1972-
SJG	J Grönroos*	Kristianstad	1928-1970
TAI	Rosa Taikon*	Ytterhogdal+	1966-
THM; T HOLM	Tore Holm*	Stockholm+	1937-1968
TKR; T KULLANDER	Tore Kullander*	Borås	1938-

*Firm acquired or reorganized under various names.
Source: Extracted from Stämplar på arbeten av guld, silver och platina, 1913-1987, Statens provingsanstalt.

\+ Firm relocated to various cities.

Glossary

Abalone Shell: Mollusk shell of the genus *Haliotis* of iridescent mixed gray, blue and green colors used frequently on Mexican silver jewelry.

Agate: Hard semi-precious stone of various colors, sometimes with a pattern or stripes.

Alabaster: A variety of gypsum and highly porous stone which is easily dyed. Used mostly in decorative objects but sometimes also in jewelry, as in Mexico.

Alloy: A mixture of two or more metals.

Alpaco: An alloy of metals, zinc, nickel, copper, and silver, imitating silver but with an off tone even when polished.

Amal: Arabic or Persian word found on old silver meaning "the work of" or "made by" followed by the name of silversmith. A Middle Age practice of marking used until the nineteenth century and seldom found on twentieth century silver jewelry unless by a major silversmith.

Amazonite: Light green semi-precious stone named after the Amazon River but found throughout the world.

Amber: Natural fossilized resin of the pine tree found in various shades of yellow, brown, and red, less frequently in other colors, used in making beads and as a stone on jewelry. Amberoid is the pressed variety in imitation of the solid natural pieces.

Amethyst: Semi-precious stone in various shades of violet. Used both in faceted and the natural state in jewelry made in various parts of the world.

Annular Brooches: Certain type of brooches in the shape of a ring which were popular in Ireland and Scotland.

Arabesque: A decorative pattern of flowing scroll work consisting of vines, leaves, and flowers, known as Eslimi in Persian and Central Asia and a recurring pattern in Arabic, Persian and some Central Asian silver products, including jewelry.

Art Deco: A decorative style succeeding Art Nouveau in 1920s which emphasized simple, often linear and curvilinear forms, and the use of exotic materials such as ebony, ivory, lacquer, bronze, and chrome, showing strong Egyptian, African, Aztec, and Oriental influences.

Art Nouveau: A decorative style prominent during the 1890 – 1910 period emphasizing curves, spirals, undulating forms, and stylized naturalistic motifs, particularly female figures. Influenced by both the Symbolism and Arts & Crafts movement as well as reflecting Egyptian, Persian, and Oriental, particularly Japanese, influences. Also known as "Jugendstil" in German speaking countries and "Stile Liberty" in Italy.

Arts & Crafts Movement: A movement that was a reaction to industrialization and mass production, emphasizing craftsmanship, craft aesthetic, and simple functional designs. Influenced by the theories and ideas propagated by Ruskin and Morris in England and named after the Arts and Crafts Exhibition Society founded in 1882 in England.

Assay: The analytical test used to determine metal content and silver fineness.

Aventurine: Translucent variety of quartz in various shades of green, showing a mix or spray of other substances.

Bail: The loop or connecting ring of a pendant which holds the chain passed through it.

Baguette: A gemstone with a rectangular cut.

Basse Taille: Enamel work whereby translucent enamel is poured over the cut surface of a metal base, giving depth and a three-dimensional look. Used frequently in modern Norwegian enamel jewelry.

Bench Mark: The silversmith's mark consisting of a symbol, initials or a name on the product. The same as the maker's mark but not necessarily a trademark.

Bezel set: A setting where the collar of the metal is so shaped that it embraces the stone.

Biomorphic: Designs based on free form and irregular shapes such as amoebic forms found in nature. Originally associated with the Surrealist school and works of Yves Tanguy and Hans Arp.

Cabochon: A facet-less cut stone with a flat bottom and polished dome-shaped face.

Cairngorm: Yellowish, sometimes cloudy stone similar to citrine and of the quartz family. The gray variety is also known as smoky quartz.

Cameo: A stone, coral or shell carved to render a design in relief. (See Intaglio.)

Carnelian: A semi-precious stone in orange to reddish brown of the quartz family used frequently in the Mediterranean and Middle Eastern jewelry.

Cartouche: A geometric box or symbol that frames the maker's mark or other writings and initials.

Casting: (See p. 13.)

Cat's Eye: An stone which has an internal reflection resembling an eye.

Chalcedon: Translucent semi-precious stone of the quartz family in blue or gray. The same as carnelian and chrysoprase which are in red and green.

Champleve: A technique of enameling where enamel is poured into the cut and carved areas of the base metal. Basse taille is a variety of champleve work whereas cloisonne is enamel within the wire cells created on the metal surface. Used frequently in Oriental and some European jewelry.

Chatelaine: A metal clasp or brooch with chains to which several useful items are attached. Usually worn at the waist.

Chrysoprase: Translucent stone of the quartz family in green color. The same as carnelian and chalcedony which are reddish brown and blue.

Cinnabar: Red lacquer pigment applied in many layers and carved. Used frequently in Oriental, particularly Chinese jewelry.

Citrine: A yellowish stone of the quartz family.

Claw Setting: A stone setting in which the stone is held by metal prongs slightly folded over its edges.

Clip: Similar to a brooch which has hooked teeth for fastening instead of a pin stem. Fur clips usually have two pin stems. Out of fashion after 1940s.

Cloisonne: Enamel decoration accomplished by pouring enamel into a raised compartment of a pattern on the metal base or the surface of the object and then fired to solid form.

Coral: A sea organism in various shades of red used in jewelry. Large corals of good grade and color have become increasingly rare and expensive. Sensitive to acids and heat and may fade in color after long wear.

Crystal (Rock Crystal): Colorless quartz used frequently in modern Scandinavian jewelry. Amethyst and citrine are the color variety of rock crystal.

Damascene: A metal surface decoration and finish derived from the name of the city Damascus which is reputed to have been a center for this type of

work in the Middle Ages. A form of niello work.

Die Stamping: A die with a cut pattern or motif which can be repeatedly used to reproduce the same pattern on metal base. Used in the mass production of silver jewelry.

Diopside: A transparent green stone used frequently in modern Finnish silver jewelry.

Dragon: An ancient motif used on Oriental and sometimes Celtic jewelry.

Electroplating: A base metal with its surface covered by a coating of another metal using electrolysis, such as silverplate over nickel.

Electrum: A natural alloy of gold and silver used in ancient times to make coins, ornamental objects, and jewelry.

Embossing: A decorative technique where the pattern or patterns are stamped into the surface of the metal.

Engine Turned: A method of decorating the surface of the metal using a lathe. Machine engraved or textured surface.

Engraving: A technique of creating a design on the base metal using an engraving tool.

Estate Jewelry: Previously owned, usally older, jewelry offered for sale.

Facet: Small surface on a stone either occurring naturally or mechanically cut.

Farman: Persian word meaning royal order or decree but widely known in reference to the Tughra or the Ottoman sultan's seal which was used as assay mark on silver products. (See Tughra.)

Feldspars: A family of stones formed of silicate minerals. Moonstones, Amazonite, aventurine, and labradorite are sub-group varieties.

Festoon: A chain or set of chains decorated with pendant drops, usually set with stones.

Filigree: A technique where shapes and

patterns are created by using fine silver or gold wires.

Findings: Various parts such as fasteners used to complete a piece of jewelry.

Fleur-de-Lis: An stylized floral symbol meaning "flower of light" in French and widely used as a city mark as well as a trademark. See Myer's trademark in Chapter 2.

Fobs: A piece of jewelry or chain from which another piece, such as a watch, can be suspended.

Foil backing: A thin metal plating or coating used on the back of gemstones or glass to enhance their brilliance and appearance.

Fraternal Jewelry: Jewelry that incorporates the emblem or symbol of an organization, such as the Masonic Order or Shriners, including the jewelry of college fraternities and sororities in the U.S.

Fretwork: Cutting and piercing of elaborate and intricate patterns in silver vessels and sometimes jewelry where the remaining portion forms the openwork design.

Garnet: Orange to deep red faceted stone used widely but found frequently on Bohemian jewelry.

Girdle: The outer edge or periphery of a cut stone.

Goldstone: Synthetic stone with copper background and gold flakes.

Granulation: Minute grains of gold or silver applied to the surface to create a pattern. First used by the Phoenicians, later perfected by the Etruscans, becoming a distinct feature of Etruscan jewelry.

Guilloche Enamel: A decorative technique using translucent polychrome enamel to cover the surface of a piece of jewelry

Hallmark: An English term having found common usage when referring to a stamp on precious metals indicating quality, place of manufacture, and manufacturer. The national silver standard (hallmark) is different from trademark and maker's mark, though both may be incorporated as part of the stamp.

Handarbete: Swedish for handmade.

Handarbeit: German for handmade.

Hematite: Heavy and highly reflective stone with iron mineral, used widely on silver jewelry, particularly rings.

Intaglio: A stone whereby a pattern is cut and engraved into its surface, creating concave recess such as the ancient seals.

Ivory: The tusk and teeth of elephants and other large land or sea mammals used widely but particularly in Oriental jewelry. Should not be confused with bone which is also used in Oriental jewelry and is softer and less compact and dense. Use of new ivory is highly regulated by international agreements and a significant portion of new products in the market are made of illegal ivory.

Jade: Usually refers to two different types of stones: jadite, a hard stone in a variety of colors ranging from white to black, but frequently in green; and nephrite which is of greater abundance and lower quality, primarily in various shades of green. Should not be confused with other colored stones. True jade has a hardness of 7 or better and cannot be marked with a nail or knife.

Jasper: Opaque stone of the quartz family, usually in red or brown.

Kinetic Jewelry: Commonly refers to jewelry with moving or rotating parts sometimes designed so that there is motion inside and outside of the piece of jewelry while it is worn.

Labradorite: A gray stone, a variety of feldspar used in early twentieth century European jewelry.

Lapis Lazuli: A blue stone with flakes of iron pyrite, used widely but particu-

larly in Persian, Afghan, and Central Asian jewelry.

Lavaliere: Similar to pendant.

Locket: A box type of ornament in various shapes which housed photographs, locks of hair, or other precious mementos. Frequently used as a pendant but also found on bracelets and fobs.

Lost Wax Method: An ancient but still practiced method of casting in which a mold is made of wax and then covered with soft clay which when baked will "lose" the wax and become a solid mold that can be used to accept the molten metal in casting. The process is also referred to as Cire-Perdu.

Loup: A folding pocket magnifying glass of varying strength though the jeweler's loup is usually of a ten-fold magnifying power (10X).

Maker's Mark: The mark of the manufacturer or silversmith. Also referred to as the bench mark but not necessarily a trademark.

Malachite: Opaque green stone with vine patterns, used widely but particularly in Russian, English, and Scottish jewelry.

Marcasite: Shiny, faceted iron pyrite stones, often used with silver jewelry to give the illusion of diamonds.

Marquise: Faceted oval shape stone, also referred to as navette cut.

Mexican Jade: Colored onyx or alabaster resembling jade and frequently used in Mexican jewelry.

Mizpah Jewelry: A type of gift jewelry popular in the nineteenth century and still made today, given at the time of separation with the word "Mizpah," meaning "God watch over you," written on it. See Mizpah in Chapter 2.

Moonstone: Translucent stone with waxy or milky luster, a variety of feldspar, found frequently on European jewelry.

Moss Agate: An agate of the quartz family, usually translucent with a moss pattern in it.

Mother-of-Pearl: The inner surface or the nacreous layer of the mollusk shell with pearly and iridescent color used in jewelry, particularly inlaid work.

Niello: An inlay decoration on silver, also called damascening.

Obsidian: Volcanic glass of high vitreous luster in a variety of colors but usually jet black, used in Native American and Mexican jewelry.

Onyx: A variety of agate often colored black but also in other colors.

Opal: A milky stone with flames and flashy speckles, widely used.

Parure: Usually a complete matching set of jewelry which includes necklace, bracelet, brooch, and earrings. Demi-parure is a partial matching set.

Pave Set: Small stones set on the surface of the metal base to create a pattern or contrast.

Pavilion: A portion of a gemstone below its outer edges, referred to as a girdle.

Pearl: Formation of a secretion in an oyster, called nacre, that creates the round as well as irregular beads known as pearls. Culturing pearls involves inducing this secretion by implanting an irritant in an oyster. The practice dates back to medieval China, but the technology for harvesting on a commercial basis was developed by K. Mikimoto in Japan in 1893. Most twentieth century pearls are cultured pearls with freshwater pearls usually having irregular shapes.

Pebble Jewelry: Usually refers to the Scottish jewelry which used native stones on silver and was popular during the Victorian period.

Peking Glass: A glass originally handmade in China to imitate jade in its variety of colors, a form of art glass cut with various designs sometimes with several layers of color.

Phoenix: A mythological bird used as a motif in ancient Egypt, and also part of Zoroastrian and Chinese folklore, which is sometimes found as a motif on modern silver jewelry, including those made in Europe.

Pierce Work: Similar to fretwork, usually accomplished with machinery.

Plique-à-Jour: A type of cloisonne enamel work with no backing, similar to stained glass, where the hard enamel is held in place by the metal frame. Used frequently in Art Nouveau and Art Deco jewelry.

Repoussé: A decorative technique whereby a surface pattern is produced by hammering, punching, and shaping the reverse side of the metal.

Quartz: Crystalline silica found in a variety of colors, constituting a broad family of stones including crystal, rose quartz, citrine, and amethyst.

Rhinestone: Originally, faceted rock crystals and in the twentieth century made of clear or color glass with or without foil backing.

Rose Quartz: Pinkish quartz found frequently in Scandinavian jewelry.

Sard: Carnelian stone with a uniform reddish brown color, found frequently in Mediterranean and Middle Eastern jewelry.

Sardonyx: A banded Sard.

Sautoir: A long chain which usually terminated with a tassel or pendant and extended below the waist.

Scarab: A beetle-like insect used frequently as a motif in ancient Egyptian arts which became a popular motif with several schools of decorative arts and jewelry, such as the Art Deco jewelry. In ancient Egypt, the scarab was a symbol of longevity.

Scarf Pins: A long, needle-like pin with a fancy terminal at one end, usually a

tube-like fastener at the other end for inserting the pin, used by both men and women on scarfs and cravats (ties). With long, modern ties, tie tacks and bars became popular, replacing the scarf pin used by men. Also known as a stick pin.

Smoky Quartz: A grayish or smoky color brilliant stone of the quartz family. Also known as Cairngorm.

Sodolite: A bluish stone with speckles, frequently used in its natural state in Scandinavian jewelry.

Stones of the Month: A particular stone which is universally associated with a particular month with minor variations in certain countries, and a designation based on historic religious and cultural superstition which has survived and been internationally commercialized in modern times.

January: Garnet, rose quartz
February: Amethyst, onyx
March: Aquamarine, red jasper
April: Diamond, rock crystal
May: Emerald, chrysoprase
June: Ruby, carnelian
July: Pearl
August: Peridot, aventurine
September: Sapphire, lapis lazuli
October: Opal, tourmaline
November: Topaz, tiger's eye
December: Turquoise

Stones of the Zodiac: A particular stone associated with each of the 12 planets on the imaginary belt of planets in the heavens, a designation based on historic religious and cultural superstition which has survived and been internationally commercialized in modern times.

Aquarius: Turquoise
Pisces: Amethyst
Aries: Red carnelian, red jasper
Taurus: Orange carnelian, rose quartz
Gemini: Citrine, tiger's eye
Cancer: Chrysoprase, green aventurine
Leo: Rock crystal

Virgo: Yellow agate or citrine
Libra: Orange citrine, smoky quartz
Scorpio: Sard or blood carnelian
Sagittarius: Chalcedony, blue quartz
Capricorn: Onyx, cat's eye

Tiger's Eye: Golden brown stone with iron oxide forming a wave pattern and sometimes resembling an eye.

Tongue Clip: A pronged snap clip used for suspending watches or chatelaines.

Tortoise Shell: The shell backing used in hair ornaments during the Victorian era and sometimes in jewelry such as Art Nouveau or some modern jewelry.

Tourmaline: A large family of stones occurring in variety of colors and quality, with the green shade used most frequently.

Trademark: A legally registered and protected mark identifying the manufacturer.

Tuğra (Tughra): The seal of the Ottoman ruler or sultan, rendered in near indecipherable calligraphy and used as assay mark on Turkish silver. Each Tughra includes the name of the reigning ruler and its documented use dates back to as early as the 1340s. The use of Tughra was discontinued with the establishment of modern Turkey after the Ottomans' defeat in WWI.

Turquoise: Opaque stone found in blue to greenish shades with some impurities. Called Persian turquoise when in its pure and uniform sky blue color.

Vermeil: Silver jewelry with a gold plating.

Vinaigrette: A small container with a perforated top which originally held aromatic vinegar or scents.

Website: A page on the Internet containing information or promoting a product.

Zoomorphic: Designs in the shape of animals or parts of their bodies.

Bibliography

The primary sources used in writing this book include many catalogs; over approximately 1,800 correspondences with manufacturers, silversmiths, government agencies, museums, and experts in the relevant fields; and the references listed below which are limited to only those sources which were directly or indirectly utilized in researching and writing the text.

Abbey, Staton. *The Goldsmiths and Silversmiths Handbook,* Van Nostrand, 1952.

Acta Archaelogica, various volumes.

Adair, John. *The Navajo and Pueblo Silversmiths,* University of Oklahoma Press, 1975.

Aksoy, Şule, et al. *Osmanli Padişah Fermanlari* (Ottoman King's Seals), 1986.

American Indian Art Magazine, various issues.

Andrén, Erik. *Swedish Silver,* Gramercy Publishing Co., 1950.

Arbman, Holger. *The Vikings,* Barnes & Noble, 1995.

Arts of Asia, various issues.

Arizona Highways, various issues.

Assay Office of Great Britain. Hallmarks on Gold, Silver and Platinum.

Baker, Lillian. *Art Nouveau & Art Deco Jewelry,* Collector Books, 1981 and 1992.

Bassman, Theda and Michael. *Zuni Jewelry,* Schiffer Publishing, 1992.

Becker, Vivienne. *Art Nouveau Jewelry,* E.P. Dutton, 1985.

Bly, John. *Miller's Silver & Sheffield Plate Marks,* 1999.

Bennet, Edna Mae and John. *Turquoise Jewelry of the Indians of the Southwest,* Turquoise Books Co, 1973.

Blair, Claude. *The History of Silver,* MacDonald & Co. Ltd., 1987.

Brooklyn Museum. *Contemporary Industrial and Handwrought Silver,* catalog, 1937.

Bruton, Eric. *Hallmark and Date Letters on Silver, Gold, and Platinum,* N.A.G. Press, 1944.

Carpenter, Charles H., Jr. *Gorham Silver 1831 – 1981,* 1982.

Carre, Louis. *Les Poinçons de L'Orfèvrerie Française,* n.p., 1928

———. *Guide de L'Amatur d'Orfèvrerie Française,* n.p., 1929.

Cartlidge, Barbara. *Twentieth Century Jewelry,* Abrams, 1985.

Cera, Deanna Farneti, et al. *I Gioielli della Fantasia (Jewels of Fantasy),* Idea Books, 1991.

Cederwell, Sandraline, and Hal Riney. *Spratling Silver,* Chronicle Books, 1990.

Chadwick, Nora. *The Celts,* Penguin, 1971.

Chamberlain, Marcia. *Metal Jewelry Techniques,* Watson-Buptill Publications, 1976.

Cirillo, Dexter. *Southwest Indian Jewelry,* Abbeville Press, 1992.

Coleman, Elizabeth Ann. *The Opulent Era,* Brooklyn Museum in Association with Thames and Hudson, 1990.

Connoisseur, various issues.

Culme, J. *The Dictionary of Gold and Silversmiths, Jewellers and Allied Traders, 1838 – 1914.* Antique Collectors' Club, 1987.

Cunliffe, Barry W. *The Celtic World,* Crown, 1986.

Darling, Sharon S. *Chicago Metalsmiths,* Chicago Historical Society, 1977.

Davidov and Dawes. *Victorian Jewelry: Unexplored Treasures,* Abbeville Press, 1991.

Davis, Mary L. and Greta Pack. *Mexican Jewelry,* University of Texas Press, Austin, 1989

De Castres, Elizabeth. *A Guide to Collecting Silver,* Bloomsbury Books, 1985.

Divis, Jan. *Silver Marks of the World,* Hamlyn, 1976.

D'Orey, L. *Five Centuries of Jewellery.* Portugal's National Museum of Ancient Art, 1995.

Drucker, Janet. *George Jensen, A Tradition of Splendid Silver,* Schiffer Publishing, 1997.

Duval, Paul-Marie, and Christopher Hawkes, eds. *Celtic Art in Ancient Europe: Five Protohistoric Centuries,* Academic Press, 1976.

Duncan, Alastair. *Art Deco,* Thames and Hudson, 1988.

Dybdah, Lars, et al. *Nordisk Smykkekunst (Nordic Jewellery),* Nyt Nordisk Forlan Arnold Busck, 1995.

Eluere, Christiane. *The Celt: Conquerors of Ancient Europe,* Abrams, 1993.

Ensko, Stephen G. C. *American Silversmiths and Their Marks,* 1927.

——————. *American Silversmiths and Their Marks II,* 1937.

Ensko, Guernsey Cook, and David R. Godine. *American Silversmiths and Their Marks,* Stephen Publisher, Inc., 1989 (see above).

English, Helen W. Drutt, and Peter Dormer. *Jewelry of Our Time: Art, Ornament, and Obsession,* Rizzoli Publishing, 1995.

Ettinghausen & Oleg Grabar. *The Art & Architecture of Islam 650 – 1250,* Yale University Press, 1994.

Fallon, John P. *Marks of London Goldsmiths and Silversmiths, 1837 – 1914,* Barrie & Jenkins, 1992.

Forbes, J. S. *Hallmark,* Unicorn Press, 1999.

Foscue, Edwin J. *Taxco: Mexico's Silver City,* Southern Methodist University Press, 1947.

Fossburg, Jorunn. *Draktsølje,* Universitetsforlaget, 1991.

Funder, Lise. *Dansk Sølv,* Nyt Nordisk Forlag Arnold Busck, 1999.

Gabardi, Melissa. *Art Deco Jewellery 1920 to 1949,* Antique Collectors' Club, 1989.

Gere, Charlotte. *American and European Jewelry, 1830 – 1914,* Crown Publishers, 1975.

Gere, Charlotte, and Geoffrey C. Munn. *Pre-Raphaelite to Arts and Crafts Jewellery,* Antique Collectors' Club, 1996.

Gluck, Jay & Sumi, eds. *A Survey of Persian Handicraft,* Bank Meli, 1977.

Greenbaum, Toni. *Messengers of Modernism: American Studio Jewelry 1940– 1960,* Montreal Museum of Decorative Arts in association with Flammarion, 1996.

Green, Miranda. *Celtic Art,* Sterling Publishing Co., 1997.

Green, Robert Alan. *Marks of American Silversmiths,* Murphy, 1977.

Gregoretti, G. *Jewellery Through the Ages,* 1970.

Grousset, Rene. *The Empire of the Stepps, A History of Central Asia,* Rutgers Univ., 1970.

Hallmarks and Date Letters on Silver, Gold, and Platinum, N.A.G. Press, 1977.

Harper's Bazar, various issues.

Hase-Schmundt, Ulrike von, et al. *Theodor Fahrner Jewelry, Between Avant-Garde and Tradition,* Schiffer Publishing, 1991.

Haslam, Malcolm. *Art Deco,* MacDonald and Co., 1987.

——————. *Arts and Crafts,* MacDonald and Co., 1988.

——————. *Marks & Monograms, the Decorative Arts 1880 – 1960,* Collins & Brown, 1995.

Haycraft, John. *Finnish Jewelry and Silverware,* Otava, 1962.

Hayden, Arthur. *Chats on Old Silver,* Unwin, 1915.

Herodotus (tr.). *The History,* Prometheus Books, 1992.

Hinks, Peter. *Nineteenth Century Jewellery,* Faber and Faber, 1975.

—————. *Twentieth Century British Jewellery 1900 – 1980,* Faber and Faber, 1983.

Hiort, Esbjørn. *Moderne Dansk Sølve (Modern Danish Silver),* Museum Books, 1954.

Hogan, Edmond P. *An American Heritage, A Book About the International Silver Company,* Taylor Publishing Co., 1977.

Holland, Margaret. *Silver, An Illustrated Guide to Collecting Silver,* Octopus Books Limited, 1973.

Hughes, Graham. *Modern Jewelry,* Crown Publishers, 1968.

—————. *Modern Silver Throughout the World, 1880 – 1967,* Crown Publishers, 1967.

—————. *The Art of Jewelry,* Viking Press, 1972.

Jackson, Charles James. *English Goldsmiths and Their Marks,* Macmillan, 1921.

Jareb, James. *Arts and Crafts of Morocco,* Thames and Hudson, 1995.

Jewelers' Circular-Keystone/Heritage, various issues.

Jewelers' Circular-Keystone Brand Name & Trademark Guide, JCK, 1965 – 1994.

Jewelers' Circular-Keystone (originally Jewelers' Circular), Trade Marks of the Jewelry and Kindred Trades. JCK, 1896 – 1950.

The Jewelers' Dictionary, Jewelers' Circular-Keystone, nd.

Jones, Edward Alfred. *Old Silver of Europe and America,* Batsford, Ltd., 1928.

Jones, K.C., ed. *The Silversmiths of Birmingham and Their Marks, 1750 – 1980,* N.A.G. Press, 1981.

Kalin, Kaj. *Lapponia Jewelry: Suomalainen Kansainvälinen Koru (Lapponia Jewelry: International Jewelry from Finland),* Painotyöt Art-Print Oy, 1990.

Kalter, Johannes. *The Arts and Crafts of Turkestan,* Thames and Hudson, 1985.

—————— et al. *The Arts and Crafts of Syria,* Thames and Hudson, 1998.

Karlin, Elyse Zorn. *Jewelry and Metalwork in the Arts & Crafts Tradition,* Schiffer Publishing, 1993.

Kaleidoscope, various issues, 1928 – 1933.

Kramer, Samuel Noah. *History Begins at Sumer,* Doubleday, 1959.

Krekel-Aalberse, Annelies. *Art Nouveau and Art Deco Silver,* Thames and Hudson, 1989.

Kraus, E. H. and C. B. Slawson. *Gems and Gem Materials,* McGraw-Hill, 1947.

Kürkman, Garo. *Ottoman Silver Marks,* Mathusalem Publications, 1996.

Lanllier, Jean, et al. *Five Centuries of Jewelry in the West,* Arch Cape Press, 1983.

Lapidary Journal, various issues.

La Plante, John D. *Asian Art,* Wm. C. Brown, 1968

Lassen, Erik. *George Jensen Silversmithy, 77 Artists, 75 Years,* Smithsonian Institution, 1980.

Luke, Catriona. *Celtic Gold,* Michael O'Mara Books, 1996.

Lee, Sherman E. *A History of Far-Eastern Art,* Abrams, 1964.

Lewin, Susan Grant. *One of a Kind: American Art Jewelry Today,* Abrams, 1985.

Lloyd, Steton. *Early Anatolia,* Penguin Books, 1956.

Mack, John, ed. *Ethnic Jewelry,* Abrams, 1988.

Madsen, Karl. *Thorvald Bindesbøll,* 1934.

Martin, Scott V. *Guide to Evaluating Gold & Silver Objects,* SM Publications, 1996.

Metal Arts, various issues, 1928 – 1930.

Metalsmith, various issues.

Meilack, Dona Z. *Ethnic Jewelry, Design & Inspiration for Collectors and Craftsmen,* Crown Publishers, 1981.

Metropolitan Museum of Art. *Modern Europe,* Metropolitan Museum of Art, 1985.

—————. *The Islamic World,* Metropolitan Museum of Art, 1987.

—————. *Contemporary American Design by Manufacturers, Designers and Craftsmen,* Metropolitian Museum of Art, (catalog), 1938.

Møller, Osvald. *Carl M. Cohr, 1860 – 1925,* 1960.

Møller, Viggo S. *Henning Koppel,* 1965.

Moro, Ginger. *European Designer Jewelry,* Schiffer Publishing, 1995.

Morrill, Penny. *Silver Masters of Mexico,* Schiffer Publishing, 1996.

Morrill, Penny, and Carole Berk. *20th Century Handwrought Jewelry and Metalwork,* Schiffer Publishing, 1995.

Morton, Phillip. *Contemporary Jewelry: A Craftsman's Handbook,* Holt Rhinehart & Winston, 1970.

National Jewelers' Trade and Trademarks Directory, 1918 – 1919, The National Jeweler, 1918.

Norwich, John Julius. *Bysantium: the Decline and Fall,* Alfred A. Knopf 1995.

Newman, Harold. *An Illustrated Dictionary of Jewelry,* Thames and Hudson, 1981.

Nielsen, L. C. *Georg Jensen,* Fr. Bagge Printers, 1921.

Olmstead, A. T. *The History of the Persian Empire,* University of Chicago, 1948.

Orientations, various issues.

Ornament, various issues.

Paine, R. T., and Alexander Soper. *Art and Architecture of Japan,* Penguin Books, 1960

Parker, Jean. *The Sterling Silversmiths Guild of America,* 1948.

Pavitt, Nigel. *Turkana, Nomads of the Jade Sea,* Harvill Press, 1999.

Peters, F. E. *The Harvest of Hellenism,* Barnes & Noble, 1995.

Peterson, J. *Vikingetidens Smykker,* 1928.

Phillips, Clare. *Jewelry From Antiquity to the Present,* Thames and Hudson, 1996.

Pickford, Ian, ed. *Jackson's Hallmarks,* Pocket Edition, Antique Collector's Club, 1994.

Poutasuo, Tuula ed. *Finnish Silver,* Teema Oy, 1989.

Pullee, Caroline. *20th Century Jewelry,* Mallard Press, 1990.

Registrering Af Navnestempler For Arbejder Af Aedle Metaller 1893 – 1988, Statens Kontrol med Aedle Metaller, 1988.

Rainwater, Dorothy T. *American Jewelry Manufacturers,* Schiffer Publishing, 1986.

—————. *American Silver Manufacturers,* Schiffer Publishing, 1988.

Raulet, Sylvie. *Art Deco Jewelry,* Rizzoli, 1984.

Reno, Dawn E. *American Indian Collectibles,* House of Collectibles, 1988.

Rezazadeh, Fred. *Costume Jewelry,* Collector Books, 1998.

Romero, Christie. *Warman's Jewelry 1st Edition,* Christie, Wallace-Homestead, 1995; and 2nd Edition, Krause Publications, 1998.

Sataloff, *Art Nouveau Jewelry,* Dorrance & Company, 1984.

Schiffer, Nancy. *Jewelry by Southwest American Indians: Evolving Designs,* Schiffer Publishing, 1988.

—————. *Silver Jewelry Designs: Evaluating Quality,* Schiffer Publishing, 1996.

Schumann, Walter. *Gemstones of the World,* Sterling Publishing, 1977.

—————. *Minerals of the World,* Sterling Publishing, 1992.

Schwartz, Walter. *Georg Jensen, en Kunstner, Hans Tid og Slaegt (Georg Jensen, an Artist, His Time and Heritage),* Georg Jensen & Wendel Inc., 1963.

Schweiger, Werner. *Wiener Werkstätte (Design in Vienna), 1903-1932,* Thames and Hudson, 1990.

Shatz, Sheryl Gross. *What's It Made Of? A Jewelry Materials Identification Guide,* published by the author, 1991.

Silver, various issues.

Silver of a New Era, Int'l Highlights of Precious Metalware from 1880 to 1940, Zilveren Kruis Groep, 1992.

Smithsonian Institution. *Art Treasures of Turkey,* Smithsonian Institutions, 1966.

Solodkoff, A. *Russian Gold and Silver,* 1981.

Somaini, Luisa, and Claudio Cerritelli. *Jewelry By Artists in Italy 1945 – 1995,* Electa/Gingko, 1995.

Stefansson, J. "The Vikings in Spain From Arabic and Spanish Sources," in *Sag Book of the Viking Club,* Vol. VI, 1909.

Sullivan, Michael. *Chinese Arts in the Twentieth Century,* Univ. of California Press, 1959.

Talanova, Olga, ed. *Along The Great Silk Road* (Russian & English text), Kramds, 1991.

Tardy, *International Hallmarks on Silver,* Tardy, 1985.

Tarkastustleimat Suomessa Jalometallituotteet (Precious Metal Marks), T.T.K., 1984.

Thage, Jacob. *Danske Smykker/Danish Jewelry,* Komma & Clausen, 1990.

Thorn, C. Jordan. *Handbook of American Silver and Pewter Marks,* Tudor Publishing Co., 1949.

Truman, Charles. *Sotheby's Concise Encyclopedia of Silver,* Conran Octopus, 1993.

Turner, Ralph. *Contemporary Jewelry, A Critical Assessment, 1945 – 1975,* Van Nostrand Reinhold, 1976.

—————. *Jewelry in Europe and America: New Times, New Thinking,* Thames and Hudson, 1996.

Umur, Suha. *Osmanli Padişah Tuğralari (Ottoman King's Tugras),* 1980.

US Patent and Trademark Office.

Vogue, various issues, 1942 – 1957.

Weber, Christianne. *Schmuck-der 20er und 30er Jahre in Deutschland,* Arnoldsche, 1990.

Webster, R. *Gems in Jewellery,* Northwood, 1975.

Welch, Stuart Cary. *Persian Painting,* George Braziller, 1976.

Westin, Ann. *Torun, Conversation with Vivianna Torun Bülow-Hübe,* Carlsson Borkförlag AB, 1997 reprint.

Widman, Dag. *Sigurd Persson: en Mästare i Form,* Carlsson Borkförlag AB, 1994.

Wilcox, Donald. *New Design in Jewelry,* Van Nostrand Reinhold, 1970.

Willetts, William. *Foundations of Chinese Art,* McGraw-Hill, 1965.

Woolley, C. Leonard. *The Sumerians,* Barnes & Noble, 1995. Out of print 1st edition recommended.

Wright, Barton. *Hallmarks of the Southwest,* Schiffer Publishing, 1989.

Wright, Margaret Nickelsen. *Hopi Silver: The History and Hallmarks of Hopi Silversmithing,* Northland Press, 1976.

Wyler, Seymour B. *The Book of Old Silver,* Crown Publishers, 1977.

Untracht, Oppi. *Jewelry: Concepts and Technology,* Doubleday, 1985.

Victoria & Albert Museum, *Modern Artists' Jewels,* Victoria and Albert Museum, 1984.

Zaczek, Laid. *The Art of the Celts,* Parkgate Books, 1997.

Zapata, Janet. *The Jewelry and Enamels of Louis Comfort Tiffany,* Abrams, 1993.

Index

COLLECTOR BOOKS

Informing Today's Collector

*For over two decades we have been keeping collectors
informed on trends and values in all fields of antiques
and collectibles.*

DOLLS, FIGURES & TEDDY BEARS

4707	A Decade of **Barbie Dolls** & Collectibles, 1981–1991, Summers	$19.95
4631	**Barbie Doll** Boom, 1986–1995, Augustyniak	$18.95
2079	**Barbie Doll** Fashion, Volume I, Eames	$24.95
4846	**Barbie Doll** Fashion, Volume II, Eames	$24.95
3957	**Barbie** Exclusives, Rana	$18.95
4632	**Barbie** Exclusives, Book II, Rana	$18.95
4557	**Barbie,** The First 30 Years, Deutsch	$24.95
5672	The **Barbie Doll** Years, 4th Ed., Olds	$19.95
3810	**Chatty Cathy** Dolls, Lewis	$15.95
5352	Collector's Ency. of **Barbie** Doll Exclusives & More, 2nd Ed.,Augustyniak	$24.95
2211	Collector's Encyclopedia of **Madame Alexander** Dolls, Smith	$24.95
4863	Collector's Encyclopedia of **Vogue Dolls**, Izen/Stover	$29.95
5598	**Doll Values**, Antique to Modern, 4th Ed., Moyer	$12.95
56101	**Madame Alexander** Collector's Dolls Price Guide #25, Crowsey	$9.95
5612	**Modern Collectible Dolls**, Volume IV, Moyer	$24.95
5365	**Peanuts Collectibles**, Podley/Bang	$24.95
5253	Story of **Barbie**, 2nd Ed., Westenhouser	$24.95
5277	**Talking Toys** of the 20th Century, Lewis	$15.95
1513	**Teddy Bears & Steiff** Animals, Mandel	$9.95
1817	**Teddy Bears & Steiff** Animals, 2nd Series, Mandel	$19.95
2084	**Teddy Bears, Annalee's & Steiff** Animals, 3rd Series, Mandel	$19.95
5371	**Teddy Bear** Treasury, Yenke	$19.95
1808	Wonder of **Barbie**, Manos	$9.95
1430	World of **Barbie** Dolls, Manos	$9.95
4880	World of **Raggedy Ann** Collectibles, Avery	$24.95

TOYS, MARBLES & CHRISTMAS COLLECTIBLES

2333	Antique & Collectible **Marbles**, 3rd Ed., Grist	$9.95
5353	**Breyer Animal** Collector's Guide, 2nd Ed., Browell	$19.95
4976	**Christmas Ornaments**, Lights & Decorations, Johnson	$24.95
4737	**Christmas Ornaments**, Lights & Decorations, Vol. II, Johnson	$24.95
4739	**Christmas Ornaments**, Lights & Decorations, Vol. III, Johnson	$24.95
4649	Classic Plastic **Model Kits**, Polizzi	$24.95
4559	Collectible **Action Figures**, 2nd Ed., Manos	$17.95
3874	Collectible **Coca-Cola Toy Trucks**, deCourtivron	$24.95
2338	Collector's Encyclopedia of **Disneyana**, Longest, Stern	$24.95
4958	Collector's Guide to **Battery Toys**, Hultzman	$19.95
5038	Collector's Guide to **Diecast Toys** & Scale Models, 2nd Ed., Johnson	$19.95
4651	Collector's Guide to **Tinker Toys**, Strange	$18.95
4566	Collector's Guide to **Tootsietoys**, 2nd Ed., Richter	$19.95
5169	Collector's Guide to **TV Toys** & Memorabilia, 2nd Ed., Davis/Morgan	$24.95
5360	**Fisher-Price Toys**, Cassity	$19.95
4720	The Golden Age of **Automotive Toys**, 1925–1941, Hutchison/Johnson	$24.95
5593	Grist's Big Book of **Marbles**, 2nd Ed.	$24.95
3970	Grist's Machine-Made & Contemporary **Marbles**, 2nd Ed.	$9.95
5267	**Matchbox Toys**, 1947 to 1998, 3rd Ed., Johnson	$19.95
4871	**McDonald's** Collectibles, Henriques/DuVall	$19.95
1540	Modern **Toys** 1930–1980, Baker	$19.95
3888	**Motorcycle Toys**, Antique & Contemporary, Gentry/Downs	$18.95
5368	**Schroeder's Collectible Toys**, Antique to Modern Price Guide, 6th Ed.	$17.95
2028	**Toys**, Antique & Collectible, Longest	$14.95

FURNITURE

1457	American **Oak** Furniture, McNerney	$9.95
3716	American **Oak** Furniture, Book II, McNerney	$12.95
1118	Antique **Oak** Furniture, Hill	$7.95
2271	Collector's Encyclopedia of **American** Furniture, Vol. II, Swedberg	$24.95
3720	Collector's Encyclopedia of **American** Furniture, Vol. III, Swedberg	$24.95
5359	Early **American** Furniture, Obbard	$12.95
1755	Furniture of the **Depression Era**, Swedberg	$19.95
3906	**Heywood-Wakefield** Modern Furniture, Rouland	$18.95
1885	**Victorian** Furniture, Our American Heritage, McNerney	$9.95
3829	**Victorian** Furniture, Our American Heritage, Book II, McNerney	$9.95

JEWELRY, HATPINS, WATCHES & PURSES

1712	Antique & Collectible **Thimbles** & Accessories, Mathis	$19.95
1748	Antique **Purses**, Revised Second Ed., Holiner	$19.95
1278	Art Nouveau & Art Deco **Jewelry**, Baker	$9.95
4850	Collectible **Costume Jewelry**, Simonds	$24.95
3722	Collector's Ency. of **Compacts**, Carryalls & Face Powder Boxes, Mueller	$24.95
4940	**Costume Jewelry**, A Practical Handbook & Value Guide, Rezazadeh	$24.95
1716	Fifty Years of Collectible **Fashion Jewelry**, 1925–1975, Baker	$19.95
1424	**Hatpins** & Hatpin Holders, Baker	$9.95
1181	100 Years of Collectible **Jewelry**, 1850–1950, Baker	$9.95
4729	**Sewing Tools** & Trinkets, Thompson	$24.95
5620	Unsigned Beauties of **Costume Jewelry**, Brown	$24.95
4878	Vintage & Contemporary **Purse Accessories**, Gerson	$24.95
3830	Vintage **Vanity Bags** & Purses, Gerson	$24.95

INDIANS, GUNS, KNIVES, TOOLS, PRIMITIVES

1868	Antique **Tools**, Our American Heritage, McNerney	$9.95
5616	Big Book of **Pocket Knives**, Stewart	$19.95
4943	Field Guide to Flint **Arrowheads & Knives** of the North American Indian	$9.95
3885	**Indian Artifacts** of the Midwest, Book II, Hothem	$16.95
4870	**Indian Artifacts** of the Midwest, Book III, Hothem	$18.95
5685	**Indian Artifacts** of the Midwest, Book IV, Hothem	$19.95
5687	**Modern Guns**, Identification & Values, 13th Ed., Quertermous	$14.95
2164	**Primitives**, Our American Heritage, McNerney	$9.95
1759	**Primitives**, Our American Heritage, 2nd Series, McNerney	$14.95
4730	Standard **Knife** Collector's Guide, 3rd Ed., Ritchie & Stewart	$12.95

PAPER COLLECTIBLES & BOOKS

4633	**Big Little Books**, Jacobs	$18.95
4710	Collector's Guide to **Children's Books**, 1850 to 1950, Jones	$18.95
5596	Collector's Guide to **Children's Books**, 1950 to 1975, Jones	$19.95
1441	Collector's Guide to **Post Cards**, Wood	$9.95
2081	Guide to Collecting **Cookbooks**, Allen	$14.95
5613	Huxford's **Old Book** Value Guide, 12th Ed.	$19.95
2080	Price Guide to **Cookbooks & Recipe Leaflets**, Dickinson	$9.95
3973	**Sheet Music** Reference & Price Guide, 2nd Ed., Pafik & Guiheen	$19.95
4654	**Victorian Trade Cards**, Historical Reference & Value Guide, Cheadle	$19.95
4733	**Whitman Juvenile Books**, Brown	$17.95

GLASSWARE

5602	Anchor Hocking's **Fire-King** & More, 2nd Ed.	$24.95
4561	Collectible **Drinking Glasses**, Chase & Kelly	$17.95
4642	Collectible **Glass Shoes**, Wheatley	$19.95
5357	Coll. **Glassware** from the 40s, 50s & 60s, 5th Ed., Florence	$19.95
1810	Collector's Encyclopedia of **American Art Glass**, Shuman	$29.95
5358	Collector's Encyclopedia of **Depression Glass**, 14th Ed., Florence	$19.95
1961	Collector's Encyclopedia of **Fry Glassware**, Fry Glass Society	$24.95
1664	Collector's Encyclopedia of **Heisey Glass**, 1925–1938, Bredehoft	$24.95
3905	Collector's Encyclopedia of **Milk Glass**, Newbound	$24.95
4936	Collector's Guide to **Candy Containers**, Dezso/Poirier	$19.95
4564	**Crackle Glass**, Weitman	$19.95
4941	**Crackle Glass**, Book II, Weitman	$19.95
4714	**Czechoslovakian Glass** and Collectibles, Book II, Barta/Rose	$16.95
5528	Early American **Pattern Glass**, Metz	$17.95
5682	**Elegant Glassware** of the Depression Era, 9th Ed., Florence	$19.95
5614	Field Guide to **Pattern Glass**, McCain	$17.95
3981	Evers' Standard **Cut Glass** Value Guide	$12.95
4659	**Fenton** Art Glass, 1907–1939, Whitmyer	$24.95
5615	Florence's **Glassware Pattern Identification** Guide, Vol. II	$19.95
3725	**Fostoria**, Pressed, Blown & Hand Molded Shapes, Kerr	$24.95
4719	**Fostoria**, Etched, Carved & Cut Designs, Vol. II, Kerr	$24.95

COLLECTOR BOOKS
Informing Today's Collector

3883	**Fostoria Stemware**, The Crystal for America, Long/Seate	$24.95
5261	**Fostoria Tableware**, 1924 – 1943, Long/Seate	$24.95
5361	**Fostoria Tableware**, 1944 – 1986, Long/Seate	$24.95
5604	**Fostoria**, Useful & Ornamental, Long/Seate	$29.95
4644	**Imperial Carnival Glass**, Burns	$18.95
3886	**Kitchen Glassware** of the Depression Years, 5th Ed., Florence	$19.95
5600	Much More Early American **Pattern Glass**, Metz	$17.95
5690	Pocket Guide to **Depression Glass**, 12th Ed., Florence	$9.95
5594	Standard Encyclopedia of **Carnival Glass**, 7th Ed., Edwards/Carwile	$29.95
5595	Standard **Carnival Glass** Price Guide, 12th Ed., Edwards/Carwile	$9.95
5272	Standard Encyclopedia of **Opalescent Glass**, 3rd Ed., Edwards/Carwile	$24.95
5617	Standard Encyclopedia of **Pressed Glass**, 2nd Ed., Edwards/Carwile	$29.95
4731	**Stemware Identification**, Featuring Cordials with Values, Florence	$24.95
4732	**Very Rare Glassware** of the Depression Years, 5th Series, Florence	$24.95
4656	**Westmoreland Glass**, Wilson	$24.95

POTTERY

4927	**ABC Plates & Mugs**, Lindsay	$24.95
4929	**American Art Pottery**, Sigafoose	$24.95
4630	**American Limoges**, Limoges	$24.95
1312	**Blue & White Stoneware**, McNerney	$9.95
1958	So. Potteries **Blue Ridge Dinnerware**, 3rd Ed., Newbound	$14.95
1959	**Blue Willow**, 2nd Ed., Gaston	$14.95
4851	Collectible **Cups & Saucers**, Harran	$18.95
1373	Collector's Encyclopedia of **American Dinnerware**, Cunningham	$24.95
4931	Collector's Encyclopedia of **Bauer Pottery**, Chipman	$24.95
4932	Collector's Encyclopedia of **Blue Ridge Dinnerware**, Vol. II, Newbound	$24.95
4658	Collector's Encyclopedia of **Brush-McCoy Pottery**, Huxford	$24.95
5034	Collector's Encyclopedia of **California Pottery**, 2nd Ed., Chipman	$24.95
2133	Collector's Encyclopedia of **Cookie Jars**, Roerig	$24.95
3723	Collector's Encyclopedia of **Cookie Jars**, Book II, Roerig	$24.95
4939	Collector's Encyclopedia of **Cookie Jars**, Book III, Roerig	$24.95
5040	Collector's Encyclopedia of **Fiesta**, 8th Ed., Huxford	$19.95
4718	Collector's Encyclopedia of **Figural Planters & Vases**, Newbound	$19.95
3961	Collector's Encyclopedia of **Early Noritake**, Alden	$24.95
1439	Collector's Encyclopedia of **Flow Blue China**, Gaston	$19.95
3812	Collector's Encyclopedia of **Flow Blue China**, 2nd Ed., Gaston	$24.95
3431	Collector's Encyclopedia of **Homer Laughlin China**, Jasper	$24.95
1276	Collector's Encyclopedia of **Hull Pottery**, Roberts	$19.95
3962	Collector's Encyclopedia of **Lefton China**, DeLozier	$19.95
4855	Collector's Encyclopedia of **Lefton China**, Book II, DeLozier	$19.95
5609	Collector's Encyclopedia of **Limoges Porcelain**, 3rd Ed., Gaston	$24.95
2334	Collector's Encyclopedia of **Majolica Pottery**, Katz-Marks	$19.95
1358	Collector's Encyclopedia of **McCoy Pottery**, Huxford	$19.95
3837	Collector's Encyclopedia of **Nippon Porcelain**, Van Patten	$24.95
2089	Collector's Ency. of **Nippon Porcelain**, 2nd Series, Van Patten	$24.95
1665	Collector's Ency. of **Nippon Porcelain**, 3rd Series, Van Patten	$24.95
4712	Collector's Ency. of **Nippon Porcelain**, 4th Series, Van Patten	$24.95
1447	Collector's Encyclopedia of **Noritake**, Van Patten	$19.95
1037	Collector's Encyclopedia of **Occupied Japan**, 1st Series, Florence	$14.95
1038	Collector's Encyclopedia of **Occupied Japan**, 2nd Series, Florence	$14.95
2335	Collector's Encyclopedia of **Occupied Japan**, 5th Series, Florence	$14.95
4951	Collector's Encyclopedia of **Old Ivory China**, Hillman	$24.95
5564	Collector's Encyclopedia of **Pickard China**, Reed	$29.95
3877	Collector's Encyclopedia of **R.S. Prussia**, 4th Series, Gaston	$24.95
5618	Collector's Encyclopedia of **Rosemeade Pottery**, Dommel	$24.95
1034	Collector's Encyclopedia of **Roseville Pottery**, Huxford	$19.95
1035	Collector's Encyclopedia of **Roseville Pottery**, 2nd Ed., Huxford	$19.95
4856	Collector's Encyclopedia of **Russel Wright**, 2nd Ed., Kerr	$24.95
4713	Collector's Encyclopedia of **Salt Glaze Stoneware**, Taylor/Lowrance	$24.95
3314	Collector's Encyclopedia of **Van Briggle Art Pottery**, Sasicki	$24.95
4563	Collector's Encyclopedia of **Wall Pockets**, Newbound	$19.95
2111	Collector's Encyclopedia of **Weller Pottery**, Huxford	$29.95
3876	Collector's Guide to **Lu-Ray Pastels**, Meehan	$18.95
3814	Collector's Guide to **Made in Japan Ceramics**, White	$18.95

4646	Collector's Guide to **Made in Japan Ceramics**, Book II, White	$18.95
2339	Collector's Guide to **Shawnee Pottery**, Vanderbilt	$19.95
1425	**Cookie Jars**, Westfall	$9.95
3440	**Cookie Jars**, Book II, Westfall	$19.95
4924	Figural & Novelty **Salt & Pepper Shakers**, 2nd Series, Davern	$24.95
2379	Lehner's Ency. of **U.S. Marks** on Pottery, Porcelain & China	$24.95
4722	**McCoy Pottery**, Collector's Reference & Value Guide, Hanson/Nissen	$19.95
1670	**Red Wing Collectibles**, DePasquale	$9.95
1440	**Red Wing Stoneware**, DePasquale	$9.95
1632	**Salt & Pepper Shakers**, Guarnaccia	$9.95
5091	**Salt & Pepper Shakers** II, Guarnaccia	$18.95
2220	**Salt & Pepper Shakers** III, Guarnaccia	$14.95
3443	**Salt & Pepper Shakers** IV, Guarnaccia	$18.95
3738	**Shawnee Pottery**, Mangus	$24.95
4629	Turn of the Century **American Dinnerware**, 1880s–1920s, Jasper	$24.95
3327	**Watt Pottery** – Identification & Value Guide, Morris	$19.95

OTHER COLLECTIBLES

4704	Antique & Collectible **Buttons**, Wisniewski	$19.95
2269	Antique **Brass & Copper** Collectibles, Gaston	$16.95
1880	Antique **Iron**, McNerney	$9.95
3872	Antique **Tins**, Dodge	$24.95
4845	Antique **Typewriters & Office Collectibles**, Rehr	$19.95
5607	Antiquing and Collecting on the **Internet**, Parry	$12.95
1128	**Bottle** Pricing Guide, 3rd Ed., Cleveland	$7.95
4636	**Celluloid** Collectibles, Dunn	$14.95
3718	Collectible **Aluminum**, Grist	$16.95
4560	Collectible **Cats**, An Identification & Value Guide, Book II, Fyke	$19.95
4852	Collectible **Compact Disc** Price Guide 2, Cooper	$17.95
5666	Collector's Encyclopedia of **Granite Ware**, Book 2, Greguire	$29.95
4705	Collector's Guide to **Antique Radios**, 4th Ed., Bunis	$18.95
5608	Collector's Gde. to Buying, Selling, & Trading on the **Internet**, 2nd Ed., Hix	$12.95
3880	Collector's Guide to **Cigarette Lighters**, Flanagan	$17.95
4637	Collector's Guide to **Cigarette Lighters**, Book II, Flanagan	$17.95
4942	Collector's Guide to **Don Winton Designs**, Ellis	$19.95
3966	Collector's Guide to **Inkwells**, Identification & Values, Badders	$18.95
4947	Collector's Guide to **Inkwells**, Book II, Badders	$19.95
5621	Collector's Guide to **Online Auctions**, Hix	$12.95
4862	Collector's Guide to **Toasters** & Accessories, Greguire	$19.95
4652	Collector's Guide to **Transistor Radios**, 2nd Ed., Bunis	$16.95
4864	Collector's Guide to **Wallace Nutting Pictures**, Ivankovich	$18.95
1629	**Doorstops**, Identification & Values, Bertoia	$9.95
4717	Figural **Nodders**, Includes Bobbin' Heads and Swayers, Irtz	$19.95
5683	**Fishing Lure** Collectibles, 2nd Ed., Murphy/Edmisten	$29.95
5259	**Flea Market Trader**, 12th Ed., Huxford	$9.95
4945	**G-Men and FBI Toys** and Collectibles, Whitworth	$18.95
5605	**Garage Sale & Flea Market Annual**, 8th Ed.	$19.95
3819	**General Store** Collectibles, Wilson	$24.95
5159	Huxford's Collectible **Advertising**, 4th Ed.	$24.95
2216	**Kitchen Antiques**, 1790–1940, McNerney	$14.95
4950	The **Lone Ranger**, Collector's Reference & Value Guide, Felbinger	$18.95
2026	**Railroad** Collectibles, 4th Ed., Baker	$14.95
5619	**Roy Rogers and Dale Evans** Toys & Memorabilia, Coyle	$24.95
5367	**Schroeder's Antiques Price Guide**, 18th Ed., Huxford	$12.95
5007	**Silverplated Flatware**, Revised 4th Edition, Hagan	$18.95
1922	Standard **Old Bottle** Price Guide, Sellari	$14.95
5694	Summers' Guide to **Coca-Cola**, 3rd Ed.	$24.95
5356	Summers' Pocket Guide to **Coca-Cola**, 2nd Ed.	$9.95
3892	**Toy & Miniature Sewing Machines**, Thomas	$18.95
4876	**Toy & Miniature Sewing Machines**, Book II, Thomas	$24.95
5144	Value Guide to **Advertising Memorabilia**, 2nd Ed., Summers	$19.95
3977	Value Guide to **Gas Station Memorabilia**, Summers & Priddy	$24.95
4877	Vintage **Bar Ware**, Visakay	$24.95
4935	The W.F. Cody **Buffalo Bill** Collector's Guide with Values	$24.95
5281	**Wanted to Buy**, 7th Edition	$9.95

Schroeder's ANTIQUES Price Guide